Public Discourse in America

Public Discourse in America

Conversation and Community in the Twenty-First Century

EDITED BY JUDITH RODIN AND
STEPHEN P. STEINBERG

PENN

University of Pennsylvania Press

Philadelphia

10   9   8   7   6   5   4   3   2   1

Published by
University of Pennsylvania Press
Philadelphia, Pennsylvania 19104-4011

Library of Congress Cataloging-in-Publication Data
Public discourse in America : conversation and community in the twenty-first century / edited by
Judith Rodin and Stephen P. Steinberg.
    p.   cm.
  ISBN 0-8122-3741-2 (acid-free paper)
  Includes bibliographical references and index.
  1. Political culture—United States.   2. Rhetoric—Political aspects—United States.
3. Conversation—Political aspects—United States.   4. Political participation—United States.
5. Civil society—United States.   6. Popular culture—United States.   7. Rhetoric—Social aspects—
United States.   8. United States—Politics and government—2001–   9. United States—
Civilization—1970–   10. United States—Social conditions—1980–   I. Rodin, Judith.
II. Steinberg, Stephen P.
E902 .P83   2004
808.53'0973—dc21   2003053741

To the members of the Penn National Commission on Society, Culture and Community, who shared willingly of their expertise and insights and graciously exemplified engaged and productive public discourse at its best.

Contents

Contents

Prologue: The Work of the Penn National Commission

Judith Rodin

The Penn National Commission on Society, Culture and Community originated in widely expressed concerns about the declining quality and effectiveness of public discourse, the increasing coarseness of public culture, and the growing separation and isolation of groups and individuals in the United States and abroad. When I first convened the Commission in late 1996, I challenged its members to address the "polarization, over-simplification, and isolation . . . that are increasingly characteristic of contemporary social and political discourse." In the years that followed, the fifty leading thinkers, scholars, writers, political leaders, and experts who made up the Commission's membership sought to understand the problems of contemporary public discussion and behavior and to foster more engaged and thoughtful conversations about contemporary social issues nationally and internationally. Between December 1996 and November 1999, the Commission deliberated over the course of six thematically linked, semi-annual plenary meetings held in Philadelphia, Chicago, Washington, D.C., and Los Angeles.[1] These discussions, and the conclusions and recommendations that emerged from them, bear even greater resonance in the wake of the complex and staggering events that the United States, and many other countries, have experienced in the new millennium. In undertaking these deliberations, the Commission's members joined in the belief that academic and professional leaders from a broad spectrum of fields have a responsibility to bring their expertise and insights to bear on the major social and cultural issues of our day: not to score some quick rhetorical points in the political and culture wars but to deepen our collective understanding of a neglected phenomenon: the centrality of public discourse and effective discourse leadership in a democratic society.

At the time of the Commission's founding, which was generously supported by what is now known as the Atlantic Philanthropies, few issues loomed larger than the apparently rapid deterioration of public discourse and public behavior in the United States. But this alleged decline has been an enduring concern throughout, at least, the past half century. Indeed, the problem that the Commission faced was almost the same one that the historian Daniel J. Boorstin encountered during the 1960s, an earlier period of social fragmentation, cultural conflict, and uncivil discourse: "The spirit of dissent stalks our land. It seeks the dignity and privilege of disagreement, but it is entitled to neither. All over the country on more and more subjects we hear more and more people quarreling and fewer and fewer people debating. How has this happened? What can and what should we do about it?"[2] I believed when I convened the Commission—and its findings have only deepened my belief—that in such times, major social and cultural institutions throughout our society, particularly the leading international research universities, bear a special responsibility to foster the kind of engaged and vibrant public discourse that builds a sense of community despite deep disagreements—and even "dissents"—about the directions and policies of that community. Fortunately, the University of Pennsylvania's educational philosophy, dating back to its founder, Benjamin Franklin, stresses the unity of the theoretical and the practical, and this ethos made the Penn National Commission a natural extension of the University's history and contemporary identity.

Early in its plenary discussions, the Penn National Commission concluded that incivility is not a new phenomenon, notwithstanding the widespread popular alarm over uncivilized behavior and language that had given rise to the Commission's creation. Rather, incivility appears to have been a constant feature of American culture from its founding, though greatly amplified by the last century's dramatic changes in the technologies of mass communication, the economic dynamics of mass markets, and laissez-faire governmental policies. Through a series of exciting plenary discussions, the Commission identified and explored three primary factors that tend to make uncivil behavior stand out at this time—not because such behavior is more prevalent, but because we have failed to balance and surround it with the kind of robust and engaged public discourse that is essential to a democratic society: a *Culture of Intolerance* expressed in the dogmatism and ideological polarization that dominate our public discourse; a *Failure of Leadership* in the continuing dialogue between and among leaders and their constituencies; and the *Fragmentation of Communities* in which race, class, ideology, ethnicity, and special interests divide and subdivide rather than unify civic life. In addition to their work in plenary sessions, Commission members examined these problems through deliberative working groups on *Culture and Public Behavior*, on *Leadership in a Democratic Society*, and on *Community in the Twenty-First Century*. These working groups greatly deepened the Commission's insights into the complex social and cultural context of public discourse, the nature of effective discourse leadership on major public policy issues, and the central role increasingly played by cultural institutions in building inclusive communities where discourse is modeled and fostered. As you will see in the course of this volume, these insights have important implications for improving public discourse in the United States.

During its wide-ranging discussions, the Working Group on Culture and Public Behavior, chaired by Neil Smelser, described how the norms of public discourse and behavior operate, and articulated the competing demands of deliberation and reflection that must be integrated to construct a normative vision of public discourse and behavior in which democratic engagement and civic hope both have their place. The Working Group on Leadership in a Democratic Society prepared a set of case studies analyzing the role of discourse leadership on specific public policy issues. In reviewing the working group's analyses, chair Michael Schudson underscores the important role that institutional leaders must play in framing and facilitating discussion of our collective civic agenda. The Working Group on Community in the Twenty-First Century, chaired by Joyce Appleby, identified several factors essential to constructing viable community infrastructures—particularly in troubled communities— and reinventing the notion of community for the twenty-first century. The working group explored the ways in which a variety of entities— grassroots community organizations, local museums, libraries, universities, community foundations, and the Internet—could contribute to the strengthening of community and public discourse, and identified, among the dozens of institutions interviewed, exemplars for constructing a vision of twenty-first century community. Our plenary deliberations and working group activities were supplemented by commissioned research projects, papers, and literature reviews that identified the characteristics and practices of productive public discourse, explored the dynamics of political apology, forgiveness, and reconciliation, highlighted the characteristics of and obstacles to effective discourse leadership, and focused attention on the emerging importance of cultural institutions in providing opportunities for productive public discourse. Several of these studies are included in this volume.

Together these materials ask a series of important questions about the condition and role of public discourse in our democracy: What is the present state of public discourse and how has it changed, if at all, over time? In what respects does it fail to approach our widely held, but often unarticulated, ideal of "reasoned and reasonable" public deliberation? What are the features and underlying principles that characterize exemplary, productive public discourse at the beginning of the twenty-first century? How and why does public discourse work when it works well— and why does it so often fail when we need it most, as in our nation's so often aborted "national conversation" on race? What are the characteristics of effective discourse leadership on the part of individuals and professionals in politics and the media? What institutional practices promote communities that foster strong and productive public discourse? Is a strong community associated with good discourse practices? Can exemplary discourse practices be used to reintegrate isolated subcommunities into a larger society or to bridge barriers of hostility between communities? Taken as a whole, the Commission's answers to these questions articulate an important—and unexpected—vision of the state of public discourse in America today, and of its central importance at the beginning of the twenty-first century. The central elements of this vision are as follows.

- An energized, inclusive, and ultimately, productive—but not necessarily civil or even comfortable—public discourse is essential to the functioning of any successful democratic society.
- Incivility and polarization in public discourse, especially in political discourse, are not *new* features of our public culture, nor have they dramatically worsened over the course of American history.
- While not qualitatively *worse* than in the past, public discourse *has* been fragmented and thinned by many modern social and technological developments, and therefore, the task of thickening it—essentially, creating more examples of productive public discourse—should be undertaken as an important civic endeavor.
- Such a thickened public discourse must integrate our traditional democratic procedural mechanisms and emphases on rational argument and evidence—all necessary to ensure productive outcomes—with an openness to narrative, emotion, and honest dialogue, which are likewise necessary for *all* citizens to participate and take ownership.
- A surprising set of social and cultural institutions—museums, libraries, schools, colleges and universities, professional sports, the military, and even the Internet—are now emerging as centers of discourse communities, in which citizens of different backgrounds come together across boundaries of difference. Alas, too often the professional staffs and lay leaders of these institutions are unprepared for their new civic responsibilities.
- The centrality of public discourse, the importance of thickening it, and the relative unpreparedness of many citizens and leaders to engage effectively in it, place a new and higher premium on exemplary discourse leadership—by civic and political leaders, by the media, and by professional and lay leaders in nongovernmental organizations, cultural institutions, and higher education.
- The ultimate importance of improving public discourse in these ways lies not in the eudaemonistic value of "talk for talk's sake," but in its indispensable role in the creation of inclusive and effective communities, where citizens of different backgrounds, origins, and ideologies can contribute to the collective tasks of our shared communal existence—as was so dramatically underscored by the events of 11 September 2001 and their aftermath.

This volume includes much of the original research and analysis produced for and by the Penn National Commission, and it highlights the major findings and recommendations of the Commission to create a more robust and productive public discourse. More important, it aims to start a conversation—among scholars, practitioners, and the general public—about the centrality and effectiveness of public discourse in American society. That conversation began in the engaged discourse among the members of the Commission, but it was their wish that it not end there. It is a conversation that is as old as our republic and as new as the twenty-first century technologies by which we can now each participate in it.

In 1787, Benjamin Franklin told the members of the Continental Congress that they had come together "to consult, not to contend, with each other."[3] But we know they *did* contend with each other, sometimes strongly and uncivilly, about the most fundamental conceptions of human liberty, community, and government. Yet the founding fathers also recognized their common situation and shared task, the pressing necessity of designing a workable government. Despite their profound and sometimes painful differences, they made their contentious discourse *productive* by remaining engaged, whether they won or lost the day's argument, and by staying committed to their common endeavor. It is to further such productive engagement with each other, an engagement that recognizes, values, and contextualizes our deepest dissents and disagreements—a kind of public engagement of which there was no greater exemplar than Franklin himself—that this volume is dedicated.

Introduction: Incivility and Public Discourse

Judith Rodin and Stephen P. Steinberg

In the midst of America's current "War on Terrorism," it is sometimes difficult to recapture the mood and worries that dominated our public life only a few short years ago. The events of 11 September 2001 and the subsequent sense of renewed national unity and relative consensus on a new national imperative have, as wars will, swept away many of the civic and media preoccupations that seemed so unalterable and important just the day before. And while new elections and new policy controversies have already begun to revive the polarized political discourse of the late 1990s, such displays of incivility and partisanship have been pushed, for the moment, a bit farther toward the margins of public life.

Yet, at the end of the twentieth century, the belief that incivility pervaded public life was widespread. In a widely cited poll published by *U.S. News and World Report* in 1996, 89 percent of Americans thought incivility was a serious problem, and 78 percent thought that the problem had gotten worse in the 1990s.[1] Social fragmentation and individual isolation prompted Robert Putnam's evocative article "Bowling Alone," a phrase that many have come to see as a succinct metaphor for contemporary America.[2] In 1996, the *Washington Post* reported that Americans were becoming a nation of suspicious strangers. Not only had they lost confidence in government and institutions, but they increasingly mistrusted each other. In every generation since the 1950s, this mistrust has grown. Nearly two out of three Americans believe that most people cannot be trusted. Just a few decades earlier, a majority believed the opposite.[3]

Such divisiveness deeply affects society. It breeds mistrust, fragments communities, isolates citizens, and polarizes the discussion and treatment of almost every public issue. In this climate, stagnation and incivility seem to overwhelm and drown out the kind of thoughtful public discussion and debate that we expect to produce positive change. These concerns about incivility and divisive social dynamics have led to repeated calls for "civic renewal," the revival of "civil society," the restoration of a sense of national unity, and recommitment to traditional American values.[4]

At the heart of these widespread calls for renewal, restoration, and revival are four recurrent observations (or allegations) about public life.

First, the claim is made that our political and social discourse is highly polarized, uncivil, and unproductive. Second, our political and social leaders are viewed as more interested in following public opinion than in imagining bold, new solutions to old problems. Third, our communal life is seen as increasingly fragmented into ever smaller and more highly politicized units. Fourth, a breakdown in public mores, tolerance, and self-restraint is lamented, and a blurring of the boundaries between private and public discourse is felt to influence dramatically and negatively every aspect of our public culture.

Yet, despite all the attention and public outcries that follow the most egregious incidents of incivility and intolerance, it remains unclear whether this widespread concern is an overreaction to a few, exceptional cases during a period of rapid social and technological change or an important and accurate diagnosis of a social and cultural illness. Certainly, claims of incivility and a frayed civil society are widely assumed to be true. But the hasty assumption that our society has entered an unusual period of uncivil and self-destructive behavior warrants skepticism. Indeed, the strong sense of renewed national unity and shared community after 11 September 2001 (most notably in New York City, of all places) argues powerfully against those who would see a society in dissolution. Rather, recognition of a common situation, that "we are all in this together," whether it occurs in the national or local consciousness, remains the cornerstone upon which all communities are built—especially those, such as America, that are composed of diverse populations with widely divergent values, perspectives, and experiences.

These dissonant impressions of our public life—discordant and polarized one moment, unified and civil the next—suggest that something more complex and interesting is at work in the relationships between civic life, politics, media, contemporary culture, leadership, and public discourse. The new strains and pressures upon these intersections will only grow as the nation works through its post-9/11 challenges. No doubt, the strength, diversity, and openness of American society for decades to come will be shaped—if not distorted—by the intense pressures now in play. Likewise, we can anticipate—and already see ample evidence—that the nature and quality of our public discourse will play a major role in shaping our future sense of community, security, and liberty. Thus, while seemingly more "civil" and unified, America's current domestic and international situation makes the three-year study undertaken by the Penn National Commission on Society, Culture and Community in the late 1990s far more relevant than one might at first have thought.

Public Discourse and Democracy

Incivility is not new. Intolerance, rapid social change, political polarization, and failures of leadership can be found in almost every era of

American history. One need only look at the vicious and "uncivil" attacks on presidents such as Jefferson, Lincoln, Cleveland, and the first Roosevelt to find ample precedents. Not only is the potential for uncivil discourse deeply embedded in basic American political tenets, its current manifestations have deep roots in historical and social changes. As the late Robert H. Wiebe explains in his contribution to this volume, democratic skepticism regarding authority has deep roots in American history. Although this skepticism has waxed and waned through the centuries, it is often misrepresented as a recent phenomenon. Wiebe also identifies several other primary historical tensions in public discourse. Some argue, for example, that the establishment of rules and standards for public deliberation will necessarily exclude some participants, while others argue that an absence of deliberative rules is an "invitation to chaos"; some endorse making all information publicly available as a democratic ideal, while others think processing tools and filters are essential to organize information in a democratic context; some place the dearest value on the equality of individuals before law, while others see the health of groups in the United States as a key measure of democracy's strength. As Wiebe summarizes, it is not necessary that those who would improve public discourse take a "side" in these fundamental debates, but they must be aware of these tensions as they proceed.

The current state of incivility in public discourse "is the product of a century of change," Thomas Bender explains, during which U.S. public culture was transformed. "Thick" interdependencies between social life and politics have given way to a "thinning" of public discourse, in which politics is estranged from people's lives, values, and social experiences. In its heyday, "nineteenth-century political culture . . . was marked by intense partisan identities, strongly competitive parties, and a politics of spectacle." Political culture was both intensely masculine and white—indeed these racial and sexual exclusions were central to the definition of the citizen and the public sphere. Bender argues that politics in this historical context was "both more and less than a civic right . . . it was, at least in part, a form of entertainment." Nineteenth-century political culture, that is, had a thick texture: politics was embedded in social life, and it helped form and narrate everyday experience.

This thick interdependency of politics and social life has thinned considerably since the nineteenth century, due to a variety of social transformations. Bender notes that the thinning of public discourse was in part an unintended consequence of reformers' efforts against the "spectacle" of American mass democracy and the parties' stranglehold over politics. These reformers, who privileged reasoned argument over "blind partisanship," had achieved much of their program by the 1920s, when "parties were weakened and independent voters became respectable." While these reformers were "rightly interested in promoting reasoned argument" in public discourse, they "wrongly reduced the political being to the merely cerebral." This undercut the "wholeness of political life" that characterized the nineteenth century and, indeed, classical notions of democracy as celebrated by the Greeks. As a result of these developments, Bender notes, voter participation began its century-long decline in the early 1900s, and parties today have very little role in policies or candidate selection. This thinning of political and public culture has "isolated politics from everyday life."

Other changes that Bender attributes to the 1920s contributed to the thinning of American political culture as well, including the press's adaptation of a standard of "objectivity" rather than explicit party loyalty; the assumption, inspired by Walter Lippmann, that a "passive public" drawn to consumer culture can be manipulated by political "experts"; and the emergence of survey research and advertising as models for political "sales" campaigns. "In the nineteenth century, entertainment and politics were fused," writes Bender. "In the twentieth century, one displaced the other." These changes have together diminished the importance and centrality of politics to public life, and have estranged politics from citizens' social lives and values. Bender cautions, however, that nostalgia for the thick political culture of the nineteenth century is emphatically the "wrong mood" for a discussion of public discourse. Public culture in the nineteenth century relied centrally on numerous social exclusions and was not as "civil" as we might imagine, judging from the Lincoln-Douglas debates alone. Nevertheless, Bender concludes, we do need to "recover by alternate means" some of the functions that parties used to perform in order to thicken public discourse. "Competing and diverse public narratives" must be created to sustain political commitment and meaning and "steady the electorate." And "an institutional space continuous with social life" is needed, where public matters can be engaged.

Fundamental historical transformations have created a context for public discourse and civil society in the twenty-first century that differs vastly from the circumstances of the country's founding, and from the nineteenth-century political heyday that Bender documents. Today, the largely silent assumptions of white, male, relatively elitist leadership in society and politics, insulated from close public scrutiny, have been supplanted by a long series of electoral reforms (e.g., direct election of senators, the elimination of racial and property qualifications, the growth of the primary system, women's suffrage, and the voting rights reforms of the 1960s), by the dominant role of public opinion polling, by televised political advertising, and by a "soundbite" public culture. The founders assumed that we would continue to live in relatively stable and homogeneous communities—geographically dispersed and predominantly rural and agricultural. Instead, we live in an increasingly transient, urban, heterogeneous, and kinetic society that challenges traditional notions and capacities of communities.

The capacity of many of our political and professional leaders for independent action and strategic vision often seems to have been vitiated by the overwhelming influence of mass constituency opinion, financial incentives, and ideological extremism. Indeed, the political arena is often viewed as a barometer for public discourse. Democratic political consultant Paul Begala has described politics in the late 1990s as "certainly more uncivil," if "not dirtier," than at any time in U.S. history. He attributes the decline in political civility to the end of the Cold War, which left political strategists searching for ways to cast their candidates in heroic light, and to the technological revolution and the 24-hour news cycle, which impede thoughtful, reasoned political analysis by journalists.[5] This view is shared by Begala's fellow Texan and Republican counterpart Karl Rove: "The whole mindset within the Beltway has deteriorated. I don't know whether it's Watergate . . . [or] Clinton-Gore . . . [or] Nixon . . . [or] Vietnam . . . [or] what it is. . . . And I worry about that, frankly, almost as much as I worry about the lack of candidates' ability to share a message and to do so in a way that people find inspiring and positive."[6] The result, as former New Jersey Senator Bill Bradley put it, is that:

On some levels, our political process is at a standstill. Democrats and Republicans both march along the well-worn paths of symbolic politics, waving flags labeled "welfare," "crime," "taxes," to divide Americans and win elections. Republicans cling to the illusion that government is the problem, even the enemy of freedom, and that less government and free markets will automatically relieve fears of working Americans. Democrats, on the other hand, cling to old programs like worker retraining, without ever stopping to ask whether those fragmented programs are actually working to change lives for the better or whether jobs are available for the workers that we're retraining. Underlying the paralysis of government, I think, is a collapse of trust and a rising polarization.[7]

Our political leaders have certainly become trapped in a seemingly endless cycle of polarized and unproductive behavior, ever more constrained in their ability and willingness to affect the caliber of public discourse. But perhaps the most significant consequence for a democratic society is the apparent impact on citizens' engagement with, and even interest in, the politics of their own government. As Bradley described it:

Politicians lob negative TV ads and campaigns that are richly financed by special interests and wealthier Americans, and a growing part of the American electorate becomes disinterested. Witness, in 1996, less than half of those eligible even thought it was worth voting for the president of the United States of either party. So democracy is paralyzed and polarized not just because politicians are needlessly partisan. The process is broken at a deeper level and it won't be fixed by replacing one set of elected officials with another any more than it was fixed in 1992, 1994, or 1996. Citizens at a very gut level believe that politicians are controlled by special interests who give them money, by parties which crush their independence, by ambition for higher office that makes them hedge their positions rather than call it like they really see it, and by pollsters who convince them that only the focus group phrase can guarantee them victory. Thought is a risky endeavor.[8]

There have been, of course, numerous efforts to reverse these trends in our political culture. Among the best known is the "deliberative poll" model developed by James Fishkin and used in a series of "national issues" broadcasts on PBS and elsewhere around the nation and abroad. Fishkin's format aims to determine what the opinion of a representative sample of the populace would be if they were given both the factual background and the opportunity for rational deliberation to make an informed and well-considered decision.[9] The behavior of politicians themselves has been the focus of an ongoing monitoring project led by Kathleen Hall Jamieson on "Civility in the House of Representatives," where the recent upsurge in political incivility and ideological polarization was first dramatized in the wake of the 1994 Congressional elections.[10]

Many observers and political practitioners have pointed to the need for clearer "rules of engagement" in political discourse. "The crux of it is . . . you have to have both parties agree to a common set of rules," said Karl Rove. "In the politics of personal destruction—and people in my profession are the worst proponents of it—you have to have candidates and handlers and media firms and a political structure that says there are commonly accepted rules of engagement, and [that] this [behavior] isn't one of them. But we don't have that now, and we certainly don't have it in the form of media. . . . The rules of engagement clearly don't say, 'Hey, we're not going to engage in something that is beyond the pale.' There is no 'beyond the pale' in politics anymore."[11] Indeed, some have argued that the unprecedented commercialization of almost every facet of culture has all but eliminated the boundaries that once separated a vaguely definable "private" sphere from public scrutiny or exposure. Today, the dynamics of mass-market media, financial influence in politics, and flourishing technological innovation have opened virtually any area of life including, for example, higher education, criminal justice, and health care, to commercial exploitation. As Kevin Phillips put it, "The politicians are just caught up in pandering to the people who have the money. . . . The whole money ethic permeates politics when capitalism is that successful and when money is allowed to flow into politics almost without hindrance. It then creates the yardstick for politicians . . . [who say] 'Hey, that's what I need to cozy up to? That's where I'm going to get re-elected or not get re-elected? People in my district don't mind it, because they sort of want the same thing, too. And I do look out for local industries more than others.' I just think the permeation of this is enormous."[12]

In contemporary society, the influence of the media in shaping culture and discourse cannot be underestimated. Media have blurred public discourse and private conversation, creating forums for debate and discussion that America's founders could not have imagined. Contemporary news norms focus on attack, assertion, and problems, as opposed to the virtues of compromise, constructive argument, and solutions, which are generally considered fundamental to civil discourse. In this regard, mainstream media are reporting in ways that debase and confuse the electorate and create the impression of a poorly motivated government, and the result is an erosion of public confidence.

In all these examples and contexts, the conditions on which our idealized visions of deliberation, leadership, community, and culture are based have changed in fundamental ways. In some cases, change has occurred over extremely long periods and reflects large-scale social, economic, and cultural dynamics. These long-term and fundamental social and technological shifts have thrown the fundamental capacities of our democratic society into question. Yet it is essential to recognize that each of these changes has an equally important positive dimension. For example, opinion polling is arguably a great boon to the realization of a truly representative democracy in which the will of the people actually matters. The diversification of leadership in every realm of endeavor has brought new and different voices into public discourse—voices that are often willing to challenge the received wisdom and accepted social and cultural attitudes of earlier, more homogeneous, times. The relaxation of cultural norms has produced an environment in which much greater freedom of expression and creativity is possible. Technological advances in computing and communications have vastly increased public awareness of important issues and developments, and forced leaders to be more accessible and responsive to their constituents. Communities are more diverse, and awareness and openness to cultural and social differences is generally greater.

The challenge of these new conditions is to ensure that the positive consequences of irreversible social, cultural, and technological changes outweigh the negative consequences. Notwithstanding nostalgia for an imagined past of coherent communities and families, no conceivable coalition of forces can restore the eighteenth- and nineteenth-century world—or even that of the 1950s. They have been swept away by the forces of the past half century. We do have the capacity, however, to use new forces of mass communication, globalization, democratization, and urbanization to create vital communities and discourse.

Nor can uncivil discourse or troublesome private behavior and morality simply be moralized, censored, or legislated out of existence. Instead, it is necessary to thicken public discourse, in Bender's phrase, by surrounding and submerging uncivil behaviors with a wealth of constructive and energetic public debate. As Alexis de Tocqueville noted, citizens are not a public unless they have work to do. They will come together into a tentative engagement only if they have shared issues and conflicts to resolve. The social task is not to make people like each other or feel at one with each other, or to change private morals and behavior. Rather, it is to find common purpose that brings disparate communities and perspectives together, and to model a robust, positive public discourse that will muffle uncivil and unproductive discourse.

Conversations on Race

The national dialogue and public policy debate on race and affirmative action crystallizes both the extreme difficulty and the critical importance of finding more productive ways to talk about race in America. But surprisingly, debates and so-called "national conversations" about race and affirmative action rarely take advantage of what we know about effective and engaging public discourse. Instead, they tend to seek consensus or a uniform answer, and rarely employ principles of good public discourse identified by David Ryfe, such as reciprocity (engaging different views) and radical difference (respecting the rights of individuals to speak in the voice of any of the groups to which they belong, or in none of those voices).

Christopher Edley reviews the multiple contexts and policy measures broadly grouped under the term "affirmative action." Speaking about race isn't "rocket science," he concludes. "It's harder than rocket science." Attempts to speak generally about policy are complicated by the complexity of specific policy settings and, more importantly, by deeply held differences in values and perceptions that underlie conversations and arguments about affirmative action, merit, and identity. Edley recommends that leaders who speak about race and affirmative action must become "relentless teachers" on race in America, and must strive to cultivate new leaders who might continue the conversation.

Changing the discourse on race and affirmative action is one way to invigorate public discussions of the subject. Another is to change the forum for that discourse. One of the Penn Commission's plenary meetings, moderated by Drew Faust, used President Clinton's "national conversation" on race as an example by which to tease out ineffective and exemplary discourse practices on race and affirmative action. The President's national conversations ranged from traditional town meetings to formal forums on social and public policy issues to relatively unfocused conversations in a wide variety of local settings with disparate groups of participants.

Participants find that many conversations on race and affirmative action tend to break down before they begin, as Jay Rosen describes, and thereafter fall into ideological polarization, clichés, and sound bites. Leaders and conveners of public discourse on race, for example, may frame the conversation in their initial comments—or even in the arrangement of the room—in such a way that some views are excluded from discussion or contemplation before discourse actually begins. President Clinton, for example, introduced one of his conversations on race by belittling the concept of "tolerance" as an approach to race relations and endorsing the "celebration" of difference instead, and this frame unduly limited the conversation that followed.

Participants note that the proper context should be established for a conversation on such a contentious topic before the conversation begins. Sponsors of public discourse on race should be responsible and publicly trusted—for example, foundations, academic institutions, or perhaps civic journalists. A neutral third party should be responsible for format, organization, and structure. National conversations should attract a representative public. The leader of the conversation should be carefully chosen and without self-interest in the outcome, and should not have a public profile sufficient to affect or sway the conversation. The setting for the conversation (e.g., the number of participants, physical situation, and the presence of the media) should be carefully considered. Multilevel conversations on the same topic can occur in multiple formats—from "representative" national forums to regional and local conversations—to achieve greater saliency and participation.

Once conversations on contentious topics such as race begin, they will defer to a "debate among fixed positions model" unless goals and new rules for the conversation are clear at the outset. Participants clarify the differences between "debate," "performance," and genuine "conversation" in which changes and evolution in one's position are invited, accepted, and anticipated. Too often, participants note, conversations on race follow a debate or a performance model rather than a genuine conversational model in which views might change over time. "What we've especially attended to is the distinction between an effort to persuade, or a performance, and an effort to learn, or conversation," said Cass Sunstein. "And what we've been trying to attend to is how there's a place in public and private life for performance, which is often what television is about. But there's also a place in public life, as well as in private life, for a conversation in which people try to learn things from one another."[13] Participants conclude that such a "learning model" for discourse on race and affirmative action would enrich the conversation and move it away from entrenched and embattled positions between adversaries. As Faust describes it, the learning model of public discourse "resists polarizing or assigning participants and leaders to one side or another," but perhaps "creates other positions along a spectrum that will allow for more easy movement, for those who are willing to undertake movement about what they believe."

In terms of goals and outcome, conversations on fractious issues such as affirmative action, abortion, or immigration should aim to achieve a more informed public understanding of complex issues, not necessarily to convert audiences to a predetermined position. To achieve this will require a more conscientious and self-conscious effort on the part of cultural leaders from all walks of life to model productive public discourse. As Sunstein summarizes, "We do have consensus, I've discerned, on a variety of principles. . . . One is that it's very important not to attack the good faith of one's opponents. One is that factual issues are important, but occasionally not decisive to [the] resolution of policy issues. One is that affirmative action is only one of a range of racial issues, and it's unfortunate that it's received so much attention. One is that it's extremely difficult to argue from first principles. One is that when first principles are shared, it is possible to mediate strategic questions for factual questions. That's a sign of hope. And the last, in a way the most interesting, I think, is the great difficulty of extracting the issues of substance from the issues of process. There's a real lesson in that."[14]

Whether they seek the job or not, athletes have emerged as revered role models, especially for young people, and inevitably contribute to the tenor, content, and quality of public discourse on race. Indeed, as Richard Lapchick notes, "Sport has become one of our culture's broadest common denominators." It is a public context and place where people of very diverse backgrounds converge as fans, players, and sports followers. Athletes are bestowed a prominent role in shaping public discourse and standards, yet as Lapchick cautions, they are not "natural" leaders of public discourse simply because they "can nail a 30-foot jump shot." Rather than attempt to discredit or marginalize athletes as role models for children, a number of leaders are examining how sports and athletes can positively contribute to the resolution of vexing social issues—in sports and in society—such as race relations, drugs, and gender violence. They are also training athletes to become leaders in public discourse on difficult questions. The Center for the Study of Sport in Society at Northeastern University, which Lapchick founded in 1984, supports projects aimed at ending racism in sports, understanding the relationships between athletics and violence, and grappling with the complex interactions of business, athletic competition, and entertainment that characterize modern professional sports. Project Teamwork, which trains athletes in conflict-resolution and diversity-training skills, won the Peter F. Drucker Award as the nation's most innovative program leading to social change. The cultivation of athletes as public leaders is especially valuable, Lapchick notes, because using athletes and the "context of sport" to lead conversations puts people at ease to talk about difficult subjects such as racism and gender violence. Writes Lapchick, "Sport, from youth sports through the pros, . . . has a small but vital role to play by having a positive impact on public behavior."

Americans also need to reconsider the most basic terms and concepts around which the discourse on race unfolds. For example, Richard Rodriguez explains, they need to challenge their concept of race as a "black and white" issue that excludes "brownness" and racial identities that do not fit into this rhetorical dichotomy. Noting that he was "reinvented in 1973 by Richard Nixon," who presided over the creation of new racial categories, such as "Hispanic," for the U.S. Census, Rodriguez introduces "brownness" as an "impurity" and a disruption in the U.S. conversation on race, which is typically organized along a black and white polarity. Inevitably, as Rodriguez describes, assimilation and racial mixing occur. The "multicultural" ideal comforts Americans who want to maintain a sense of racial boundaries and separateness, but it belies the complex cultural, personal, and social interactions and appropriations between ethnicities and races that will increasingly characterize this century.

The Importance of Discourse Leadership

Throughout the nation's history, Americans have expected political leaders to initiate and direct a strong and productive public discourse. It is all too easy to look with nostalgia at our founding generation as the once-and-only period of greatness in American public discourse and deliberation. Yet, as Michael Schudson observes, there has not been an *absence* of leadership in recent contexts so much as significant change in the conditions surrounding leadership, and these shifting conditions have made leadership more difficult to achieve under traditional models. "Leaders today must learn to operate in a climate of distrust; in a context of diversity and multiple authorized voices; in a global society where their locus of effective control is much narrower than the world forces impinging on them; and in a public soundbite culture where communication is invariably intense and rapid," Schudson explains. Leaders must also contend with intense publicity and public scrutiny; traumatic events of recent history, including political assassinations and Watergate, that have undermined faith in leadership; and a political system that has diminished political leaders' autonomy. Schudson concludes, "Leaders require new models and must learn how to operate" under novel social conditions.

These conditions create at least three paradoxes for leadership in a democracy. The "paradox of complexity" requires that leaders master and understand complexity, yet communicate clear paths and alternatives. They must see complexity yet simplify their messages to make—and communicate—decisions. (President George W. Bush's simple, straightforward, and effective rhetoric in the wake of the 11 September 2001 terrorist attacks—contrasting so dramatically with the complexity and uncertainty faced by our nation's leaders at that particular moment—provides a powerful example of this paradox.) The "paradox of diversity" means that a leader must bring to the table relevant stakeholders that represent the diversity of viewpoints in our thinner public culture.

This diversity increases the democratic legitimacy of decisions but decreases the speed and efficiency of decision-making. As a wider array of stakeholders play legitimate and necessary roles in making decisions, no leader can safely presume consensus—or even common purpose. The "paradox of accountability" obliges a leader not only to lead, but to change the meaning of leadership itself. With a contemporary view of leader as bridge-builder or boundary-crosser, leaders must regularly engage with the public and with mediating institutions. All these conditions, however negative their effects on public discourse may seem, are not insurmountable, particularly if leaders view them as positive challenges that emerge out of long-term and in many cases very positive social changes.

As a striking example of the complexities and, in some respects, the failure of leadership, Derek Bok analyzes the "great health care debate" of 1993 and 1994. Considered by the public to be a serious national issue, health care reform was the centerpiece of the first Clinton campaign and seemed to be a winner out of the starting gate. As Bok notes, however, "The health care debate is in many ways an illustration of a process of deliberation that is increasingly evident, albeit in less spectacular form, whenever important legislation is proposed affecting large numbers of people." A national debate, because of an increasing number of vocal interested parties and the accessibility of the media, can quickly become formidable. Because of the extraordinary wealth of ideas and opinions, reality can be obscured. Whether a useful debate about important policy issues can even take place under these conditions is questionable. The health care reform debate was confused by the large number of participating groups in Congress, a media barrage by special interest groups, and muddy messages from the White House about the Clinton plan. As the debate intensified, substantive news coverage, perhaps encouraged by a passive public, devolved—thinned—into stories about competing groups, political strategies, and counterclaims. Without effective presidential leadership, a legislative campaign of this magnitude was doomed. As Bok concludes, the President made several critical errors. First, he tried to do too much too soon. Reform of this scale might have been more fruitfully introduced in stages. Second, the President used a task force, headed by his wife, that operated in secret. This tended to exclude voices that might have helped create a more viable plan. Lastly, the President did too little to explain the plan to the public, in part due to a perception that the issues involved were too complex for the media or the public to grasp and contemplate. Nonetheless, Bok cautions, skillful leadership may not have led to successful reform either. Other forces, including budget deficits, opposition to tax increases to fund the plan, and an electorate lacking confidence in its government, may also have soured the plan's reception.

The Role of the Professions and Institutions in Public Discourse

In the absence of traditional political leadership that initiates and maintains public discourse, nontraditional leaders and institutions have begun to take a more active role in shaping civil society. Professionals from many fields and social institutions play a largely unexplored role in leading public discourse and using robust dialogue to bridge differences, ease hostilities, and strengthen communities. The professions bring to public dialogue their specific expertise and, in many cases, a commitment to public service. Professions that derive their authority from specialized information can furnish not only basic information about specific contested issues, but also rigorous analysis of that information. This can take the form of advising political officeholders and candidates, testifying before public committees, appearing on news programs, and teaching, for example. In this capacity, the expert is more of a counselor than a leader. Beyond these functions, professionals can contribute to public discourse by examining their own roles in shaping its norms and dynamics.

Jay Rosen explains that journalists are increasingly aware that they not only "report" on the events of civil society and public discourse, but in critical ways shape those events as well. Analyzing the "public journalism" or "civic journalism" movement, Rosen asserts that "the relevant questions are not whether journalists are competent, ethical, and professional, but whether the craft as a whole is serving the public interest," which means the stake we all have in making democracy work. By understanding that "the press is an active agent in public life, not a passive observer," Rosen writes, journalists around the country have blazed trails in news coverage to initiate and enrich public discourse. Public journalism now has significant support from external organizations. One of the earliest examples of civic journalism comes from the *Wichita Eagle* in Kansas, where editor Davis Merritt, in 1990, was disgusted by the spectacle of the 1988 presidential campaign. For the 1990 Kansas gubernatorial campaign, Merritt shifted the focus of campaign coverage from politician-driven to citizen-driven. The *Eagle* promised readers "the opportunity to understand in great detail the candidates' positions on every major issue Kansas faces." Using its own knowledge of the community, supported by polling data, the *Eagle* focused its coverage on ten key concerns, gave each a long background piece, and included a weekly feature on a topic, a summary of the candidates' positions, and anything new on the topic from the campaign that week. As Rosen notes, the exercise set a standard. "The rules for candidates were clear: Say something meaningful about the key issues; and we'll report it and keep reporting it."

In essence, the press issued an "invitation" to experience and participate in public life, cultivate a meaningful dialogue, and address people in their capacity as citizens. Hundreds of other journalists and editors have followed suit, and civic journalism has gained support from print and broadcast media, foundations, think tanks, and academicians. At its best, civic journalism promotes robust public discourse. As a profession, journalism is in a position to lead and is giving the public a way to participate in its governance and in society. In addition, public journalism—though not unilaterally lauded—shows that experimentation can work, even in the face of resistance, which is an important precept that can drive innovations in public discourse.

Paralleling the important role of the professions in fostering a more robust and productive public discourse, major institutions in every area of society—corporations, professional sports, popular media, the military, and others—play a little-recognized but powerful role in shaping public behavior. These institutions have developed more active and self-conscious leadership roles to influence public discourse and culture. And when their leadership fails—as it did dramatically in some notable corporate CEO scandals in 2002—the impact of their failure of leadership reverberates widely throughout our society. Such institutions also can be proactive in expanding the participants in social dialogues as well as the range of subjects and issues that are open for public discussion.

Probably the modern cultural medium that speaks most loudly and pervasively about the American skepticism and antagonism to authority is cinema. Neil Gabler calls moviegoing a "cultural declaration in the national conversation" and notes that citizens have thought of the movies as "the medium that belonged to them." If citizens feel the political system is unresponsive, they find solace in popular culture, and movies in particular, as "expressions of public will against all the forces that seem to disregard us," Gabler argues. Although the kinetic world of film rarely presents public discourse in its content, Gabler finds that the structure and underlying message of film have profoundly shaped political discourse and public culture. The media often present public affairs, policy debates, and issues as "plotlines"; political candidates are expected to share personal stories or "narratives"; Americans look to leaders to be individual "heroes" who find quick resolutions to problems. In this environment, argues Gabler, it becomes more difficult to separate the "dramatic form" from substance; as a result, discourse becomes uninformed, intolerant, and unrealistic in its desire for heroic, individual solutions to complex problems. "[T]he purpose of the cinematic mode of discourse is not to resolve our differences," Gabler writes, "but to make us feel better about ourselves, which is not insignificant. But it is not the same thing as confronting our problems and meeting our challenges, either. . . . For those who want to encourage better public discourse, who want to stimulate a rational exchange of ideas, the challenge is to usher us from the movie theater into the real world, from the darkness of wish fulfillment into the light of reason. Until then, the movie will just keep on rolling."

Talk of Reconciliation

Given more effective, better prepared, and more knowledgeable discourse leadership, and the institutional commitments to support it, can public discourse be a vehicle to create diverse and inclusive communities across boundaries of difference? Indeed, can such discourse facilitate the healing and reunification of societies torn by racial and ethnopolitical conflict? Perhaps the most definitive attempt to use public discourse as an instrument of reconciliation in the wake of race conflict and human rights violations was the Truth and Reconciliation Commission (TRC) of South Africa. The work of the TRC, as its vice-chair Alex Boraine describes, makes clear that truth-telling can promote reconciliation. By using personal narrative (an important feature of the engaging public discourse described by Ryfe), both victims and offenders gave "meaning to their multilayered experiences of the South Africa story." Oral tradition and the media, both central to the TRC process, effectively communicated the Commission's proceedings to the public.

One of the main goals of the TRC was to "restore the human and civil dignity of victims by granting them an opportunity to relate their own accounts of the violations of which they are victims." Unlike an amnesty committee, the TRC focused on the victim, not the perpetrator. As Boraine describes, the TRC traveled throughout the country to give "voice to the voiceless," and people responded to find release from personal burdens and to affect the "life and work and future of their country" as well. Dialogue, the TRC believed, would yield a social truth or narrative truth, rather than factual evidence. Boraine explains, "We felt that one of the ways in which to bring about restoration, and reconciliation, was to engage in truth-telling, to take oral tradition very seriously, to empower our people—ordinary people—to come and tell their stories, not only victims and survivors but also perpetrators." While "truth" in and of itself does not produce "reconciliation," Boraine clarifies, it is its prerequisite: "It seemed that however grotesque that truth was, knowing it" and telling it was part of the national healing process.

At the same time, while the narratives provided knowledge, victims needed acknowledgment from the offenders of their accountability, both those who participated openly and those who did so from the sidelines. To acknowledge publicly that thousands of South Africans have paid a very high price for the attainment of democracy affirms the human dignity of the victims and survivors and is an integral part of the healing of the South African society. For South Africa after apartheid, reconciliation was not only a moral imperative but a practical necessity, if its citizens were to live together peacefully and with stability. "We need to acknowledge the wounds but have to go beyond this truth to a possibility of the wounds being cleansed and closed and the victims being restored," Boraine told the Commission. To demand forgiveness would be wrong, but to hold it out "as a choice and as a possibility" may be viable.

Elaborating on Boraine's insights concerning the TRC, Graham Dodds analyzes the largely unstudied phenomenon of political apology more broadly as a form of public discourse. He finds that political apologies, which are becoming increasingly common, can satisfy a wronged community or people by offering them a representative who symbolizes the collective that harmed them; by putting things on public record; by rendering the offender vulnerable while empowering the offended party; by being well-timed—not too close or too distant from the offense; by providing, when appropriate, compensation; and by complementing legal action. Apology, Dodds concludes, is a specific and important type of discourse. "Apologies are a prime example of discourse thickly conceived. While early accounts of discourse limited its formal contents to rational argument, more recent accounts accept that discourse can and often does contain elements beyond mere rational argumentation." These discourses of reconciliation and apology can help us imagine what a more productive public discourse would be like.

What Is Good Public Discourse?

What would such a "good," more productive and engaged, public discourse look like? David Ryfe reviews the scholarly literature on good public discourse to identify its key features. Ryfe finds that, traditionally, good discourse has been interpreted solely as rational argument—impartial, disinterested, and evidence-based. But in the past twenty years this view has come to be seen as overly sterile, exclusive, patriarchal, and inadequate to describe the varied motivations and forms of public discourse. Good deliberative discourse today integrates rational argument with narratives, personal experiences, expressions of emotion, and empathetic listening.

Ryfe identifies six principles intrinsic to this conception of "postmodern argument." "Formal democratic procedures" are the basic set of individual rights undergirding a vibrant civil society. These include formal equality, freedom of expression and association, and freedom of the press. These rights secure a space for individuals to participate in public life. "Grounded rationality" means that public discourse ought to be characterized by the practice of advancing claims, providing evidence, and developing counterarguments. But this process of reasoning ought not to be abstracted from concrete human relationships. Instead, it should be grounded in those relationships and sensitive to the role of emotion in establishing connections between people. The principle of "reflexivity" calls for constant reflection on the values, assumptions, and terms on which propositions are made. "Reciprocity" holds that participants in public deliberation must go beyond "mere toleration of different views." They must actively engage with these views, as tolerance too easily slips

into isolation. Reciprocity denotes a middling condition between "tolerance" and "respect," the latter of which is difficult to achieve. The principle of "radical difference" asserts that individuals have the right to speak
in the voice of any—or none—of the groups to which they belong. Majority groups ought to recognize that subordinate groups may view the
world differently. Finally, "moderation" links reflection and reciprocity.
Public discourse should be characterized by modesty in the assertion of
claims and in the assumed generalizability of personal experience. A
public discourse fashioned along these lines will be argumentative—but
argumentative in a way that strives to achieve greater inclusion and
stronger communal bonds.

Thickening Public Discourse

While direct interventions to improve public discourse may meet with resistance, there are several practical possibilities for thickening and improving public discourse, possibilities that might overwhelm incivility
and ineffective public discourse with constructive and positive discourse.
This thickening can be achieved in schools, for example, by invigorating
courses in history, civics, and government at all levels and increasing
student interaction and participation with government and politics. It is
also possible to accomplish this through the media, by increasing the
number and type of discussions and debates during campaigns; by examining the treatment of conflict and grievance in organizational life in
the United States; and by giving more of a voice to social movements
and "the voiceless"—those for whom many others speak and act, but
whose own political life is relatively unorganized and infrequently heard
directly.

   David Ryfe examines the activities of sixteen discourse organizations
involved in "the cultivation of good deliberation." The organizations in
Ryfe's study are nationally focused, discourse-based (meaning that discourse is a principal tool and outcome of their activities), and publicly
focused on community-wide issues. Ryfe concludes that discourse organizations understand there is no such thing as one ideal form or format of
good discourse; rather, effective public discourse is inherently rooted in
context, and different kinds of contexts demand different kinds of conversations. In particular, discourse organizations have learned that conversations about values ought to be organized differently from conversations
about actions. For instance, disagreements between pro- and anti-abortion
activists are not likely to be reduced by the distillation of more policy information or the convening of a debate. In the same way, conversations
about action plans and policy proposals generally assume that fundamental values are already shared.

   Regardless of goal, discourse organizations understand that good public discourse almost always begins with relationship-building. No public

conversation can succeed unless the participants share a minimal recognition of some aspect of common values, purposes, or experiences. This is true as much for community groups oriented to civic education as it is for groups geared to policy discussions. Even the most action-oriented discourse organizations build time into their formats for sharing experiences. Ryfe discovers, however, that discourse organizations have trouble integrating deliberative and representative models of politics into a unified format. This is one of the most crucial dilemmas facing these organizations. As Ryfe explains, this form of politics, with its stress on coalition-building and bargaining, is in many ways antithetical to the deliberative ideal: a community of individuals reaching, if not political consensus, then at least political compromise, through dialogue. To capture the imagination of a wide public, these organizations will either have to form stronger links to the political system or convince a skeptical public that conversation without this link is still worthwhile.

In a panel discussion with the Penn National Commission, representatives from four exemplary discourse organizations included in Ryfe's analysis—America*Speaks*, the Common Ground Network for Life and Choice, the Kettering Foundation, and the Study Circles Resource Center—shared elements they have found essential to creating and sustaining meaningful dialogue about complex, and often controversial, issues. Several of the panelists recalled their surprise at the ease with which participants in public discourse will engage in reasoned and productive conversation if, quite simply, they are "invited" to do so, which they rarely are. Most participants in these organizations' programs have had many debates with one another, and are not interested in more debates or "talk for the sake of talking," as Carolyn Lukensmeyer of America*Speaks* would describe it. Panelists underscored, however, that if organizers invite potential participants to join a conversation that will be "different" and then "make sure that it is different," productive discourse will develop. Panelists also emphasized that discourse programs must clarify the link—whether at the local or national level—between "talk and action," as Martha McCoy of Study Circles describes. Organizations convening effective public discourse must take care to ensure that participants are sitting and talking with a group of citizens who are diverse in race and ethnicity, sex, geography, ideology, age, and other features. While high-profile organizations that are linked to particular constituencies and missions, such as the AARP or the NAACP, may provide participants, it is important that these participants do not sit with their own special interest group and talk only to the like-minded.

Among other features, successful public discourse begins with ground rules and well-trained moderators who can heavily facilitate conversations, as necessary. Bob McKenzie of the Kettering Foundation notes that while discourse is a "natural act," performed successfully each day over mundane debates such as where to go to dinner, "we tend to forget that we know how to [deliberate] when we get into politics." McCoy similarly observes that good talk "doesn't just happen." Ground rules establish a tacit contract between participants as to how they will treat each other in the course of conversations. For example, Common Ground convenes pro-abortion and anti-abortion citizens and encourages them to identify areas of common values and shared social concerns. The organizers make clear to participants that the conversation is not an occasion to try to "convert" the other side to another point of view. McCoy similarly has concluded that good public discourse "begins where people are," with an opportunity for participants to talk about how they have experienced important issues in their lives. In contrast, an invitation for participants to "talk about affirmative action," or other major social issues, will most likely reproduce old debates and arguments. All panelists agree that good public discourse evolves over time, as citizens develop genuinely rich and more complex relationships with one another. "Drive-by" conversations or one-time programs will not substantially change social dynamics or, to be sure, national policies.

Indeed, as the contributions to this volume suggest, some of the obstacles to more productive and engaged public discourse are embedded in the paradoxes and antinomies of the American political tradition itself. By birthright, Americans live in a democracy that guarantees rights of free speech and treasures deliberation and discourse. But—paradoxically—these values can actually impede the ability of Americans to maintain high standards of public discussion. The value that Americans place on free speech, writes Neil Smelser, leaves the door ajar for "debased or deteriorated discourse and behavior." Further, correction of such discourse and behavior is precluded by "the very democratic principles we embrace." Other constraints on the improvement of civil discourse include the notion of public and private spheres: "Since the line between private and public is ambiguous and continuously contested," Smelser writes, "citizens and groups resist intervention . . . by claiming that the item under question is private." That areas considered private are particularly protected from intervention constitutes a political strategy in itself. Smelser identifies a "general American cultural principle: a skepticism about, and possibly an antagonism toward, authority and authorities" as another constraint on good public discourse. In American democracy, skepticism toward authority makes interventions on matters of expression difficult.

Creating Community Through Public Discourse

The Penn National Commission's working group on Community in the Twenty-First Century discovered that, just as new nongovernmental organizations are emerging to help foster and facilitate public discourse, a variety of cultural and philanthropic institutions not usually thought of in this context are emerging as the centers of effective and inclusive discourse communities. For example, Joyce Appleby reports that museums and foundations are reconceptualizing their missions and what it means to be a community. Increasingly, they are engaging in active outreach and serving as loci for public discourse in their geographical communities. These community-building efforts begin with political action and social engagement, often filling the vacuum left by public officials and policies that are less responsive to citizens' and communities' needs. As Appleby writes, "Museums, many of them anchored to buildings in deteriorating urban zones, have reconceptualized what museums are for, reaching out to families through their children. Even more remarkable, they are laying out paths to participation in our national culture through the byways of ethnic identities." Museums have converted apparent liabilities into assets, building on their downtown locations, for example, to reinvent themselves as centers for urban renewal, town forums, and community gatherings. None of these changes has evolved naturally, Appleby clarifies. They have emerged out of years of thinking about the challenges posed by an increasingly mobile and fragmented population. For foundations, Appleby writes, "community-building has become the mantra of the past decade, the catchphrase for efforts to close the distance between knowledgeable professionals and the poor families they serve." Foundations have responded to urban decay, including unchecked violence, toxic environments, fleeing jobs, deteriorating schools, and public indifference, by establishing and funding community-based programs. In addition to financial backing, foundations offer guidance in how to create sites for community gatherings, and expertise in formulating plans for community action. Whatever their ultimate success, these efforts at community-building among museums and foundations demonstrate that, internally and in our society at large, major institutions can be proactive in expanding the participants in public discourse as well as the range of subjects and issues that are open for public discussion. Appleby's review of new initiatives by museums and foundations illustrates, for other professions and institutions, the ways in which they can move beyond narrow concepts of "mission" to create spaces and forums for robust public discourse.

Universities have a long and storied history as havens for free speech and the free exchange of ideas. They are also tasked with molding and shaping future leaders. Students, faculty, and the public continue to look to colleges and universities to mediate public opinion on controversial issues and to exemplify rational and reasoned deliberation. As Don Randel explains, however, universities need critically and self-consciously to evaluate their own community practices before they can claim a leadership role in the broader civil society: "there is more that we need to do at the heart of our universities if we wish to claim the ability or perhaps even the right to teach others about community. We must first teach one another and by that method (if not alone) teach our students. Who would dare to embark on a community-building enterprise outside the university and claim that the goal was to replicate the degree to which their own department or university functions as a community? Who would dare to say with a straight face that the only trouble with our political institutions is that they do not exemplify community, civil discourse, and other values as well as the faculty of their own university?"

Arguably, institutions of higher education have become complacent in recent years, much to the detriment of public discourse. Rather than hiding in ivory towers, college and university leaders must keep "relentlessly articulating the university as a marketplace of ideas," in the words of Judith Rodin. From the "intellectual heart of an issue," Rodin says, come creative solutions. Learning to tolerate even the most difficult of different opinions and constantly engaging and re-engaging parties in dialogue are critical steps to creating and sustaining discourse on campus. College and university leaders, by virtue of their professions and with the power of their institutions, must make a difference by example. They must practice good citizenship, Rodin concludes, by becoming meaningfully involved with their communities and setting and establishing standards for good public discourse. "If we can actualize the potential of universities to define civility and community for the twenty-first century," Rodin observed in the plenary, "I believe the universities can be truly powerful forces for the opening of a robust discourse and the changing of public culture. Universities can set the standards, help to describe the standards, train the leaders and the citizens, demonstrate the rewards, and provide the inducements that really will foster a more robust and diverse and civil public discourse."[15] The service professions—clergy, medicine, law, and the military—are also qualified to lead debates on highly contentious subjects. The public service ethos requires these professionals to devote themselves to the welfare of others and not to be absorbed exclusively in themselves. Such professions attract people already inclined to think beyond themselves, and leaders among them might foster the capacity for "enlarged thought" (Kant's phrase for taking the standpoint of others) among their members.[16]

One of the newest forms of community involves people who cannot see each other or hear each other. They may live next door to each other, or thousands of miles away. They may know each other well, or they may have never met. As Lawrence Lessig described, these new patterns of community are generated from computers and Internet technology, which have opened up new vistas for public discourse, and new ways of thinking about community.[17] Much-touted virtual or cybercommunities, however, rarely meet the standards of genuine community or productive public discourse. Interactions over the Internet typically involve quick visits, unidirectional actions, or exchanges of abbreviated messages rather than sustained dialogue and long-term commitment. Many of the most popular so-called communities are actually formed around sites (such as eBay and Amazon) that engage visitors primarily in commercial transactions or simplistic polls and other kinds of additive processes. Most important, so-called cybercommunities often lack the most crucial element of true communities: the existence of real "work to do together" that brings members together, despite their differences, to deal with a shared situation or circumstance. When it is well planned and wisely used, however, the architecture of cyberspace has enormous potential to create new forms of community and robust public discourse. Stephen Steinberg identifies several types of individuals whose community engagement would be especially well served by Internet technology. These include the geographically isolated; the differently abled, for whom communication technology yields more active participation; the nonnative speaker; the person with an odd or crowded schedule; the physically immobile; and the hypermobile.

Steinberg reports on the work of a Discourse Technology Project that sought to imagine online community "from the ground up" in the light of what we have learned about the relationship between productive public discourse and inclusive, engaging communities. He describes online communities in which visitors and participants move toward deeper involvement over time, while gradually shedding their anonymity, to become fully identifiable and richly described citizens of cyberspace. During a "curious visitor" get-acquainted stage, viewers could peruse publicly available content, and could view, but not participate in, "general public" discussions. They could join the community by submitting a personal profile. During a "welcome newcomer" phase, visitors would be given newcomer status and access to members-only privileges and conversations. They could ask even the most rudimentary questions about issues in heavily facilitated "safe haven" conversations, and participate in online exercises and role-playing to reinforce community standards. "Full-fledged" members could avail themselves of all community privileges and services, and contribute feedback at all levels. After participating in the cybercommunity for a certain length of time, and having received a sufficient level of positive feedback about their participation, an individual would be eligible for community leader status. A virtual community designed along these lines would remedy many of the shortcomings in current cybercommunities by emphasizing incremental levels of participation and commitment to the community, a formal process for learning the rules of online discourse, robust identities over empty anonymity, and the creation of "work to do together" that binds participants over the long term.

The essays in this volume present a fresh and unconventional view of incivility and the alleged crisis in public culture that has been the topic of much moralizing and condemnation in recent decades. Incivility is not a new phenomenon, notwithstanding the complaint that we have entered a uniquely negative phase of public life. Incivility has, however, been amplified by changes in the social and economic context, including the emergence of new technologies, mass media, and other transformations that have thinned public discourse and life. Nostalgia for an imagined past of robust public discourse, however, will do little to thicken public discourse and encourage a more vibrant civil society. Nor can uncivil, intolerant, or unproductive discourses simply be censored or legislated out of existence. Rather, this volume proposes that such discourse must be submerged in or surrounded by many sites for good public discourse.

But the meaning of "good" public discourse has changed, apace with changes in the underlying social and political context of public discourse in the United States. Public discourse today is still rooted in reasoned and rational argument, but increasingly encompasses narratives, personal experiences, and empathetic listening. Discourse fashioned along these lines will be argumentative—but argumentative in a way that achieves greater inclusion and recognizes the new challenges to public life posed by diversity and other changes. Such a productive public discourse plays an important enabling role in the critical faculties of any democratic society. As Steinberg describes in his Epilogue to this volume, "faculties" in this sense are the essential capacities by means of which a democratic society carries out its key functions, including conflict resolution and problem-solving, civic education, and social and political interaction.

In the absence of effective traditional political leadership of public discourse, new institutions, professions, and communities have assumed more visible roles in these activities, along the way creating new kinds of "communities of conversation." There is great cause for optimism on the frontiers of civil society—in museums that have revitalized their missions to become vanguards of community organizing, in discourse organizations that facilitate public conversations and "teach" the art of public discourse to participants, in the potential to use new technologies to create cybercommunities among participants who may live next door or thousands of miles away, and in communities that thicken public culture and model exemplary discourse. If we can continue to mobilize leaders, institutions, and citizens to create and engage in the kind of discourse described in this volume, there is the potential in this new century to strengthen the fundamental fabric of society and build a more cohesive and inclusive public life. While the challenges remain formidable, real opportunities abound in the post-11 September 2001 consciousness.

Part One
Public Discourse and Democracy

Chapter 1

The Thinning of American Political Culture

Thomas Bender

To what causes can we attribute the current condition of American public culture?[1] Is the manifest impoverishment of American public discourse recent in origin? It is easy enough to construct a narrative of decline. One has only to recall Lincoln and Douglas and compare recent examples with their closely reasoned debate and the attentive audience to whom they spoke. But it is equally easy to undermine that narrative. Their famous series of debates was hardly the whole story of nineteenth-century American political culture. Nineteenth-century politics was rife with insult; reasoned argument was often eclipsed by spectacle, liquor, and corruption. Even if Americans historically have been drawn to jeremiad, a simple narrative of decline, which inevitably imputes moral failure, actually offers little help in understanding our present circumstances. We will do better to focus on specific changes in political culture and the larger social and cultural patterns that help to define it.

In his recent and important book *The Good Citizen: A History of American Civic Life*, Michael Schudson undertakes a more precise and historical examination of the condition of public life, past and present.[2] Arguing against the notion of decline, Schudson outlines a succession of different configurations of the institutions, practices, and values of American public life, from the seventeenth century to the present. He tracks the shifts in principles of authority in politics (from personal to interpersonal to impersonal), and in the geography of politics and public life (from town to city to suburb, technoburb, or edge city). And he finds that hierarchy and obligation have receded as operative values in favor of an emphasis on rights. Instead of decline, he describes successive restructurings of American civic life, each of which involves a recalibration of citizenship and civic practice. His approach is compelling, and his conclusion is comforting. We are not so badly off as we might have thought. My own analysis shares with Schudson's a focus on changes in the circumstances or contexts—the larger public culture—in which political culture is embedded and out of which it is formed. No less than Schudson, I fail to find sufficient illumination in the jeremiad. Yet, unlike him, I am persuaded that the reconfigurings result in a less vital civic life and an impoverished politics.

To some, the explanation for the dissolution of serious and effective public discussion is the presence of difficult issues, issues that are hard to discuss—abortion, religion, race, and more. I grant the difficulty of these issues, but there is no point in a politics that must avoid the difficult issues of the time. Nor is there reason to believe that democracy is somehow inherently unable to address such issues. What we suffer derives from long-term changes in our social and cultural life that establish the underlying conditions, or stage, for political discourse. Some of these changes were driven by broad social transformations, but others were the result, ironically, of efforts by educated elites to "reform" public life. Such changes in the framing conditions of public discussion are more important in explaining our contemporary disappointment with civil society than the particular content of our public issues. Were the arena of public culture organized differently (and more fairly), we might well be able to address difficult issues in more democratic and politically effective ways. To identify the historical roots of our present politics, I will sketch a few themes and episodes that reveal changes in the shape of our public culture and in the relation of politics to social and cultural developments.[3]

Nineteenth-century political culture in its heyday, between roughly 1830 and 1890, was marked by intense partisan identities, strongly competitive parties, and a politics of spectacle.[4] Political culture was intensely masculine and it was white. Racial and sexual exclusion was not accidental, but central to the "standing" of the citizen, to use Judith Shklar's term.[5] Political affiliation, moreover, was part of personal identity. Rarely did one change parties. Political rhetoric was not designed to convert voters; rather the clambakes, torchlight parades, and militaristic party rhetoric aimed to mobilize voters whose votes were predictable. Almost all who cast ballots voted a straight ticket. Indeed, such ballots were available in preprinted form.

The press was integral to this political culture. It was financed by the parties—directly, not by advertising—and it was openly partisan. The press and party rhetoric constructed a worldview that nurtured the political identity of white male citizens, and it offered those citizens a narrative interpretation of American history and political life. These narratives, bizarre as they often were, had an important role in sustaining political commitments; they gave meaning and significance to public life. Party activities and symbols also had a social function;they formed social solidarities.

Politics, thus, sustained social life and social life flowed into politics. This double movement of group identification was important. Politics not only reflected presumably preexistent group identities, but political practices contributed to their formation.[6] We may today be expecting too much of civil society in asking for the formation of local social groupings without the support of locally organized political parties. Politics was both more and less than a civic right and obligation; it was, at least in part, a form of entertainment. This quality of American political life was widely recognized by foreign visitors as the predominant form of entertainment in the United States. The "spectacular" model of politics constituted an important ritual of legitimation that sustained popular support for constitutional government, and it produced high levels of citizen participation. It was not uncommon for 80 percent of eligible voters to go to the polls.

I want to emphasize the "thick" texture of nineteenth-century political culture. Politics was embedded in social life, and it helped give form to everyday experience. Such is no longer the case. These thick dimensions of nineteenth-century political culture, clearly missing today, were valuable, but they did not necessarily promote rational argument. There is much that is appealing in this thumbnail description of nineteenth-century political culture, but there is too much that is disturbing to permit us to recall it with nostalgia. Not only were the Lincoln and Douglas debates a rare event, but racism, sexism, voter manipulation, and the spoils system were commonplaces.

A bit more than a century ago, this incarnation of American politics became the target of political reformers. These reformers, except for being exclusively male, might be understood as the social equivalents of highly educated, civic-spirited professionals or academics today. Without self-consciousness, they referred to themselves as the "best men."[7] And they felt that intelligence and learning, their personal and class capital, had insufficient weight in American politics, a politics of mass democracy and spectacle. Post-Civil War politics, they thought, gave too much power to quantity over quality. The numerous ignorant voters in immigrant communities, organized by bosses and duped by partisanship, had more clout than did the educated. Charles Eliot Norton, a leader among the reformers and a Harvard professor, complained: "The principle of equality is extended into regions where it has no proper validity. Our public life, our literature, our journals, our churches, our amusements, our politics, all exhibit a condescension to the crowd. . . . There is a lack of independence and of leading."[8]

Some of the reformers, the noted journalist E. L. Godkin among them, proposed compromising universal male suffrage—the great historian Francis Parkman did the same[9]—claiming that democracy did not imply the vote. Godkin and his ilk also rejected the ideal of positive government that had been so evident in the Civil War and Reconstruction, turning instead to laissez-faire theories of political economy. Essentially, if the government did nothing, it did not matter if the rabble—their phrase for the increasingly organized working class—won some power in it.[10]

Their version of reformed politics presumed that informed citizenship and reasoned argument, not corruption and blind partisanship, should define a smaller but proper civic life. By 1920, much of their program had been achieved. Parties were weakened and independent voters became respectable. Reformers made the world safe for the educated, independent voter. But at the same time, elitism and disdain for the less well educated made the world of politics less welcoming to the immigrant and working class voter. "Discouragements" to participation were even more substantial for the African American citizen.[11] Like Jürgen Habermas in our time, the reformers, rightly interested in promoting reasoned argument, wrongly reduced the political being to the merely cerebral. There was a loss of that wholeness of political life that had been recognized and celebrated by the Greeks and writers who have affirmed that classical tradition, most notably in our century, Hannah Arendt. The meaning—and thus the significance and appeal—of politics was narrowed.[12]

With these developments, voter participation began a decline that has been steady ever since, save for the reversal in the New Deal era when workers, African Americans, and immigrants were drawn into Democratic Party politics.[13] One might fairly argue that nearly all the past century's progressive proposals for campaign and election reform have weakened parties and the idea of partisanship. Today, parties have very little role in the selection of candidates or the determination of policies. They have lost their monopoly on political information to the more objective coverage of mass journalism; government is increasingly reduced to administration, particularly fiscal administration; and influence is achieved through particularistic, organized interests that supply the money politicians need for their post-party, mediated campaigns. In fact, the ritual and talk that was so prominent before reform has been displaced by the weakening of partisanship and the growth of mediated politics—leading to the overrepresentation of those interests that are able to supply campaigns with the funds they require for such a politics. In their quest for a more honorable and reason-giving politics, reformers rejected the social and symbolic aspects of partisanship. Whatever the potential gains in rational discourse, this thinning isolated politics from the everyday life that had importantly structured political identification, meanings, and responsibility. It made for greater voter volatility, and candidates appeared in the media outside any defining context. This combination made voters vulnerable to a new kind of political opportunism at the hands of both individual candidates and organized interests.

These political developments, as I have suggested, went hand in hand with changes in the press. Many of the late nineteenth-century reformers were, like Godkin, journalists, and they pressed the idea of an independent, objective press, free of party affiliation. In 1850, 95 percent of the press was partisan, which meant not only that the newspaper had a political disposition, but also that it was directly funded by a political party. The *New York Times*, with its now more than a century old commitment to objective news, expressed in the motto "All the news that's fit to print," was and is a model of this new journalism. Advertising made this revolution possible. Most of us favor "objective" news, but it was clearly the older connection between politics and the press that Alexis de Tocqueville praised as the foundation of American democracy.[14] Moreover, there is increasing evidence, most notably in the powerful argument of C. Edwin Baker, that advertising's role in supporting the press seriously limits the diversity of opinion and the rigor of reasoned discourse.[15] With the dissolution of partisanship, of party narratives in the press and on the stump, and of the social aspects of party life, it became harder for citizens to feel much like members of parties and therefore responsible to some larger body or movement. Today, two-thirds of voters split tickets, and about 40 percent of the electorate identify themselves as independent.

Such is the thinning of our political culture. But that is only part of the problem. In itself, the replacement of a ritualistic politics with the politics of education ought not to have had seriously negative consequences. But in conjunction with a series of other developments, all of which I will associate with the 1920s, the change helped transform politics in a way that effectively displaced the political and the seriousness entailed by the political. Our public culture is impoverished because it has ceased to be political, or, put differently, because it is no longer a site for serious political work.

Soon after World War I, Walter Lippmann published *Public Opinion* (1922). It was characterized at the time by John Dewey as "perhaps the most effective indictment of democracy as currently conceived ever penned." Lippmann followed in 1925 with *The Phantom Public* and Dewey responded in 1927, with his only work of political philosophy, *The Public and Its Problems*.[16] What was the nub of this extraordinarily important debate which, in my view, announces the democratic dilemma of our century? During the war, Lippmann had been excited by the possibilities of expertise and deeply disappointed in the capacity of the public. How could the citizen understand the demands of modern society and government? A vision of citizen participation that was plausible in the age of Jefferson was now an anachronism. Instead of Jefferson's faith in the competent citizen, Lippmann despaired of the incompetent public so easily manipulated by propaganda during the war. He proposed to accept what he found; let the political theorists and practitioners assume an incompetent passive public, one drawn to the new consumer culture. Let government be managed by insiders and experts, with a regular plebiscite-like vote of confidence.

Dewey acknowledged that abundance and entertainments threatened the centrality of politics in the common life of Americans, but he insisted that the passive public was historically created, not an essential condition of modernity. Effective competence, he argued, was circumstantial, not innate. He proposed that the public, nourished initially at the local level in communities connected by voice, by the same face-to-face problem-solving associations that Tocqueville observed, could and should find itself and become the basis for a participatory democracy, one in which experts serve the public rather than displacing it. He deeply believed that there was an intelligence of democracy.[17] Unfortunately, Lippmann's vision of an incompetent public predicted the future better than did Dewey's call for a revitalized public. Lippmann's assumptions were precisely represented in mainstream political science, especially in the behaviorist and pluralist movements that followed World War II. Elite and academic lack of faith, even deep fear of mass democratic publics in the 1940s and 1950s, contributed to the demobilization of the more inclusive public of the New Deal era.

Parallel developments of a broader, cultural sort contributed further to the weakening of the public culture and the displacement of reasoned discourse. The repeal of reticence, to use Rochelle Gurstein's phrase, inflated private matters and pushed public matters to the margins.[18] Personality replaced both character and issues.[19] Exposure of private vices undermined the public's business, which is, in Dewey's formulation, those private acts that affect collective life. There were, of course, good reasons to expose the private realm—secrecy cannot and ought not be wholly trusted. But with public discourse already weakened by the dissolution of partisanship in parties, the new sensibility and the sensational journalism that sustained it emptied the public culture of much of its political content. In the nineteenth century, entertainment and politics were fused; in the twentieth century, one displaced the other.

Democracy and public life, already thinned, were further diminished by advertising and survey research. In the 1920s, Edward Bernays, the founder of modern advertising, remarked that businessmen learn to use the pageantry and spectacle of politics for their sales campaigns, but politicians, he complained, learn nothing from business, nothing from those who "study the public and manufacture products based on this study." It was amazing to him that "the very men who make their millions out of cleverly devised drives for soap and cars, will turn around and give large contributions to be extended for vote getting in an utterly inefficient and antiquated fashion." Fifty years later, such a charge would seem fantastic. The voter is treated as a consumer and the political content of electioneering has been diminished to the vanishing point.[20] The same broad social developments provided both the opportunity and the need for marketing and advertising of products and candidates. Modern selling, for example, depended upon the dissolution of locally based and socially embedded or connected patterns of production and consumption. Likewise, modern vote-getting as marketing depends upon the dissolution of the continuing social affiliations and traditional political narratives represented by parties and the partisan press.

It is revealing that Paul Lazarsfeld's classic voter study, *The People's Choice*, published in 1944, was initially conceived as a study of consumer choice. The availability of funding for voter studies prompted the change of focus, which Lazarsfeld accepted because he felt the choice in the two domains was essentially similar. The point was made a few years later with startling candor by Rosser Reeves, an ad man and GOP adviser. He characterized the man in the voting booth hesitating between two levers as no different from the consumer who was "pausing between competing tubes of toothpaste in a drugstore."[21] Lazarsfeld's work produced what he called "the law of minimal effect," which had quite a significant effect on campaigning and advertising. He concluded that opinions of the consumer and the voter could not be changed by advertising. Rather, the point of advertising and campaigning must be to associate a product or a candidate with beliefs already held by the voter or consumer—as often as not beliefs with no use value in the case of products and no political meaning in the case of candidates.[22] To my mind, the most consequential implication of this use of word and image in a manner disconnected from narrative explanation is that it obfuscates the relation between cause and effect. That obfuscation is fatal not only to reasoned discourse, but more consequentially, to political solutions of any kind.

My conclusion is brief and prescriptive. The age of parties is past; we ought not lament that. We ought not long to restore them. Yet we need to recover by alternate means two of the functions they performed. First, we need public narratives competing in a diverse public culture to sustain political commitment and meaning. Such narratives steady the electorate and make citizens less vulnerable to media manipulation. Second, we need an institutional space continuous with social life where public matters of interest to diverse individuals and groups can be engaged by them directly. Such practical civic education is the foundation of responsible public life. There is, however, a third necessity, one noted by Alexis de Tocqueville. Citizens are not a public unless they have work to do. They will come together into a tentative engagement only if they have work to do together, conflicts to resolve. Any localized, face-to-face public must be empowered, for it is only the real-life give-and-take of politics that can nourish the enlightened self-interest that so impressed Tocqueville. He never fully elaborated the concept, but in it one finds an essential, but difficult to calibrate combination of assertion of interest, respect for difference, and commitment to civic responsibility—learned by practice, not precept.[23] Political work in public is both the means and the end. We need it to bridge difference, not to erase it. Since social distance breeds contempt, whether in political or cultural life, we must shorten that distance. The work of public life is not to make people like each other or to feel at one with each other, but to enable them to continue to work with each other as new issues emerge. Dewey may have been right: only more democracy can cure the problems of democracy.

Chapter 2
Primary Tensions in American Public Life

Robert H. Wiebe

This essay has two objectives: to identify important tensions in contemporary American public life that relate specifically to the improvement of public discourse, and to state those tensions in a way that stresses the necessity of recognizing and grappling with them. Advocates of better public discourse do not have to agree on a single position or side, but each of these tensions needs to be taken seriously in the discussion of civil society in a democracy. The purpose of the essay's back-and-forth format is to express unresolved debates and tensions that have played out repeatedly in American history and could continue indefinitely.

Setting the Rules for Public Discourse

Without rules on civility and the resolution of conflicts, public life deteriorates into a jungle of passions, one side argues. Without a focus on the common good and rules for deliberation, public exchanges are merely expressive, not deliberative. To be effective, democracy requires a rational structure. Thoughtful, knowledgeable people, the argument goes, have the ability and hence the obligation to define what constitutes a healthy public life.

No rules are neutral, the counter-argument goes, and invoking code words such as "rationality" will not make them so. Rules on civility and deliberation that suit some people—the comfortable, educated elite, for example, or members of a dominant group—block access for those who bring a different background, style, and intelligence to public life. By the same token, the keepers of the rules, especially the agencies of the state, only serve the interests of those powerful enough to reach them. Hence rules in a genuine democracy must be negotiated among all participants. If there is such a thing as the common good, it needs to emerge out of the democratic process itself. A certain messiness, a certain risk, is a small price to pay for an inclusive public life.

Letting the rules of civility and deliberation emerge out of the democratic process is an invitation to chaos, the first side replies. Democratic deliberation requires restraint: it is not therapy for everybody's frustrations.

Without some enforced rules, public exchange becomes a dog chasing its tail: deliberation cannot even begin. Moreover, study, expertise, and knowledge matter. Trained minds do see more and understand better than untrained ones, and their very training protects them against most of those hypothetical biases that critics claim would exclude groups from participation.

Of course public exchanges must begin somewhere, the second side responds. What really matters is recognizing the exclusionary tendency in any set of a priori rules: all rules must always be open for renegotiation. As for those superior minds competent to set the rules, the public in a democracy will let them know if they need their help. People will not be shy to ask for help when they need it, if that is what they really get.

Informing Citizens About Public Life

The guiding principle is simple, one argument goes. Come as close as possible to making all information available to the public in a democracy. Public life cannot thrive without an informed public. Though "all" information is obviously a fiction and an unattainable standard, it is a serious fiction. Do not withhold information about public figures and public affairs because somehow it seems irrelevant to genuine public concerns. A public figure's reputation is never an excuse to suppress information. Make it a cardinal rule of the news media to resolve all matters of doubt in favor of providing, not withholding, information. Store government records in ways that allow them to be retrieved as citizens request them. Narrow the concept of national security so drastically that only the most self-evident cases qualify as confidential—and then for the least number of years.

For three reasons, disclosure of all information is an unacceptable guide, another argument goes. First, long before something resembling this goal is reached, the public will have drowned in information. "All" means dump all available junk on people who have neither the time nor the skill to sort among it for useful information. If an informed public is the goal, access to all information guarantees failure. Second, an absence of filters for the flow of information is equivalent to an absence of public values. We do not need to pretend that relevance and rationality are mysteries: there are principles governing both, and both should filter the flow of information. We should not pretend there is no such thing as public decency. An overwhelming majority of the public knows better. We should explore the boundaries of decency, not ignore them. Third, informing the public requires correcting for the bias of wealth. An unmodified "all information" policy surrenders the public to the rich and the powerful. For evidence of this we need go no farther than the advertising leverage that big business possesses, or the error of *Buckley v. Valeo* (1976), which struck down campaign spending limits as unconstitutional impediments on political speech. "All information" translates into all the information that privilege and money can buy.

In reverse order, the first side responds that *Buckley* is not a mistake; it is only incomplete. Obsessing about money actually distracts from the real issue: diversity. Let money buy what it can, but open more and more outlets for competing voices so that all sides are heard. Second, the history of free speech is strewn with obsolete standards of decency and discarded assumptions of relevance that at one time suppressed information that we would now consider essential to the public agenda. Finally, remember the principle of the garage sale: one person's junk is another's treasure. We do need to develop and refine processing tools that will enable citizens to sort and sift quantities of data efficiently, but we should never narrow the range of that data.

Processing tools are a euphemism for limitations, the other side replies. Do not pretend they are something else; simply be self-conscious about the most sensible limitations for an informed public deliberation. And do not invoke the history of free speech as if it were necessarily a straight line, forever allowing more and more information with fewer and fewer restraints. Certain kinds of speech may deserve levels of protection that others do not—this is Cass Sunstein's proposition.[1] Finally, until those hypothetical outlets for public expression come into existence, money orchestrates access to information and *Buckley* must go.

American Society—Groups or Individuals?

America's dearest tradition, one argument goes, is the equality of individuals in public affairs and before the law. Construing America in any other terms violates the essential meaning of its democracy. For various purposes—countries of origin for immigrants, age levels for social services, and the like—categories of convenience make sense. All of them are mutable and none interferes with the individuality of each person in the group. Where, on the other hand, culturally constructed categories—of race in particular—take priority over individuals, we establish our reality by fiat: "I was reinvented in 1973 by Richard Nixon," Richard Rodriguez writes.[2] Assigning rights and rewards on the terms of culturally created categories not only diminishes the humanity of winners and losers alike, it also distorts public policy by turning faddish social categories of the moment into its building blocks. It is one thing to punish tobacco manufacturers as knowing poisoners; it is an entirely different thing to create a category of nicotine addicts and compensate them for inhaling.

No one lives outside a context, an alternative argument begins. Everything we are, everything we know, is mediated by cultural contexts. Even in a democracy, individuals are the supreme category of convenience. Hence, as Robert Putnam has argued, we measure democracy's strength not by the state of its citizen atoms but by the health of its groups—its social capital.[3] Public policy always involves a search for the best groupings. In fact, that is how justice is meted to individuals: by not treating them individually. Some contexts we choose; many—probably the most important—we do not. Those, in effect, we inherit. In the United States, race and gender define the inherited categories with the most profound consequences. Fairness in contemporary policy and public life depends on a concentrated effort to redress these group legacies.

Groups matter because they sustain individuals, the first side replies. Putnam does not expect everybody in a bowling league to emerge with the same democratic stamp: individuals take it from there. The law may categorize, but individuals go to jail. By the same token, individuals live out the consequences of group compensation. How is it possible to factor into policy the significance—historical, contemporary, or otherwise—of race, class, and gender in the cases of a penniless nineteen-year-old white woman from the West Virginia mountains and a penniless nineteen-year-old black man from Cabrini-Green in Chicago? New arbitrary categories cannot overcome the sins of earlier arbitrary categories; they simply generate new inequities requiring ever newer corrections. If we believe in a society of free individuals, then we should free individuals.

The fact that individuals live, breathe, and die as individuals falls somewhere between the solipsistic and the ho-hum, the other side responds. What is unacceptable is the translation of this routine truth into the glorification of what Michael Sandel has called "the unencumbered self."[4] This glorification of the individual, furthermore, is a quite recent cultural phenomenon, one that Robert Bellah has also publicized in his own way.[5] By ignoring the contexts of our lives, both of these writers explain, we impoverish them. In the same fashion, by ignoring the group basis for injustice, we cripple our capacity to correct it. Most Americans most of the time understand that Jim Crow, restrictive covenants, and union exclusions did not operate by forming a long line and appraising afresh each individual. Groups have created other groups who, as groups, have suffered grievances that now demand group redress. Public policy must reflect this historical reality.

EDITORS' NOTE: We can only surmise how the late Robert Wiebe would have concluded this working paper, had he lived long enough to prepare it for publication. Yet we are struck by two implications that may be drawn from his argument. First, historical perspective is absolutely necessary in contextualizing the pro-and-con of contemporary political and cultural debate—a tension that Wiebe clearly regarded as primary and inevitable. Without historical perspective, one inevitably feels condemned to a Sisyphian dynamic of polar oppositions that makes even democracy's strongest advocates sometimes despair of its chaotic and wasteful excesses. Second, an appreciation of the dialectical character of these debates strongly suggests the need to look for an alternative, if not a synthetic, position. Only partisans of one polarization or the other can truly be comfortable in choosing between such reified positions. While acknowledging that no alternative can do away with the dynamics imposed on us by such primary tensions, David Ryfe's review of the contemporary literature on public discourse points to a model that begins to integrate the most valuable aspects of each pole: the need for rational and efficient decision procedures to ensure that public discourse is productive (else citizens will find it merely "talk for talk's sake" and stay home) and openness to the relational and emotive aspects of public discourse to ensure the participatory character of democracy so necessary to its legitimacy and credibility.[6] As Wiebe implies in his introductory paragraph, no democracy—certainly not American democracy—can function without integrating aspects of each polar position into its essential character. No wonder the dialectical debate seems endless and unproductive—it must be. The worst possible outcome would be for one side or the other to gain permanent ascendancy. In the tension lies America's greatest strength and flexibility—of which no scholar was more profoundly appreciative than Robert Wiebe.

—*Judith Rodin and Stephen P. Steinberg*

Chapter 3
Deliberative Democracy and Public Discourse

David M. Ryfe

Why Deliberation? Deliberative Democracy and Its Critics

Of all the ways to organize a democracy, a reliance on public discourse and communication is better than its alternatives. Yet, surprisingly, our liberal political tradition leaves little room for political deliberation or communication in public life.[1] The framers of our Constitution had a particular distaste for political talk outside of governmental institutions.[2] Even today, John Rawls, the leading liberal thinker of the last half-century, conceives of no fundamental place for deliberation in his ideal model of politics.[3] Instead, for Rawls, as for most other liberals, politics is confined to the procedural sphere between the state and the citizens. Liberals like Rawls believe that the primary danger faced by political society is not that it is too fragmented—fragmentation is a defining aspect of a plural society—but that the state may unduly constrain individual rights. In mainstream liberalism, it is the protection of rights, not public discourse, that assures a good democratic politics. So long as individuals have an equal right to form preferences and get those preferences heard by the larger public, a democratic polity has achieved its primary goal.[4]

The liberal tradition has been drawn upon to level several criticisms at deliberative democrats: (1) they misconstrue the purpose of politics, which ought to be oriented to the protection of individual rights rather than to the establishment of cultural harmony; (2) they assume self-interest and issues of power can be erased in politics; (3) they misjudge the interest and willingness of individuals to participate in politics in more than minimal ways; (4) they inappropriately seek to make consensus on substantive views a standard of political legitimacy; and (5) they do not have an adequate appreciation for the possibility of social disorder when competing comprehensive substantive claims are deliberated.[5] According to their critics, deliberative democrats place too much importance on social harmony and political participation, often at the expense of individual rights. Most damningly, they conceive of the good society as one in which everyone gets along, and everyone participates in a free and equal manner in public discussions, rather than as one in which individuals bear the right to be let alone.

If for liberal thinkers deliberative democracy is theoretically unsatisfying, for social choice theorists it is practically unrealistic. Highly influential in contemporary political science, social choice theory approaches politics as a process of interaction between social agents intent on securing their personal ends.[6] Lacking full information, these actors opt for strategies that, as Herbert Simon has put it, are "satisficing"; that is, that offer "good enough," if not optimal, outcomes.[7] On the basis of this view, William Riker has argued that, even if deliberation were theoretically preferable, better political outcomes would not emerge from more, and more open, discussion, for several reasons.[8] First, many issues are so complex that different and often competing choices can be made, even on the basis of the same set of values. Second, choices among the range of issues that might be deliberated upon are impossible to order in a rational way. Thus, there is no rational means of choosing to act on one issue rather than another at any given moment. Finally, in any particular deliberative session, leaders may move the discussion in irrational ways by controlling the agenda.[9] Riker concludes that even if deliberative democracy could be justified in theory, in reality it cannot achieve the ends it desires.

For scholars who draw upon the work of Friedrich Nietzsche and his postmodernist followers, it is the process, not the outcome, of deliberative democracy that is faulty. Donald Moon notes that arguments for deliberative democracy are inherently circular: they depend upon common rules and principles which themselves must be up for discussion.[10] This discussion, however, will likely end when it is realized that any set of rules by definition will exclude some people from the deliberative process. Peter Berkowitz extends this point, to argue that power in a deliberative process will naturally flow to those who are more capable in the "deliberative arts"; that is, deliberative democracy is set up to reproduce the status of exactly those kinds of people who argue for it most vehemently, the "professors and pundits . . . who by virtue of advanced education, quickness of thought, and fluenc[y] of speech, can persuade others."[11] Strangely, deliberative democracy ends in a process that may be deliberative, but at the expense of broad public participation.[12]

These various challenges go to the core of the deliberative enterprise. If it is true that deliberative democrats have misjudged the boundaries of the political, have misinterpreted human nature and the inviolability of comprehensive doctrines, and have overestimated the likely results of deliberation, then a focus on good public discourse as a cure for the ills of public culture is also misguided. Deliberative democrats have offered several arguments in their defense. These responses make clear the fundamental assumptions, principles, and goals of the deliberative enterprise.

The Deliberative Defense

Deliberative democrats begin by drawing upon the communitarian insight that people live in communities, not as autonomous individuals.[13] Far from being independent of social ties, individuals gain a sense of themselves only in relation to others.[14] They are, in the parlance, socially constructed. Though significant disagreement among members of a community is possible, it is always expressed in the context of shared cultural traditions. The problem, as deliberative democrats see it, is that in the United States these cultural traditions have become fragmented.[15] Absent a shared culture, moral disagreements become intractable, and ultimately erode the very possibility of achieving good political outcomes.[16] Unlike conventional liberals, deliberative democrats view communication as key because it offers the only avenue for expressing and negotiating deep moral differences, and for reconnecting people to their shared cultural traditions.[17]

If the outcomes of such deliberation are never fully rational, as Riker points out, deliberative democrats nonetheless defend political outcomes achieved through deliberation in two ways. First, they argue that open deliberation will lead to more rational outcomes than will choices made through other mechanisms. And second, even if deliberative conversations are not fully rational, they still privilege a mode of reasoning and argument that is preferable to other ways of making public claims.[18] These responses stem directly from the work of John Stuart Mill, who suggested that free and open deliberation in a "marketplace of ideas" will strengthen arguments.[19] Increasing the variety of participants in the public's conversation will broaden the reasoning capacity of society as a whole. This increased variety will also pressure individuals to justify their preferences by giving reasons to others.

The outcomes produced by deliberation will also be more legitimate.[20] Berkowitz may be correct that deliberative democratic procedures may end in simultaneously reproducing and masking the power of elites. But representative mechanisms can be implemented to preclude this possibility.[21] Moreover, it is unclear that other forms of democratic decision-making would curtail the power of elites any more than deliberative democracy. Opening political discourse to greater public scrutiny might at least increase the scope of consensus, and thus achieve greater legitimacy. Talk, as opposed to voting or bargaining, forces individuals to justify their political positions to others.

Finally, a few deliberative democrats go further still, to argue that deliberation in and of itself produces better citizens.[22] This notion, drawn from Aristotle, and more immediately from republican theories of political participation, assumes that social interaction cultivates prudence, a constraint of the passions, and concern for others.[23] Participation in a deliberative exchange will force individuals to consider a range of opposing viewpoints and to hone their cognitive abilities through use of argumentative skills. Deliberation also roots individuals in a social world, since arguments are developed on the basis of shared cultural norms. With its narrowly constrained, procedurally oriented political universe, conventional liberalism denies the possibility that a public culture might alter individual values. Many deliberative democrats, in contrast, view the enlightenment of individuals to be the best reason for a revitalized public discourse.

Taken together, these defenses of deliberative democracy represent the best case to be made for revamping American public discourse. Public discourse is good, its advocates claim, because it is the only way to deal with deep moral disagreement. It leads to more rational outcomes than other methods of decision-making, establishes political legitimacy, and creates better citizens. Though inspired by real-world concerns, this argument has been made on the basis of theory, not practical circumstances.

Deliberation for Whom? Social and Cultural Challenges to Good Discourse

Few theorists of deliberative democracy have attempted to connect their principled defenses of deliberation with empirical data on the real world.[24] This split between theory and data is unfortunate. It presents an obstacle to moving from a defense of deliberation in general to a set of specific deliberative principles. Even if the theoretical argument for deliberative democracy is valid, it is still unclear who it is valid for, under what conditions, and guided by which principles. Deliberation may be good for the United States in theory, but several social trends raise practical questions.

ECONOMIC INEQUALITY

It is by now widely known that poverty in the United States, and economic inequality generally, increased during the 1980s.[25] While the income of the richest one-fifth of Americans increased by an average of 25 percent during the 1980s, poverty increased in the same period from 11.4 percent of the population to 14.4 percent.[26] As poverty increased, the absolute numbers in the middle classes declined more than 5 percent.[27] It is less well known that wealth inequality over the history of the United States has been relatively stable.[28] This is not to diminish the importance of economic inequality, only to set the issue in a larger perspective. Inequality may not have been much greater in the 1990s than it was in the 1890s, but it is a persistent aspect of American socioeconomic relations.

This inequality affects public deliberation in several ways. First, economic inequality is firmly associated with levels of political knowledge.[29] Lower socioeconomic status (SES) is strongly correlated with low levels of political knowledge, low access to political information, and low interest in politics. SES is also strongly associated with levels of political participation.[30] Without economic security, poorer individuals are less likely to participate in any kind of political activity, from voting to calling their representatives. Finally, lower SES is also connected to lower education levels, which in turn result in greater political intolerance.[31] Lacking skills of argument perceived to be appropriate to the public sphere, and the mobility necessary to gain a wider view of the world, poorer people are generally less tolerant of others than people with greater economic means. Any form of public deliberation must speak to these basic economic realities underlying political life.

SOCIAL FRAGMENTATION

Several indicators also suggest that the United States is socially dislocated at both the local and national levels, primarily along racial and ethnic lines. The isolation of the inner city from the suburb is well documented.[32] Within suburbia itself, however, exclusivity has been a continuous trend since the nineteenth century. Just as Anglo-Saxons moved to the exterior of the nineteenth-century city to escape the Irish, so whites today use a variety of devices, such as rent controls, land use ordinances, and open discrimination, to sequester their suburbs from people of color.[33] In recent years, this trend has evolved into the creation of gated communities.[34] While not pervasive—Thernstrom and Thernstrom point out that the integration of blacks and whites is actually higher than it has ever been—the very presence of these communities is ample reminder of the continuing desire for racial separation.[35] Moreover, social isolation has been intensified by the erosion of public spaces and the "malling of America."[36]

This social fragmentation challenges models of good public discourse in three ways. First, isolated social groups may have fewer interests and experiences in common. Widely divergent interests produce less common ground for public deliberation. Second, levels of trust may be much weaker between groups that have little contact with one another.[37] Lack of trust makes it more difficult to initiate and sustain a public conversation. Finally, social fragmentation exacerbates long-standing traditions of discrimination.[38] This decidedly illiberal sentiment has been confirmed in a number of surveys.[39] Americans judge others on the basis of group stereotypes and discrimination, which often produce very illiberal kinds of engagement in the public space.[40]

This illiberalism mixes in unpredictable ways with liberal values. Although social fragmentation is greater than one might like, much of the empirical data suggests that Americans of every stripe still hold to a basic set of liberal values.[41] Most notably, Americans believe in the possibility of individual success, in formal individual rights, and in the protection of private property, whatever their ethnic, racial, and class differences, and despite a predisposition to ethnoculturalism. The contradictory nature of the American value system (Rogers Smith has described it as at once liberal, republican, and ethnocultural)[42] explains many of the contradictions in our public discourse. Americans, particularly white Americans, advocate social policies to help the disadvantaged—but only if these policies are not framed in the language of groups.[43] Americans look fondly on new immigrants, but only if they ascribe to a set of "typical" American values and cultural habits.[44] Any viable theory of deliberation must take account of this complex assortment of liberal and illiberal values.

POLITICAL PRIVATIZATION

Finally, deliberative democrats must confront the basic fact that while they belong to a country of joiners, Americans have rarely been interested in conventional political institutions. People today generally do not vote, let alone participate more fully in politics, and this is nothing new.[45] Certainly, the party period of the late nineteenth century was characterized by enormous participation, particularly in election seasons, but this has not been the norm in U.S. history.[46] Even the interest in electoral politics created by parties in the nineteenth century is anomalous in some respects. Citizens voted, campaigned, and paraded, but knew little about political issues and did not play a significant role in choosing nominees or setting party agendas. Voting rates increased during the New Deal, but by the 1960s they declined once again and have stayed roughly the same ever since.

Of course, voting rates are not the only register of political participation. But they do indicate that politics for Americans historically has been a private affair, pursued in local associations, concerned with personal issues. Even in the nineteenth-century heyday of political parties, most individuals participated in local clubs and associations, rarely straying from their neighborhood or city. This fact should inspire humility among deliberative democrats. Concerted attention to politics seems to go against the American personality. Any principle that requires a demonstrable and continuous effort by citizens to participate in public affairs is likely to founder. Principles of deliberation must speak to people as they are, rather than imagine them as they will never be.

GLOBALIZATION

After World War II, the national economy slowly gave way to an international order, in which multinational conglomerates straddle the globe, unconstrained by the old rules of the Cold War.[47] If American society is fragmented and stratified today, the global order promises more of the same. Because globalization is beyond the purview of individual nation-states, national political leaders find it very difficult to formulate policies to soften its impact. Individual countries often find themselves at the mercy of international economic forces—and the upheaval they bring to local cultures and traditions.

Institutional Challenges to Good Public Discourse

Aside from economic inequality, political privatization, social fragmentation, and the emergence of globalization, the structure of our political institutions presents the greatest obstacle to revising public discourse.

INTEREST-GROUP POLITICS

The rise of interest groups in Washington is well documented, and in the past twenty-five years, their influence has exploded.[48] In 1992, there were over 7,000 lobbyists registered with the Senate, a jump of over 4,000 in fifteen years.[49] This explosion of groups and lobbyists has changed the nature of politics. Once conducted by relatively stable, if exclusive, groups from business, labor, and the government, today politics resembles more a medieval bazaar.[50] Issues of every kind are contested, debated, and negotiated by a cadre of professional lobbyists expert in the ways of Washington politics. Interest-group politics threatens the implementation of good discourse in several ways. Professionalism itself often serves as a means by which to exclude ordinary individuals from politics.[51] What's more, the abstract, instrumental, and often technical language of professional lobbyists often contradicts the more familiar, private, informal language that ordinary Americans use in political discussions.[52] Finally, the quest to win—to pass or defeat a bill, elect a member of Congress, or raise money—becomes the sole goal of political interaction, and this undercuts rational, reasoned discourse.

THE ENTREPRENEURIAL POLITICIAN

In theory, the framers imagined Congress as an ideal body of public deliberation. Populated by the "best men" and governed by the rule of law, Congress was supposed to function as the primary deliberative forum for our nation.[53] Though it is more open and inclusive than in the past, the modern Congress rarely lives up to this image. To ensure inclusiveness, Congress has relaxed rules of decorum and debate, expanded the number of subcommittees, and increased the staff size of both committees and individual members. Virtually self-nominated, members of Congress today must constantly work to further their careers.[54] While their staffs handle more of the substantive work of deliberation, members concentrate on the things that will keep them in office: raising money, campaigning, and publicizing themselves. Consumed by this effort, members of Congress rarely rise to the level of principle, let alone moderate a healthy public conversation.[55]

The presidency has done little better. Woodrow Wilson first imagined this institution as a central national rhetorical force.[56] Seeing Congress as an inferior deliberative body, Wilson believed that the president ought to preside over a national conversation about large principles. In practice, Wilson's model of the rhetorical presidency devolved quickly. By the post–World War II period, Daniel Boorstin could talk about the rise of "image politics" in presidential communication—a form of artificial publicity designed to sell presidents as products rather than to lead public dialogue.[57] Image politics has become so ingrained in presidential communication that whole departments are dedicated to the purpose.[58] Thus, publicity techniques have made it easier for presidents to sell themselves, but at the cost of a serious national dialogue.

From Parties to Political Consultants

It is unclear whether the fragmentation of Congress and the selling of the presidency can be attributed to a third trend in national politics—the replacement of parties by political consultants—but the three processes have at the least paralleled one another. The demise of the parties, a process that began in the Progressive period, is well established.[59] By the 1960s few voters identified themselves as strong party advocates. Largely running outside the party structure, candidates asked political consultants to administer their campaigns and to provide political advice. This trend became especially strong with the advent of television campaigning.[60] Of course, consultants have long played a role in politics.[61] But the demise of the parties and the rise of television campaigning have put the modern political consultant at the heart of the political process.[62]

As in the case of professional lobbyists, political consultants have contributed to a rationalization of political language. Hired to elect specific candidates, they rarely take a larger view of the public good. Their use of negative advertising is a case in point. Despite the fact that most commentators agree—even most political consultants agree—that negative ads corrode the public discourse, consultants routinely turn to this method of political communication. Why? Because it works. As Stephen Ansolabehere and Shanto Iyengar have documented, negative ads succeed not by attracting people to a candidate's message, but by depressing support for opposing candidates.[63] Negative ads work precisely to the extent that they reduce popular participation and support for the political process.

The other primary technique employed by political consultants—opinion polling—is little better. Catering to the needs of politicians who could no longer rely on parties to gauge public support, pollsters soon became a staple of modern political communication. Scholars have offered trenchant critiques of polling, indicting it as everything from a manipulation of the public to a denigration of public discourse.[64] Despite these criticisms, polling has become more, not less, central to modern campaigning and governance. Indeed, along with negative advertising, it represents a primary feature of a modern political discourse that is more rationalized and strategic than ever before.

MEDIA SPECTACLE

Finally, the media have played a decisive role in transforming political deliberation into spectacle. It has long been known that the media "frame" politics in particular ways.[65] They tend to focus on events rather than process, personalities rather than issues. They tend to divide issues into two sides, to use official sources to represent these sides, and to play up the opposition between them.[66] In the past twenty years, the organization of the media and their impact on the news has changed demonstrably. When the networks were taken over by larger conglomerates in 1985–1986 (NBC by General Electric; ABC by Capital Cities and later Disney; CBS by Loews and later Westinghouse and Viacom), they became more closely connected to the global corporate economy.[67] At the same time, cable and satellite television have greatly expanded the media environment.[68] Once insulated from the demands of profits and ratings, television news today is a money-making machine. In a more competitive environment, and charged with attaining high ratings, television news has adopted many of the entertainment techniques it was once loathe to embrace.[69] In this environment, the distance between news and entertainment has shrunk. Television news is today more dramatic and emotional than in the past. Star reporters convey this dramatized news in a variety of quasi-news formats, from news magazine shows to talk shows.[70] Changes in the newspaper industry have also made it more focused on the economic bottom line and more inclined toward entertainment and personality, rather than conventional politics or journalistic expertise.[71]

In the context of other strong political institutions, this commercialization of the news would not merit much comment. A strong party structure would compensate for the inadequate reporting of the news media. However, this commercialization has taken place in an institutional vacuum. With the withering of the parties and the fragmentation of other political institutions, the news media have become the central site of political deliberation.[72] Where once the parties and elected officials served as primary intermediaries of political discourse, today reporters serve that function. The result has been a spectacularization of political talk: a talk that is simplified for dramatic effect, polarized, and inflammatory, rather than reasoned, moderate, and reciprocal.

Together, these features show us a political world that has largely become disconnected from ordinary citizens. It is, paradoxically, a more democratic world in that many more groups vie for political influence than in the past. But it is a democratized politics conducted by professional lobbyists, politicians, consultants, and reporters. Trained in the "game" of politics, these actors drain from political discourse all but the most strategic talk. Citizens enter into this dialogue primarily in the form of polls, a common currency wielded by all sides in the competition to define and interpret political issues. The result of their interactions is a rationalized, competitive, strategic form of political dialogue that leaves little room for the realization of robust public discourse. These social and institutional challenges do not exclude good public discourse, but the brute facts do serve to temper the elegant theory of deliberative democracy. Recognition of the clash between theory and reality will produce more clearly defined, pragmatic principles of good public discourse.

Part Two
Challenges of Public Discourse

Talking About Race

Chapter 4

Affirmative Action and the Culture of Intolerance

Christopher Edley, Jr.

What kind of conceptual structure can we discern in all the policy disagreements about affirmative action, and about race more broadly?
Imagine a matrix, and for the rows think of education, employment, and
contracting; for the columns, think of a range of tools or interventions
that one might adopt in each of those contexts.[1] The columns start on
one end with soft measures like outreach and recruitment, and then simply making race a consideration in an admissions decision; they move to
somewhat firmer measures—a thumb on the scale, or some kind of a
bonus—to still firmer measures, perhaps a numerical goal, and ultimately at the other end a set-aside and, at the extreme, a quota. Specifying all the cells in the matrix, we see clearly that there is a multitude of
contexts and tools by which immutable characteristics like race or gender
might play a role in decision-making. Consider a single context, such as
employment. If one concludes that it makes sense to take race into account in at least some employment circumstances, this raises further
questions. When you say employment, do you mean hiring, or do you
also mean promotion? If you mean promotion, what about layoffs? An
initial problem when it comes to making general policy statements is the
mind-numbing complexity of specific policy settings. The most important conclusion, for me, is that talking about race and affirmative action
is not rocket science. It's harder than rocket science.

Moreover, we cannot simply work through the details of a single cell of
this matrix as though it were independent of the others. Clearly there
has to be some search for the deeper issues and values at stake if we hope
to construct reasoning that is coherent and even persuasive, rather than
ad hoc and seemingly arbitrary. I have posed the deeper question this
way: Do you believe there is a moral cost to making decisions about people based upon their immutable characteristics, like color or gender?
There are at least three ways of answering that question. Some people
think, "Yes, there is a moral cost, and the moral cost is so great that we
should never be willing to pay it." This is the color-blind perspective. At
the other end of the spectrum, there are some people who think that

paying attention to color or gender is really no different from paying attention to other factors by which we sort people and allocate benefits and burdens when we make public policy—factors such as geography, income, and athleticism, for example. Gender and race are simply other variables that one could rationally use in making decisions to optimize some objective. The middle ground position is that there is a special moral cost, but we ought to be willing to pay that cost in at least some circumstances. Those who take that middle position are then drawn into argument about what specific circumstances might justify paying attention to race.

The first position, that there is a cost and it is always too great a cost to bear, is distinguishable from the second and third positions, and has logical coherence. Indeed, it has moral coherence. In our arguments about race, and about affirmative action in particular, it is important to understand value differences between the first position, especially, and either the second or third. One possible explanation is that people who hold the first position are simply less concerned than I am about effectiveness. They might say, "I'm against discrimination; I'm in favor of racial justice, but I'm not particularly concerned with consequentialist arguments about what kind of tool is needed in order to achieve it, because I have a higher principle of color-blindness that to me is more important than instrumental arguments about what measures might be needed in order to achieve equality." I am enough of a utilitarian to feel uncomfortable with that position, but I understand it. There are people who hold a moral position that has nothing to do with an instrumental calculation about effects. Showing somebody who has that perspective a new social science study on race is not going to influence them at all. On race, the role that your evidence has in argument depends a bit on the moral position of the opponent. It is therefore useful to clarify the distinction between moral positions in the discourse on race.

The next difficult question is this: If you believe that there is a moral cost, but that it might sometimes be worth paying, then when? Within the legal framework, the most obvious answer is that the moral cost is worth paying to remedy discrimination. The difficulty, of course, is we have huge disagreements about what discrimination is—how to define it, how to measure it, and when its legacy of lingering effects is sufficiently attenuated to say that discrimination no longer provides a moral predicate for social or legal practice. Some believe that it is not discrimination unless there is an identifiable victim and racial animus dripping from the lips of a perpetrator. On the other end, people believe that any kind of observed social or economic disparity is discrimination. They do not have to see animus or intent. Color-coded inequality is evidence enough of discrimination. There is of course a range of positions between these extremes. The simple statement, "I'm against discrimination," is at best a platitude and at worst an obfuscation, because the difficult issues that divide us are not about opposition to discrimination. They are about the difficult moral choices involved in defining and measuring it, and deciding what we are going to do about it. Choosing a definition of discrimination, as is well known to those who study race, involves making commitments familiar to political philosophers. For example, focusing on individual culpability, on the one hand, or focusing on ideals about community, on the other, entails a basic choice and commitment about political philosophy. Part of the problem with defining discrimination is that the communal impulse and the traditional liberal, individualistic impulse both run deep in American political culture. Therefore, a legal or policy position that embraces only one of those two alternatives will inevitably open itself to serious disagreement—and indeed we see extremists on either side of these debates.

There is a third deeply difficult issue. If we accept that remedying discrimination, however defined, might provide a justification in certain circumstances for paying attention to race or gender, is remediation the only available justification? Diversity and inclusion are other possible rationales for paying attention to race and gender, and they are logically and morally distinguishable from the antidiscrimination rationale. Does diversity provide a sufficient moral justification for paying attention to color? Again, underneath our disagreement about that question are disputes about how the world is and what we want it to be. The Fifth Circuit Court of Appeals, in the 1996 *Hopwood* case involving affirmative action at the University of Texas, wrote that notwithstanding the Supreme Court's 1978 decision in *Regents of the University of California v. Bakke*, diversity had never been a compelling interest to justify race-conscious measures in university admissions and public institutions. We accept the notion that universities should care about inclusion and diversity, but paying attention to diversity on the basis of race is as irrational in the admissions process, the three-judge panel argued, as paying attention to hair color, weight, or blood type. Those judges are living on a different planet from the one I am on. In evaluating the kind of community that should be created on campuses, they obviously differ with university leaders around the country, who value diversity on campus. The *Bakke* issue in higher education was directly addressed by another federal appellate court in litigation involving the University of Michigan, with results contrary to *Hopwood*, and the issue will now be addressed by the Supreme Court.

Others argue that remediation and diversity conflict with merit. There are huge disagreements about this issue, too. One set of arguments concerns the instruments that measure merit. The tests are not overwhelmingly good predictors of what they claim to predict—for example, the SAT's prediction of first-year performance in college. The correlation coefficient of about .4 explains about 16 percent of the variation. That's about as good a predictor as weight in predicting height—adequate but not great; not as solid as you want when making really important decisions in your own life. And I emphasize that it is not a good predictor for anyone—not just for minorities, but for anyone. Furthermore, why is performance in freshman courses any kind of merit that we want to predict in the first place? A second line of argument holds that merit depends on mission. College administrators and presidents may feel that inclusion and diversity are important because they contribute to the educational mission of our institutions, and because we are trying to prepare leaders. That is fine, but defining the mission of an institution is a deeply contested process—at least if anyone is paying attention to it. Most college and university presidents nowadays say that inclusion promotes the institutional mission, but the Fifth Circuit in *Hopwood* did not seem to believe that. Apparently the Board of Regents at the University of California under Governor Pete Wilson and Ward Connerly did not believe it either—or at least did not believe it very seriously. When the Regents in 1995 prohibited race-conscious affirmative action in admissions, they acknowledged the value of diversity, as the *Hopwood* court did in Texas the following year, but seemed to believe it was worth having only if it occurred by accident as the institution pursued other, race-blind goals with race-blind tools. The Regents subsequently reversed their policy, but by then a state ballot initiative, Proposition 209, had inserted the ban on voluntary public sector affirmative action in the state's constitution, making the policy change moot for now.

So where is the evidence that diversity is compellingly important? Supporters of diversity cite dead social philosophers, which is not really much better than citing dead judges. There is disagreement of an empirical sort regarding the contribution that inclusion can make in an institution, as well as disagreement with respect to the values and mission that the institution should pursue. Since the mid-1990s, there has been a flurry of research on the benefits of racial diversity in education. Some of this is cited in the briefs and court opinions in the Michigan affirmative action case, *Grutter v. Bollinger* (2002), including an amicus brief by the Civil Rights Project at Harvard, summarizing the research literature.

Even if we cross the hurdle of agreement that there are at least some circumstances in which we should pay attention to race or gender, the appropriateness of race-conscious measures in a given context, to take one example, will depend to a great extent on the details of that context, as will the nuances, that is, the details of the tool's design. We have this notion, certainly in the law, that you should not unnecessarily trammel the interests of bystanders and white guys; do not gratuitously deprive them of various benefits and opportunities. Do it carefully, or at least think about it carefully, and try to minimize the extent to which you impose burdens. That makes sense, and of course, it follows directly from the assumption underlying our very first hard question, namely, that there is a moral cost to considering race. So, how do you design a tool to minimize that moral cost? How much do we care about the fact, say, that a certain kind of small business contractor does not get an opportunity to bid on a certain subset of Air Force contracts. Is that a little problem, or a big problem that we should worry about? Obviously, this is another sharply contested question. How do we feel about an emphasis on inclusion and diversity when it comes to promotion, as compared with layoffs? Even if we think it is important to have diversity within the high school, is it important to have diversity within the faculty of the business education department of that high school? There is much room for argument—it is not all black and white.

I am persuaded beyond any shadow of a doubt that if one peels away the platitudes and the ugliness and the heated words in so much of the debate on race, one can identify, in a fairly systematic way, some sharp disagreements of an empirical sort and some sharp disagreements regarding values. It also seems obvious that our differences with respect to perceptions of the world and our differences with respect to values are both rooted in, and in turn generate, the distance between our communities. Our perceptions and values are shaped by our experiences. Our experiences are shaped by our communities. And our communities are separate. If differences in perception and values animate the ugly policy battles, and those differences are rooted in the separateness of communities, what do we do about discourse on race? Conversation about race is fine, but interracial civility is not an end in itself. Public discourse on race, therefore, needs to be not about civility, but about justice. It needs to be not about the discussion gap, but the opportunity gap and the investment gap. But bold measures to address the opportunity gap will be stillborn because so many of our policy discussions on the social and economic challenges facing the country are poisoned by color, usually appearing as subtext. As long as the political face on various economic and social challenges is black or brown or yellow, our politics is poisoned and the possibility of consensus is handicapped. But the answer is not to ignore color, pretending that policy discourse can be race-blind. An opportunity agenda that does not confront the problem of connecting communities so that we create the possibility of bringing values and perceptions together will not work. The difficult truth, I believe, is our conundrum: We cannot have racial justice without having equal opportunity, and we cannot have racial understanding without closing the opportunity gap. As I said, this is harder than rocket science.

The second piece of a successful conversation on race is this: If we are going to have conversations, what kind of conversations will they be? Some kind of conversion experience gives a person religious faith. I do not think that conversion comes from a sermon, or a legal brief. Something else happens to create faith. This kind of shift in values—this conversion, and this transformation—is what we need to be about with respect to racial and ethnic justice. What are the secular analogues of that kind of transformative experience? What experiences and conversations will have a transformative effect on people's sense of community, a transformative effect on people's sense of us and them? With that transformation comes the possibility of bridging the gulf in perceptions and values. I was a very strong proponent of the "national conversation on race" thesis when I worked at the White House, provided that it was coupled with serious policy debate and initiative. Then I left, and I concluded that it was all wrong. I concluded that Bill Clinton would not do it, could not do it, that no political leader could do it, in part because talking about race necessarily almost inevitably means you are going to upset at least 40 percent of your audience. As it turns out, most political leaders, be they presidents of countries or presidents of universities, would just as soon avoid topics guaranteed to upset 40 percent of the audience. They would rather talk about something else, and there is no shortage of subjects. Once in a while presidents do it anyway. It's called Leadership with a capital L. When it happens, we applaud, and we write books about it. But we shouldn't expect it as a matter of course. Additionally, most of these leaders are busy. There is the issue of race, yes, but there is also the Middle East, social security, the economy, and so forth and so on. The sustained conversation and attention to race required by the complexity of the subject make it difficult to figure out what a leader can practically do. It is so very hard to talk about race. Context and nuance matter so much. Platitudes can be not only unhelpful but poisonous. Furthermore, the possibility of sustained engagement on a complicated issue like race when working through the media is sharply limited.

National leaders who want to address race and affirmative action must engage in a process that has five elements. First, relentless teaching is necessary about where America is on race—discrimination, disparities, demography, and especially history. Speak authoritatively about it. Second, relentless teaching is needed about the ways in which color poisons our consideration of various policy problems. Expose these areas, and deal with them constructively. And in doing so, model for the nation how to wrestle with these difficult value divisions, which we are not skilled at doing. Third, leaders need to articulate and share their vision of racial and ethnic justice in the twenty-first century, and they need to explain that vision and explain why their vision is preferable to alternative visions. Leaders must provide clarity and moral teaching. Fourth, leaders need to look around the country and identify those examples of leadership and those programmatic examples that to them represent the promising paths toward achievement of that vision: What should the federal government do? What should the president of the University of Pennsylvania do? What should the pastor of the local church do? What works and why? How do we make concrete progress toward that vision? Fifth and finally, leaders on race need to recruit and sustain and nourish other, new leaders. They cannot transform race relations alone. Other people need to exercise leadership. When I give speeches on this subject around the country, I am struck by how hungry people are for help in figuring out how to address problems of race. They know it is hard, and they do not know what to do. As a nation we are not practiced at discussing difficult issues. Most of the time when somebody comes up to me to talk about a very complicated issue like race or abortion, I try to change the subject. I am tired, and life is hard. Instead, when we talk about the subject, we usually do it with people who are relatively like-minded. We engage in what I call choir practice. We practice our melodies. We practice our harmonies. And it just sounds so good and feels so good. Choir practice is great. But instead, what we need to be doing is missionary practice: figuring out how to talk to people whose values and experiences are different, figuring out how to build a connection to peoples whose experiences and whose communities are different from our own.

Chapter 5
The North American

Richard Rodriguez

It is instinctive in humans, as it is in other warm-blooded creatures, to fear the swallower. I had an uncle who came from India and who feared being deported by U.S. immigration officials because he feared India would swallow him—consume, devour him again—without respect for his person or his life's journey, a journey that brought him to Sacramento, California, where he wished to remain. An American. Americans have lately taken up a Canadian word—multiculturalism—as a talisman against the notion of the swallower. But America has always been the swallower, our national culture has been omnivorous. I believe the United States of America swallowed me a long time ago. It may be that I am about to swallow you.

There is something unsettling about immigrants because they can seem to overturn America—or they can seem to undo America. At the very point at which Americans think we have a communal identity, at the very point at which we think we know who we are—we are Protestants, culled from Western Europe, are we not?—then new immigrants appear from Southern Europe or from Eastern Europe. Suddenly we don't know exactly what the latest comers mean to our community or our identity, how they fit. Thus are we led to question our identity. After a generation or two, the grandchildren or the great-grandchildren of immigrants to the United States will romanticize the immigrant, will see the immigrant as precisely the meaning of America, to see the immigrant—who comes and remakes herself in this new land—as the figure who teaches us most about what it means to be an American. The immigrant, in mythic terms, travels from the outermost rind of America to the very center of the country's mythology. None of this, of course, do we say to the Vietnamese immigrant who serves us our breakfast at the hotel. In another forty years, we will be prepared to say of the Vietnamese immigrant, that he, with his breakfast tray, with his intuition for travel, he alone realizes the meaning of America.

In 1997 the Gallup Poll conducted a survey on race relations in America. The pollster found that race relations in America strained as respondents ascended an economic ladder. For example, college-educated blacks were pessimistic about interracial relationships. But the poll was only concerned with white and black Americans. No question was asked of the Vietnamese man who served me breakfast today in the hotel. There was certainly no reference to the Chinese grocer at the corner. There was no reference to the Guatemalans in San Francisco or to the Salvadorans who re-roofed my Victorian house. None at all. That is because the American conversation about race has always been an abstract in white and black. What I represent, in my public life, is a kind of rude intrusion into the black-and-white conversation. Though I was born in San Francisco, I assume the outsider's task of unsettling the United States of America. I have listened to the black-and-white conversation for most of my life and it had nothing to do with me. I was supposed to attach myself to one side or the other, without asking the obvious questions: What is this white-and-black dialectic? Why does it admit so little reference to anyone else?

Brown does not represent a third race, but rather some blurring of racial distinction. I am speaking to you in American English that was taught me by Irish nuns, immigrant women, in California. I wear an Indian face; I answer to a Spanish surname as well as this California first name, Richard. You might wonder about the complexity of historical factors, the collision of centuries, that creates Richard Rodriguez. My brownness is the illustration of that collision, or the bland memorial of it. I stand before you as an impure-American. An ambiguous-American. I address you from the pride of my impurity. In the nineteenth century, Texans used to say that the reason that Mexicans were so easily defeated in battle was because we were so dilute, being neither pure Indian nor pure Spaniard. In the nineteenth century, Mexicans used to say that Mexico, the country of my ancestry, joined two worlds. José Vasconcelos, the Mexican educator and philosopher, famously described Mexicans as *la raza cosmica*, the cosmic race. In Mexico what one finds as early as the eighteenth century is a predominant population of mixed-race people. The *mestizo* predominated over the pure European and the pure Indian. Also, once the slave had been freed in Mexico, the intermarriage rate between the Indian and the African in Mexico was greater than in any other country in the Americas and has not been equaled since.

Race mixture has not been a point of pride in the United States. Americans speak more easily about diversity than we do about the fact that I might marry your daughter; you might become we; we might eat the same food. We settle more easily on the Canadian notion of diversity because it preserves the notion that we are separate, that our elbows do not have to touch, much less merge; that I need not become you, that I can remain Mexican, whatever that means, in the United States of America. I would argue that instead of adopting the Canadian model of multiculturalism, the United States might begin to imagine the Mexican alternative of a *mestizaje* society, and move away from the multicultural safety that Canada offers, and all fear of swallowing, of being swallowed.

I was born in Mexico, therefore—though I wasn't. I was born in San Francisco to Mexican immigrant parents. But I was reinvented in 1973 by Richard Nixon. Nixon had instructed the Office of Management and Budget to determine the major racial and ethnic groups in this country. (Can you imagine the bureaucratic deliberation over the phone books of America?) The Office of Management and Budget came up with five major ethnic or racial groups. The groups are, in no order of preference, white, black, Asian/Pacific Islander, American Indian, and Hispanic.

I call myself Hispanic.

The interesting thing about Hispanics is that you will never meet us in Latin America. You may meet Chileans and Peruvians and Mexicans. You will not meet Hispanics. If you inquire in Lima or Bogotá about Hispanics, you will be referred to Dallas. For "Hispanic" is a gringo contrivance, a definition of the world that suggests that I have more in common with Argentine Italians than I have with American Indians; that there is an ineffable union between the white Cuban and the mulatto Puerto Rican. Nixon's conclusion has become the basis for the way we now organize and understand our society. As a Hispanic, I will say with some irony that a recent statistic from the Census Bureau interests me very much. The Census Bureau tells us that by the year 2003 Hispanics will outnumber blacks to become the largest minority in the United States. While I admit a competition exists in America between Hispanic and black, I insist that the comparison of Hispanics to blacks will lead, ultimately, to complete nonsense. For there is no such thing as a Hispanic race. There is no Hispanic race in the world. In Latin America, you see every race of the world. You see white Hispanics, you see black Hispanics, you see brown Hispanics who are Indians, many of whom do not speak Spanish because they resisted. You see Asian Hispanics. To compare blacks and Hispanics, therefore, is to construct a fallacious equation.

Some Hispanics have accepted the fiction. Some Hispanics have too easily accustomed themselves to impersonating a third race, a great new third race in America. But Hispanic is an ethnic term. It is a term denoting culture. So when the Census Bureau says by the year 2060 one-third of all Americans will identify themselves as Hispanic, the Census Bureau is not speculating in pigment, but rather is predicting how by the year 2060 one-third of all Americans will identify themselves culturally. The black Dominican today who identifies himself as Hispanic is identifying himself in terms of culture rather than by race, and that is revolutionary. For a country that traditionally has taken its understandings of community from blood and color, to have so large a group of Americans identify themselves by virtue of language or fashion or cuisine or literature is an extraordinary change, and a revolutionary one.

Is there, in fact, a Hispanic culture? Henry Cisneros, the ex-mayor of San Antonio, gathered together a group of Hispanic politicians in the mid-1990s to try to determine whether there was a Hispanic political agenda, for, indeed, there is a Hispanic caucus in Washington modeled on the African American caucus in Washington. After two weeks the group that Henry Cisneros convened could not come up with an agenda. There is no Hispanic politics. What unites the eighth-generation New Mexican, who considers himself a Spaniard, with the white Republican Cuban with the black Puerto-Rican with the Guatemalan Indian who arrived in San Diego yesterday with the Mexican American gang kids who speak Spanglish in East L.A.? What singular culture is there in this diverse company?

Some Hispanics speak Spanish. Some do not. Some are Catholic. Many are becoming Evangelical Protestants. Some are white. Some are brown. Some are black. The more I think about it, the more I think there are only two considerations common to Hispanics. First, this business of impurity, that we are making America an impure place. The second thing that unites Hispanics is that we (those of us who are not of Europe) look south when we consider the past. That is our revolutionary gift to America, the cultural inheritance that we bring to this country. Hispanics are changing the contour of the United States because we are north-south people. The United States has traditionally written its history east to west, has begun its history at Plymouth Rock and has ended up at Venice Beach, a country that has always understood itself in one direction only. Suddenly, there are millions of Americans who see themselves along a north-south trajectory. That is a revolutionary regard.

After the North American Free Trade Agreement (NAFTA) was signed by the presidents of Mexico and the United States and the prime minister of Canada, the *New York Times* called me to ask if I would write something on NAFTA. I said I couldn't write anything on NAFTA, because I've never met a North American. But then I thought, actually, I do know one North American. He is a Mexican from the state of Oaxaca in southern Mexico. He impersonates an Italian chef in a restaurant in the Napa Valley for about nine months of the year. He is trilingual. He is a Mixteco Indian. His first language belongs to that tribe. His second language is Spanish, the language of his Colonial oppressors. His third language is a working knowledge of English, because, after all, he works here. He deals with two currencies, two codes of justice, two views of the human condition.

The North American knows thousands of miles of dirt roads and freeways. He knows where to hide in the United States, because he is, after all, illegal when he crosses the dangerous border. On the Mexican side, he knows how to hide from the Mexican federal police who are always trying to steal his money. He wires his money home by Western Union, he puts the rest in his shoes. In Mexico, he lives in a sixteenth-century village where the Virgen de Guadalupe floats over his wife's bed. In Napa Valley, too, he hears Madonna, "the material girl." He is the first North American. He sees this hemisphere whole. He is a peasant from Latin America. At the Harvard Business School, meanwhile, there is much talk about this new North American, this transborder reality. Harvard conceives the pan-American as a new idea, patented by MBAs, but the peasant has known the idea all his life.

There is a quarrel going on in California about mythology: Which myth applies? What does California mean? What is California? For a long time the United States labored under the impression that California was the Far West. "Go west, young man." Go west, young man, and change the color of your hair and go to Gold's Gym, get a new body, lose weight, become a movie star, Botox your name, become Rock Hudson. But, as early as the 1860s, California was finitude. We had come to the end of the road in California to discover that America was a finite idea. I think the innovation in California results from that idea of finitude— land's end. Americans have been trained by their maps to believe that everything will be OK if we move west. But having arrived at the end, what do we do? We look to the sky. It is no coincidence that so much technological innovation is happening along the strip of land that stretches from North County, San Diego, all the way to Redmond, Washington. Why there? Why are people entering cyberspace with such frenzy at the western portal? Because restlessness continues and because the land has come to an end. But has it? Today—in about an hour from now—a procession of planes will land at LAX from Asia. The flights originate in Asia. We are sort of glad to see Asians, but we don't have any more room in California. We've come to the end of things in California. But the Asian says, "Well, you know, I've always thought this was where America begins. I thought this was where the continent begins." What would the history of America look like if it were written in reverse, from west to east? Have we even imagined such a history?

People in Mexico go to el Norte not because they want to find a new future; they go to el Norte because they want a dreary job working at a dry cleaner's in L.A. They work to sustain the past. People climb to el Norte without experiencing the same sense of disconnection from the past that the Western traveler felt. If one travels east to west, one follows the light of day; one leaves the past behind. If one travels north and south, one begins to resemble a monarch butterfly or a whale. One moves with seasons. Laborers who worked six months of the year in the North and returned south every year infuriated Americans, because Americans didn't understand what that north-south journey might mean. Americans could only imagine disruption. Discontinuity. A new day. But now Americans are becoming north-south people. There are grandmothers in Minnesota who live not by some east-west calendar, but by a north-south calendar. They spend summer in Minneapolis and winter in Florida. All over the country I meet teenagers who are not traveling between coasts, as we used to imagine youth's journey in America, but between hot and cold, between desert and tundra—the new extremities of the country, the new way the country exists in the American imagination.

To my mind, nothing else Bill Clinton accomplished compares to NAFTA. The notion given to the United States by this trade agreement is that the United States is related to Canada, is related to Mexico. Northern Mexico looks like San Diego these days. Northern Mexico is filled with Gold's Gyms and Hard Rock Cafes, shopping centers. Everybody wants to be an American in northern Mexico. And South Texas is becoming very Mexican. That circumstance surprises Americans because our notion of community never extended beyond our borders and certainly never extended south. Look at the map now—the Hispanic map of the United States of America—and one of the weirdest things you will notice is the reconquest of the Spanish Empire. Florida, Colorado, New Mexico, Arizona, Texas, California, and Nevada are Hispanic—just as they were in the early eighteenth century.

I know there are concerns about diminished civility and social fragmentation in the United States, and especially in a city like Los Angeles. But there are uses of incivility, too. The formation of a society does not happen easily. It does not happen when all of us feel good about each other, and it does not happen because we all like each other. Coca-Cola commissioned a commercial to run at Christmas time wherein a utopian population, in various ethnic costumes, in mutual respect and good will, sing a hymn to Coca-Cola. All of us in America have been encouraged thus to believe in a relative and banal multiculturalism. But the real working out of inevitability more often happens at some Frontage Road franchise where the red-headed waitress has to communicate with the Mexican fry-cook, and she doesn't have all the right words, and neither does he. And so their cooperation—entirely pragmatic—ends up sounding like this: "Dos huevos, over easy, side of salchiche!"

In 1992, Los Angeles endured one of the great urban riots of American history, a terrible event that began as a black-and-white altercation, but within hours drew Korean shopkeepers, then Salvadoran women who wrestled with Mexican women outside Kmart for looted boxes of Pampers. You cannot have a black-and-white riot in a multiracial city. The most interesting thing about that riot was the way the city got formed from the terror of those days and nights. On the West Side of the city, that first Thursday, one saw neighborhoods on television that one had never visited. L.A. was famous, after all, as the city of separate suburbs, and separate freeway exits. The interesting thing was the way those distant neighborhoods drew closer and closer and closer together. By about four A.M., people on the West Side began to hear fire sirens, began to smell smoke. For the first time, Los Angeles realized it was one city. This realization did not come from good feeling. It came from terror. People resorted to their closets for guns. People came to realize the street they live on is, in fact, connected to every other street.

Sometimes I stand on the line between San Diego and Tijuana, and I talk to the kids who are beginning their American lives. I do not talk to them about Benjamin Franklin or Tom Paine. They've never heard of the Bill of Rights. They are coming, they say—many of them illegally—because there is a job in Glendale waiting for them or there is a grower near Tracy who needs them to pick peaches. That's it. They are not coming for welfare. They are not coming for famous freedoms. There is no politician who will tell the truth about these young men and women. The truth is that we cannot stop them from coming. The fact is there is a 2,000-mile border that cannot be defended. Americans continue to worry about illegal immigration. But the poor cannot be stopped. The poor, worldwide, are mobile. We of the middle class do not know how to stop them, how to keep them out of our society, and the truth is that we don't want to keep them out of our society. These Mexican kids know that. They know we will hire them to sit patiently with our dying mother. They know we will hire them to spade the moats around our rose bushes. They know we will hire them. In Mexico, in the realm of the public, the politician will say one thing and everyone will assume the opposite to be true. The Mexican judge says, "five years"; the family of the defendant calculates one year or despair. The price of the jar of baby food says 50 pesos and it might be 50 pesos or it might be 10. Nothing is what it seems in the public realm. Mexicans transfer this knowledge to America. They know that public utterance of prohibition means one thing and private welcome means another. There is work in San Diego if you can make it across.

In the 1970s, people began to believe that L.A. might not be a West Coast city with palm trees and beachfront, but might, in fact, be a northern desert city with Indians, sand, sirocco. The moment the mythology of that city began to change from blond to brown—Los Angelinos began to make the best of inevitability. They began to bring cactus into the house. They took the curtains off the windows and extolled the beauty of desert light. By adopting a desert aesthetic, Los Angeles attempted to transform something fearful; to make beautiful something that was fearful. Fear is not always met with withdrawal; sometimes fear is met by a kind of seduction. One solution to the fear of the advent of a brown population is to cast the brown man or woman in a soap opera; to call him the newest, sexiest; to fall in love with her. We lock up black males at a disproportionate rate because we are afraid of black males and we don't know what to do with black males—that's why we dance to black music. We end up marrying Chinese women. We also don't know what to do with empowered Western women who are more like black males than they are like Chinese women. In the great ancient societies, France would marry England—the king would pawn his daughter to England—as a way of making England part of the family. We are giving each other our daughters. We are marrying each other as much out of fear as of yearning.

People ask me all the time, "Do you envision another Quebec forming in this country from all of this immigrant movement? Do you see a Quebec forming in the Southwest, for example?" No, I don't see that at all. I do see something different happening with the immigrant population, which is as much as ten years younger than the U.S. national population, and which is more fertile than the U.S. national population. I see the movement of the immigrant as the movement of youth into a country that is growing middle-aged. Immigrants are the archetypal Americans at a time when we—U.S. citizens—have become post-Americans.

Once more along the border: I met three boys from a group called Victory Outreach, an evangelical Protestant group that works with young people who have serious drug or gang problems. Here they were (five hundred years after Columbus), here were these three Indians who told me that they were coming to the United States of America to convert the United States of America to Protestantism. This doesn't sound like Quebec. This sounded like immigrants are bringing America to America—a gift.

I was at a small Apostolic Assembly in East Palo Alto a few years ago, a mainly Spanish-speaking congregation, along the freeway, near the heart of the Silicon Valley. This is the other side. It used to be black East Palo Alto. It's quickly becoming Asian and Hispanic Palo Alto—the same story. There was a moment in the service when newcomers to the congregation were introduced to the entire group. They brought letters of introduction from sister churches in Latin America. The minister read the various letters and announced the names and places of origin to the community. Everyone applauded. And I thought to myself: It's over. The border is over. These people were not being asked whether they had a green card. They were not being asked whether they're legally here or illegally here. They were being welcomed within this community for reasons of culture. There is now a north-south line that is theological, and it cannot be circumvented by the U.S. Border Patrol.

The deepest fear Americans conceive of the South right now is not of the separateness of the South, but that people of the South will replace us, that they want us, that they want to be us, that they want our food, that they want our culture, that we will be swallowed. One Monday, a few years ago, *Monday Night Football* originated from Monterrey, Mexico—a northern Mexican metropolis with all the charm of Pittsburgh in the 1930s. The pre-game show began with a serenade by a group of *mariachis*, singing in Spanish. What the *mariachis* sang was this: The Dallas Cowboys are our team. They are Mexico's team. And I thought, does anybody at ABC News know about this? Do any of us realize that the Dallas Cowboys are about to be devoured?

Americans continue to believe that Canadian multiculturalism is going to make everything come out all right. Multiculturalism is not going to make everything come out all right. You—here I address America—you are going to end up with Mexican grandchildren.

I was on a BBC interview show, and a woman introduced me as being "in favor" of assimilation. I am not in favor of assimilation any more than I am in favor of the Pacific Ocean. If I had a bumper sticker, it would read something like ASSIMILATION HAPPENS. One doesn't get up in the morning, as an immigrant child in America, and think to oneself, "How much of an American will I become today?" One doesn't walk down the street and decide to be 40 percent Mexican and 60 percent American. Culture is fluid. Culture is smoke in the air. You breathe it. You eat it. You notice culture or you don't. Elvis Presley goes in your ear and you cannot get Elvis Presley out of your mind. He's in there. I'm in favor of assimilation. I'm not in favor of assimilation. I recognize that it exists. L.A. has become Mexican, which is what it always was. L.A., this monstrous city that we identify now as the immigrant capital of America, has three times the miscegenation rate of the American average. I was in Merced, California, a few years ago, which is a town of about 75,000 people in the Central Valley of California. Merced's two largest immigrant groups now are Laotian Hmong and Mexicans. The Laotians have never in the history of the world, as far as I know, lived next to the Mexicans. But there they are in Merced, and they are living next to the Mexicans. They don't like each other. I was talking to the Laotian kids about why they don't like the Mexican kids. They were telling me this and that—the Mexicans do this and the Mexicans don't do that—when I suddenly realized these Laotian kids were speaking English with a Spanish accent.

I remember when once Bill Moyers asked me how I thought of myself, as an American or Hispanic. I said, "I'm Chinese." And that's because I live in a Chinese city and that's because I want to be Chinese. Well, why not?

Yes, I think it's a celebration of utopianism. I do think distinctions exist. I'm not talking about an America tomorrow in which we're going to find black and white no longer the distinguishing marks of separateness. But for many, many young people that I meet, it sounds almost Victorian to talk about their identity that way. They don't think of themselves in those terms. And they're already moving into a world in which skin or tattoo or ornament or movement or commune or sexuality or drug are the organizing principles of their identity. And the notion that they are white or black simply doesn't apply to them. And increasingly, of course, you meet children who really don't know how to say what they are anymore. They simply are too many things. We're in such a world, in such an America, already. What will we say—that we still live in a black and white America? I mean, what do we say to Tiger Woods, who insisted he's not African, because that would deny his mother's existence? I met a young girl in San Diego the other day at a convention of mixed race children, among whom the common habit is to define one parent over the other. In most white and black marriages, the habit is to define black over white. But this girl said that her mother was Mexican and her father was African. I said, "What are you?" She said, "Black-xican." And I think to myself, "You know, the vocabulary that the Spanish empire has, the recognition of multiplicity of possibilities, we do not have in this society—we do not have words to describe who we are anymore. And I tell you, if we rely on the old vocabulary, we are doomed because no one is using it anymore. They're inventing their own words."

So, what myth do we tell ourselves? You know, I think the person who got closest to it was Karl Marx. Marx predicted that the discovery of gold in California would be a more central event to the Americas than the discovery of the Americas by Columbus. He goes on to write that the discovery of the Americas by Columbus was only the meeting of two tribes, essentially, the European and the Indian. But he said, "You know, when gold was discovered in California in the 1840s, the entire world met." For the first time in human history, all of the known world gathered. The Malaysian was in the gold fields alongside the African, alongside the Chinese, alongside the Australian, alongside the American pioneer, etc., etc., etc.

For the first time—and with calamitous results—the whole world was seeking gold in the same place at the same time, and they were at each other's throats. People were murdered and so forth. But that was an event without parallel, and it is, I think, the beginning of modern California and why California, today, really is our mythology. It provides the mythological structure for understanding how we might talk about the American experience as not being biracial, but the experience of the recreation of the known world in the New World.

Sometimes the truly revolutionary things that are going on in this society are happening almost regardless and almost without anybody being aware of them. We are going to wake up one day, and it's all going to be changed, and we're going to say, "When did it all change? Why didn't the *New York Times* tell us it was going to happen? Where was Maureen Dowd when we needed her?" She was going on about Bill Clinton's sex life.

There is no black race. There is no white race either. There are mythologies, and I'm in the business—insofar as I'm in any business at all—of demythologizing these identities, and suggesting their complexity and the dynamism of individuals to meet and learn and fall in love with people different from themselves.

So I come to you as a man of many cultures. I come to you as a Chinese, and unless you understand that I am Chinese, then you've not understood anything I've said.

Chapter 6
Sports and Public Behavior

Richard Lapchick

Sport has become one of our culture's broadest common denominators. We see more in the newspapers about sports than we see about news, the arts, or culture; weekend television is glutted with sports entertainment, not to mention the all-sports networks. Politicians and ministers use sports jargon to explain the world and morality. College coaches are paid more, in some cases much more, than college presidents. Male professional athletes make what seem to be preposterous salaries; fans cannot count on those professional athletes being on the same team for the next year because of free agency. Fans of a hometown team cannot even count on the hometown team being in the hometown the next year because of all the stadium relocation issues.

On average, we read of about two athletes a week who have had some problem with the law, whether it is drugs, alcohol, violence, or gender violence. Many say that sports institutions breed lawless men who have no regard for the society that they come from and only care about themselves. It is easy to understand how the public becomes cynical about our games and the people who play them. It is equally easy to understand the widespread claim that so many people make that athletes should not be leaders or role models for our young people. Some of America's finest sportswriters warn that sport is bringing the apocalypse to our doorsteps. This essay looks at what I consider to be the biggest problem in sports today: race and the way it affects media coverage and perceptions of athletes as role models and leaders. I will then propose some solutions to the problems of sports institutions, so that athletes can better serve as leaders and perhaps create a vision for children that they cannot see now in front of them.

When I was growing up, everybody told me I was going to be in the NBA. My dad, Joe Lapchick, was the first great big man in professional sport. My father played for the Original Celtics in the 1920s and 1930s, when there were no integrated teams. They regularly played a team called the Renaissance Five, which was the great black team of the era. Race riots erupted in five of the games they played because some people were not willing to watch what was happening when blacks and whites played together. In 1950, when I was five years old, my father brought Nat "Sweetwater" Clifton to the New York Knickerbockers, one of the first black players in the league. We lived in Yonkers, New York, and I looked outside my bedroom window to see my father's image hanging from a tree and people picketing outside our house. For the next three years, I would sometimes answer the phone, my father not knowing I was on the other line, and hear someone say "nigger lover." I did not know what it all meant until much later, but obviously it was about him bringing a black player into the NBA.

Years later, when I was teaching at a college in Virginia in 1978, my son Joey, who was five years old, came into my office and said, "Daddy, are you a nigger lover?" I was stunned and stepped back for a minute and asked Joey what he meant, and he said, "I don't know, but some man just called me on the phone and told me you were one." It was as if the circle had closed around the three generations of Lapchicks. I received the call because I was the national chairperson of the coalition of groups that had come together to boycott South African sport, when the first South African team was coming to the United States for the Davis Cup. Apartheid was not a major issue in the United States at the time. I went to Nashville, where the matches were going take place, to help build the protest and also to announce, on behalf of the African governments, that they would boycott the Los Angeles Olympics if this team were allowed to come. When I flew back to Virginia that night, I felt maybe for the first time in my life that I had done something worthwhile. The next night I was working late in my office. At 10:45 there was a knock on the door. I assumed it was the campus security police, but instead it was two men wearing stocking masks who proceeded to cause liver damage, kidney damage, a hernia, a concussion, and carve "nigger" in my stomach with a pair of office scissors.

As an activist in the area of race relations, I knew that some type of violence was always a possible consequence, but I never expected what followed. The police accused me of self-inflicting the wounds for either personal publicity or to try and enhance the image of the anti-apartheid movement, and asked me to take a polygraph test. I consulted with the various civil-rights leaders around the country who were in the coalition, and they unanimously said I should not take the test. When I publicly said that, I knew that a large number of people would, from that point on, doubt my sincerity. I also said that I understood for the first time what it must be like for a woman who had been sexually assaulted to be asked to prove that through a lie detector. As a result, I also received more than 150 letters and phone calls from women around the country who had been raped. These letters and calls, coupled with my experience, helped me better understand what it is like to be raped and then to be asked to prove that you were raped. And that insight ultimately led to some of the programming done today at Northeastern University's Center for the Study of Sport in Society on the issue of men's violence against women.

When I went back to Nashville, I realized that I was the issue, not South Africa. Everybody was wondering, "Did Lapchick do it? Didn't he do it?" They did not really care if this team from South Africa was coming. I flew to Washington, took a polygraph, and flew to New York where I was examined by a medical examiner. But before we released the information, a South African Ministry of Information official came through New York and held a press conference at the United Nations. The scandal that became known as Muldergate, after Minister of Information Connie Mulder, that toppled Mulder and his prime minister, was just beginning to break, and he was being grilled on it. When he was asked, "What do you consider the successes that you've had this year?" he said two things: that the Davis Cup matches were going to be held and "the destruction of Richard Lapchick." I had asked the American Justice Department in to investigate a triangular relationship between the Virginia police, the Virginia Ku Klux Klan, whose grand wizard was welcomed as a guest of state in South Africa five weeks after the attack, and the South African security forces.

For years, sport has been viewed as the ideal playing field by both blacks and whites. People in their fifties and sixties in the black community will discuss for hours athletes like Joe Louis, Jackie Robinson, Arthur Ashe, and Muhammad Ali. They are heroes and pioneers, in the black community and in many segments of the white community. I think that whites generally still view sports as a level playing field for people of color, but African Americans know that opportunities to become sports executives are extremely limited, and that, fifty years after Jackie Robinson broke the color barrier, not very much has changed in executive positions.

Sport's most visible positions at the professional level are player, coach, and general manager; at the college level, they are student athlete, coach, and athletic director. It may be hard to recognize from newspaper and television coverage, but the percentage of African Americans playing basketball, football, and baseball is actually declining in professional and college sport, and has been since 1991. But a significant number of African Americans continue to play the games. In 2001, African Americans were 13 percent of Major League Baseball players, 78 percent of the NBA, and 67 percent of the National Football League; at the college level in Division I, African Americans were 56 percent of basketball players, 46 percent of football players, and 3 percent of baseball players. Jackie Robinson had two dreams—one was to increase opportunities for African Americans as players, and the other was to increase their opportunities as managers and executives. The second part of his dream is overwhelmingly unfulfilled. At the beginning of the 2001 seasons, Major League Baseball had six African American managers and one Latino manager out of thirty, or 23 percent; the NFL had three out of thirty, or 10 percent; the NBA had nine, or 31 percent—by far the best showing. The worst record is in college sport, where only 4.7 percent of head coaches in Division IA football were African American in the 1999–2000 school year. In the 1999–2000 school year, whites held 95.9 percent of the college athletic director positions, African Americans held 2.4 percent, and women held 9 percent.

The factor that is hardest to measure, however, when we talk about race is attitude. I believe that athletes are being unfairly stereotyped all across America. The conviction that athletes are poor role models and bad leaders for children is fueled by media images, which are themselves fueled by racial stereotypes. Some white people who used to express openly their racial stereotypes about intelligence, work ethic, drugs, violence, and gender violence now express them about athletes, consistently and regularly in the press, and when Americans think about athletes they generally think about black athletes. I spoke at an elite Ivy League university in 1996 to 25 career diplomats, all ambassadorial rank or higher. I asked them to write down five words to describe American athletes. They all mentioned attributes that we would read in the sports pages concerning athletic ability, but every one of the 25 diplomats also used one of the following words: dumb, violent, rapist, or drug user. This list came from reading America's sports pages during a single year of being in this country and absorbing the images presented there. I get requests for an average of three interviews a week from the media to talk about athletes as bad role models, and one or two a month about coaches who are negative leaders for their young people. I have never been called to make a comment on a good-news story about athletes. When I suggest good-news stories to writers who have called me to talk about bad news, the conversation quickly goes silent. When I say, "Why won't you write it?" they say that "good news won't sell." How do they know? It is so rare that they put it in the newspapers.

But when something goes wrong with a player, watch out for the national consequences. The fan base in the United States is mostly white. They read about our athletes through a media filter primarily created by white male journalists and writers. There are only two African American sports editors on major American newspapers. In 2002, there were only nineteen African American columnists at major newspapers in the United States. According to the National Association of Black Journalists, 90 percent of our daily newspapers do not have a single African American sportswriter on their staff. The result can be a reinforcement of white stereotypes of race, because so many athletes are African American. I do not mean to suggest that all white writers are racist, but they have been raised in a country where stereotypes, study after study shows, prevail: many white people think blacks are more violent, less hardworking, more dependent on welfare, less intelligent, and more inclined to use drugs. In sports, the less hardworking stereotype translates into African American athletes being called "natural athletes," as if they do not have to work hard to attain the skills that they display for us on television.

Our athletes are coming from a generation of youth cut adrift from the American Dream. When the Center for the Study of Sport in Society started in 1984, we would talk about balancing athletics and academics, telling young people to make sure that they get the academic preparation, just in case they are among the 9,999 out of 10,000 who won't make it to the pros. Today the issue for young people has little to do with balancing academics and athletics; it is about balancing life and death. Increasingly, athletes who are recruited to college and, later, to pro teams have witnessed a violent death. If a child in America is killed every two hours by a handgun, chances are that colleges are going to recruit players who have seen this violence or know people to whom it has happened. Colleges are increasingly recruiting fathers and mothers to our college campuses and our athletic departments—people who have one or two children by the time they get to campus. Are colleges ready to help this group of people adjust to the life that we hope that they will have on our campuses, or later on pro teams?

Colleges and the pros are going to get athletes who commit acts of gender violence. Perhaps the single most prevalent stereotype about athletes today is that, because they are athletes, they are more inclined to be gender-violent. There have been, of course, too many cases of athletes who have committed acts of gender violence, but there has never been a study done anywhere in the United States that has proven statistically that athletes are more inclined toward gender violence than non-athletes. Every time a story appears on an individual athlete and gender violence, the media refer to a Northeastern University study that originated at the Center, but that we did not allow to be published in our name, because it was based on so few cases and the researchers did not control for the three main factors that are predictors of gender violence (alcohol, tobacco, and the male's attitude toward women). The study came up with 65 cases of gender violence, using campus judiciary or campus police reports, on ten Division I campuses over a three-year period—13 were athletes and 7 were basketball and football players. I knew exactly what would happen if we published the study. The press would not say, "Athletes committed 13 out of 65 cases of gender violence over three years on ten Division I campuses." Instead they would say, "We don't know whether this one athlete at this school is representative of other athletes, but 20 percent of all campus acts of violence against women are committed by athletes." This conclusion would be based on a mere 13 cases. "Most are committed by basketball and football players," would be allowed to imply a finding about all African American college athletes, based on only 7 cases. A version of that story has appeared in the American media countless times.

In 1994, however, 1,400 men killed their significant other or wife. Throughout the 1990s, an average of three million American women were the victims of battering each year. For the last five years, nearly 100 athletes a year were accused of sexual assault, but on an average day, 8,200 women are battered in America and 2,345 American women are raped. The problem is about American men, including male athletes. It is not just about athletes. Formal legal complaints of sexual harassment have been brought against corporations such as Astra and Mitsubishi, but none of the stories about these cases talked about the climate created in their plants where men felt entitled to abuse women. In contrast, every time I read a sexual harassment story involving an athlete, the story somewhere discusses why athletes are more inclined toward violence, or how the culture of athletics contributes to sexual violence and harassment. Since we are talking mostly about African American and Latino men, such speculation is fueled by stereotypes. Writers say that athletes are trained to be violent, and that we can expect that to carry over into our homes. If that is the case, why don't we expect the police, the Army, the Navy, the Air Force, and the National Guard, who are trained to use lethal force, to come home and kill? It is a preposterous idea that a college football player who is aggressive on a Saturday is going to come home and be aggressive in his home. Violence might happen, but not necessarily because he is one of the 50,000 college football players engaged in the sport.

Academically, colleges are going to get athletes who have literacy problems. The press discusses this extensively. Once a year—and never in our sports pages—I will see a story about how many college freshmen now coming to our campuses have to take remedial English and math that doesn't refer to athletes. Sports teams are going to have athletes who use drugs. As we keep reading about this problem, the coverage creates an image in our mind of who our athletes are. None of the stories talks about the fact that there are 1.9 million cocaine users in the United States and 2.1 million heroin users, that 6 percent of the American adult population consumes an illegal drug once every month, and that within the 18 to 24 male age group, that figure jumps to 13 percent. The press, however, continues to zero in on athletes.

All this coverage reinforces stereotypes and creates the idea that athletes are very poor leaders and role models. But athletes can be positive role models in affecting the lives of our youth. Children have chosen them to be leaders, whether or not athletes want the job. Children have said to us, "We want athletes to help us." The Center for the Study of Sport in Society opened in 1984 with hopes of training athletes to be spokespeople and leaders on various issues for young people. The Center has spent 18 years trying to change the discourse on sport and to help sport live up to its ideals. Many people have a lofty view of what sport is or what it can do, but frequently those ideals have not been met. We want sports and our athletes to reach children who are in deep crisis. We can help them believe in what they cannot see. Children see what is in front of them, on the edges of despair, and often see no source of hope.

We see these young people every day and observe how they act with each other. Lou Harris conducted a study for the Center in 1990 on youth attitudes toward racism, and his documentation showed us what we already knew: that our children have learned to hate each other on the basis of how they look and what they believe in. But it also showed their desire to participate in changing those feelings. They were not comfortable or happy with the hostility they felt. When asked whom they want to reach out to them, the group most frequently mentioned was athletes, at the professional, college, and even high-school level—not because of their fame, not because of their athletic accomplishments, but because young people thought that athletes were caring individuals. The Center developed Project Teamwork after seeing the results from the Harris survey. This program arranges for trained athletes to go into schools to work with kids on issues of race relations. Teamwork members are ambassadors against prejudice and they systematically train students in conflict resolution and diversity-training skills. This program won the Peter Drucker Award as the nation's most innovative program leading to social change and was named by the Clinton administration as one of its models for conflict resolution. It is now part of an AmeriCorps-funded Athletes in Service to America program. We offer training services to avert gender violence, and these have now been brought to over 85 campuses. When we first started the program, schools did not even want us near their campuses, because they were afraid that if the program came to their campus, they would be indicting themselves.

The Center created the National Consortium for Academics and Sports, which has 222 university members around the country. Upon joining, members agree that any athlete who goes to their school on a scholarship and does not graduate can come back at the expense of the university to finish his or her education. In exchange for tuition and fees, the athletes have to give us ten hours a week of community service on the issues that I have described. Since the Consortium started, we have had more than 22,000 athletes return to complete their educations in this program. They have worked with over 10 million children in the community service and outreach program, donating 10 million hours of their time, and the schools have put up over $150 million in tuition assistance. The Center and the Consortium have succeeded, in part, because sport captures people's imaginations, their loves, hates, and passions. Communicating in the context of sport—working with athletes to deliver the message—puts people at ease when difficult, contentious subjects are being discussed. But we do not believe that because someone can nail a 30-foot jump shot or smash a ball across a volleyball net he or she is competent to talk about the deep, penetrating issues troubling our youth. We have to train athletes and help them learn those skills.

The following proposals for professional sports are based on my belief that professional sports organizations have a unique place in our community, and unique responsibilities. Yet professional sports organizations have hardly lived up to this potential. If we imbue them with an expanded sense of responsibility, the beneficiaries will include the owners, the administrators, the players, the fans, and most important, our children. Because athletes are role models, I propose that we hold athletes to a higher standard than we apply to other people. Among my recommendations is that we hire into our franchises leaders and decision-makers who have a sense of ethical and moral responsibility. These leaders have to be a diverse group, and they must understand the times and conditions that their players are coming from, including some of the problems I have described. We must create ongoing programs for the personal development of players and the front-office staff. We cannot expect the players, if we do not know what kind of college or high-school educations they have received, to be model citizens or to lead the conversation on race. We have to create rookie orientation programs. The NBA has a very systematic one, and the NFL has developed a version of it. The NBA brings all their rookies together for five days with experts who talk about, among other things, drugs, alcohol, HIV, relationships, sexual harassment, gender violence, financial planning, continuing education, and career development. All professional sports leagues need to adopt a life-readiness plan for athletes, who are going to play an average of only three to four years in professional sport. What are they going to do afterward? We need to offer them continuing education and career planning so that players can decide that there is going to be a life after professional sport, to give them internships that will be real and meaningful, and to provide counseling for their families. Just like all of us, they are going to have problems in their homes, but because of the public spotlight, they might not be the best at handling them. I propose very emphatically a cultural transition program for Latino ball players coming into Major League Baseball. Each league and the team offices need to adopt programs on diversity, not only for their players but for the front offices and coaching staffs, to get them out there as leaders so they can speak effectively to young people about issues of race and gender violence.

The National Consortium adopted a zero-tolerance position on gender violence at its 1996 annual meetings. If an athlete is convicted of an act of gender violence at one of the 222 universities in the Consortium, they will be banned immediately for a year. After a year of counseling and other steps, they can apply for reinstatement. If they are convicted twice, they will be banned for the rest of their college careers. Professional teams need to take this issue of violence against other persons more seriously as well. We must let our athletes know that they have choices to make, that the actions they take entail consequences. The leagues also need to strengthen their drug policies, provide greater substance abuse assistance to current players, and include additional drugs on the proscribed list. The issue of steroids and performance-enhancing drugs, for example, is very prominent in Major League Baseball. The leagues and teams and players associations, most importantly, have to get more directly involved in the communities where our teams play, to expand the outreach efforts of their players and train them to talk about the issues, and to promote and support urban youth sports programs. Males who live in cities are one-third less likely than suburban kids to have youth sport opportunities and females are one-eighth as likely to have them. Finally, pro teams need to work closely with the media to get more positive examples of athletes before the public, especially when there are so many athletes doing positive things as leaders. Most professional athletes have private foundations that work in communities. Most are deeply religious, family-centered people. Sports pages skew this reality.

Children will look to athletes for leadership, whether athletes are prepared to be leaders or not. Despite its problems, sport has an undeniable power in American culture. Each year President Clinton invited the Center to bring our National Student Athlete Day award winners to the White House. In 1996, the event was scheduled for April 5, but on April 3, Commerce Secretary Ron Brown died in a plane crash. We fully expected that the awards visit would be canceled, but it wasn't. I said, "Mr. President, the fact that you would honor these people on this particular day, with personal and national tragedies before you, brings even more honor to these award winners." And he said to me, "Richard, I needed this today." Even for a president, sports can bring good news that can lift the weight of the world. It is a powerful gift if we use it to help alleviate the spiritual poverty that affects so many of our children. That spirit is the antidote to the loneliness and the feeling of being unwanted that so many young people live with today. We can give them that richness of spirit that is being part of a team, counting on somebody else to deliver the goods for you. It doesn't matter what race your teammates are; sometimes it doesn't even matter what gender they are. If they are your teammates, you can expect them to do something good for you. Sport, from youth sports through the pros, has a role to play in leadership and public discourse. It has a small but vital role to play by having a positive impact on public behavior, because if our children have learned how to hate, sports can help teach them how to love again. If they are waging war on one another, sports can certainly give them tools to make peace.

Chapter 7

Performance, Debate, or Productive Conversation? Imagining an Exemplary Conversation on Race

A Roundtable Discussion with Members of the Penn National Commission

Led by Drew Gilpin Faust

What would effective public discourse on contentious topics such as affirmative action and race look like? The Penn National Commission on Society, Culture and Community addressed this question at its 4 June 1998 plenary meeting, drawing on examples of discourse on affirmative action from President Clinton's initiative to create a "national conversation" on race. The President's 1997–98 national conversations ranged from traditional town meetings to formal forums on social and public policy issues to relatively unfocused conversations in a wide variety of local settings with disparate groups of participants. By examining these and other examples, the Commissioners teased out widely applicable principles for more productive public discourse on divisive topics. They looked at the specifics of one subject of national conversation and debate—affirmative action and race—to identify strengths and weaknesses in the more general processes of public discourse. The Commissioners did not debate the substance of various affirmative action stances, but rather considered the processes, assumptions, and conventions by which affirmative action is discussed. General insights concerning effective—and ineffective—public discourse on divisive topics such as affirmative action emerged through the Commissioners' close scrutiny of the national conversation on race.

The Importance of Discourse Leadership: Goals, Context, and Loading the Dice

The Commission identified the act of discourse leadership itself as an undervalued yet critical component of leadership in contemporary society. "Leading a conversation doesn't necessarily come to mind when we think of the task of leadership," noted Judith Rodin. She invited the Commissioners to imagine "a moment when ideas and policy proposals are taken as possibilities to be explored rather than trial balloons to be shot down, in which leaders are expected to learn as much from their conversations as they're expected to teach others, and in which followers feel empowered— not only because their leaders listen, but also because they respond thoughtfully and learn from them." By these standards and others, leadership of public discourse on race and affirmative action, as well as other hot-button topics, is lacking, overlooked, and much needed.

Throughout their deliberations, the Commissioners affirmed Jay Rosen's insight that "the biggest breakdown point in conversations about affirmative action is right at the beginning." Commissioners observed that many assumptions—about public discourse on affirmative action, the goals of the discourse, and desired outcomes—are structured into choices made long before the conversation begins. The "goals of the conversation are very tied up with the context in which it takes place—the audience, the arrangement of participants, and who the participants are," moderator Drew Faust summarized. Rosen explained that "certain decisions about the conversation are made beforehand and are already in place as the event opens. The first is reflected in the design of the room." Having a panel of experts or people with well-known positions situated at the front of a room, for example, imparts a very different message about the event to follow than, say, having discussants at a round table surrounded by smaller tables. The first example establishes an "experts speak to the masses" model, while the second would privilege a more intimate conversational model between presumed equals. James Fishkin asked, "Who is in the room and how did they get there? And then, how are they going to talk? It's very difficult for 500 or 600 people to talk about something. If you have a context where you have some small-group discussions and some large occasions, and you have an effort to provide information and get the questions answered that people will have, and you have some guarantee that if the group, whether it is representative or not, is at least diverse enough so that different viewpoints get a hearing, then you begin to approach some of the conditions for a more successful deliberative discussion."

Conversations on race are also predetermined and framed by introductory comments about the event that invariably embed ideological and other assumptions. Leaders of conversations on factious topics, for example, may introduce forums with comments that, in effect, tell an audience what they can or cannot think and feel. As Neil Smelser commented, "It's always counterproductive to tell the audience how they ought to be feeling during the course of the event. It's somewhat condescending and imparts a kind of unequal tilt to everything that goes on." Jean Bethke Elshtain agreed that prefatory comments that frame and introduce a conversation can eliminate central categories of belief from the discussion right at the outset. President Clinton, for example, introduced a conversation on race in Akron, Ohio, by commenting, "I don't like the word tolerance" to describe race relations. Elshtain challenged this remark as "a very quick way to derogate hundreds of years of political history and the hard-won achievement of toleration." Fishkin found troubling the tendency to frame conversations on contentious topics by airing competing "soundbites and headlines" that "reduce our public dialogue to messages worthy of fortune cookies or bumper stickers."

Derek Bok observed that discussions on race often assume as a given what is in fact culturally contested. While many assume that race is a problem in the United States, he observes, "the majority of whites believe that the problems of blacks are largely of their own making, and that the societal problems have—perhaps not entirely, but to a substantial extent—been removed." David Bromwich elaborated a similarly unstated presumption among leaders in discourse about hot-button topics such as affirmative action that "qualified opinion, educated, enlightened opinion, not blind and superstitious, is on one side. Therefore, if someone is not on that side, their opinions—which have to be listened to, because they're part of our diversity and so on—come from ignorance, prejudice, and other such self-blinding obstructions to true judgment. I don't feel that way about affirmative action. I do not feel that qualified opinion is on only one side. But there are issues I feel that way about, too. If you feel that way about an issue, you may call for many sorts of discussion, but not a conversation."

Commissioners and guests called attention to a disingenuousness, perhaps unintended, in the leadership of public discourse on race. Richard Daynard likened the leader of the conversation to a law school professor using the Socratic method: "It often has a disingenuous element to it, conscious or unconscious, on the part of the professor, where you're questioning the student and the assertion is that it's really open. It's the student and the text and the only test is reason. But the professor knows, and you know, what he or she wants pulled out. And you keep going until it happens." Edna Ullmann-Margalit sensed in some of President Clinton's national conversations an unstated but structuring tension between the goal that the conversations would model respectful conversation and the audience's—or the media's—desire to "see blood. They want a real fight; otherwise it's not interesting," she said. Media coverage and attention is often at cross-purposes with thoughtful, deliberative public discourse, especially insofar as it privileges "real fights" and soundbite distillations of views on complex topics.

Rosen observed that when a forum or conversation is introduced, as were many of the national conversations on race, through video clips or summaries of different stances on affirmative action and race, an assumption is made that "to have a conversation about ethnicity and diversity is to negotiate and hear from various already pre-set positions," rather than an assumption that the conversation might create new positions altogether. An alternative framing of the conversation, Rosen speculated, would be to have voices of people who describe ambivalences, confusions, and complexities in their views of affirmative action. One voice might say, "The more I think about this, the harder it is to make up my mind," or "The thing that I'm always struggling with when I think about affirmative action is . . ." or "I used to think this way, but now I think that way." These ambivalent statements might all be "equally representative of people's experience" as the firm declaration of an opinion, Rosen noted, "but would be representative of deliberation itself, rather than a contest of the committed" or the prevailing model of political discussion as a "debate among fixed positions."

The Commission concluded that the proper context must be established for a conversation on such a contentious topic. Sponsors of conversations should be responsible and publicly trusted—for example, foundations, academic institutions, or perhaps civic journalists. A neutral third party should be responsible for format, organization, and structure. National conversations should attract a representative and well-informed public. The leader of the conversation should be carefully chosen and should be without self-interest in the outcome or a profile sufficient to affect or sway the conversation. The setting for the conversation should be carefully considered (e.g., the number of participants, physical setting, and the presence of the media). Multilevel conversations on the same topic can occur in multiple formats—from "representative" national forums to regional and local conversations—to achieve greater saliency and participation (e.g., White House commissions, White House conferences, town meetings, local forums, and so forth).

The Role of Facts in Public Deliberation

Panelists discussed the status and value of "facts" in contentious debates on race and affirmative action. Derek Bok observed that academicians and other experts need to play a more active leadership role in explaining the intricacies and realities of affirmative action policies, especially as applied in university admissions decisions. Said Bok, "In a democratic society we ought to try to be as clear about the underlying facts that we're discussing as we can be." Universities, he elaborated, "ought to recognize our own failure in making that happen. And I would argue that the most basic facts, starting with what the purpose of affirmative action is, the degree of preference that is actually given, the effects of affirmative action on grades and retention, the consequences of affirmative action once people graduate and go out into society, are simply not known." Amy Gutmann cautioned, however, that the facts are "necessary, but not sufficient" on a topic such as affirmative action, because "people are deeply divided on values here. We can't just talk about facts. We also have to talk

about the political values at stake, which is bound to be a political deliberation." Faust added that facts, often distorted and/or irrelevant to the
topic at hand, can become "a weapon to silence everyone else in the
room." Faust noted the "big gap between the useful information and
how it gets marshaled in discussions. For the most part, people just issue
facts from their mouths that have nothing to do with anything under discussion." She concluded by asking, "How can we make rules or principles about how facts should be used" in public discourse? "It's not just
that we don't have them, but that they're being used in ways that are not
entirely productive."

Performance, Debate, or Productive Conversation?

As Rosen suggested, there are many possible goals or purposes for public
discourse, especially on contentious issues, yet these goals are often unexamined, moving by default to the "debate among fixed positions"
model. The Commissioners agreed that in public discourse and public
conversations, especially on the issue of race, conveners and participants
need to think constantly about intended goals and outcomes. The Commissioners discussed the need for greater clarity and, in some cases, inventiveness concerning goals and outcomes for public discourse. Overall,
the goal needn't be to win the argument, or persuade others to one's own
point of view, or even to reach consensus. On certain deeply contentious
issues, the goal is perhaps not to change minds, but to find ways to work
together or at least to minimize friction over clashing beliefs and values.
Michael Schudson pointed to Search for Common Ground, an organization that brings together pro-life and pro-choice communities, whose
goal is not to change anyone's mind, but to "just not be bombing each
other. They really expect everyone to leave the meetings without having
changed their opinion at all. It's another outcome," entirely, from consensus or conversion.

Martin E. P. Seligman echoed Rosen's distinction between a debate
with fixed positions or a performance of predetermined views, and a
genuine conversation where new positions and insights may emerge. "I
think it's useful to ask yourself: What are the best conversations you've
ever had? And I think one element in our memory of our important conversations is, we thought things we never thought before. And so in that
context, I want to distinguish between a performance and a conversation. And I think success of a conversation occurs when the speakers say
things they've never said before and think things they've never thought
before and the audience does as well. And I think we're seeing a national
performance on race, not a national conversation on race."

Different goals for public discourse on race suggest different criteria of
success, yet because goals are often unclear and/or unexamined in public

discourse, so too are the criteria for success unclear and confused. Cass Sunstein identified several possible goals for a conversation on race, each of which would suggest a different criterion for success: "One . . . purpose would be to promote better policy outcomes. Another would be to promote broader and greater participation in democratic politics. A third would be to provide just an outlet for hostility and rage. A fourth would be to give people a sense of the ground they share. A fifth one would be to produce a better understanding of the diversity of views that our fellow citizens actually hold. A sixth would be to produce a better understanding of the issues. And a seventh would be to attract viewers or voters, either their attention or their affection."

Martin Marty identified three primary modes of public discourse and different criteria of success: "Argument, which is always guided by the answer: 'I have an answer; I've got to defeat you; I've got to embarrass you; I've got to annihilate you; I've got to convince you, convert you, or get you out of here.' Performance, which we see plenty of. But conversation, we genuinely don't know." While there are plentiful examples of performance and debate in the public discourse on race, the Commissioners echoed popular observations that genuine conversation in the public sphere is almost nonexistent. Smelser elaborated, saying that in the best conversations "we don't know where they're going, and we don't have an outcome in mind. There are many, many possible outcomes in a conversation. It has that kind of free exploratory quality that defies a lot of the structuring that goes into" most forums on race and affirmative action.

In a genuine public conversation, Fishkin asserted, "I don't think the criterion for success should be whether people change their minds." Instead, Fishkin imagined a conversation in which views are aired, and concerns are expressed and then answered. That criterion "begins to move toward a Habermasian ideal speech situation," in which the criterion of success is the "completeness or incompleteness with which perspectives are responded to. If a diversity of views and arguments is answered by other arguments, then at least you have some real deliberation, not in a soundbite, but in somebody really being able to express their concerns from their social perspectives, and, so, a modestly complete deliberative discussion." With "mutual understanding," Fishkin asserted, "you would get some movement, and you would get people thinking things they hadn't thought before. If you can create a social context where the listening as well as the talking occurs in groups of manageable size that are sufficiently diverse or representative, you would get, on many issues, movement of opinion. And when you don't get movement of opinion, at least you'll get some mutual understanding, which is itself a useful product." In short, the Commissioners emphasized the important distinction between performance and productive conversation. Conversations on

race, Faust summarized, are not about "simply displaying already existing commitments," but, ideally, about a willingness to "amend or move
from them."

A Learning Model of Public Discourse

The Commission concluded that exemplary discourse, especially on affirmative action and race, might adopt a learning model of public discourse.
Moderator Faust detected some "disagreement about whether people
have to come to these discussions [national conversations on race] ready to
change their positions, or if they have to come simply ready to learn, even
if they're not going to move." Rosen characterized the learning model as
an alternative to debate and deliberation. Under the learning model,
"people aren't required to give up their positions, aren't required to pretend to have none or to find common ground. But they would conduct
themselves in such a way that at the end of the process they would know
something that they didn't know at the beginning of the process, either
about themselves and why they believe what they believe, or about their
opponents, or about what's possible." The learning model of public discourse assumes, Rosen observed, that affirmative action, for example, "is
a kind of a mess inside of a problem. We're groping, and therefore, a
learning model is the right one, as against the 'winning' model of discussion" or debate. Under a learning model of public discourse, participants
may change their perspectives or opinions through the act of deliberation,
or they may at least have more information at the end, and a deeper understanding of different views, even if they do not arrive at new opinions
or conclusions. The learning model of public discourse resists polarizing
or assigning participants and leaders to one side or another, but creates
other positions along a spectrum that will allow for easier movement for
those who are willing to undertake movement about what they believe.

Part Three
Leading the Public's Conversation
Studies in Contemporary Discourse Leadership

Chapter 8
Leadership in a Complex Democratic Society

Michael Schudson

Some features of good leadership are no doubt constant across societies and organizations. Leaders of any country, whether monarchy or democracy, will do better if they demonstrate courage, wisdom, and passion. Leaders of any organization, whether a hierarchical, top-down military organization or a hospital or engineering firm where administrative leaders must rely on the technical expertise and sometimes prickly egos of their subordinates, will do better when they have vision and integrity. In any situation, leaders will be measured by whether they effectively accomplish their goals, maintain their legitimacy while doing so, and exemplify some virtues along the way.

Leaders in a democracy face additional demands and operate under additional constraints. Even leaders of hierarchical organizations inside a nation with a strong democratic culture operate on a short leash. What is leadership in a democracy? There is a saying, attributed to Lao-tsu, that "of a true leader, the people will say, 'We did it ourselves.' " This is especially so in a democracy where all are enjoined to participate in self-governance. Citizens in a democracy seek good policy outcomes, but they also seek democratically legitimate policy processes. The measure of leadership's success in a democracy is not only whether decisions achieve a good end but whether, in the process of decision-making, all relevant views are aired, all relevant views are listened to, citizens feel that the decision-making process is fair, and public understanding increases. Leaders today must learn to operate in a climate of distrust; in a context of diversity and multiple authorized voices; in a global society where their locus of effective control is much narrower than the world forces impinging on them; and in a public soundbite culture where communication is invariably intense and rapid. These conditions generate at least three paradoxes for leadership in a democracy.

The Paradox of Complexity

It is the leader's job to clarify complex issues, and this requires simplifying. It is also the leader's job to indicate the consequences, trade-offs, and values at stake in complex issues, and this requires not oversimplifying. It is a leader's job to know when to turn to experts, and when to turn away from them. Leaders must accommodate expertise without bowing to it. Not only does a complex world make the instrumental tasks of leaders more difficult, it also puts a premium on a leader's skills in communication. Leaders must see into and see through complexity but communicate clear paths and alternatives, incorporating an educational dimension in everything they do.

The Paradox of Diversity

It is the leader's task to bring relevant stakeholders to the decision-making table. The diversity of viewpoints represented at the table should reflect the diversity of viewpoints of the people affected by decisions. This increases the democratic legitimacy of decisions but decreases the speed and efficiency of decision-making. It may increase the chances that a significant decision will be practically successful, but it may also decrease the chances that a bold decision will be made. Academic literature on leadership widely acknowledges that today's leaders must be connectors, bridgers, or boundary crossers, rather than giants who look down on others.[1] It is also coming to be recognized that leaders who share authority build their own authority. "By granting work associates more authority to get the job done and tools to make it happen, a manager becomes more authoritative," Michael Useem writes.

> With their relationships to customers, patients, and the public more clearly established, one's associates acquire a greater incentive to respond. With responsibility for decisions more clearly delegated, everyone on the management tree acquires a stronger wherewithal to act. With accountability more clearly pinpointed, they also acquire a better reason to perform. And with the results delivered and reputation enhanced, one places oneself in a position to acquire more power to get an even bigger job done. The same is true for leadership. It is not just how many followers one has; it is also how many leaders one has created among them. The more leadership in the ranks, the more effective is one's own.[2]

What remains underanalyzed in the academic leadership literature, nonetheless, is just how a leader brings people to a sense of their own authority. Even leaders who bridge as well as command, listen as well as direct, consult as well as act decisively, share authority as well as exercise it, must demonstrate the moral vision and steadfastness that motivate people to give their best. The authority of leadership at some point must be not only that of a collaborator or an editor but also, as the word implies, an author.

Today, more stakeholders than ever before play legitimate roles in decision-making, and the very term "stakeholder" has a broad currency. No leader can safely presume consensus because more and more people and groups, with more and more conflicting interests, demand to be consulted. Political theorist Benjamin Barber argued in 1975 that the short supply of leadership has to do most directly with the absence of consensus on national purpose: "There are today no leaders, only heads of factions; there is no leadership of ideas, only a competition of ideologies; there is no consensus, only an unstable balance of opposing interests."[3] This is rhetorical. It might have been written (and probably was) in any decade of our history. But Barber's general point is well taken: leaders do not exist in a vacuum; in a democracy, they personify and articulate group purposes. They lead by listening, they initiate by responding, they inspire by their sensitivity to the public. If groups have no coherent or identifiable purposes, the possibility of leadership is denied.

A lack of common purpose is a strength of contemporary culture even as it is an impediment to older styles of paternalistic leadership. There is a new cultural recognition of elements of the American mosaic that had essentially no place in public discourse a generation ago: evangelical Christians, gays and lesbians, Latinos, Asians, and other new immigrant groups. Most important, astonishing, and troubling for older elite patterns of leadership, African Americans and women have achieved civil rights and political power. It is less than forty years since the Civil Rights Acts of 1964 and 1965 began to change the politics of race in this country and an organized women's movement began to champion new relations between men and women at home, in the workplace, and in the legislatures. All this contributes to what some observers fear is a lack of common national purpose that makes leadership difficult. This does not imply that we should want to recover the national unity of the 1930s, made possible by a great depression, or of the 1940s, made possible by a world war, or of the 1950s, made possible by the complacency of old-boy parties and community elites. It means instead that leaders require new models and must learn how to operate under novel social conditions.

The Paradox of Accountability

Leaders will be judged by how they live up to cultural conventions about leadership (the man on the white horse, the charismatic leader, the inspiring moral leader) even if these conventions betray the highest ideals of democratic leadership. The more that leaders stay mindful of their responsibilities for broad consultation and inclusion, for not oversimplifying, for connecting and listening, the more they imperil their chances of maintaining an image of leadership that people respect. A democratic leader is obliged not only to lead but to change the public meaning of leadership. This requires leaders' regular engagement, with the public and mediating institutions, in education about leadership. The leadership of democratic discourse entails educating the public about the assumptions around which our public life operates. Leaders can be agitators not only in favor of certain policies but also in favor of certain understandings congenial to democracy. For instance, the assumption that the press is adversarial to government may lead public officials to hide activities or to act distrustfully of the media, which then encourages the press to be adversarial and distrustful. The assumption that the press, along with government, seeks to make democracy work could establish a better relationship between the two.

One thing that follows from the public accountability of leaders is that democratic leadership must withstand the test of the publicity principle: that is, leaders must act as if what they do and the way they do it may be on the front page the next day. This is a basic principle of democratic leadership, made more acute in recent years. Great things have been accomplished while violating it, and any theorist of democratic leadership must ultimately grapple with examples like the Constitutional Convention, which arrived at its extraordinary product in secrecy, or Franklin Roosevelt's efforts to draw the United States into World War II without candidly addressing the American public on the issues at stake. Leaders will often be tempted to take shortcuts around democratic participation, openness, and accountability, but as American political culture has grown more democratic, this is more and more difficult to manage. Publicity enters decision-making sooner and more relentlessly than ever before. Prudence as well as democratic values call for leaders to mind the publicity principle.

There are perils and opportunities in publicity. Leadership must include skill and leadership in the art of publicity itself; publicity cannot be an afterthought of leadership. Publicity should not be what happens to leaders—it should be part of what leaders do. This is a point no one neglects. The combination of an aggressive news media, government prosecutors and inspectors newly created or newly empowered by government ethics legislation, increasingly restrictive ethics laws for public officials and others, increasing numbers of whistle-blowers in government (and in corporations) encouraged by norms of disclosure, honesty, and freedom of information, and increasing numbers of private watchdog organizations on the left, the right, and the good government center, all have helped to build what Suzanne Garment calls "a self-reinforcing scandal machine."[4]

Leaders today also must confront perennial democratic ambivalence about leadership, exacerbated by several traumatic shocks in the twentieth century to faith in political institutions. The founders of the United States distrusted government only slightly less than they feared anarchy. They approved a Constitution that they believed in only because it sought to blend a necessary level of energy in government with a large number of checks upon it, checks internal to the federal government in the separation of powers, checks written into the Bill of Rights, and checks in a federal system that continued to locate most political power in the separate states. Their distrust in government would soon be coupled with a distrust of the people who dared aspire to run it; the vote-seeking politician has never enjoyed a high reputation in America. Even in the heyday of the American political party in the nineteenth century, an antiparty mentality inherited from the founders could not be entirely expunged.

A perennial distrust of politicians and government was exacerbated by John F. Kennedy's assassination—and the assassinations of Robert Kennedy and Martin Luther King, Jr., to follow. The President's assassination, as Garment observes, "played a large role in arranging the discontents of those years into a pattern of systematic suspicion about established institutions."[5] We should not overestimate the importance of a single event to explain broad social and cultural changes; nevertheless, the nation was truly traumatized on 22 November 1963. Something that could not happen here happened here, and no ethics law, no good will, no investigative reporting, and no political reforms could ever put this humpty dumpty together again. The traumatic events of the 1960s, Watergate, and a succession of what were widely perceived as failed presidencies (Johnson, Nixon, Ford, and Carter) helped torpedo public confidence in government. Confidence levels, as measured by opinion polls, declined rapidly between 1964 and 1974 and have by no means regained the levels of the early 1960s. In 1964, 75 percent of Americans trusted the federal government to do the right thing most of the time—compared to 15 percent in 1995. But a general deterioration of traditional cultural authority was also underway. Confidence in universities dropped from 61 percent to 30 percent, 55 percent to 21 percent for major corporations, 72 percent to 29 percent for medicine, and 29 percent to 14 percent for journalism.[6]

All these developments at the intersection of government, legislation, and media have increased the personal risks and hazards for someone who dares embark on a political career. The scandal machinery has also contributed to a general public cynicism about politics. On the other hand, recall where the scandal machinery came from: the rise of investigative reporting when government was epitomized by Lyndon Johnson's lies to the American public about Vietnam and Richard Nixon's contempt for the media and the democratic process; from the rise of public interest organizations dedicated to the protection of individual rights against governmental arrogance and intransigence on voting rights for African Americans, equal employment opportunity for women, access to welfare for the poor, and consumer rights against corporations. These reforms may have had some unintended and unfortunate consequences, but they sought to repair real shortcomings of the political system.

This essay has focused on formal political leadership, but leadership in other fields shares the challenge of a worldwide cultural shift in which deference to traditional cultural authority has declined. Take the case of American medicine where, in the past thirty years, "the discretion that the profession once enjoyed has been increasingly circumscribed, with an almost bewildering number of parties and procedures participating in medical decision-making."[7] Historian of medicine David J. Rothman goes on to cite a large number of contributing factors, chief among them that after World War II physicians became more connected to hospitals and hospitals less connected to religious, ethnic, and neighborhood communities. This increased the "professional isolation and exclusivity" of doctors. The symbolic measure of this isolation was the rapid decline of the house call, which represented less than one percent of doctor-patient contacts by the early 1960s. Then, after the enactment of Medicare and Medicaid in the 1960s, government became the primary purchaser of medical services and newly scrutinized the self-regulation of the medical profession—often finding that organized medicine operated as a self-protective guild more than a self-policing profession. At the same time, as part of the rights revolution spawned by the civil rights movement, patients' rights became an activist watchword and by 1972 the American Hospital Association adopted a Patient Bill of Rights. Dramatic changes in medical practice ensued—in 1960 a minority of physicians informed patients when they had cancer; by 1980, informing the cancer patient was the rule. An orientation toward rights entered medical practice and, with it, both an increase in bureaucratic and legal controls over medical decision-making and a growing climate of distrust.[8] Contemporary medical practice suffers from a newly intensified vulnerability to the market, but also from a newly institutionalized accountability to the individual patient, community and media review of the ethics of practice, and governmental oversight. Leadership in medicine is directed more than ever by the requirement that it must listen to, please, or placate a wide range of publics.

Questions and Conclusions

There are leadable moments just as there are teachable moments. They cannot be predicted. The leader just knows how to use them or has the good luck to fall into them. How can we measure the success of leadership in a democracy? Certainly there is no consensus on measures. One leading academic authority on leadership judges Margaret Thatcher the most impressive democratic leader of the postwar world while others, who found her policies unwise and in some measure even antidemocratic, would fundamentally differ. What might be good measures of leadership? Clearly, if democracy is an important part of this consideration, measures must include some way to evaluate not only the quality of policy outcomes but the quality of the policy process—perhaps the frequency with which discussion responds to the concerns of each participant, the extent to which the process of deliberation itself offers an outlet for discontent, the extent to which people discover common ground they had not seen before, or the extent to which participants become informed.

What is the role of leadership in getting more people involved in the democratic process? How does leadership operate in ways to model rather than stand opposed to democratic forms? How does leadership sustain a conversation over time? What research should be undertaken to improve our understanding of leadership? How do leaders find psychological and social support in a culture that seems increasingly suspicious of them? How do leaders themselves learn? How do they change course? American social critics have worried about the decline, absence, or insufficiency of leadership for a long time. In the 1830s, many mourned the passing of the founding generation and doubted that we should ever see their like again. In 1888, the British ambassador James Bryce published his anatomy of American politics, with its famous chapter, "Why Great Men Are Not Chosen Presidents." In France and Italy, he observed, "half-revolutionary conditions have made public life exciting and accessible," in Germany a strong civil service cultivated fine statecraft, and in England an aristocratic tradition drew men of wealth and leisure to politics. Recruitment to American public life was not enhanced by any of these factors but ensnared in the corruptions of party politics.[9] One would have to say that Bryce's observations were perfectly fair—and yet they did nothing to anticipate the vitality of American leadership in the century to come or the failures of leadership in the European nations that seemed to him at the time to produce more capable leaders. Leaders of institutions, whether they wish it or not, must also be leaders of democracy in a democracy. They will not only guide their own organizations but also exercise a "civic imagination," in Jay Rosen's phrase,[10] making space for and setting a model of intelligent public talk. Every leader of an institution is, by voice or by silence, a participant in a general public conversation. That public conversation must concern itself with democracy and, indeed, with the place of leadership in a democracy. Great leaders will not only engage that civic discourse, but promote it.

Chapter 9
Political Leadership in the Great Health Care Debate of 1993–1994

Derek Bok

The United States enjoys the dubious distinction of having the highest health care costs in the world while being the only major democracy with a substantial fraction of the population still lacking basic medical insurance. On several occasions in the last century, Congress seriously considered plans to provide universal health coverage. In each case, determined opposition led by physicians, big business, and Republican lawmakers blocked the proposals. In 1992, however, with the election of President William Clinton, all the auguries seemed to favor major reform.

Rising health costs threatened to put American business at a disadvantage in world markets and thus made corporate executives receptive to a plan that might shift health costs to the government. Growing segments of the medical community expressed a desire to consider reforms; even hospitals seemed interested in some scheme that would spare them the heavy burden of giving free medical care to the uninsured. Most important of all, large majorities of the public rated health care reform among the most urgent problems facing the nation and voiced support for a plan that would provide medical insurance for all Americans. Buoyed by this widespread concern, Harris Wofford rode the health care issue to a surprise victory over Richard Thornburgh in an interim race for Senate in Pennsylvania during 1991.

The Clinton Health Care Reform Initiative

Moved by these favorable signs, candidate Clinton made health care reform a centerpiece of his campaign platform. His election seemed to present an excellent chance to translate his promises into law. True to his word, he moved quickly to address the issue by announcing early in 1993 that he would assemble a task force of experts to review the subject and construct a plan that he could propose to Congress. To underscore his commitment to the effort, the president took the unprecedented step of naming his wife, Hillary Rodham Clinton, to head the task force.

Months later, after deliberating under a cloud of secrecy, the task force produced its report. Numbering more than 1,300 pages, the final document detailed a complex plan that would guarantee a defined package of basic health care benefits to all Americans. President Clinton announced the plan to the Congress in a widely acclaimed speech on 22 September 1993. In forceful tones, he urged the lawmakers "to fix a health care system that is badly broken . . . giving every American health security— health care that is always there, health care that can never be taken away."[1] During the days that followed, Mrs. Clinton appeared before Congress to respond to detailed inquiries from one committee after another. Pictures of the first lady sitting alone before a battery of lawmakers coolly answering questions on a subject of extraordinary complexity won her widespread applause. Moved by all the favorable publicity and anxious for reform, large majorities of the public expressed support for the president's plan. In the words of TV analyst William Schneider: "The reviews are in and the box office is terrific."[2]

At that moment, the chances for sweeping reform seemed greater than they had ever been over the long, trying history of health care legislation. But appearances proved to be deceiving. After a year of innumerable committee hearings, reports, negotiations, trial balloons, and arguments from every quarter, Senate Leader George Mitchell announced on 26 September 1994 that health care legislation was dead, at least for that session of Congress. After all the publicity and all the talk, the failure to produce even limited reform seemed to epitomize the breakdown in government and political leadership that many Americans fear.

The Great Debate

The health care debate is in many ways an illustration of a process of deliberation that is increasingly evident, albeit in less spectacular form, whenever important legislation is proposed affecting large numbers of people. On such occasions, it is now common not merely to debate the issues in Congress but to engage the people directly in ways that resemble an election campaign. Members of Congress, of course, return to their districts as they have always done to talk with constituents. But Congressional leaders, along with the president, speak directly to the people through televised speeches and appearances on talk shows. Interest groups also participate more and more actively by televised ads, electronic messages, and other forms of modern technology to reach the public and urge them to communicate with their representatives in Congress. When one adds media reporters, talk show hosts, op-ed writers, and expert commentary of various kinds, a major piece of legislation, such as Clinton's health care plan, can set off a national debate of formidable proportions.

Ideally, such a debate ought to display certain characteristics. It should provide opportunities for all points of view to be presented. No participant should be too weak to present ideas effectively or so powerful as to dominate the discussion through superior organization and resources. In addition, for the marketplace of ideas to operate effectively, issues and arguments must be joined in some fashion so that misinformation, faulty reasoning, and false issues can be winnowed out and the controversy reduced to the essential questions, backed by enough reliable information and arguments for citizens to arrive at reasoned conclusions.

With these requirements in mind, what can be said about the quality of deliberation in the United States? Surely, there are valid reasons for concern. Major public issues tend to be more and more complicated and difficult to understand. The extraordinary wealth of ideas and opinions so characteristic of America can add to the confusion. Some major participants in the debate—especially powerful interest groups—may have much more money than other interested parties and thus enjoy a substantial advantage in carrying out an effective mass campaign of persuasion. Of course, the media are there to help the public sort out the problems and understand the proposals and the relevant arguments, but reporters often seem more interested in describing the political tactics and conflicts than in discussing the substance of complex policy issues. Finally, although no debate of this kind can succeed without an attentive, interested public, Americans seem increasingly uninterested in politics and distrustful of what they hear from politicians and public figures. Can a useful debate about important policy issues take place under these conditions? Can it do much to help clarify options, inform judgment, and contribute to wise results consistent with the broad desires of the people?

The health care debate of 1993–94 provides an instructive, albeit a somewhat extravagant case through which to ponder these questions. Much space and time were devoted to the issues by newspapers, TV stations, and radio talk shows. More than $100 million is said to have been spent on the legislative campaign by the many interest groups concerned with health care reform.[3] Most of this amount was devoted to media efforts to communicate with the public. Innumerable fliers, direct mail appeals, TV spots, and newspaper advertisements were directed to citizens by interest groups on every side of the question. If there was ever a marketplace of ideas for public policy, the health care debate was surely a spectacular example.

Yet in the end, this vast effort at persuasion exhibited all the weaknesses characteristic of public discourse today. The debate was confused throughout by the large number of participating groups in Congress. Instead of simplifying the discussion by developing a single Democratic plan, several committees and even individual senators and representatives took it upon themselves to introduce separate reform plans, creating a daunting array of options for the public to follow and understand.

By the end of the Congressional debates, 27 different legislative proposals had been advanced, which in turn were identified in the media by 110 different names.

Interest groups spent large sums communicating with the public, but most of their efforts seemed designed less to inform than to arouse latent fears and anxieties and to reinforce existing views. "This plan forces us to buy our insurance through those new mandatory government health alliances," complained a prototypical wife, Louise, in a celebrated series of TV ads paid for by the Health Insurance Association of America. "Run by tens of thousands of new bureaucrats," added husband Harry. "Having choices we don't like is no choice at all," replied Louise. "They choose, we lose," both concluded with evident disapproval. According to a study by the University of Pennsylvania's Annenberg School for Communication, 59 percent of all the television ads were misleading. In addition, most of the broadcast health reform ads concentrated on attacking a position rather than advocating one. A high percentage of the ads "impugn[ed] the goodwill and integrity of those on the other side of the issue." Again and again, the same exaggerated themes were repeated. According to one side, the Clinton plan amounted to "involuntary euthanasia" and deprived families of their choice of a doctor. According to the other, "unless the Clinton plan is passed, millions of Americans will have no access to health care."[4]

Ultimately, opponents of the Clinton plan proved more effective than supporters. Many Americans were highly skeptical of government intervention and fearful that it would squander large amounts of money. The suspicion that all government programs are wasteful offered tempting opportunities for opponents to exploit through communications such as the Harry and Louise ads. They also caused the president's advisors to back away from trying to explain important parts of the Clinton plan to the public. "Whatever you do," warned one internal White House memo, "don't get caught up in the details of the policy."[5] Every effort was made to avoid any suggestion of increased taxes (other than tobacco taxes) or to intimate that more government bureaucracy might be required. As Theda Skocpol has observed, "Promoters of the Clinton Health Security Plan tried to avoid discussing the alliances as new sorts of governmental organizations. Instead of telling Americans as simply and clearly as possible why this kind of governmental endeavor would be effective and desirable, their accommodation to the public's distrust of government was to pretend that President Clinton was proposing a virtually government-free health security plan."[6]

In the end, the White House strategy did more to increase public misunderstanding than to promote the president's plan. Weeks after the president unveiled his proposal, large majorities of Americans still had no comprehension of what health alliances did or why they were needed. Nor could they understand how the Clinton plan could insure millions of Americans who lacked health care coverage without increasing taxes. Amid the suspicion that surrounds all government initiatives, 80 percent of the public concluded that health costs would rise more than the president claimed; 54 percent believed that costs would rise "much more." Similarly, although only 25 percent of Americans claimed to understand what a health alliance was, 65 percent assumed that the president's plan would result in more bureaucracy.[7]

The only hope of bringing clarity to the debate lay in the media. To their credit, reporters did make a serious effort to inform the discussion and enlighten the public in the early stages of the campaign. Major newspapers devoted lengthy columns, even entire pages, to trying to explain the details of health care alliances, employer mandates, and other intricacies of the Clinton proposal. With support from the Robert Wood Johnson Foundation, NBC aired a long program explaining the issues on prime time. The *New York Times* ran a 16-page special supplement on health care reform. Other newspapers provided extensive coverage of their own. After the president's initial speech to Congress, however, in September 1993, media attention increasingly turned from the substance of the rival health plans under consideration to the conflicts and maneuvering of the different Congressional factions and interest groups that were struggling to get the upper hand. Some reporters even speculated that the health care debate was simply a smokescreen by the Clintons to divert the public's attention from the Whitewater saga.

As the number of competing proposals grew, substantive news coverage declined, and the barrage of interest group claims and counterclaims became more strident. Only about one-quarter of the newspaper stories and less than one-fifth of the television coverage focused on the substantive issues under consideration. Reporters tended not to mention the several areas of agreement between Republicans and Democrats, such as the need for some kind of insurance pool and for some means of allowing workers to take their health insurance with them when they changed jobs. Gradually, a sense of confusion overcame American voters. Eventually, a majority came to feel that Congress should abandon the effort and start again from the beginning the following year.[8]

The public itself surely bears some responsibility for the quality of the debate. If the media came to concentrate more on the political maneuvers of opposing factions, the tactics of powerful interest groups, and the clashes within the Democratic party, it is because many readers and viewers found these subjects more interesting than the numbing details of alternative proposals for reform. If the plight of the uninsured was not fully appreciated, part of the explanation must be that the poor and uninsured rarely bothered to vote, let alone make an effort to understand what was at stake and to communicate their views to Congress.

A Failure of the Marketplace of Ideas

Whoever is ultimately responsible for the quality of the health care debate, the end result was depressing. According to reliable surveys, the public was even more confused about health care by the end of Congress's deliberations than it was when President Clinton first presented his plan to Congress in September 1993.[9] The public's reaction proved highly significant. In a survey of lawmakers after the plan met its end, three-quarters of the members of Congress polled asserted that public opinion was a "very important" factor in the outcome of the deliberations. The problem, then, was not that Congress was unresponsive to its constituents. The difficulty was that the marketplace of ideas had failed to produce a working consensus. Months of intense competition to persuade Americans only succeeded in sowing confusion about the underlying facts and creating uncertainty about the proper solution.[10]

Not everyone will be convinced that the health care debate was seriously deficient. Those who opposed the Clinton plan may believe that, despite all the confusion and exaggeration, the public came to understand the problem quite clearly. Behind the glitter of President Clinton's brave promises, opponents argue, his plan would have produced more government regulation, a larger federal bureaucracy, higher health costs, and little or no improvement in the quality of care. According to these critics, members of the public who opposed the plan were correct.

Since the Clinton plan was never tried, no one can be sure what results, good or bad, might have ensued. Nevertheless, there are objective reasons for questioning the quality and effectiveness of the debate, whatever one thinks of the plan's merits. Despite the millions of dollars spent on communicating with the public, voters remained ignorant or confused about many key facts. Americans never understood the government's role in Medicare and the cost that it entailed—a confusion nicely illustrated by a constituent's angry letter to Representative Pat Schroeder urging her to "keep the government's hands off my Medicare." Three months after President Clinton's initial speech, 56 percent of the public was still confused on the vital point of whether his plan guaranteed that workers would retain their health care coverage if they changed jobs. Over 70 percent continued to believe that the government spent less on health care than on humanitarian foreign aid. Most people thought that children had better access to health care than the elderly, despite the existence of Medicare. Only 25 percent of Americans said that they knew what a health alliance was, even though these institutions were a critical part of Mr. Clinton's proposal.[11]

The health care debate also failed to throw light on a critical problem that affected the attitudes of most Americans toward health care reform. Large majorities of the public felt that the principal cause of high medical costs was the existence of waste, fraud, and greed within the health care industry. Accordingly, they were persuaded that adequate reforms could be financed by curbing these abuses. This impression was not misguided on its face. Doctors' incomes in the United States are 50 to 200 percent higher than they are in other advanced democracies. The General Accounting Office has estimated that fraud accounts for as much as 10 percent of the total health care bill. Studies show that American hospitals are much more heavily staffed than hospitals in other industrial nations and that the country is oversupplied with expensive medical technologies. Further studies estimate that up to 20 to 25 percent of all medical procedures in the United States are unnecessary.[12]

Despite such evidence of waste, no effort was made to tell the public why it was not possible to pay for extending health care to the uninsured by curbing unjustified expenditures. The Clinton rhetoric even reinforced popular feelings by accusing insurers and pharmaceuticals of making excessive profits. Since no one bothered to explain, it is little wonder that the public's principal reason for rejecting the Clinton plan was that it would cost too much.

A final commentary on the health care debate emerges from a *Wall Street Journal* article appearing in 1994 entitled, "Many Don't Realize It's the Clinton Plan They Like." The article reported the results of a *Journal*-NBC poll asking respondents their reaction to a health plan that contained all the features of the Clinton proposal without revealing that it was the president's plan. Respondents were also invited to evaluate the four other plans under consideration in Congress, again without identifying the sponsor of the plan to the readers. When the results were tabulated, 76 percent saw "some" or "a great deal" of appeal in the Clinton proposal, a much more favorable response than that given to any of the other plans. This result occurred at the very time that other polls were reporting a majority of Americans opposing the Clinton plan.[13]

The health care debate, of course, is not representative of all public discussions of policy questions. Few legislative issues are as complicated, and none has ever provoked such massive efforts to influence the views of American voters. Still, the differences are ones more of degree than of kind. The principal features of the struggle over health care—the grassroots lobbying, the appeal to emotion, the media's preoccupation with controversy and tactics, the inattention of the public—are all common to most important legislative campaigns involving topics of direct interest to ordinary people. As a result, the lessons one draws from the history of the Clinton plan have implications for the entire democratic process in this country.

The Role of Leadership

How important was the president's leadership in this case? How could he have improved the debate and helped the public reach a better understanding of the issues? Is there anything he might have done that would have secured the passage of major health care reform? To carry through a legislative campaign of this magnitude, effective presidential leadership was clearly essential. Because the issue touched every American and involved such vital interests, public opinion was bound to be important, and the president would have to use his bully pulpit to maximum advantage. His power to command attention and attract an attentive audience would clearly be vital to overcoming the doubts and confusions spread by powerful adversaries.

From this standpoint, the president's performance can be criticized on several grounds. First of all, one can argue that he attempted to do too much, too soon, in view of his weak popular mandate (43 percent of the popular vote in 1992). Perhaps it would have been better to seek reform in steps, starting with such popular items as covering children and providing portability of health care benefits. In this way, he could have broken a huge subject down into manageable pieces that could be understood by the American people in the course of a public debate that might have taken several years.

Another criticism involves the president's use of a task force, headed by his wife, that operated in secret. This process tended to shut out voices that might have helped create a more viable plan—voices of knowledgeable persons in the administration who feared to criticize the work of the first lady, voices of critics of a managed competition approach who were excluded from the Task Force, voices of interest groups and politicians who, had they been consulted more frequently, might have exposed the political vulnerabilities of the eventual plan. Secret deliberations and exclusion of contrary voices are hardly a viable way of crafting a major reform in an environment in which the president has limited influence over Congress, powerful opponents, and a public distrustful of government and its capabilities.

Finally, once the plan was introduced, the president did too little to explain it to the people. Indeed, at the urging of advisors, the Administration denied that the plan would cost any more than what could be raised by "sin" taxes and avoided discussing how such important items as the proposed health care alliances would actually operate. In an atmosphere of crisis or during a time of maximum trust, a leader may gather support for an important proposal without explaining important details. But this was not President Clinton's situation. By saying so little about costs and the alliances, he allowed his adversaries an open field to convince an already skeptical public that his plan would cost the taxpayers money and create another large, unwieldy federal bureaucracy.

Despite these shortcomings, it is one thing to criticize the president and quite another to maintain that skillful leadership would have secured the passage of major health care reform. While faith of this kind is appealing, a hard look at the evidence suggests that passing major health care reforms in 1993 and 1994 represented a gargantuan task that might well have stymied any president. To begin with, there were huge deficits in the budget and heavy opposition to any tax increases (other than sin taxes). As a result, Clinton was forced to devise a plan that could not buy off opposition by increasing benefits. In addition, he faced a public with little or no confidence in the government's capacity to function effectively. Hence, he had to try to reform the health care system without seeming to add to official bureaucracy. Furthermore, he was operating within a climate of acute distrust toward politicians. Thus, he had to propose a vast reform in a highly complicated and sensitive field of activity without being able to ask people to take anything on faith. Finally, he had to contend with interest groups that would spend millions trying to convince the public that his ideas were dangerous, wasteful, and not workable. Could any leader make his way through such a minefield and have the Congress enact a major health care reform?

A Dilemma of Democracy

The health care debate reveals a dilemma for democracy and public debate that is far from new but grows with time. The issues that a modern government must face seem increasingly complicated. Health care is an apt illustration. In addition, the quality of debate—although richer in information than before—is more confusing as more and more voices enter in, many of them highly partisan and with goals quite different from the pursuit of truth and the public interest. Under these circumstances, the burden on the voters to understand the issues and arrive at an informed opinion is greater than ever, precisely at a time when voters are increasingly uninterested in government and cynical about the value of citizen participation.

Ideally, the inherent complexity of the issues calls for greater trust in elected representatives to work out enlightened solutions, with the public concentrating more on electing the best and ablest candidates to serve them. Instead, because the public so distrusts the legislature, lawmakers rely increasingly on public opinion to guide their actions, which in turn leads interest groups to devote more money and effort to influencing grassroots opinion for their own advantage. In such an environment, inspired leadership, though always desirable, is hardly something one can count on to offer more than temporary, occasional relief.

Is there some way of making policy proposals, using voices other than those of politicians, that would command greater trust from the public? Bipartisan commissions with eminent members have been tried but only occasionally with success. Universities have sought to give objective opinions in the health care field by issuing newsletters on medical problems that try to give reasoned summaries of what is known and not known to counteract the swirl of confusing reports about so many issues of appropriate care. Are there adaptations of this principle that might work for at least some issues of public policy, such as global warming?

A second question worth exploring is whether there is some way of creating more useful, informative discussion in the media. As economists have shown, market forces will lead to underinvestment in public affairs discussion because private firms cannot capture the social value in a democracy of increased public enlightenment on policy questions. The United States government allocates far less to public affairs programming than any other advanced democracy. As a result, one can argue that greater investments are needed—much greater than the amounts allocated to public affairs broadcasting on NPR or public television. Can one imagine a way to create and finance programming that could help offset the tendency in the media—so clearly illustrated in the health care debates—to veer off into a preoccupation with tactics and political conflict? Could such programming be kept objective and free from political influence? Could it be made interesting enough to capture a reasonable segment of the viewing audience?

Finally, hasn't the time come to respond to the growing apathy and cynicism of the public by making much more determined efforts to prepare Americans as active, engaged citizens? Clearly, this is a task that has been sorely neglected in recent decades. In schools, it is sacrificed to the preoccupation over preparing a workforce for the global economy. In universities, it is rarely discussed as an explicit aim of undergraduate or professional education. In the media, civic journalism has confronted the issue directly, but there is much opposition to such methods from powerful sources. Amid this neglect, political participation has declined from one generation to the next since 1960. By now, barely one-third of American citizens aged 18–30 even bother to vote in presidential elections.

What has never been tried is a concerted effort at all levels to recognize active citizenship and engaged public discourse as major goals of democratic society, to be pursued simultaneously at many levels and in many forms. Perhaps the most important opportunity for effective leadership by political leaders is to put this challenge on the agenda and stimulate an active discussion in many quarters on how citizenship and civic virtue can best be cultivated and strengthened throughout American society.

Chapter 10
Part of Our World:
Journalism as Civic Leadership

Jay Rosen

Some years ago, while watching the *CBS Evening News*, I was startled to hear Dan Rather say, "And that's part of our world tonight." Mr. Rather then thanked me for watching, but it was I who wanted to thank him—for frank acknowledgment of what he and his colleagues actually do. They give us part of the world, a version of it; and there is no scandal in saying that this artifact, the news, is something journalists make, which means it can be made poorly or well. The point may seem simple, or even simpleminded; and yet it is a good starting point for any discussion of journalism and our public culture. It allows us to name what journalists do well: present a version of events that bears the mark of mind and the stamp of belief. "And that's part of our world tonight" is a very civil thing for an anchorman to say. It admits: "This is not the final word, or the whole truth, or a mirror we've made, just the best we could do in crafting our nightly report." Freed from some of its grander pretensions ("Expect the world," says the *New York Times* in its current ad campaign; "And that's the way it is," spoke Walter Cronkite from the chair Rather now holds), the news is made simultaneously more human, more artful, more reliable—in fact, more real. It is easier to trust in a journalist's version of events than a journalist who says: "I deal not in versions. My trade is the truth."

On the other hand, to say the news is made is not to say the news media make it up. In 1922 Walter Lippmann likened the news to "a beam of a searchlight that moves restlessly about, bringing one episode and then another, out of darkness into vision."[1] By picturing the people who shine the beacon here and there—using their judgment, including their judgments about us—we adopt a more humble but more compelling image of the journalist. With this image there is much we can do. Once we realize that the news is made, rather than found, we can ask what it looks and feels like when it is made well. We can ask what "well" means, from a variety of perspectives. How does the political community at large, ritually invoked in that newsroom battle cry, "the public's right to know," know when the journalism we are getting is the one we need in order to navigate the public world and take our place within it? Here is a matter too important to be left to journalists alone, in the same way that health is too vital to be delegated to doctors.

American journalism has taken on the trappings of a profession: we train journalists in some of our best universities; we expect from them, as they expect from themselves, certain standards of conduct; and we give them wide latitude in deciding what right conduct shall mean. I teach in a journalism department at a research university in the media capital of the world. We do not require of our students, nor do we offer ourselves, any courses in "democracy for news professionals." We do not ask them to inquire deeply into the requirements of a healthy public culture, a workable sphere of discussion, a politics we can respect, a government that comes as near as possible to the ideals of the American republic. We, and the schools to which we compare ourselves, do not insist on teaching these things because we have something to teach in their place: how to be a competent professional. But once we think of journalism as a curriculum in itself, a daily tutorial in the events of our time, then all the teachings of that curriculum fall open to examination. From this angle, the relevant questions are not whether journalists are competent, ethical, and professional, but whether the craft as a whole is serving the public interest.

In the words of historian Christopher Lasch, democracy is best defended "not as the most efficient but as the most educational form of government." All the institutions that help make democracy work are educational, in Lasch's sense, and this includes the press. Typically, when we debate press performance, we fix on a handful of familiar problems: inaccuracy, bias, or a rush to judgment; a fixation on scandal and sleaze; stories that are bungled amid others that are missed; and news that signals little more than a commercial formula at work.[2] But a more vital debate would reach deeper: to the lessons we receive from journalists as they educate us to a sense of the world. What kind of instruction should we expect, along with our daily diet of information? In presenting what can only be a part of our world, what parts should journalists take care to include and highlight? Beyond sound reporting, a profession in whose standards we can trust, what can we ask of a press that is both a private business and a public actor?

The Press as an Actor

I use the word "actor" with some hesitation—and to make a point. The hesitation is that American journalists are reluctant to describe themselves as anything more than observers or commentators. And for good reason. There is a difference between doing journalism and doing politics; between conveying the scene to others and striding across it as one of the players. The press box, set apart from the public stage, is not an imaginary locale. By reserving a place for journalists in their capacity as chroniclers, we expect them to tell us about the world, not rearrange it to their liking. There is a good deal of common sense in the American contributions to journalism: traditions of objectivity, independence, and detachment. But if there is honor in these traditions, there is no dishonor in calling them part of our political tradition, one way in which we realize our aspiration to live together as freethinking citizens who try to solve their problems through democratic means. When news crews show up in a Senate hearing room, the room becomes a different kind of space, inviting a different kind of politics; and no one wise in the ways of power can ignore this fact. In a broader and deeper way, the news is always getting mixed up with our public and popular cultures, returning "us" to us with all of our excesses and discontents, but also setting out a pattern, amplifying a tone, and inviting particular behaviors. This is all part of journalism's hectic and varied curriculum.

This tenor of thought—which understands journalism as an education in democracy and politics, as well as a maker and molder of our public climate—is not entirely foreign to the American press, although it is a minor chord. It can be heard clearly in these passages, both from mainstream journalists with considerable experience. Katharine Seeyle, reporter for the *New York Times*, writes in a 1995 article, "Modern American culture is loud and adversarial, and politics reflects the culture. And the ever-adversarial, conflict-seeking press helps shape the politics." Robert MacNeil, former anchor of the *MacNeil-Lehrer News Hour* on PBS, said in a 1995 speech: "We have to remember, as journalists, that we may be observers but we are not totally disinterested observers. We are not social engineers, but each one of us has a stake in the health of this democracy. Democracy and the social contract that makes it work are held together by a delicate web of trust, and all of us in journalism hold edges of the web. We are not just amused bystanders, watching the idiots screw it up."[3] These statements go beyond the acknowledgment that news is not a mirror of events to reveal a deeper truth: the press is an active agent in public life, not a passive observer.

Journalism and Leadership

These claims concerning the agency of the press raise the tricky but not impossible question of leadership in journalism, for anyone acting on our common life can try to find a way of telling our story that helps us own and improve it. Most journalists would probably admit that they can occasionally expect leadership in their profession. If asked what this means, they might reply that the press can employ its editorial voice to awaken public conscience, warn of possible dangers, and recommend a course of action. The press can be an opinion leader, as long it labels what it is doing "opinion." Beyond that, it can take the lead in exposing corruption, documenting the abuse of public trust, bringing hidden or suppressed facts to light. Investigative reporting is leadership because it can lead (indirectly) to reforms. Finally, by focusing on matters that might otherwise escape notice, the press can lead by example. It can say to the community: "We're giving time and space to this story because we believe it's important, whether or not others agree." These observations would probably exhaust the common meaning of leadership in American journalism. They do not exhaust the possibilities, however. If reporters like Seeyle understand that the "press helps shape the politics" we have, can't they begin shaping the politics we need? If an accomplished broadcaster like Robert MacNeil knows that social trust is a "delicate web" that journalists, among others, uphold, can't he and his colleagues also try to strengthen that web? And wouldn't these be responsible acts of leadership for an institution that claims a duty to the public good?

My answer would be "yes," but it is not my answer alone. David Broder of the *Washington Post*, arguably the most respected political journalist of our time, wrote a provocative column on the press over a decade ago: "We cannot allow the [1990] elections to be another exercise in public disillusionment and political cynicism. . . . It is time for those of us in the world's freest press to become activists, not on behalf of a particular party or politician, but on behalf of the process of self-government."[4] Broder explained what he meant by "activists" in a 1991 lecture that elaborated on his column. There he described a "bleak political landscape" where citizens "tell us that they are disgusted by the campaigns they are offered in this country." Along with the political consultants, whose power was rising in the campaign system, journalists had become a "permanent part of the political establishment." Both groups characteristically denied "any responsibility for the consequences of elections." This was disingenuous at best, dishonest at worst, for the fact was "we have colluded with the campaign consultants to produce the kind of politics which is turning off the American people."

Broder asked himself what he could do. "If we are going to change the pattern, we in the press have to try deliberately to reposition ourselves in the process. We have to try to distance ourselves from the people we write about—the politicians and their political consultants—and move ourselves closer to the people that we write for—the voters and potential voters." Broder proposed that journalists should treat the campaign period as part of a longer drama, "embracing both elections and government" and centered on the American people rather than the candidates and their advisors. The campaign should be treated as the property of the voters, a time when they "have a right to have their concerns addressed and their questions answered by the people who are seeking to exercise power." So "let their agenda drive our agenda," Broder explained. Journalists should represent the public in the political process, rather than just bring the process home to a public already disaffected with it. Why do all this? Because the situation was not beyond remedy. Broder held to a belief that the American people were not "apathetic or unconcerned"; nor were they "selfish or indifferent." They were simply tired of seeing politics treated as a "sport for a relative handful of political insiders." Broder closed on a personal note. "I would like to leave some better legacy than that behind when I get out of this business."[5]

What is this speech, if not an act of leadership? Broder, a prominent figure in his field, diagnoses a problem, implicates himself and his colleagues in it, and tries to imagine a way out. He lays forth an "alternative proposition" that is both practical and, if this is not too strong a term, visionary. It is visionary because it refuses to accept what is as the horizon of what could be—in politics, in public discourse, and in journalism. The hope that election campaigns might become the "property" of citizens, a time when their concerns are fairly addressed, is a prescription for a better politics and a better press. Broder thought that this enlarged vision, if embraced by his colleagues, might bring changes to political reporting, which might also affect politics. After all, he said, journalists had already "colluded" with political professionals to produce a dreary dialogue dominated by the maneuverings of insiders. Perhaps the press could move away from one kind of cooperation toward another: finding and amplifying citizens' concerns during election season, asking for a response from candidates, then persisting in this aim as balloting gives way to governing. Broder's rhetorical leadership had some tangible effects, most notably in the experiment that has come to be known as civic or public journalism.

Birth of a Notion: The Public Journalism Movement

In 1990, out in the plains of Kansas, Davis Merritt, editor of the *Wichita Eagle*, had begun refashioning his newspaper's approach to political coverage much as Broder would envision. Merritt was a 35-year veteran of the newspaper world who had spent time in Washington during the Watergate era. The newspaper's feature, "Where They Stand," was more than a handy voters' guide. The rules for candidates were clear: say something meaningful about the key issues, and we'll report it and keep reporting it. This was a powerful use of political space. Deploying the threat of a blank appearing under a candidate's name was the *Eagle*'s way of being tough on the candidates. Here, however, toughness doesn't become an end in itself, as so often happens in political reporting. A candidate can avoid the penalty of white space by cooperating in a process that will help voters make up their minds.

Merritt's 1990 experiment recognized that beyond information, the press sends us an invitation to experience public life in one manner or another. Reflecting on what this invitation should say was perhaps the most daring thing the *Eagle* did. The experience should be participatory,

Merritt and his staff said. It should cultivate a useful dialogue about issues. It should address people in their capacity as citizens, in the hope of
strengthening that capacity. It should try to make public life go well, in
the sense of making good on democracy's promise. These "shoulds"
were acts of leadership by a local newspaper. And they would eventually
form the core of public journalism as a philosophy. As Merritt wrote
about the 1990 voter project: "We had deliberately broken out of the
passive and increasingly detrimental conventions of election coverage.
We had, in effect, left the press box and gotten down on the field, not as
a contestant but as a fair-minded participant with an open and expressed
interest in the process going well. . . . We had a new purposefulness: revi-
talizing a moribund public process."[6]

In the fall of 1992, the *Charlotte Observer* took this "new purposefulness" further with its own experiment in election coverage. Like others
in journalism, executive editor Rich Oppel was dissatisfied with press
performance in past campaigns, particularly with horse-race polling. In
1992, Oppel and publisher Rolfe Neill were determined to try something
different. The *Observer* set out to amplify and extend the "new political
contract" outlined two years earlier by Merritt and described in strik-
ingly similar language by Broder. In a front-page column entitled, "We'll
help you regain control of the issues," Oppel announced the paper's intentions: "We will seek to reduce the coverage of campaign strategy and
candidates' manipulations, and increase the focus on voters' concerns.
We will seek to distinguish between issues that merely influence an election's outcome, and those of governance that will be relevant after the
election. We will link our coverage to the voters' agenda, and initiate
more questions on behalf of the voters."[7]

Oppel's column represents a coming clean that was long overdue in
campaign journalism. First, he admits that politics-as-strategy is a narrative device that was bringing diminishing returns; then he declares that
his newspaper will be consciously applying a new device: a "focus on voters' concerns." He acknowledges that the temporal frame—the definition of political time—that ordinarily shapes campaign coverage is too
narrow, focusing as it does on "issues that merely influence an election's
outcome." He then announces the choice of a new frame: matters of
"governance that will be relevant after the election." He admits that
question-asking is an important public function that can be performed in
several different ways. The way the *Observer* chooses is to "initiate more
questions on behalf of the voters." In the same passage, Oppel concedes
that "covering politics" and "having an agenda" are not mutually exclusive. He grasped that if journalists are to be seen as actors, it is reasonable to expect from them a kind of agenda.[8]

But what should that agenda be? How can journalists justify it to wider
audiences? What sort of rhetoric should they employ in doing so? Such
questions confound the profession's view of itself. Almost all the key

tenets in the journalist's ethical code emphasize, not civic action, but professional detachment: the maligned but still influential doctrine of objectivity, the related emphasis on fairness and balance, the separation between the news columns and the editorial page, the watchdog role, the adversarial stance, the principle of ignoring consequences in deciding what's newsworthy. None of these ideas offers guidance to the people Broder tried to address: professionals willing to acknowledge their influence in politics and to use it on behalf of "genuine democracy in this country."

If these early experiments in civic journalism were to continue, a lot of work lay ahead. Some of the work was intellectual: finding a coherent philosophy for a press that might elect a different path. Some of it was practical: experimenting with a revised approach that fit the constraints of daily journalism. Some of it involved mobilizing like-minded people to form something resembling a movement. And some of it was institutional: finding money and organizational support to further a rising spirit of reform.

Public Journalism: Getting a Fix on the Phenomenon

Public journalism (also known as civic journalism) came to the attention of the American press in the years 1993 to 1997. The profession had some trouble coping with the development because public journalism was not a single phenomenon, but a broad pattern of activity that moved in many directions and relied on multiple sources of support. Among the key players were: editors and executives and newspapers and broadcasts outlets, along with reporters and producers who worked under them; foundations (chiefly, the Kettering Foundation, the Knight Foundation, and the Pew Charitable Trusts) that provided funding for research, conferences, and experiments in the field; think tanks like the American Press Institute and the Poynter Institute for Media Studies, where important get-togethers were held; companies (Knight-Ridder was the most prominent but not the only one) that exposed the journalists in their employ to the ideas behind public journalism and urged them to take it seriously; professors (like me) at journalism schools, who undertook research and advanced the thinking behind public journalism, often in interaction with working professionals.

To complicate the picture further, the range of experiments that fell under the heading of "public journalism" went considerably beyond the election-year projects I have described. The *Herald-Dispatch* in Huntington, West Virginia, helped convene a group of citizens (900 showed up for the first meeting) to discuss what might be done about a faltering economy and the flight of young people from the area. The citizens organized themselves into task forces that examined what needed to be done in different areas, such as economic development, job training, and education. The newspaper pledged to help out by reporting on how similar-sized communities had coped with massive job loss and by opening its pages to ideas and opinions generated by the ensuing civic discussion. A media partnership in Madison, Wisconsin, brought newspapers, TV stations, and public radio outlets together to sponsor televised public forums where citizens could deliberate, grand-jury style, on important policy questions, with background materials printed in the newspaper. The forums examined health care, land use, public education, the federal deficit, and other pressing problems, with citizens—rather than experts—in the lead role. Editors and reporters at the *Dayton Daily News*, faced with the imminent shut down of a major defense plant and the loss of thousands of jobs, hired an architect to complete a rendering of what the plant might look like if converted to civilian use, while simultaneously reporting on what it would take—from government, business, labor, and the community itself—if the jobs were to be saved. The editorial pages of the *Spokesman-Review* in Spokane, Washington, were redesigned to become more open public forums. In Spokane, the editors ventured out into the community and found people who had something to say, but lacked the skills or courage to say it. The editors acted like writing coaches, helping ordinary citizens gain a voice in the community, rather than relying on the "usual suspects" who dominate public debate. The *Charlotte Observer* adopted a problem-solving focus in its "Taking Back Our Neighborhoods" series, which examined the crime rate in the hardest-hit sections of town. The paper asked residents there to deliberate about the causes and consequences of crime, then profiled these neighborhoods in depth—without whitewashing the realities of street crime on the one hand, or exploiting it for lurid headlines on the other. The paper then highlighted what local residents had to do for themselves, what city government could contribute, and what the community as a whole could do to help, moving from neighborhood to neighborhood with news that spoke of problems and possible answers. This is but a sampling of hundreds of experiments that put into practice the ideas behind public journalism.

Conclusions and Lessons from Public Journalism

I have not given here a complete (or even balanced) picture of public journalism. There is plenty more to say in fair criticism of the idea and the experiment; but I will leave that to others. Destructive patterns in our common life include the deterioration of public talk and a faltering sense of community amid a host of pressing challenges—especially the challenge of living together in a diverse and complex society, where competing notions of the good are inevitable. What is not inevitable is a public climate of perpetual warfare and rampant incivility, problems that are particularly apparent in the way we do politics and conduct our national discourse.

What forms of leadership are required to steer our way out of our current discontents? How can the spirit of community be revived, without getting overly romantic about it? What are the cultural patterns that engender civic values and shape behavior in the public square? What would a better national dialogue look and sound like, if one can be imagined and brought to life? Public journalism offers the following lessons.

LOOK TO THE PROFESSIONS

As people are constantly reminding me, journalism is a business. It needs to turn a profit in order to survive in an increasingly commercialized and competitive environment. This is an unarguable fact, but it is not the only relevant fact. Most people who choose journalism as a field do not make that choice seeking money, power, or fame. I have asked several hundred of them in my travels about the field. They often say they went into journalism to "make a difference," or to right wrongs, or, in a favorite phrase, to "comfort the afflicted and afflict the comfortable." Never has a journalist said to me: "I chose this field because my passion is . . . objectivity!" Never have I heard: "I am by nature a neutral person, so I thought journalism would be best for me."

Despite all the constraints and pressures they face, most journalists feel a strong duty to the public good. This is what makes their craft, which is a business, also a profession. Professions matter because they profess things. They legitimate themselves around a commitment to the public interest and democratic values; and if they sometimes define this commitment in self-serving fashion, we do them (and ourselves) no favor by treating the professional's claim to public service as merely a sham.

Rather, if the professions are not serving the public as well as they might, we should look to what they profess, for we will find there the rhetorical ground on which a renewed commitment to the common good can be based. Public journalism is a way of taking seriously the journalist's identity as a professional. It accepts this claim in good faith. But it does not assume that what people in the press do and say is adequate to the times, or faithful to the values that drew them into the field. Instead, it argues with the profession about what journalism ought to profess.

What civic identity means within any given profession—law, medicine, accounting, education, commerce, public administration, social work—will vary with each field of endeavor. But it should also move with the times, since what we need from professionals will change as our problems alter and grow. Public journalism is an example of that. It does not appeal to everyone in the press, or even a majority. It does not offer a ready-made template for other fields. But it is a useful reminder that professionalism is not dead or deaf to democracy's call. If we take the professions more seriously than some professionals do, we might awaken their slumbering potential for public good.

ENLARGE THE LANGUAGE OF DEMOCRACY

Democracy, as John Dewey relentlessly declared, is a way of life, not just a system of government. When Dewey declared that the only cure for the problems of democracy was more democracy, he did not mean we should vote on everything. He meant that discovering what democracy demands is a never-ending inquiry. In particular, it requires fresh and varied attempts to speak and think like a democrat, while going about all the other business of life. Public journalism offers another way to talk about democracy as the ultimate end the press should serve. Not the only other way, or the one right way, but just a different way—one that we hope is more attuned to the times. What other democratic dialects need to be spoken now—in what haunts and by whom? What does it mean to be a democrat—and a movie producer? And a doctor? And a pollster? Questions like this may have heuristic value, if nothing else. And there is always the chance they will turn practical in surprising or fruitful ways.

CALL FOR AN EXPERIMENTAL SPIRIT

Public journalism says to professionals in the press: try stuff and learn from what you have tried. It has to proceed this way because, in truth, no one knows exactly how to fortify civic identity in the craft or renew its commitment to public values. When you don't know how to move forward, there are two choices: you can pretend you know, or you can experiment. What Dewey called the "quest for certainty" is everywhere the enemy of the kind of patient inquiry and piecemeal reform he thought appropriate in a democratic society—which to him meant a community of learners.

We might profitably imagine what an "experimental" spirit would look like in various corners of society where our key concerns resonate. Without prescribing the "stuff" to be tried, we can still say "try stuff" in a more than a cursory manner. We can do this by imagining what the atmosphere would be like in any public sphere where a spirit of experiment is needed. We can find out who is experimenting in a genuinely "civic" way—and who is not, but could be.

Make Resistance Revelatory

Public journalism invites a good deal of criticism. Some of it, no doubt, is due to the fuzzy or even wrongheaded direction in which the experiment has sometimes moved. But much of it reveals in its intensity and dismissive tone a reflexive quality that has overtaken the mind of the American press. The elite press, in particular, was overly quick on the draw, as it attempted early on to wave away public journalism as a gimmick or fraud—or worse. In the process, however, even the most shallow critiques revealed where the critic stood on some key questions: What does civic purpose mean in journalism? What should the power of the press be used for? What is the best way for this profession to serve democracy? What is the political role of a journalist?

Any answer that was given to these questions actually contributed to the experiment. Why? Because speakers had to move into public and declare themselves on something larger than the latest scandal or missed story. Resistance to public journalism thus revealed how far the movement had to go to engage the mind of the press. But it also displayed the contents of that mind, which made the challenge of finding a civic identity for journalism easier.

Chapter 11
Modeling Public Discourse in Popular Culture

Neal Gabler

In attempting to examine how the movies have portrayed public discourse and how that portrayal may affect the broader public discourse, it is important to recognize that the movies themselves are a form of that discourse. Most obviously and narrowly, the movies have addressed a range of subjects, from sexual behavior to race to war to social responsibility to juvenile delinquency to such other pressing issues as fending off an alien horde bent on conquering the Earth or destroying humongous monsters trampling through cities and overturning public transportation systems, or deflecting asteroids headed directly toward our planet.

There is, however, another less obvious and more general way in which the movies have become a form of discourse, this one having less to do with the specific content of any single film than with the act of moviegoing itself. Almost from the inception of the movies in the last century, moviegoing has constituted a cultural declaration in the national conversation. Ordinary citizens flocked to the movies, recognizing that the medium belonged to them in a way no previous art or entertainment had. Movies were not only accessible and relatively inexpensive, they had none of the cultural pretensions and prohibitions attached to so many other arts, and none of the cultural condescension, either. You could chat at the movies. You could neck at the movies. You could eat at the movies. And the vestiges of these activities remain, to this day, in what I have described as "the Whitmanian slurp of soda and the crunch of popcorn." Imagine going to the opera or to the symphony or to the ballet lugging your box or bag of popcorn. It is just not done.[1]

In a sense, moviegoing has always been a slightly subversive activity. It subverts the elitist idea of what art is supposed to be, which is why elitists frequently condemn the movies on aesthetic grounds and why moralists continue to condemn them on moral grounds. To this day, conservatives cannot countenance the fact that having commandeered the country's political agenda, they have not been able to commandeer its cultural agenda. What those who criticize popular culture do not understand is that there may be a cause and effect relationship between their cater-wauling about the debased state of American popular culture and the embrace of that culture by the general populace. Critics fail to recognize this nose-thumbing, contrarian, democratic impulse that moviegoing expresses, especially among the young, but it is among the main reasons why there are still 20 million people who go to the movies each week. "Perhaps the single most intense pleasure of moviegoing," the critic Pauline Kael once wrote, "is this non-aesthetic one of escaping from the responsibilities of having the proper responses required of us in our official (school) culture. . . . It's the feeling of freedom from respectability we have always enjoyed at the movies."[2]

If conservatives fail to recognize the cause and effect relationship between their disapproval and public approval, they also fail to recognize another cause and effect relationship, one between the sense that our political system is unresponsive to public needs and the feeling that the popular culture is responsive. In fact, a sense of disempowerment in one arena creates a sense of empowerment in the other. Critics say constantly that Hollywood is governed by a liberal media elite that does not give the public what it wants. But no one can make the argument that Hollywood is not trying to give the public what it wants. Whether one likes them or not, the movies are Jacksonian. They are expressions of public will against all the forces that seem to disregard us.

But when we get beyond the act of moviegoing itself as public discourse and consider how the movies have portrayed such discourse, we immediately discover something: they don't. There is very little public discourse in American film. Frankly, this should not be too surprising. The movies, after all, are a kinetic medium, a medium of action. Discourse, particularly rational discourse, is not exactly going to provide nail-biting suspense. Watching public discussion is much more like watching paint dry. When we do see public discourse portrayed in the movies, it tends to present issues as a matter of conflict rather than of conflict resolution. Examples of public discourse in the movies assume that there is a truth, and that truth is thwarted by forces of ignorance or outright corruption, greed, or evil. For truth to triumph, one has to defeat the forces of ignorance or greed or evil. In the second place, one might also notice that the airing of public issues in movies is really less a matter of discussion or negotiation than of individual action. People do not band together to accomplish their ends in American films. That is what happens in the old Soviet movies of Sergei Eisenstein. In American movies, people may be inspired to act, but the inspiration is almost always an individual—a hero. In fact, the primacy of the individual may be the subtext of virtually every commercial American film.

Movies are constantly reminding us, subliminally and otherwise, of the importance of being important. Whether it is the emphasis on the star above the title or the compositions that invariably favor the heroic figure or the narratives that are driven by the hero's actions, we are being told that not to be at the center of action is to be swept to the margins. Arnold Schwarzenegger may kill dozens of bad guys in one of his films, but no one cares about them. I do not think that anyone, myself included, sits and thinks, "Does this fellow have a wife? Does this fellow have children? Does this fellow have a mother and father?" We do not care about them because we realize that they are present as fodder. They don't matter. The only one who matters is Schwarzenegger himself.

A good deal of our public discourse has been shaped in the image of the movies, and specifically, in the image of these two elements, which are so fundamental to our moviegoing pleasure: the centrality of conflict and the valorization of the individual.

The influence of cinematic images of conflict may be seen in our tendency to think in terms of plots when considering social issues. It seems that every issue is framed as a Manichaean dispute, a battle between good and bad, which favors drama over fact. This, of course, is not an entirely new phenomenon in the world of public affairs. Jeffersonians portrayed America in its infancy as threatened by demonic federalists who supported an essential authority and affected aristocratic ways. Jacksonians portrayed Americans threatened by rich, intellectual dandies; populists by Eastern banking interests and antipopulists by populists; Reaganites by free-spending liberals and Clintonites by political moralists.

But while political plots are nothing new, the mass media has intensified them, virtually demanding that issues somehow be configured as plot if they are going to get a public airing, since it is the political drama that the media love, not the dull recitation of positions and policies. That is why Ronald Reagan, in opposing the Soviet Union, invoked the specter of an evil empire, and scolded those who wanted to remove themselves from what he called the struggle between right and wrong and good and evil. That is why Arianna Huffington, in floating the presidential possibilities of actor Warren Beatty, described him as a master storyteller, someone who could frame the issues for the public in ways that would get them to care, and identified this as his chief political asset. Good, exciting plots are the ones that are most likely to get media attention for the obvious reason that those are the ones, like the movies, that are most likely to be entertaining.

In the process of turning policy debates into movie narratives, these plots are also more likely to be divorced from the politics they purport to frame than the old political plots which were designed, after all, not for entertainment value, but to sharpen political distinctions between opponents and to rally the troops. We all now take it for granted that coverage of electoral politics will consist primarily of telling us who is ahead and how he or she might stumble; the so-called horse race aspect of the campaign. Secondarily, we get the personal aspect of the campaign. This has become so much a part of American politics that every candidate is now expected to have a narrative for the media to retail. In the 2000 election George W. Bush was the prodigal son; John McCain, the war hero; Bill Bradley, the nonpolitical politician. Only Al Gore seemed to have no narrative, which may be the occupational hazard of being a vice president. He is condemned to be a sequel. The press then amends these plots almost on a weekly basis during a campaign season.

The emphasis on plot has one other consequence besides separating the dramatic form from its content, one that I believe is directly related to the movies. As anyone who listens to talk radio can attest, the emphasis on plot forces our discourse to extremes, since it is at the extremes where the greatest drama and the highest entertainment value lie. In American policy discussions, whether on *Crossfire* or *Nightline* or *Meet the Press*, or simply in a postmortem of a presidential speech or debate, we always get the pairs. They are the yin and the yang or, less charitably, the mongoose and the snake. The host pokes them a few times and we watch them go at it. Since this is the way that the media now present policy discussions, participants understand what is expected of them: combat.

But if we tend to think of policy issues in terms of plot, setting one side against another, we also tend to think of them in terms of valorous individual action—the second cinematic image mentioned above—and that also distorts public discourse. In *Who Governs?* Robert Dahl's classic study, the esteemed political theorist once described pluralist democracy as a government in which instead of a single center of sovereign power, there must be multiple centers of power, none of which is or can be wholly sovereign. In practice, this means, among other things, what Dahl called constant negotiations among different centers of power in order to make decisions.[3] Talk about noncinematic! Multiple centers of power? Constant negotiations? In the movies, there is one center of power and there are no negotiations. Anyone who negotiates is a nerd or a wimp. In short, pluralist democracy makes for a terrible plot, and Americans know it. They are exasperated by the mess this form of government inevitably entails. And they are constantly searching, not for leaders who swear their fealty to the system, but for leaders who vow to change it.

The basic appeal of H. Ross Perot was his promise that as a no-nonsense businessman he simply would not tolerate the system's red tape. He would just cut right through it. This was also the promise of candidate Donald Trump, citing his swift construction of the Wollman Ice Skating Rink in New York's Central Park as the paradigm for his prospective presidency. He explained, "You just do it. That's all. You just do it." This is not political talk, at least not the talk of a pluralist democracy. This is movie talk. It taps into one of the greatest satisfactions of the movies, the vicarious thrill of a hero overcoming every obstacle, vanquishing every foe. It is a politics of antipolitics, a politics that challenges the very basis of our democracy by replacing the democratic mess with the all-powerful hero acting for right and good.

As powerful an effect as this is, the movies may have had a more powerful effect still in public discourse. This is a result not of the movies serving as a model for public discourse, but of the movies operating as a kind of consciousness, a way of framing our reality. We usually think of policy discussions as being substantive, by which I mean that they deal with problems and they examine how we are going to solve them. Discussions present possibilities, analyze outcomes, and assess political avenues and roadblocks on those avenues. But there is an aspect of public policy that has less to do with solving problems than in making one feel as if the problems do not matter. This is an important component both in the movies and in governing, especially in this age of mass media when public officials can communicate to the public directly and often, and when marshaling public support has become more important than marshaling party support.

As the first president to take full advantage of the national media, Franklin Roosevelt understood the importance of this cheerleading function. Even before he devised a strategy of dealing with the Depression, he was massaging the public psyche, rallying the public mood, telling people they had nothing to fear but fear itself. Harry Truman and Dwight Eisenhower both largely disdained this responsibility, but John Kennedy understood it as well. He knew that his personal glamour would become the national glamour, that his self-confidence would become the national confidence. But no one understood the importance of "feel good" discourse as instinctively or had as natural a gift for it as Ronald Reagan, who had, not incidentally, come to politics from the movies. Reagan had learned a great many things from his years in Hollywood, especially about the art of performance. The most important lesson that he learned was that people flocked to the movies because they liked the way the movies made them feel. Reagan brought this basic piece of intelligence to his new profession, recognizing the affinity between what the movies did and what politics could do if only one reimagined the form—in fact, reimagined it as a movie.

Reagan's revelation was that politics and political discourse did not have to be about policy. They could be about raising spirits. This is not to say that the actions taken during his administration with his endorsement did not affect people's lives—obviously, they did. It is to say that for Reagan himself and for a good many Americans as well, the perception of the president as a genial leader made his policies largely irrelevant to them. This feature may constitute the other Reagan revolution, one that was probably much closer to his own heart than the conservative orthodoxy so often attributed to him, and one that may have much more enduring ramifications for our public discourse. Reagan turned politics into a placebo by regarding Americans not as a constituency to be served, but as an audience to be uplifted. He recognized that politics, like the movies, could itself be a form of escapism. The charm of his presidency, especially after Carter's fixation on malaise, was that there was never any malaise. Malaise makes a terrible plot as well. Who's the hero when there is malaise? Instead, it was always morning in Reagan's America.

Reagan accomplished this by reframing issues as anecdotes and stories, many of them drawn from the movies themselves. Reagan told frequently about the young gunner during World War II who was shot and whose plane was going down and who was frantic, when an older soul on the plane embraced him and said, "Don't worry, son, I'm going down with you." And Reagan always told this as if it had actually happened. In fact, it was a scene from *A Wing and a Prayer*. Reagan also created cinematic images that were impressed into our consciousness, such as the welfare queen. I've always remembered his frequently told story of the common man who invented a beer can holder and became a millionaire as a result, and everyone remembers the cinematic images of the Star Wars antimissile system. Reagan even scripted lines to "cinematize" his points. In the wake of the *Achille Lauro* seajacking in 1981, the *New York Post* wanted the headline to read, "They Can Run, But They Can't Hide," the line heavyweight boxing champion Joe Louis had used when he was going to fight the lighter, quicker Billy Cahn. The only trouble was that Reagan had not said this. So the *Post* contacted Pat Buchanan, who was then in the communications office, told him they had this "wonderful headline," and asked Buchanan to contact Reagan. Reagan then said, "They can run, but they can't hide," thus giving the *Post* its desired headline.

Reagan cinematized the presidency not only by bringing absolute narrative clarity to any situation but by making his performance before the cameras the measure of his performance in office, something that is now a permanent feature of American political discourse. One of Walter Mondale's advisers said in 1984 that in prepping for the debates they "spent more time discussing ties than East-West relations." In effect, if Reagan, as his biographer Lou Cannon has observed in *Role of a Lifetime*, saw his presidency as a movie and himself as its star, and if that meant that stagecraft replaced statecraft and presentation superceded policy, in Reagan's mind it seemed a relatively small price to pay for what Americans got in return.[4] What they got was exactly what they get from the movies: an ineffable sense of pleasure, a wonderful sense of security.

This may be the most profound effect of the movies on our public discourse. Engagement with issues increasingly gets preempted by escapist entertainment, whether it is the entertainment value of the conflict itself, or the entertainment value of pretending that the conflict can easily be resolved, or the entertainment value of whatever distracts us from the conflict altogether. Whatever the source of the entertainment, the purpose of the cinematic mode of discourse is not to resolve our differences, but to make us feel better about ourselves, which is not insignificant. But it is not the same thing as confronting our problems and meeting our challenges, either. The task is clear. For those who want to encourage better public discourse, who want to stimulate a rational exchange of ideas, the challenge is to usher us from the movie theater into the real world, from the darkness of wish fulfillment into the light of reason. Until then, the movie will just keep on rolling.

Part Four
Discourses of Reconciliation
Truth, Apology, and Forgiveness

Chapter 12

Creating a National Discourse:
Truth and Reconciliation in South Africa

Alex Boraine

There are two age-old choices that people have made and nations have been forced to make, summed up by Timothy Garton Ash in his book *The File: A Personal History*.[1] On the one side, there is the old wisdom of the Jewish tradition that to remember is the secret of redemption, and that of George Santayana, so often quoted in relation to Nazism, that those who forget the past are condemned to repeat it. On the other side, there is the profound insight of the historian Ernst Renan, that every nation is a community both of shared memory and of shared forgetting. "To forget—and I will venture to say—to get one's history wrong," writes Renan, "are essential factors in the making of a nation."[2] Historically, the advocates of forgetting are many and impressive. Cicero demanded, only two days after Caesar's murder in 44 B.C., that the memory of past discord be consigned to eternal oblivion.[3] Winston Churchill in his Zurich speech 2,000 years later recalled Gladstone's appeal for a "blessed act of oblivion" between former enemies.[4]

Those of us who participated in the historic election in South Africa in 1994 were on a mountaintop for a brief time, I think with some justification. We had come through a very bitter struggle that was almost 300 years long and accentuated and institutionalized for more than 50 years. We could be forgiven the luxury of standing on that mountaintop and rejoicing. We could not stand there very long, however. We had to go back into the valley and to work again, because there was huge baggage, economic and social, weighing very heavily on our shoulders, and there was a readiness to commit ourselves, and the government in particular, to reducing the wide gap between rich and poor, to addressing the social and economic needs of millions of people who had been discriminated against for so long. It is a huge and never-ending task.

There was another choice we had to make. What would we do about, and how would we cope with, the human rights violations that took place during that period of oppression? Do we simply consign them to oblivion? There were many who argued that way. They did not put it quite so eloquently, and I suppose they had good cause. The previous government and the security forces were adamant that we should simply forget the past and move on. It sounds very attractive. South Africa's is such a sordid past, so complicated and affecting so many. Why can't we just forget about it and focus on the future? There were also those who said that we had to take the perpetrators of these human rights violations to task—to arrest them, put them on trial, prosecute them, and punish them. This is also very understandable. Many had suffered very deeply, and they wanted their day in court. And there were others who decided that, for the sake of South Africa and its precarious unity—its fragmented and fragile democracy—we ought to see if there was a third way. We rejected amnesia and committed ourselves to remembrance. We also rejected the Nuremberg model of prosecutions and trials, partly out of political realism. Politicians seeking consensus in their negotiations also have to reach compromise, and the compromise was that in order to have a relatively peaceful election and to stop the bloodshed, we would offer a limited form of amnesty. That was part of the interim constitution, and there was no going back. But those of us who had to implement the amnesty provisions were faced with yet another choice. We could have simply said, "All right, let's opt for general provisions. Those who apply and those who qualify will be granted amnesty," and leave it at that. That was not an ideal situation—the golden mean—but we could have left it like that. But we decided against that approach as well.

Instead, we decided to put the focus not on the perpetrator but on the victim and the survivor, and to try and find a way of restoring to them their social and human dignity. We decided to give a voice to the voiceless, to the hundreds and thousands of people who had suffered for so long and had no way of telling anyone. They had been silenced. We felt that one of the ways in which to bring about restoration, and reconciliation, was to engage in truth-telling, to take oral tradition very seriously, to empower our people—ordinary people—to come and tell their stories, not only victims and survivors but also perpetrators. In order to implement the commitment to remembrance and accountability, we established the Truth and Reconciliation Commission (TRC), which has many similarities with commissions in different parts of the world. If perpetrators did not apply for amnesty they would have to risk proceedings in court. The Promotion of National Unity and Reconciliation Act 17 laid down criteria that would determine whether or not applicants for amnesty would succeed. Nearly 8,000 applied for amnesty. Thus far, only 200 people have been granted amnesty. In a recommendation in our final report, we urge that the attorney general should proceed against those who have not applied for amnesty and against those for whom there is sufficient evidence of human rights violations. One similarity between other commissions and ours is the tremendous determination and persistence of people who had been victims during this apartheid system to know the truth. It seemed that however grotesque that truth was, knowing it was part of the healing that had to take place. Essentially, the Truth and Reconciliation Commission is committed to the development of a human rights culture and a respect for the rule of law. But there is an irreducible minimum, and that is a commitment to truth. President Patricio Aylwin of Chile puts it this way: "To close our eyes and pretend none of this had ever happened would be to maintain at the core of our society a source of pain, division, hatred and violence. Only the disclosure of the truth and the search for justice can create the moral climate in which reconciliation and peace will flourish."[5] More recently, a number of mature democracies have had to face the truth as well. Switzerland has had to confront its relationship to the Holocaust, and the possessions that its banks secured during those years. Thomas Borer, who had been entrusted with the Swiss investigation, puts it this way: "Jews are not our enemies. Our history is not our enemy, but the way we deal with or not with our history, that would be our enemy." At an international conference in Geneva in December 1998, Minister Flavio Cotti, who had just relinquished the presidency of Switzerland and was then their foreign minister, said, "I've spent 10 years in government, and until last year, no one—I mean, no one—spoke of the fundamental necessity of reexamining Swiss history. Now I realize this must be done, because a country that has not really faced its past cannot decide its history."

The TRC traveled the length and breadth of the country. We met in very small townships, in large townships, in urban areas, in big cities, in church buildings, in magistrates' courts, and out of doors. The largest hearing we ever had was attended by 3,500 people in a huge iron structure in a Port Elizabeth township. Elsewhere, attendance ranged from 50 to, at other times, 500 or 1,000 sometimes very angry people, and always very deeply moved. The Commission was an experience of raw emotion, many tears, great searching, and compassion. I think that whatever else we achieved, the uncovering of the truth, which had been hidden for so long, was extremely important. Giving voice to the voiceless, enabling ordinary people to participate in the life and work and future of their own country, is a model that is obviously going to assist us in the future. It is not something that belonged only to a commission. People now really want to participate not only in the understanding of the past but also in their commitment to the future.

I'm asked on many occasions, and perhaps they put it a little more strongly than this: "Well, yes, it looks to me as though your commission has been successful in uncovering the truth, and perhaps the greatest reparation you can give to victims is the truth. But what about reconciliation? What about the deep divisions in your country?" There is no doubt that the dead hand of racism rests very, very heavily on our shoulders as a nation and as a people, and it is going to take a generation or more to achieve anything approaching reconciliation. But one thing I do know is that a country will not reconcile unless it deals with the truth of the past so that it can be avoided in the future. Reconciliation cannot be built on lies and deceit, which were characteristic of South Africa for so long. The TRC has laid some foundation stones through its work, but now it is up to the entire country, both state and civil society, to build on that foundation. To that end, in the TRC final report, we made many recommendations for how the work can be taken forward, and what still needs to be done. It is my hope that the government of my country together with the strong civil society that does exist in South Africa will make social, economic, and moral transformations, and that the faltering steps that we have taken will lead to a much greater march that will consolidate democracy and a human rights culture that has been denied us for so long.

Discussion Excerpts

Members of the Penn National Commission on Society, Culture and Community discussed Alex Boraine's presentation at the Commission's plenary meeting in Los Angeles on 18 December 1998.

MARTIN SELIGMAN: I have a psychological question about the possibility of reconciliation, and it comes from the literature on children and psychotherapy. In the field of psychotherapy, there are two very conflicting schools about what you do with severe trauma. One is Cicero's school, which is "Forget it. Let scars heal over." And the other is the Freudian catharsis school that says, "Let's find the truth." I think the evidence has actually come out quite strongly on the individual level one way rather than the other. If you have a child who has been brutally sexually abused and you have a trial in which the child recounts the abuse, the evidence is that for the child, the length and severity of the disorder is 10 times greater than if the child does not go to trial. When studies began, we thought catharsis would decrease anger, ultimately. But I think the evidence almost universally goes toward it increasing and sustaining anger. My worry here is that the way the evidence has come out within the psychological literature about these much smaller parallels suggests that the telling and retelling and reliving of the truth feeds rather than diminishes anger. So given that, I wonder what the prospects are.

BORAINE: I don't know the psychological literature. All I can tell you is the experience that I've had with these 22,000 people. We avoided having children before us because we thought that they could be abused. What we did have, however, were a number of people who had been abused as children who are now adults, because apartheid had been going on for a very long time. And we had that in private so that—you know, I don't want to suggest the media would abuse the occasion, but we didn't want to allow any opportunity for that.

I remember a man coming before us—he was in his middle thirties. He was blind. He'd been shot by the police in the face. And there were many, many instances like that, so it looked as though it was almost a deliberate tactic. This particular man was a teenager when this had happened, and he was running an errand for his mother; he was caught in the crossfire and was shot in the face. They had to help him up to the stage where we were sitting, and we always had somebody with people who came before, during, and after so as to give some kind of care, as much as we possibly could.

He told us his story, which was obviously very moving, and I was in the chair at the time, and I talked to him for a while and asked him what he felt the Commission could do to assist him, which we'd asked everyone. He mentioned one or two things—not much, very simple. So I said, "Well, is there anything else you want to say, or are you ready to go now? Because there are other people that we have to hear." He said, "No, I have to say one more thing." So I said, "Say it." And he said, "When I came here, I was blind. Now I can see."

And, of course, he didn't regain his sight. But that experience we heard over and over and over again, like a woman who came and had been brutally abused over a long period of time, severely tortured. And the result is that she was a very disturbed person. She came back the next day after having given evidence the previous day, as many did, to listen to their friends. And she asked if she could speak again. We were very hard-pressed in terms of time, but we said, "OK." And she said, "I want to tell you that for the first time in nine years, I slept through the night."

I'm not just speaking of a couple of isolated cases—I'm trying to illustrate that for some people, at least, the unburdening, their being given a voice, where they'd been silenced for so long, the breaking of their silence, seemed to be healing. And, obviously, we put people in touch with trauma clinics, psychiatrists. Wherever we felt there was a specific need, we referred people, and hopefully, that was a help. But my own experience tells me that a whole lot of people are helped by letting the poison come out.

Many people warned us that if we were going to conduct this truth commission and conduct it in public, people were going to take revenge into their own hands, particularly when they heard policemen and military people and death squads describing vividly what they had done to people. We had no single instance of that. We had psychologists on the commission, obviously, and we had doctors and we had a number of us who'd had a lot of experience in counseling. But we were terrified. And you're quite right; it's risky. But that's our experience.

SELIGMAN: What you described is really quite consistent from what we know from the literature I was talking about. In the short term, on the individual level, it's very common to see an unburdening, a great relief, but then something else takes over in the long term, which is rumination and flashbacks. And so my worry here is that we've seen a short-term effect, but now something inventive, I would suggest, needs to be done to short-circuit this very regular process, in which you've gone through the experience and rehearsed it and said it, and then it becomes lifelong fuel for rumination and flashback.

LAWRENCE LESSIG: I'd like to ask the same question at the level of the community or the people who participated in these hearings, either actually coming to the hearings or your understanding of people who listened to the hearings. Do you have any feedback or feel for how this discussion transformed the community within which the discussion was occurring, either people on the side of the former government or people who had suffered under the former government? And whether your sense was from this experience that the very discussion of it had a constructive effect on the community's effort at reconciliation?

BORAINE: I suppose that it's almost too soon to speak with any kind of dogmatic certainty about what the long-term results are going to be. We had a staff of over 300 people and, first of all, we made a decision that we would not sit in the major centers and let everybody come to us; we would go to them. So we deliberately wanted to involve the community. That is why we had thousands of people coming and many, many more thousands participating through radio, television, and the print media.

We sent an advance guard of people ahead of time to tell the community that the commission was going to be there next week. We put up notices. There were town hall meetings, and we went to the church—churches in the area of all faiths, specifically, and told the congregations and asked for their assistance and their prayers and their support and their attendance, if they felt that was going to be helpful, and to encourage people who may want to come. No one had to come. These were all volunteers. We couldn't cope with the number that really wanted to come.

I think it had an incredible impact on the community before we were even there, because people started to talk about it. And at long last they were being recognized. The thing was opening up. It's hard to describe the meetings. But many, many people from around the world came as well, apart from the press and media. Civil society in those areas took over from where we left off. When the caravan moved on, which we had to do, we didn't just simply leave; we had a number of people who were responsible for the continuing debate.

All sorts of new organizations have started as a result of this commission, some of them very critical of the commission, saying that more should have been done for the victims, for example. So our challenge to them was, "You're right. What are you going to do about it?" And as a result, they formed these support units in many of the major townships of our country. Many of the churches have become far more active than they've ever been before—high time, in my view, and overdue. But they certainly have, and that has assisted. But I think there was a national impact. There was a community impact.

AMY GUTMANN: The TRC report is distinctive in, from the very beginning, admitting that it may not have gotten the whole truth and it may not have gotten it all right—it is very open not only about the TRC's process but also in its conclusions. It takes a stand. It had to take a stand, and it should have, but it takes a stand that is admittedly open to further discussion and further argument and further criticism.

The second thing that I think is very obvious, but bears saying because it's so infrequently said, is that the measure of the success of public discourse in this case is not the ending of controversy or the ending of acrimony. In fact, it would be a bad thing if somehow, all of a sudden, people could be healed by something like the TRC. Rather, the measure of success is whether this helps South Africa move forward better than the alternatives would have, as a democracy. So I think that's one thing we should keep in mind, that the measure of public discourse should not be the end of controversy. The end of controversy would mean, by the way, the end of democracy.

JUDITH RODIN: You talk about an extraordinary set of events and a somewhat unusual way to deal with them. Can we take lessons from the way that you dealt with them and apply them to less extreme behaviors, but behaviors that, nonetheless, can rip the society apart? I'm asking myself, listening to you, whether, in the way that you've characterized it, the United States ought to go back at this? It is so consequential for our society. Before we get to the point of violence and atrocities, do you think the mechanisms that you've used can be applied here?

BORAINE: I've been asked to go, on three occasions, to Northern Ireland, and I'm going again in February. And what I've said when I've been asked that question is that you cannot take the South African model and impose it anywhere as it stands, as a model, but that there may well be mechanisms, approaches, and learnings that can be shared. At a meeting in Geneva we were discussing the distinct possibility of a truth commission in Bosnia, the argument being that there is a war crimes tribunal in The Hague, but the final word of the tribunal is punishment. And if that's all we're going to do, it's going to be very difficult to reconstruct and restore a society. The same thing is true of many countries in Africa who have chosen trials rather than a commission.

When I've talked about the Commission in the United States—and I've been addressing a number of universities in particular, both in the East and in the South—without fail, the first questions that were asked of me were from African Americans who did not ask a question. They felt— they wanted to comment and said that "we desperately need something like this in our own country." And I think the biggest tragedy of what's happening in this country is that so much has been totally neglected and focused on so little.

Every single place I've been, there's been this talking past each other, this acceptance, almost, that we've solved it. We had the civil rights movement. People are equal. Affirmative action has not worked, and we must try some other way—or it's wrong. And there doesn't seem to be any real debate that I can detect as to how to take this further.

Chapter 13
Political Apologies and Public Discourse

Graham G. Dodds

Political apologies are a way to heal, restore, and create effective discourse communities. They are symbolic acts that can promote peace and reconciliation, help to resolve social conflicts, and bring together estranged communities to facilitate peaceful coexistence.[1] Without political apologies, forgiveness and reconciliation may be impossible in some cases. As Donald Shriver notes, "Absent forgiveness and its twin repentance, political humans remember the crimes of ancestors only to entertain the idea of repeating them."[2] Similarly, Andre Dumas explains, "If there is no procedure for forgiveness, we are left with the endless circle of self-propagating vengeance. If there are no equivalents of forgiveness in the socio-political sphere, we are left with isolation which knows no pre-existence. If the community has no analogies to the rights of re-acceptance, we are left with the past, slowly forgotten and unalterable, and no clearly expressed desire for a common future."[3] This essay examines political apologies and their relationship to public discourse. Specifically, through a literature review and analysis of prominent political apologies, I examine political apologies both as a form of discourse and as a means of repairing and creating effective discourse communities.[4]

What Is a Political Apology?

The term apology derives from the "Greek root *apologos*, a story, from which *apologia*, an oral or written defense, became apology."[5] Plato's *Apology* fits this early mode of apology, with its defense of Socrates' life and teachings against the charge that he corrupted the youth of Athens. The conception of apology as defense can also be found in early English language uses of the term. For example, the *Oxford English Dictionary* finds the first use of the term apology in English in a work written by Sir Thomas More in 1533 and describes its meaning as "the pleading off from a charge or imputation . . . ; defense of a person, or vindication of an institution, etc. from accusation or aspersion."[6] Since More's time, however, the concept of apology has evolved to include elements other than active defense or justification. Whereas early uses of apology involved responding to a charge by invoking reasoned argument, later uses entail responding to a charge by invoking regret. Today's apologies occasionally retain something of the early use of justification, but increasingly their focus seems to be on expressing regret. More so than reasoned justifications, regret is seen as essential to an apology; for an apology to be effective, the offender must be sorry and must say so.[7]

Consider the following minimal formula of an apology, offered by Nicholas Tavuchis: "The offender acknowledges full responsibility for the transgression, expresses sorrow and contrition for the harm done, seeks forgiveness from the offended party, and implicitly or explicitly promises not to repeat the offense in the future."[8] The middle portion of the formula is crucial: beyond rational persuasion, moral suasion is essential, and this entails the expression of regret. Indeed, according to some accounts of apology, the expression of sorrow or regret constitutes the centerpiece of an apology; "the heart of apology consists of a genuine display of regret and sorrow as opposed to an appeal to reason."[9]

In other words, although apologies are often described in the "language of commercial exchange and conventional notions of rational self interest" (e.g., one owes another an apology), they are emphatically not mere outcomes of rational utility calculations, nor is their articulation merely a matter of dispassionate communication. As Tavuchis explains, "When we apologize, we are in the morally unsettling position of seeking unconditional pardon precisely in the context of our being categorically unworthy."[10] Apologies crucially involve emotion, normative judgment, and deeply felt human connectedness. This is especially true of apologies by nations, as considerations of national honor, prestige, reputation, and morality are paramount.[11] Such considerations are not merely manifestations of calculated realpolitik, as they often run directly counter to the dictates of rational self-interest. The apology's emphasis on emotion and regret distinguishes it from the closely related entities of justification, excuse, and defense. "In its purest expression," Tavuchis notes, "an apology clearly announces that 'I have no excuses for what I did or did not do or say. I am sorry and regretful. I care. Forgive me.' "[12]

Political Apologies as Discourse

The centrality of regret and sorrow in apologies has important implications for their status as a type of discourse. Specifically, apologies are a prime example of discourse thickly conceived. While early accounts of discourse limited its formal contents to rational argument, more recent accounts accept that discourse can and often does contain elements beyond mere rational argumentation. According to David Ryfe, this thicker conception of public discourse also includes emotion, reflection, reciprocity, radical difference, and modesty or moderation.[13] Apologies aptly demonstrate this broader conception of discourse that involves emotions. Another way to conceive of apologies is as one step in a process: "A proper and successful apology is the middle term in a moral syllogism that commences with a call and ends with forgiveness" and perhaps reconciliation.[14] This process-oriented view of apologies affords a simple way to think of their nature, but it is problematic. First, each step in this process is "acutely susceptible to miscalculation, impasse, uncertainty, and failure to achieve desired ends."[15] Second, the beginning and end of the process can be much more complicated than the above model suggests. Another approach is to consider apologies as a form of discourse between two parties: the giver and the receiver, or the offender and the offended. Tavuchis sees the apologetic discourse as "dyadic," rooted in a "relationship between the Offender and the Offended that can neither be reduced nor augmented without undergoing a radical metamorphosis."[16] Tavuchis elaborates a taxonomy of apologies:

1. Interpersonal apology from one individual to another, or *One to One*.
2. Apology from an individual to a collectivity, or *One to Many*.
3. Apology from a collectivity to an individual, or *Many to One*.
4. Apology from one collectivity to another, or *Many to Many*.[17]

Political apologies would fall under Tavuchis's fourth type—the many to the many. However, true political apologies are perhaps a more narrow category than this, since not all apologies that fit Tavuchis's fourth type would also qualify as political apologies, as I define them.

I hold that political apologies, specifically, must involve groups or collectivities, not just individuals. I mean this in terms of both who gives the apology and who receives it. Individuals may and often do articulate political apologies, but they must be acting in their capacity as the authoritative voice or representative of the collective. These apologies are not truly from the one to the many, but rather from the many to the many. Apologies in which the recipient is an individual or a small group are also excluded as political apologies. Political apologies necessarily involve significant political entities in terms of the parties who give and receive them. I hold that political apologies need not involve state actors per se. This is because I assume a broad definition of "political," as entailing relations among peoples. Thus, my analysis includes apologies offered by groups such as the Catholic Church. I exclude, however, corporate apologies on the grounds that businesses are usually mainly private, not public actors. These distinctions are perhaps arbitrary, but they are necessary to narrow the scope of inquiry here. A review of political apologies reveals that many of the hundreds of apologies concern events from World War II, and almost all of the apologies are very recent. The most prolific apologizers seem to be the Catholic Church, Japanese officials, and President Clinton.[18]

Political Apologies: Scholarship and Literature

Despite the surge in the number of political apologies, there is very little significant scholarship on the subject. In fact, even the scholarship on related subjects is fairly limited. Religion provides probably the most significant and best-developed perspective on apologies and forgiveness. An apology is essentially a "secular ritual of expiation."[19] Indeed, there are strong affinities between secular apologies and religious confession. The confessional nature of many apologies is important, especially given the Catholic Church's propensity to apologize for past wrongs. In the French Roman Catholic Church's 1997 apology for not doing more to prevent the Holocaust, the archbishop who read the "Declaration of Repentance" twice employed the image of the confessional to describe the Church's contrition.[20]

The related concept of forgiveness is particularly amenable to religious explanation and figures prominently in Christianity, Judaism, Buddhism, and Hinduism.[21] For example, based on the Torah, "Jewish law employs the term *tsedaka*, which indicates that justice essentially comprises the capacity of parties to achieve reconciliation."[22] As one scholar understands the relation between forgiveness and reconciliation in Judaism, pardon and forgiveness "bring the parties back to neutral ground. Once that is done, both parties must take positive steps to rebuild the relationship." Reconciliation "can only happen if both parties agree to resume their relationship."[23] In order to be worthy of forgiveness, Judaism holds that offenders must engage in a process of *teshuvah*, return to good standing. In Maimonides's famous codification of these "Laws of Return," several steps are necessary in order for forgiveness to follow. They include acknowledgement of wrongdoing, public confession and remorse, compensation for the victim, sincere requests of forgiveness by the victim, avoidance of the conditions that caused the offense, and acting differently when confronted with a similar situation.[24]

Given the various ways that different religions treat forgiveness, one might think that the propensity to accept apologies and to forgive would vary with religion. However, one study suggests that this is not the case. Fabiola Azar, Etienne Mullet, and Genevieve Vinsonneau studied the propensity to forgive among people from three Christian communities in Lebanon: Catholics, Maronites, and Orthodox. They found that willingness to forgive did not significantly vary among the three religions; people's religious proximity did not particularly matter, as people's willingness to forgive was not contingent on whether the offender was of the same religion; and apologies were very important in achieving forgiveness.[25] In short, the study underscores the significance of apologies for forgiveness and suggests that in practice forgiveness may be relatively constant across religious differences. Relatedly, from a more anthropological perspective, Robert Enright has shown that the development of reasoning about forgiveness is similar across different cultures.[26] Together, these two studies suggest that there is something universal about forgiveness in practice.

Apology and forgiveness also figure prominently in philosophy. In *The Genealogy of Morals*, Nietzsche argues that forgiveness is an expression of weakness and can thus be harmful or even a vice.[27] In contrast, Hannah Arendt argues in *The Human Condition* that since we have the power to remember the past but cannot change it, forgiveness is the only effective response. For Arendt, forgiveness is what makes social change possible.[28] In contemporary analytic philosophy, Jeffrie Murphy and Jean Hampton have debated whether it can be good to keep a grudge and not forgive. They reason that "if holding a grudge is the opposite of forgiveness, then it is essential to analyze the appeal and the potential (or perceived) benefits of holding a grudge. Grudge theory and forgiveness theory thus constitute mirror images of each other."[29] Murphy argues that continued hatred and anger towards wrongdoers may be appropriate, and Hampton agrees that sometimes forgiveness is inappropriate.[30]

As an academic discipline, psychology has dealt with the topics of apology and forgiveness much less than one might imagine. Still, there are several psychological studies of forgiveness that are relevant for the study of political apologies. For example, a 1990 study by Roy Baumeister and others examined forgiveness in terms of conscious acceptance of victimhood, developing from a psychological perspective the philosophical insights of Murphy and Hampton: "As a choice by the victim, forgiveness is a rejection of the victim role and a gesture of return to normalcy. The alternative is to hold a grudge against the perpetrator, thereby altering the relationship and continuing to identify oneself in terms of victimization."[31] The study identified several reasons why people choose to hold a grudge rather than forgive, including the extraction of rewards or concessions from a perpetrator, a belief that "holding the grudge will help prevent the transgression from being repeated," and wounded pride that would make "forgiving seem an admission of weakness or a loss of face." While a grudge offers some benefits, the study concludes, "it also carries costs, such as the continuation of hard, unpleasant feelings; the damage to one's health and well-being . . . and the damage to close relationships" that grudges can cause.[32]

Two other psychological studies point to real benefits in forgiving. In 1976, Dolf Zillman et al. found that apologies and other mitigating input reduced victims' "elevated physiological arousal following interpersonal transgressions in short order."[33] In 1989, researchers in Japan documented "the power of apologies in reducing victims' negative affect, thoughts about perpetrators, and likely verbal and physical aggression towards perpetrators. The effects of apologies on reduced retaliation appear to be mediated, in part, by their effects in reducing victims' negative affect and repairing victims' negative perceptions of their perpetrators."

In short, the study validated the power of apologies to create "cognitive and emotional change following interpersonal offenses."[34]

The question of the relative costs and benefits of forgiving past harms is of course crucially important for determining the restorative potential of political apologies. Drawing on research on treatment of incest survivors, Martin E. P. Seligman has suggested that remembrance of the painful past can be counterproductive.[35] The potential trauma of remembrance not withstanding, failure to deal with the problematic past can itself be traumatizing. News of the acquittal of concentration camp guards by German courts led to "violent psychological reactions in concentration camp survivors," for example, and failure to punish wrongdoers in the military dictatorship of Argentina has "driven victims to psychotherapy."[36]

Two other psychological studies touch on the question of exactly how apologies do or do not work. A 1982 study by Bruce Darby and Barry Schenkler found that children take apologies into account in determining how harshly to judge a transgressor and that "the fact of the offender's apology might not be as important as the specific qualities of that apology—such as the perceived motive and intentions of the offender—and the way in which the offended person perceives those elements of the apology."[37] Similarly, a 1991 study of public confessions by Bernard Weiner et al. found that "basic variables, such as the style with which one confesses and the timing of the confession, influence forgiveness." Building on the previous work by Darby and Schenkler, this study offered further proof that "forgiveness is strongly shaped by social events that occur after the offense itself is already completed."[38] These findings clearly have important implications for the effectiveness of political apologies.

In political science and closely related parts of the social sciences and other fields, the very small literature on political apologies tends to approach the topic in terms of the study of transitional justice. One excellent book of this sort is Martha Minow's *Between Vengeance and Forgiveness: Facing History After Genocide and Mass Violence* (1998), on which I draw extensively in this chapter. In more formal political science, there is little literature that directly touches on political apologies and forgiveness, although some parts of game theory are relevant. For example, in a 1980 article, Robert Alexrod demonstrated that "even in terms of purely pragmatic interpersonal strategies (i.e., independent of emotional effects), behavior that is nice and moderately forgiving appears to bring more benefits for the self than hostile or unforgiving behavior."[39]

In sociology, Erving Goffman's brief 1971 study of apologies in *Relations in Public* is regarded as seminal and certainly informs the work of Schenkler and Darby and others.[40] Goffman describes the peculiar workings of an apology, which he characterizes as "a gesture through which an individual splits himself into two parts, the part that is guilty of an offense and the part that distances itself from the derelict and affirms a belief in the offended rule." Apologies "split the self" into a "blameworthy part and a part that stands back and sympathizes with the blame giving,"[41] and is thus worthy of reintegration into the fold. Considerably building on Goffman's account, Tavuchis's *Mea Culpa: A Sociology of Apology and Reconciliation* (1991) is by far the best treatment of apology in the field. Much of this chapter develops further some of the many insights in his study.

Case Studies in Political Apology

In order to examine the nature and workings of political apologies more closely, this section considers four cases of political apologies in some detail: (1) Germany to Jews and Israel for the Holocaust; (2) the United States to interned Japanese-Americans; (3) Japan to Korea and China for wartime atrocities; and (4) the Soviet Union and Russia to Poland for the Katyn massacre. These four cases cover much of the range of logical possibilities, from full, repeated apologies with compensation to minimal or no apologies without compensation. They also exhibit some variation in terms of the relation of the groups involved, including both interstate and intrastate apologies. Furthermore, the workings and effectiveness of the apologies vary significantly, yet, like so many other political apologies, their subjects are rooted in the events of World War II.

GERMANY'S APOLOGIES TO JEWS AND ISRAEL FOR THE HOLOCAUST

The case of the German apology for the Holocaust is interesting in that there is no explicit apology. Albert Speer, the only Nazi leader at the Nuremberg trials to admit his guilt, wrote, "no apologies are possible."[42] Nevertheless, there are several events in postwar German history that for present purposes may be considered as de facto apologies or other ways of seeking forgiveness and reconciliation. Germany's initial response was to offer reparations and, where possible, restitution. Only West Germany paid reparations, however. The GDR, founded four months after West Germany in October 1949, regarded itself as an entirely new state and hence not responsible for the obligations of the Third Reich.[43] In contrast to East Germany, West Germany claimed a continuity with the German state(s) of the past. As a condition on returning sovereignty to West Germany in February 1952, the Allies required that the new Federal Republic adopt a uniform federal arrangement for reparations as soon as possible.[44] Germany made restitution or paid compensation for identifiable property under the Federal Restitution Law of 19 July 1957, and amendments to the law removed a ceiling on payments and stipulated that all claims were to be satisfied one hundred percent. Germany also paid compensation for "damage to life, health, liberty, property and possessions, damage to vocational and economic pursuits, losses suffered in jobs and professions and the loss to widows and orphans of their providers."[45]

In addition to reparations for individuals, West Germany also paid reparations to Israel. Not long after the initial Jewish request for reparations from Germany in 1945, West Germany began to pay (literally) for its wartime sins, largely because of its new chancellor. Konrad Adenauer, the first chancellor of West Germany, sought integration into the West, NATO, and the nascent European community. Adenauer's own religious convictions also inclined him toward reparations.[46] In April 1951, Israel and Germany began negotiations on reparations. Israel demanded $1.5 billion from Germany, two-thirds of which was to come from West Germany. "For the first time in modern history . . . a victimized ethnic group sat down to bargain with the perpetrators of its victimization for compensation."[47] Formal agreements were signed in Luxembourg in September 1952.[48] In 1965, Israel and West Germany established diplomatic relations.

In return for reparations, Israel made certain concessions, such as abandoning its claim "that it had the standing to speak for all Holocaust victims and survivors."[49] Most commentators claim that Israel was driven by both moral and economic considerations.[50] As Lily Gardner Feldman has shown, German and Israeli needs coincided. "Both sides perceived the other as uniquely capable of fulfilling simultaneous need, for only Israel could absolve Germany of past deeds, and only Germany could (and would) rescue Israel's economy."[51]

West Germany and Israel clearly saw the reparations in different terms. Israelis used the term *shilumin*, Hebrew for "recompense," to describe the payments made by Germany to Israel. "The term was borrowed from the book of Isaiah and indicated that these payments did not imply an expiation of guilt, nor did their acceptance connote a sign of forgiveness. The term embraces an element of vengeance, which at the same time can be a presupposition for bringing about peace (*shalom*)." In contrast, Germans used the term *Wiedergutmachung* to describe the payments, which means "returning to former conditions and, in a broader sense, to a former state of co-existence."[52] Moreover, West Germany saw the payments to Israel as a means of making collective payment from the German people to the Jewish people and as a symbolic expression of national guilt. Put simply, Germany paid for destroying European Jewry by subsidizing the creation of the new Jewish state.

Aside from Germany's monetary reparations, one of its most striking apologies for the Holocaust involved an action by a government official decades after the end of World War II. While in Warsaw to sign a treaty between West Germany and Poland in 1970, Chancellor Willie Brandt visited a memorial to those who died in the Warsaw ghetto uprising of 1943. At the memorial, Brandt dramatically fell to his knees, as if to express repentance for Nazi crimes against Jews. Afterward, Brandt said, "I wanted on behalf of our people to ask forgiveness for the terrible crime that was carried out in Germany's misused name."[53] After Brandt's death many years later, Richard von Weizsacker said of Brandt's action, "Nobody expected it; nobody ever forgot it."[54] In addition to the spontaneity of the act, Brandt's standing as a refugee during the Nazi years helped lend credibility to his contrition: "He was a satisfactory symbol of German repentance precisely because he had nothing of which to repent himself."[55]

The U.S. Apology to Japanese-Americans for Internment During World War II

After the Japanese attack on Pearl Harbor, President Franklin Roosevelt and others concluded that Japanese Americans posed a security threat, possibly constituting a "Fifth Column" or an "enemy within." On 19 February 1942, Roosevelt signed Executive Order 9066, calling for the exclusion and internment of all Japanese Americans on the West Coast. The exclusion and incarceration began one month later, as Congress enacted Public Law No. 503, making it a crime to disobey military orders concerning restrictions on residence in the areas which the Secretary of War had stipulated pursuant to the President's order. At first, Japanese Americans were sent to twelve temporary detention centers in California and Oregon run by the War Relocation Authority (WRA). By summer, internees were transported to what the government called "concentration camps" located in remote, inhospitable areas. Over 120,000 Americans of Japanese ancestry were interned. Two-thirds of those incarcerated were American citizens by birth whose parents had lived in the United States as permanent residents for twenty to forty years.[56] The exclusion lasted until December 1944. Japanese Americans suffered greatly during the relocation and internment. Most had to sell homes and businesses at significant losses, many had their educations disrupted, and all and had to endure bleak conditions at the camps.

Roughly twenty-six years after the camps closed, grassroots groups in the Pacific Northwest began to push for redress for the internment. At first, the idea of reparations or an apology was not popular even within the Japanese American community, as many former internees felt it would be too painful to relive their memories and that having to explain their position would be humiliating.[57] Nevertheless, more and more people came to support the idea. The first success in the push for redress came on February 19, 1976, when President Gerald Ford officially declared Executive Order 9066 terminated, thirty-four years to the day after it was enacted. In his statement on the matter, Ford called the internment a "mistake."[58]

In 1978, the Japanese American Citizens' League (JACL) asked Congress for a government apology and financial payments of $25,000 for each internee. Congressmen of Japanese background made the League's request a priority. In particular, Senator Daniel Inouye (D, Hawaii) successfully pushed to create a commission "to review and analyze the official government contention, historically accepted, that the exclusion, forced removal, and detention of Americans of Japanese ancestry were justified by military necessity."[59] The creation of a commission was seen as a needless delay by some advocates, but others saw it as a way to build consensus for redress by documenting the abrogation of due process rights.[60]

In 1981, the Commission on Wartime Relocation and Internment of Civilians held public hearings throughout the country, and 750 witnesses testified. In 1982, the Commission concluded that the policy of exclusion and internment had been wrong.[61] The Commission's 1983 report concluded: "In sum, Executive Order 9066 was not justified by military necessity, and the decisions that followed from it—exclusion, detention, the ending of detention and the ending of exclusion—were not founded upon military considerations. The broad historical causes that shaped these decisions were race prejudice, war hysteria and a failure of political leadership."[62] Based on these findings, the Commission issued its recommendations to Congress in June 1983, calling for an official apology and reparations of $20,000 for each survivor.[63]

Even though the Commission's recommendation for an official apology and compensation was nearly unanimous—one member, Republican Dan Lundgren of California, supported an apology but opposed compensation—it took five years of lobbying to persuade Congress to pass legislation enacting the Commission's recommendations.[64] In part, this was because of Congressional apathy: given the small size of the Japanese American community, their concerns, even though intensely felt, were largely lost on most members of Congress.[65] Furthermore, any legislative apology was actively opposed by many veterans' groups. Some people even defended the internment on the grounds that it was intended to protect the internees from violent attacks by other Americans.[66]

In the end, after renewed lobbying, Congress assented to the Commission's recommendations, but legislators wanted to set a very narrow precedent, and thus agreed to compensate only living internees, whether citizens or resident aliens. On 10 August 1988, President Reagan signed the Civil Liberties Act of 1988, which provided for an official government apology and $20,000 for surviving inmates alive on that day, as well as a $1.25 billion education fund. Reagan said of the legislation, "No payment can make up for those lost years. What is most important in this bill has less to do with property than with honor. For here we admit wrong."[67] On 9 October 1990, the first redress payments were made, beginning with the oldest survivors. The checks were sent with a letter from President Bush, which noted:

A monetary sum and words alone cannot restore lost years or erase painful memories; neither can they fully convey our nation's resolve to rectify injustice and to uphold the rights of individuals. We can never fully right the wrongs of the past. But we can take a clear stand for justice and recognize that serious injustices were done to Japanese-Americans during World War II. In enacting a law calling for restitution and offering a sincere apology, your fellow Americans have, in a very real sense, renewed their traditional commitment to the ideals of freedom, equality, and justice. You and your family have our best wishes for the future.[68]

JAPAN'S APOLOGIES TO CHINA AND KOREA FOR WARTIME ATROCITIES

Japan's actions during World War II have spurred a number of political apologies. While the evils of Nazi Germany are well known to Americans, the horrors inflicted by Imperial Japan on its neighbors are perhaps less familiar. In China, many people still remember the wrongs committed by the Japanese Imperial Army in Manchuria and elsewhere, when some 13 million Chinese died as a direct result of Japan's invasion and occupation of China from 1931 to 1945.[69] None is more bitterly resented than the rape of Nanking.[70] After invading Shanghai, Japan launched a massive attack in November 1937 on the Republic of China's newly established capital in Nanking. According to critic Iris Chang, "When the city fell on December 13, 1937, Japanese soldiers began an orgy of cruelty seldom if ever matched in world history. Tens of thousands of young men were rounded up and herded to the outer areas of the city, where they were mowed down by machine guns, used for bayonet practice, or soaked with gasoline and burned alive. For months the streets of the city were heaped with corpses and reeked with the stench of rotting human flesh."[71] In contravention of rules of warfare, soldiers were executed en masse, and tens of thousands of civilians were raped and killed. Arguably, the slaughter was public in order to terrorize. "While the exact toll of this bloodbath will never be known, conservative estimates based on investigations conducted right after the Second World War put the number of dead at over three hundred thousand."[72]

Japan ruled the Korean peninsula for thirty-five years, from 1910 to 1945. One of the main aspects of Japanese colonial rule in Korea that has occasioned calls for a political apology is the issue of "comfort women": women forced to serve as sex slaves for the Japanese military.[73] The policy began in the early 1930s and lasted through the war. Estimates of the numbers of women involved reach to 200,000, of whom 80 to 90 percent were Korean, many of them teenagers. They were sent to "comfort stations" in Korea, Manchuria, Taiwan, Japan, Singapore, Saipan, Micronesia, and elsewhere in the territories occupied by Japan between 1930 and 1945.[74] The policy has been aptly characterized as "a large-scale, officially-organized system of rape by the Imperial Japanese Forces" across Asia.[75]

Despite its record of abuses during World War II, Japan has paid very little in compensation and reparations. Under Article 14 of the 1952 San

Francisco Peace Treaty, Japan assumed the burden of paying reparations to various countries in Asia and elsewhere and, under Article 16, to
former POWs. When these reparations ended in 1977, Japan had paid
32.5 billion yen.[76] By way of putting that figure in perspective, however,
Japan had paid roughly forty times that amount to its own citizens for
war-related matters, such as military pensions and compensation to widows. German war reparations total over $80 billion.

Beyond Japan's allegedly inadequate reparations, the issue of its more
explicit political apologies has been and still remains highly controversial. The conventional wisdom is that Japan has yet to apologize for its
wartime abuses, despite repeated requests from its neighbors for such an
apology. But Japan has in fact apologized and done so repeatedly. Japan
has in some fashion apologized for various actions during World War II
well over a dozen times. These have included statements by Emperors
Hirohito and Akihito and Prime Ministers Nakasone, Miyazawa, Hosokawa, Murayama, Hashimoto, Obuchi, and Koizumi, as well as the national Diet. Furthermore, many of these apologies appear to articulate
deep regret and remorse. Given the numerous apologies from so many
officials, how can we account for the common perception that Japan has
not apologized?[77]

The apparent difference between perception and reality is understandable in part because most of Japan's political apologies have been
very recent. Prior to 1990, Japan said very little about its wartime actions, and when it did address its past wrongs it did so in exceedingly
vague terms. For example, even as late as 1984, Emperor Hirohito spoke
only vaguely about such things, telling the visiting South Korean President that "it is regrettable that there was an unfortunate period in this
century."[78] Against the background of so many years of silence and
euphemism, the more recent, robust apologies appear to have been
somewhat ineffective in changing perceptions.

There are several reasons that Japan for so long did not issue a political apology for its wartime misdeeds. In short, they include the lack of
closure after World War II (relative to Germany), the country's postwar
political context, Japanese racism toward China and Korea, lack of diplomatic relations with China, and the long-term domination of Japanese
politics by one party, the LDP. Conversely, recent changes in Japan's attitude toward political apology may be influenced by political apologies
abroad, including the U.S. apology to Japanese-American internees. In
the Korean context, the use of comfort women was relatively unknown
until the early 1990s, due to family shame and the aversion of South Korea's military leadership to citizen lobbying on all matters.[79]

While the decades of Japanese silence may account for much of the
failure to accord significant credit for Japan's recent political apologies,
another reason may be that the apologies of recent years may not in fact

have been all that robust. In other words, insincerity, not time, causes many people to see Japan as unapologetic. The Japanese language has a number of terms that can in some sense connote apology, ranging from mere personal regret or reflection to deep, sincere apology. Japan's recent apologies have generally used the most superficial of these terms. For example, before Murayama, Japanese prime ministers used the term *hansei* in their apologetic discourse. Similarly, the resolution passed by the Diet on the fiftieth anniversary of World War II used the term *fukai hansei*. One commentator claims that *hansei* is "a fudge word meaning 'regret' " that still enables its user "to express some measure of sorrow."[80] However, an official Japanese source claims that the term *hansei* is even less deeply apologetic than this. After Foreign Minister Michio Watanabe's remarks on 1 December 1991, the Japanese Foreign Ministry elaborated on the meaning of the Japanese words *fukahu hansei*, "which the minister had used in echo of the same word used by former Prime Minster Toshiki Kaifu in a speech earlier that year in Singapore. The word, said the Foreign Ministry, means 'self-reflection' and not 'remorse.' Under no circumstances, they said, 'did it constitute an apology.' "[81] Words with stronger apologetic connotations in Japanese include *shazai* and *owabi*.[82] On 15 August 1994, Prime Minister Murayama used the term *owabi* in apologizing for the suffering caused by Imperial Japan, but the term has seldom been used in Japan's political apologies.[83] According to one source, the use of the word *sumanai* is necessary in order for there to be (1) a recognition of the wrong as something that can and should be apologized for and (2) a true confession of guilt.[84] To date, none of Japan's official political apologies have used the strongest language possible.[85]

The evident Japanese reticence to employ strong apologetic language in its political apologies stands in striking contrast to the frequent use of fulsome apologies in other aspects of Japanese society. "In Japan, a 'sincere apology' has magical power to bring about reconciliation," and Japanese people supposedly apologize more often and more freely than do Americans.[86] The actions of various Japanese corporations suggest that this may be true. For example, industry and government officials in the 1970s literally kowtowed before victims of pollution, as in the case of the mercury poisoning in Minamata Bay. Similar scenes occurred in 1996 and 1997, when industry and government were implicated in the failure to protect Japanese hemophiliacs from HIV-tainted blood products imported from the United States. Japanese television carried vivid images of officials literally prostrate in apology for the failure. Again, these instances of fulsome apology in the business and regulatory context contrast sharply with the laconic pronouncements concerning Japan's wartime actions.[87]

If the frequent occurrence of sincere, deep apologies in other aspects of Japanese society makes Japan's lack of such political apologies seem anomalous, Japanese political opinion makes it seem stranger still. Recent opinion polls have shown that many Japanese want their government to be more contrite for the country's actions in World War II. For example, in August 1995, the *Japan Times* reported that, "According to recent media polls, most Japanese believe the nation was waging a war of aggression in the 1930s and 1940s, and they think some financial redress for the victims is necessary." In 1993, a poll by *Asahi Shimbun*, Japan's most influential newspaper, found that 76 percent thought Prime Minister Hosokawa "was right to apologize for Japan's 'aggression,' and more than half favored paying compensation to victims." And in 1995, a poll by the *Asian Wall Street Journal* found that "61 percent of Japanese, compared with 53 percent of Americans, agreed that 'Japan hasn't done enough to take responsibility for its role in World War II.' "[88]

THE APOLOGY OF THE SOVIET UNION AND RUSSIA TO POLAND FOR THE 1943 KATYN FOREST MASSACRE

The Soviet Union invaded eastern Poland on 17 September 1939, just sixteen days after the German invasion of western Poland, thus splitting the country under the terms of a secret agreement. Soon after the Soviet invasion, the NKVD, the forerunner of the KGB, rounded up between 15,000 and 22,000 Polish prisoners.[89] Many of the prisoners were reservists who had been called up after the German invasion, and many were previously doctors, lawyers, and businessmen. Shortly after they were taken prisoner, the Poles vanished; only a few were later freed by the Soviets. In 1941, Stalin told Poland that the men somehow must have escaped to Manchuria.

In April 1943, two years after Poland came under complete German control and over three years after the prisoners disappeared, the German army discovered the graves of between 4,142 and 4,500 Polish officers in the Katyn forest near Smolensk (in present-day Russia). Most of the victims had died from close range gunshots to the head or neck. Despite the evidence of Soviet culpability, the U.S. and British governments did not push the issue because they feared a separate Russian-German peace and thus did not want to compromise the unity of the Big Three by antagonizing Stalin. Absent the condemnation of its wartime allies, the Soviets blamed the Germans, saying the killings took place between August and October 1941, at which time the area was under German control. After the war, little was done about the massacre. A group of Polish exiles organized a committee to investigate the killings, which resulted in hearings in the United States and abroad in 1951 and 1952.[90] The Committee "unanimously agreed" that the Soviets had committed the massacre.[91]

Although Katyn was a continuing source of tension between Poland and the Soviet Union,[92] little more was done until 1987 when, under Soviet President Mikhail Gorbachev's policy of *glasnost*, an official Soviet-Polish commission was set up to resolve historical disputes between the countries, and Gorbachev specifically promised to cooperate in resolving the Katyn massacre. On 13 April 1990, forty-seven years to the day after German soldiers discovered the mass graves at Katyn, Gorbachev essentially admitted Soviet responsibility for the massacre, as he gave Polish President Wojciech Jaruzelski documents that indicated that the murders were the work of Stalin's NKVD.[93] Gorbachev referred to Katyn as one of the "historical knots" that complicate Soviet-Polish relations and said, "It is not easy to speak of this tragedy, but it is necessary."[94] In response, General Jaruzelski said, "The Soviet statement about the crime of Katyn is, for our people, especially important and valuable from a moral point of view. . . . For us, this was an unusually painful question."[95] Similarly, Lech Walesa termed the Soviet admission "an act of moral justice which has been awaited for a long time."[96] He said, "The thorn has been removed but the wound is still there. We must work together to let it heal."[97]

Despite the fairly positive Polish reaction to Gorbachev's 1990 admission, three barriers to fuller reconciliation soon arose. First, some critics demanded that those who were responsible for the killings should be punished, if they were still alive, although none were.[98] Second, although the documents released to Poland by Gorbachev in 1990 implicated the NKVD, the question of the degree of Stalin's personal involvement in the killings remained unresolved.[99] In 1992, however, Russian President Boris Yeltsin opened KGB archives on the 22,000 arrested Poles and made public a document from March 1940 that confirmed that Stalin's Politburo ordered the killings.[100] Third, the goodwill generated by the 1990 and 1992 admissions was in some part negated by the failure of Russian leaders to attend a ceremony in 1995. In August 1993, Yeltsin became the first Russian leader to lay a wreath at a monument to the murdered Polish prisoners, and "relatives of the victims praised Mr. Yeltsin for the gesture intended to heal wounds."[101] In 1995, however, Yeltsin and Alexander Solzhenitsyn were both invited by Polish President Walesa to lay a foundation stone for a proper cemetery near Smolensk, but neither invitee accepted, and only a medium-ranking Russian official came. Poland's *Zycie Warszawy* daily newspaper said: "Boris Yeltsin's absence leaves a deeply unsettling message. . . . There has been no apology of the kind that Germany has long since made. This day could have been a symbol of reconciliation between two nations tragically marked by communism. Instead it is a bitter shame, and Katyn forest continues to cast its dark shadow."[102]

The Work of Political Apology

How do political apologies, such as those just outlined, work? Political apologies are in many respects mysterious and not amenable to sustained, systematic analysis. This is because all apologies essentially seek to do the impossible, to undo a previous wrong, even though of course they cannot really do so.[103] Tavuchis notes that "an apology, no matter how sincere or effective, does not and cannot undo what has been done. And yet, in a mysterious way and according to its own logic, this is precisely what it manages to do."[104] Notwithstanding the mysterious nature of apologies, it is possible to gain some further clarity on how political apologies work their magic by exploring several different aspects of such apologies.

REPRESENTATION

One of the most important aspects of political apologies is the transformation of an individual into the personification of a collectivity. At some point, size and logistics preclude all members of a group from making an apology. Insofar as it is impossible for an entire nation to apologize, the nation must be personified or somehow represented by an individual or a small group. There must be "a symbolic and conceptual transformation" of the many into the few or even the one. "In other words, the collectivity must constitute itself and be perceived as a singular entity, a One in its own right with its own voice."[105] Since political apologies involve large groups on both sides (i.e., giving and receiving the apology), the need for distillation, personification, and representation is twofold.

The practical need for a representative has a number of important implications for political apologies, including their style. For example, Tavuchis notes that the discourse between or among such representatives is essentially "mutually ventriloquial speech."[106] Also, representation causes collective apologies to be fairly formal.[107] This is because representatives are not free to act according to their own beliefs; they are constrained by collective goals and practices.[108] Because the apologizer is a representative of a larger entity, the "working and tenor of the apology, typically the product of anonymous authors, must be carefully crafted . . . in order to avoid ambiguity or further offense." The conveyers of the apology must also "conform to conventional standards of decorum and protocol." All told, Tavuchis concludes, "the consummate collective apology is a diplomatic accomplishment of no mean order."[109] When both the giver and the recipient of the apology are groups, the need for formality is of course increased, as two sets of norms must be satisfied.

Representation may also limit the types of collective attributes that can reasonably be made in articulating and responding to political apologies. While some characteristics (e.g., strength, health, greed, and so forth) are as easily attributed to groups as to individuals, "others do not transfer as easily or without jarring our sensibilities."[110] For example, can we rightly attribute love, sorrow, regret, or sincerity to a group? Political apologies require exactly these types of attribution, but it is quite unlikely that every member of a community or every citizen of a state feels as the representative claims. I will shortly examine the problem of antiapologetic minorities, but for now I want to highlight a larger, related problem for political apologies. Specifically, if a political apology really includes all members of a state, then we are supposing that all members of a state can be responsible for wrongs committed by that state. For example, Germany's reparations would indicate that all German citizens were culpable for the wrongs committed by the Nazis. This is of course highly controversial. If we allow that not all members of the collectivity are so included, however, then a political apology runs the risk of legitimately being from only the state and not its people.[111]

A third important implication of the sort of representation necessary for political apologies is that the representative of the group who articulates the apology must legitimately represent that group. Tavuchis claims that the hallmark of collective apologies is their "on behalf of" character.[112] Accordingly, "an apology offered without proper credentials, that is, lacking the imprimatur of the group, amounts to no apology at all."[113] Some critics have charged that recent Japanese apologies do not count because they represent only the opinions of the people who made them, not the nation. In response to a criticism of this sort directed against one of Prime Minister Murayama's apologies, Seiichiro Noboru, Japanese Consul General in Los Angeles, claimed that "every word was in fact first reviewed and approved by the Cabinet, and it most assuredly represents the official government position."[114]

To this obvious constraint about legitimate representation, I want to add two more. First, not only is it important that the representative be legitimate, the representative must also be convincing in his or her representativeness. In other words, representatives who are not usually called upon to represent the collectivity or who usually defer to higher-ranking representatives cannot convincingly apologize on behalf of the collectivity. This condition explains Polish displeasure with the low-ranking Russian representation at the 1995 Katyn ceremony. Similarly, when the Canadian government's 1998 apology to Canada's indigenous peoples was delivered by Indian Affairs Minister Jane Stewart instead of Prime Minister Jean Chrétien, Native Women's Association President Marilyn Buffalo deemed it inadequate for that reason.[115]

Second, even if the representative is legitimate and convincing, the group in question must be authoritative and salient. In other words, apologies from subgroups within the larger group in question may not carry much weight. For example, in 1991 the Yokohama Association of Bereaved Families of War published an open letter in American newspapers deeply apologizing for starting World War II, and in 1997 a group called the Japanese Fellowship of Reconciliation apologized for Japan's actions in the war.[116] While these apologies were offered by legitimate representatives of those groups, the groups were not the salient ones. The call for an apology was directed at Japan, not at smaller groups within it. As a result, the apologies likely did little to appease Japan's critics and may even have further antagonized them by highlighting the lack of an apology from Japan as a whole. Similarly, the apology of German Christians in 1994 for the Nazi invasion of the Netherlands and the apology of an Australian Christian group in 1998 for complicity with state policies on aborigines cannot have been very effective and may even have exacerbated the respective situations.

While the above examples show small groups proactively attempting to step in to fill the void of a missing apology on the part of the greater collective, there are also cases in which the larger collective has tried—unsuccessfully—to privatize apologetic gestures. For example, Murayama's establishment in 1995 of a private compensation fund for "comfort women" was rejected in part because it lacked the imprimatur of the Japanese government.[117] Similarly, in December 1996, when Hashimoto offered a letter of apology and monetary reparations to some 500 surviving "comfort women," only six women accepted, mainly because the funds came from private sources instead of from the Japanese government.[118]

COUNTER-APOLOGETIC ACTIONS

Problematically, a group's solidarity is never complete, which complicates representation and aggregation in a political apology. In other words, there will invariably be some individuals or subgroups who do not adhere to the larger group's views, as articulated through its authoritative and legitimate representative. This disagreement is often manifested in counter-apologetic actions. This is particularly problematic in the Japanese context. One manifestation of Japanese opposition to war apologies is the annual visit on 15 August to the Yasukuni Jinja shrine, a Shinto site that enshrines Japan's war dead, including many "Class A" convicted war criminals. Prime Minister Yasuhiro Nakasone's 1985 visit to the shrine "brought outraged protests from across Asia," but since that time most high ranking officials have refrained from making official visits to Yasukuni.[119] However, government officials who are slightly more junior routinely make the trip. On the same day as Murayama's 15 August 1994 apology, which went further than any previous apology, "seven members of his coalition cabinet made a point of mourning Japan's own war dead by visiting the Yasukuni shrine."[120] In 1994, seven sitting ministers visited, knowing full well that other Asians see the visits as indicating a lack of contrition for Japan's wartime wrongs.[121]

In addition to the ritualized visits to the Yasukuni shrine, there is a history in Japan of various government officials making comments that directly contradict the sort of contrition that Japan's official political apologies have sought to convey. For example, in May 1994, Minister of Justice Shigeto Nagano was forced to resign after calling the Nanking massacre a "fabrication," characterizing the *ianfu* ("comfort women") as "public prostitutes," and referring to the war in Asia by the patriotic old name "Great East Asian War" (Dai Toa Senso).[122] In August 1994, Shin Sakurai, the environment minister, denied that his country had waged an aggressive war in the 1930s and 1940s. He also was soon forced to resign.[123]

In the German context, the controversy about President Reagan's official visit to the Bitburg military cemetery is perhaps analogous. Also, on 11 November 1988, on the occasion of the fiftieth anniversary of Kristallnacht, Bundestag President Jennings attempted to indicate the extent of German suffering during World War II in a speech to the Bundestag. His remarks were immediately met with cries of "shame," and he was forced to resign the next day, still perplexed about what he had said wrong.[124] In the American context, the controversy about the Smithsonian's Enola Gay exhibit may demonstrate how disagreement about wartime actions can detract from official pronouncements. Democracies must expect that pluralism will preclude total agreement on official declarations about matters of national morality and emotion, but the effectiveness of political apologies is diminished by official actions that contradict the attitudes expressed in such apologies.

COMMUNITY

Even if the difficulties of holistic representation can be overcome or largely mitigated, effective political apologies appear to require an even higher conception of unity. Specifically, political apologies work in part because they see not two groups (offender and offended) but because they assume both parties are in some sense members of the same group. The very meaning of the apology resides in a shared social bond between the parties.[125] Selfish or exclusionary considerations of honor or prestige may push a group to apologize, but effective apologies underscore inclusive community and oneness. As Tavuchis explains, "When we respond to the call after the offense by apologizing, we are seeking reconfirmation of our credentials as members [of the same community] by publicly recalling their unstated grounds, that is, what we apparently forgot when we transgressed."[126] Since apologies "simultaneously represent (and reenact) consummated infractions and attempts to reclaim membership, they unequivocally enunciate the existence and force of shared assumptions that authorize existing social arrangements and demarcate moral boundaries."[127] It might be objected that some wrongs by their very nature preclude a community that includes both offended and offender. Slavery, for example, appears necessarily to deny any such sameness or inclusion.

Nevertheless, apologies work in large part because they invoke the previously extant but often unspoken community that was violated by the wrong committed.

The communal nature of political apologies has implications for the content as well as the meaning of such apologies. Specifically, the need for shared understanding influences the amount of contextual information included in a political apology. Tavuchis argues that because there are multiple persons involved in collective apologies, there is less leeway for the sort of private understandings and accommodations that often characterize relations between individuals. Instead, actions must conform to widely shared sociolinguistic norms and protocols. This means that "everything counting as the apology must be spelled out; nothing can be taken for granted or remain ambiguous."[128] When both the giver and the recipient of the apology are groups, concern for clarity about meaning is compounded, as the number of persons precludes all but the most basic shared understandings. In such cases, explicit acknowledgement of all relevant contextual information is crucial.

Publicity

In addition to the implications of collectivity for meaning and content, the doubly collective aspect of political apologies may even change the nature of apology itself. When two groups are involved, the entire memberships of both groups must somehow be involved, and this requires some measure of publicity. Thus, political apologies are crucially concerned with publicity and recording apologetic overtures so as to make the apology accessible to all members of both groups.[129] According to both Tavuchis and Minow, concern with the public record is central to apologies from one group to another.[130] Tavuchis argues for the centrality of the public record in collective apologies by comparing collective and interpersonal apologies in terms of the main source of their efficacy. Whereas interpersonal apologies "realize their potential" through "sorrow and remorse," corroboration is a "necessary but insufficient condition for an authentic apology between persons." However, "the ultimate task of collective apologetic speech" is "to put things on record, to document as a prelude to reconciliation."[131]

In short, collective apologies work because they put things on a public record; sorrow and remorse are of secondary importance.[132] This point is important not only because it helps explain exactly how political apologies work their magic, but also because it means that apologies between groups are unlike other apologies, insofar as the regret that is essential to most apologies is replaced by concern for the public record. By way of lending further credibility to the claim of Tavuchis and Minow that the public record is key, consider the following remark about Gorbachev's

1990 admission of Soviet culpability for Katyn. Wanda Zadrozna, the daughter of a victim, said: "Whatever happens now, it is good that the truth will be finally written in history."[133] The emphasis on having a written apology in some examples (e.g., Japan's October 1998 apology to South Korea) underscores the importance of the public record.

EMPOWERMENT

Political apologies, like all apologies, also work because they render the offender vulnerable while simultaneously empowering the offended party. Despite their often radically different starting points, victim and villain are in some sense made equal (and amenable to reconciliation) because the latter is made low while the former is given new power. The first of these points is perhaps easier to see. We have earlier said that in proffering an apology, one is in the awkward position of seeking pardon in the context of being categorically unworthy. Apology may be viewed as "a form of self-punishment that cuts deeply because we are obliged to retell, relive, and seek forgiveness for sorrowful events."[134] In an apology "we stand unarmed and exposed, relying, in a manner of speaking, on our moral nakedness to set things right. Paradoxically, by assuming such a vulnerable stance, and only by doing so, we now unobtrusively shift the burden of belief and acceptance to the injured party."[135]

In essence, the injured party is given moral authority and thereby empowered. According to Minow, victims must have the power to choose to accept, to refuse, to ignore, or merely to acknowledge the apology.[136] Furthermore, the victim is largely able to dictate whether and to what degree forgiveness and reconciliation follow. In some cases, victims may need more than an apology before forgiving. "Forgiveness may be withheld, conditional, or granted without subsequent reconciliation," or "some kind of rapprochement may be established without forgiveness."[137] While "forgiveness may open the door to reconciliation, the nature of the relationship may well depend more on the trustworthiness of the offender than on the desires of the injured."[138]

One example may serve to underscore this point. Two years after the United Church of Canada apologized to Canada's native peoples for past wrongs inflicted on them by the Church, the All-Native Circle Conference acknowledged but did not accept the apology. The Conference credited the apology with goodwill but did not wish to belittle the gravity of the offense by forgiving too easily or quickly and thus releasing the church from the consequences of what it had done and condoned.[139] Although this political apology did not accomplish all that it wanted to, it was nevertheless "instrumental in bringing about social harmony."[140]

TIMING

Of all the factors that determine the success or failure of a political apology in enhancing public discourse, one of the most important but most difficult is timing. Basically, apologies do not work well if they are offered either too soon or too late after the wrong is committed. Instead, there must be appropriate intervals between the various phases in apologetic discourse, from the offense through call and apology to response.[141] Apologies that follow too closely after a call for an apology may be "construed as self-serving, a hollow courtesy." Conversely, the longer one waits to apologize following a call "the more difficult it is to apologize, the more carefully one's words must be chosen, and the less the apology is worth."[142]

At a minimum, an apology presupposes that the harm has stopped. After that, some time may pass before a call for an apology is issued, as was the case with Korean demands that Japan apologize for the "comfort women." After the call, the offender presumably must take some time to recognize the past action as wrongful. Furthermore, insofar as political apologies require attention to formal requirements and the articulation of all relevant contextual information, it would likely take some time to craft a good, effective apology.

While the above considerations explain why apologizing too soon is inadvisable, there are also considerations that caution against waiting too long. Even though aggrieved communities have long memories (consider the frequent invocations of centuries-old wrongs in the Balkans), apologies seem to work best if the victims are still alive; apologies presuppose an existing class of victims (or at least that their descendents are still similarly disadvantaged).[143] A brief consideration of several specific political apologies reveals that lateness may significantly diminish an apology's restorative potential. For example, after Gorbachev's 1990 admission of Soviet culpability for Katyn, Wanda Zadrozna, whose father was among those killed, said: "There is a great regret that it took 50 years and the wives of those people didn't live until this day."[144] Magda Czarnek Pogowska, whose husband survived capture by the Soviets in Poland, was bitter that the 1990 Soviet acknowledgment was delayed so long: "It was much too late."[145] In the Japanese context, Asian leaders welcomed Hosokawa's 1993 apology, but some complained that it was long overdue.[146] And after a small Christian group apologized in Jerusalem for the actions of Christians during the Crusades, Rabbi Yisrael Meir Lau, one of Israel's two Chief Rabbis, responded by saying, "Better late than never."[147]

Long-delayed apologies also run the risk of bringing up a host of thorny questions about responsibility. For example, maybe guilt cannot be intergenerational; maybe the living should not be called upon to repay the debts of the dead. Insofar as young people and new immigrants are excluded from complicity in a state's earlier wrongdoing, why should they be included in an apology? Alternatively, can the continuing failure to apologize constitute a wrong comparable to the original wrong done?[148]

Another problem in waiting too long before making an apology is that previous refusals could ruin later apologies. For example, Japan's decades of silence may well have diminished the impact of its recent apologies. In Australia, Prime Minister John Howard's initial refusal to apologize to aborigines may have detracted from his eventual apology. In France, Mitterand's 1992 refusal to apologize for French complicity in the persecution of Jews surely changed the force of Chirac's 1995 apology on the same issue. Of course, it is equally possible that initial refusals enhance rather than diminish later apologies, but the evidence does not seem to support that view.[149]

COMPENSATION

When is an apology alone insufficient? Is the symbolic power of a political apology enhanced or diminished by the inclusion of monetary compensation?[150] Minow suggests that apologies often need to be accompanied by direct, timely, and substantial actions in order to appear sincere, and compensation may be one way to do that.[151] Indeed, Ben Takashita of the Japanese American Citizens League said compensation for interned Japanese Americans showed that the U.S. government was "sincere."[152]

However, Israeli views about German compensation for the Holocaust indicate that the issue can be controversial. Israelis were not all in favor of German restitution. In fact, "when it was announced that in early January 1952, the Knesset would discuss whether or not to open these negotiations, a young and demagogic Menachim Begin led a charge against the government building. Thousands shouted from the outside, many broke windows and the building had to be cordoned off with barbed wire and guards. Begin screamed, 'What price are we going to get for grandpa and grandma?' Prime Minister David Ben-Gurion answered back, 'Let not the murderers of our people be also their inheritors!' "[153] As the Israeli reaction against compensation suggests, reparations cannot truly compensate for nonmaterial losses, such as the death of a loved one. Even insofar as reparations can compensate, some societies or groups may be unable to pay large reparations. Thus, there may be both principled and practical reasons for eschewing a close connection between political apologies and compensation.

Law

The relation of political apologies to law can also be problematic. Several authors suggest that legal remedies are often inadequate for dealing with instances of collective wrongdoing, alienation, and reconciliation, and that political apologies may also be needed. For example, Ackerman claims that law alone cannot make a nation come to terms with its own past, as that requires more ambiguity and hesitation than law may allow.[154] And Minow claims that legal responses to instances of national wrongs are usually insufficient, as those who are victimized deserve an acknowledgement of the wrong done to them and a reaffirmation of their humanity. Another commentator asks, "What is to be done in situations where putting perpetrators on trial might jeopardize a fragile new balance of law and order?"[155]

But while these and other limits of law point to an important role for political apologies, legal considerations can also limit the effectiveness of political apologies. As Tavuchis explains, "Because an apology necessarily acknowledges admission and fault (whether in a civil or criminal action), it is likely to be interpreted as acceptance of liability and grounds for compensation by authoritative third parties, in this case, legal officers and agents."[156] In some cases of withheld apologies, an apology "would have confirmed the actions in question in the sense of producing official and incontrovertible truths. As such, it would have provided strong grounds for some form of compensation and the acceptance of blame for the offenses."[157]

There are several instances of legal worries precluding political apologies. For example, Australian Prime Minister John Howard cited legal concerns as one reason for opposing an apology to Australia's aborigines.[158] In Quebec, a church apology to mistreated orphans was complicated by legal worries: Bishop Pierre Morissette, president of the Quebec Assembly of Archbishops, said that the matter was delicate because of legal considerations.[159] Also in Canada, federal officials long refused to give an apology to native peoples because of fears of setting a legal precedent.[160] In Japan, court decisions in a class action suit by "comfort women" have blocked some efforts for compensation.[161] In the American context, however, the legal effort to reverse convictions in Japanese-American internment cases helped rather than hindered efforts to obtain an official apology and compensation.

Symbolism, Repetition, and Other Factors

Several other aspects of political apologies are sufficiently important to warrant at least passing reference here. Symbolism is certainly very important in effective political apologies. For example, political apologies are often given on the exact anniversary of the harms for which they apologize. Many apologies for World War II events occurred on the fiftieth anniversary of the wrongs for which they apologize. More generally, vivid images appear to enhance the sincerity of apologies. In this context, Japan's various apologies have largely failed to placate South Korea and China in part because they lack the grand symbolism of Brandt's expression of contrition, for example. Symbolism can also inhibit apology, especially when the harms done achieve symbolic status in the national consciousness. Along these lines, "the tidy moral equation of Pearl Harbor to Hiroshima" undoubtedly makes it difficult for Japan to apologize for the former and for the U.S. to apologize for the latter.[162]

Another factor that influences political apologies is other political apologies. For example, Japan, China, and South Korea were all reportedly struck by the U.S. apology to Japanese Americans. The impact of an outside apology seems to be stronger when the relation is directly analogous. For example, calls for Australia to apologize to the aborigines were emboldened by Canada's apology to its native peoples. As one Australian apology advocate put it, "Where Canada has taken an approach of inclusion and healing, we continue down the paternalistic path of division . . . and isolation of Aboriginal people."[163] As political apologies become more and more common, pressures to be as contrite as other countries have been are likely to increase.

Repetition is yet another important aspect of political apologies. In most cases (Japan may be an odd exception), it seems that effective apologetic responses are not single apologies but rather are somehow iterated. In other words, there appear to be very few collective sins for which a single act of apology is sufficient. For example, despite favorable Polish reaction to the 1990 Soviet admission, the 1992 Russian admission, and Yeltsin's 1993 actions, Yeltsin's failure to attend the 1995 Katyn ceremony appears to have undercut the gains of the earlier apologies.

Last, it is abundantly clear that politics matter. Political considerations of all sorts affect the call for an apology, the decision to give it, the mode and substance of its presentation, and the response to it. For Germany, there was regional integration; for Japanese American internment, there was the presence of Japanese Americans; for Japan, there were Cold War pressures and the LDP's electoral dominance; for the Katyn massacre, there were various international pressures and *glasnost*. Given the enormous significance of the subjects with which they deal, political apologies are profoundly vulnerable to political constraints and influences. For this reason, a full understanding of any one case of political apology requires a deep appreciation of its political context.

Conclusion

This essay has approached political apologies both as a type of discourse and as a way to enhance public discourse. The subject of political apologies and related matters is radically understudied. Given the growth in political apologies and the potential of political apologies to heal formerly effective discourse communities and to enhance existing ones, political apologies clearly merit further study.

Future research on political apologies will have to delve more deeply into their complex nature. For example, how exactly does the call for an apology originate and become compelling, what is the impact of the relative power balance between victim and victimized on apologetic efforts, and what are the differences between interstate and intrastate apologies? Also, the consequences of political apologies need to be examined in much more detail: exactly what effect have specific political apologies had on subsequent relations and public discourse? The cases examined here suggest beneficial results, but the impact of political apologies on future discourse clearly requires further study. More broadly, it remains to be seen to what extent forgiveness and/or reconciliation can occur at the community level. However, a problem in such research is how to measure forgiveness.

Furthermore, work needs to be done to identify more clearly how this kind of discursive practice can be promoted and made effective in highly charged or otherwise polarized environments and in the achievement of reconciliation at particular stages in the resolution of protracted ethnopolitical conflicts. There is no shortage of places in which conflict and violence might be mitigated by political apologies; the Middle East, Northern Ireland, parts of the former Yugoslavia, Algeria, and Rwanda and Burundi are all places that could potentially benefit from carefully considered political apologies.[164]

Part Five
Thickening Public Discourse

Principles and Practices

Chapter 14

The Principles of Public Discourse:
What Is Good Public Discourse?

David M. Ryfe

The presence of incivility has sparked considerable interest in the nature of good public discourse. In academia, this concern has been driven, in part, by the more general turn to issues of language and discourse. The guiding assumption of much work in the social sciences and humanities today is that reality is constructed through language, or more broadly, through communication.[1] This "postmodern turn" has had two broad effects on the study of public discourse. First, the concern for language has spawned a great variety of research into the relation of language to personal and social identities. Developed in the disciplines of rhetoric, communication, sociology, social psychology, and linguistics,[2] this tradition is especially sensitive to the production of social and political inequality by linguistic categories and discourses. Second, the focus on communication and discourse has generated new, deliberative theories of democracy.[3] Advanced by scholars in the disciplines of sociology, political science, and communication, the concept of deliberation has been offered as a way of shoring up conventional liberal democracy theory, and of responding to the perceived rise of public incivility. For deliberative democrats, conventional liberalism's resources for negotiating deep social and cultural divisions are inadequate. Given the fragmentation and stratification that characterizes contemporary public life, it is not enough, advocates of deliberation claim, to confine politics to the narrow relation between the state and individuals.[4] In place of the impoverished vision of politics offered by liberalism, deliberative democrats argue that a good democratic politics depends upon good public discourse.[5] They assert that the best hope for reviving American public life lies in reconfiguring political institutions to make them more communicative. For them, it is only in a politics achieved through communication and deliberation that our public life will be revitalized.

Postmodernism and theories of deliberative democracy have generated a great deal of scholarly activity in the last twenty years. Together, they constitute the academic community's response to the rising tide of incivility in public life. Has this work developed useful theories about the relation between language and communication and political identity? Has it suggested how issues of language and identity affect our understanding of political institutions? Has it identified principles of public discourse that might reunite the personal and the institutional in such a way as to revitalize public life? Finally, has this work provided answers to the most basic question: What is good public discourse? The present essay assesses what has been accomplished in this focus on language, identity, and politics during the past two decades. It does so in a review of the major journals in communication and rhetoric, political science, linguistics, sociology, and history. The qualities that are most closely associated with good public discourse are culled from these various literatures, including articles from 45 major disciplinary journals published from 1990 to 1997. The first part of the essay ends with a list of several principles widely viewed as worthy of inclusion in a vibrant public discourse. Prescriptions for overcoming challenges to the realization of good public discourse are discussed in the second part.

What Kind of Deliberation?

In theory, a vibrant public discourse is supposed to negotiate moral disagreements, lead to more rational outcomes, establish political legitimacy, and create better citizens. In practice, it must accomplish these goals in the face of economic inequality, social fragmentation, and political apathy. What kind of deliberation might achieve these ends? The short answer is argumentation. The overwhelming consensus in the literature is that argumentation is the best deliberative model for public discourse. This is true in rhetoric, where argumentation has been a subfield of the discipline since its founding.[6] It is true in sociology, communication, and history, where Jürgen Habermas's communicative model of rationality has been dominant.[7] And it is true in linguistics, where Paul Grice's conversational maxims have guided much research.[8] Social psychologist Michael Billig has even argued that thinking itself is basically argumentative.[9] Postmodern complaints about the inescapability of irrationality and the abuses of reason have revised, but not overcome, argumentation as a model of good public discourse.[10]

These revisions have specifically focused on overly abstract and rationalistic descriptions of argumentation found in key texts. Habermas's suggestion that ordinary language is inherently rational has been hotly contested by Thomas McCarthy.[11] Similarly, Grice's four maxims of conversation—that it be informative, based in evidence, relevant, and clear—have been relaxed by Sandra Harris.[12] In both cases, researchers have moved to a conception of argument much closer to that which Stephen Toulmin and Chaiz Perelman outlined some time ago.[13] They envisioned argument as pursued in context, in ambiguous, face-to-face situations and, thus, critically shaped by forms of persuasion not necessarily grounded in logic or rationality. Though still rooted in the work of Habermas and Grice, notions of argument advanced in the literature today are responsive to a postmodern world of contingency and plurality.

What does postmodern argument look like? This question drives much of the current research. While no consensus exists, bare outlines of agreement have emerged. Postmodern argument, like all forms of argument, is principally based in reason.[14] That is, it advances clearly stated propositions, provides evidence for those propositions, and produces counterarguments that are also based in evidence.[15] While it may not reside in individuals, as Immanuel Kant suggested, and may even be manifested in many ways, reason is nonetheless a principal aspect of public communication and of the Western tradition.[16] Even in a world of plurality, contingency, and irrationality, the literature still clearly embraces reason as the best method for communicative interaction.

But if reason is endemic to argument, so are several other qualities. Perhaps the most hotly contested notion is that argument also entails emotion.[17] Traditionally, reason has been sharply distinguished from emotion by its impartiality and detachment. Recently, scholars have challenged this dichotomy. Observing that reason is often associated with the masculine, and emotion with the feminine, many feminist theorists have protested that the dichotomy, and the privileging of reason over emotion, serves male domination.[18] Language scholars have demonstrated how this domination takes place in linguistic interactions.[19] While persuasive, this argument says little about the positive value of emotion in public discourse. If reason has been deployed to reinforce male power, one might remedy the situation simply by affirming that women are as rational as men, and continue to exclude emotion from public deliberation.

Robert Frank makes a more proactive case for the role of emotion in argument. According to Frank, individuals engaged in public deliberation are often asked to act in ways that are contrary to their self-interest. In these cases, emotions may be key to gaining their assent.[20] Guilt, anger, envy, or love can motivate individuals to act in other than narrowly rational ways. Moreover, emotion may lead individuals to make inferences as to the character of others, which, in the absence of better information, may produce assent.[21] Thus, emotion is central to commitment in argumentative interactions, and commitment may encourage actions that would be unlikely if deliberators adhered to strict rationality.

Frank's argument has been supported by empirical research. In a book-length study involving several case studies, Douglas Walton shows that emotion can be employed in conversational arguments to both bad and good effect.[22] On the one hand, appeals made on the basis of pity, threats, ad hominem attacks, or popular sentiment may be grossly misleading and dangerous.[23] On the other hand, if used in proper contexts, especially when no verifiably correct position is available, arguments based on emotion may steer actors toward a resolution of conflicts. In a smaller study based on survey data, Elizabeth Theiss-Morse and her colleagues have demonstrated that appeals to emotion are often the only way to get participants' attention.[24] Further, while emotions may be associated with intolerance, this study found that they also play a crucial role in helping individuals evaluate their environment. According to these studies, emotion is central to good public discourse because it helps to establish relations between people, assists individuals in evaluating and acting on complex issues that have no clear solution, and, in the absence of other motivations, sustains individual commitment to the deliberative process.

Narrative is one way of importing emotion into public deliberation. Just as emotion has been distinguished from rationality, storytelling is often opposed to reason. Unlike reason-giving, storytelling is designed to persuade by moving people emotionally rather than intellectually. Stories appeal to values rather than facts, emotions rather than reasons. The power of a story often derives from the narrator's ability rather than the reasonableness of its claims. For these reasons, advocates of strict argumentative rationality often dismiss the value of storytelling to public discourse. This view has recently been revised. Deborah Schiffrin has found that storytelling may be crucial to sustaining dialogue.[25] Strict rationality often operates in an aggressive manner. Rational argumentation is pursued in a kind of verbal combat, with one side always trying to undermine the position of the other. In analyses of naturally occurring conversational arguments, Schiffrin has found that storytelling allows a kind of relational deliberation. Participants who tell stories do not try to undermine one another; rather, they employ stories to justify their claims to truth through appeal to broad values or common experiences. By inviting others to share a common understanding based in experience rather than reason, actors in a narrative mode achieve a kind of collective identity.[26] Narratives put actors in a stronger relation to one another, and spur commitment to that relationship far better than strict reason-giving.[27] Narrative thus supports a form of relational reasoning that privileges equality, participation, and community.

In terms such as "relational reasoning," it is apparent that the most recent literature seeks to develop a synthesis of concepts once viewed as oppositional: reason versus emotion, facts versus stories, and objectivity versus subjectivity. In so doing, it ignores two concepts that have traditionally been used to describe good public discourse: tolerance and politeness. The long-standing liberal ideal of tolerance[28] suggests that even if people do not respect alternative views, they must accommodate themselves to those views or risk violence.[29] This notion has been attacked from a number of angles. Conservatives see in tolerance a decay of moral virtue; democrats view the term as a mere mask for social and economic inequality; and postmodernists suggest that tolerance is anathema to true diversity.[30] The gist of these complaints is that tolerance is too weak to sustain dialogue under conditions of deep moral disagreement.[31] It is as likely to end in withdrawal and isolation as in sustained communication. While respect may not be achievable, deliberative democrats argue that individuals must still engage with one another. Reciprocity is the term used to describe this engagement.[32] Reciprocity is a middling-term between tolerance and respect. Under conditions of reciprocity, individuals actively engage with rather than simply tolerate the views of others. Unlike respect, which requires an active appreciation of alternative views, reciprocity merely guarantees that individuals will concede the existence of those views, and commit to engage with them. Reciprocity, that is, demands a form of engagement between isolation and appreciation.[33]

Politeness has been attacked on similar grounds. Penelope Brown and Stephen Levinson have argued that politeness, expressed in a variety of ways, is a universal feature of human communication.[34] For Nina Eliasoph, this is exactly the problem.[35] In a study of citizens' groups in the Northwest, Eliasoph found that the requirement of politeness in public interactions often led group members to avoid potentially divisive topics. While perfectly willing to state their views in private settings among friends, group members were wary of confronting controversial issues for fear of causing pain to others.[36] To prevent this from happening, they simply avoided talking about much of the political world, thereby setting narrow boundaries on the political. Eliasoph's study suggests that politeness is likely to hinder rather than facilitate dialogue on difficult problems.

Good public discourse, then, implies reason and emotion, reciprocity and a willingness to confront difficult issues—even if it seems impolite to do so. Martha Nussbaum also believes that it requires compassion.[37] Drawing on ancient Greek thought, Nussbaum urges a reconsideration of the fragility of human life. As the ancient Greeks understood so well, life often ends in tragedy—despite the best intentions—for no other reason than simple bad luck. Given the fragility of human existence, Nussbaum contends that it is rational to be compassionate. Bonding with others will not eradicate one's fragility (this can never be done), but allows individuals to share risk and assist one another when things go wrong. Where modern forms of instrumental rationality seek to eliminate risk, Nussbaum advocates a form of practical rationality that leaves room for a good measure of compassion.

Robert Wuthnow makes a similar argument. Compassion, Wuthnow claims, is perfectly rational, not because of the old maxim that to help others is to help oneself, but because it is a singular guarantee of individuality. Wuthnow employs the metaphor of gift exchange to make his case.[38] Gift exchanges help to sustain a particular image of a relationship between two people. They bring that relationship into being and create the expectation that it will continue in the future. By giving gifts, persons reveal both an interest in being a certain sort of person, and in perpetuating a particular kind of social relationship. Similarly, in a complex society, persons who perform an act of compassion have the satisfaction of knowing that they are contributing to the life of another member of the group, and thus to the persistence of that group's reality. They confirm an image of themselves and sustain an image of the group.

For all its attractiveness, it is difficult to assess this claim. On the one hand, social choice theorists have demonstrated repeatedly that under conditions of information scarcity, real individuals rarely choose to be compassionate.[39] This is especially true in collective deliberations, where responsibility for actions is often borne by a few, while benefits flow to many. On the other hand, scholars have found that an image of a compassionate society often sustains the self-identity of committed activists.[40] These activists demonstrate that compassion is rare, but present, in the public culture. Whether these activists are an aberration or the seed for a renewed flowering of social commitment is unclear. It is clear, however, that along with recent attention to emotion and narrative, Nussbaum and Wuthnow's appeal to compassion is made not to contradict traditional understandings of individualism and rationality, but to broaden them.

Principles of Good Public Discourse

In the past twenty years, as I have described, the definition of good public discourse as rational argument has been revised, although not supplanted, by postmodernism and other critiques. Impartial, disinterested argumentation has come to be seen as overly sterile, exclusive, patriarchal, and inadequate to describe the variety of motivations that inspire public deliberation. In place of strict rationality, academic research seems to be moving toward a conception of postmodern argument. Six principles are intrinsic to this conception.

1. **Formal Democratic Procedures.** This principle, retained from the liberal tradition, specifies a basic set of individual rights necessary to create a vibrant public sphere. These include principles outlined in the Bill of Rights: formal equality, freedom of expression and association, and freedom of the press. These procedures are meant to secure a space within which individuals may participate in public life. While much of the recent scholarship has been dedicated to revising liberalism, the need for formal democratic procedures has continued to enjoy great support.
2. **Grounded Rationality.** This is less a principle than a method of argumentation. It suggests that public discourse ought to be charac-

terized by the practice of advancing claims, providing evidence, and developing counterarguments. But this process of reasoning ought not to be abstracted from concrete human relationships. Instead, it should be grounded in human relationships and be sensitive to the role of emotion in establishing connections between people. Storytelling is an ideal way of grounding public discourse because it generalizes experience, spurs commitment, allows individuals not trained in the skills of argument to participate in public discourse, and establishes the legitimacy of truth-claims on other grounds when the relevant facts do not do so. Public discourse is as much about establishing and maintaining relationships as it is about winning arguments. The line between abstract and grounded rationality cannot be fixed, but must be negotiated continually in context.

3. **Reflexivity.** This principle is derived from discussions of the postmodern condition, defined as hyperplurality, contingency, and complexity. In this context, constant reflection on a proposition's values, assumptions, and terms is required not only because truth is relativized under these conditions, but also because situations change so rapidly that values and assumptions may not hold over time. Such reflection is required not only at the level of individuals, but at the level of the system generally. That is, mechanisms must be put into place so that values and assumptions may be constantly interrogated within institutions as well as by individuals.

4. **Reciprocity.** This principle suggests that actors in public deliberation must go beyond mere toleration of different views; they must actively engage with these views in the course of dialogue. Tolerance too easily slips into isolation, and respect is difficult to achieve. Reciprocity functions as a middling term between these two, implying that while respect may not always be achievable, engagement with alternative views is necessary. Under conditions of social fragmentation, it seems plausible to work toward this goal.

5. **Radical Difference.** Through the 1970s and 1980s, scholars often called for the recognition of difference, by which they meant that majority groups ought to recognize that subordinate groups may view the world differently. The notion of radical difference goes farther, asserting that individuals must have the right to speak in the voice of any of the groups to which they belong. That is, an elderly, African American, working-class female should be allowed to speak as a member of any of these groups, or the many others she belongs to—and she should be allowed to switch voices, to speak as a female at one moment and an African American the next, or to refuse to speak in any of these voices.

6. **Moderation.** This principle links the notion of reflection to reciprocity. Given the difficulty in finding solutions to complex issues, public discourse should be characterized by modesty in both the

assertion of claims and the generalizability of personal experience. Given the level of fragmentation in our society, care should also be taken to moderate one's rhetoric so as to develop reciprocal relationships with others.

These six principles flow directly out of debates on deliberative democracy and public discourse, and speak to the reality of American society and politics. Taken together, they describe public deliberation as a space of formal equality, reason-giving, and relationality. According to these principles, individuals will advance arguments; they will link arguments to their personal experiences; they will be recognized as individuals with group affiliations rather than as representatives of particular groups; and they will advance claims but also seek to establish commonality. A public discourse fashioned along these lines will be argumentative—but argumentative in a way that strives to achieve greater inclusion and stronger communal bonds. If actual people took these principles as guides to discourse and deliberative action, what form would their interactions take?

The Form of Deliberation: Debate, Family, or Therapeutic Discussion?

Few scholars have described or assessed actual forms of good public discourse.[41] Most present either an analysis of naturally occurring conversations, or discuss principles abstracted from forms of deliberation. However, three models of public discourse are implicit in much of this discussion. They are deliberation as debate, family discussion, and therapy. The model of debate is most prevalent in the field of rhetoric, where argumentation is taken most seriously. It is also a naturally occurring model of political communication, especially during election seasons. The family model is implicit in much of the communitarian literature. It imagines bonds of history, tradition, and affection transforming an impersonal society into a community. Finally, the therapeutic model has usually been criticized in academic analyses of contemporary public discourse. None of these deliberative forms alone is likely to realize our six principles of public discourse, but each illuminates some qualities of public discourse that speak to these principles. Instead of debating the merits of the models, it is perhaps better to focus on the qualities characteristic of each, and the ways in which those qualities may help to realize our deliberative principles in actual public discourse.

Debate is a long-standing model of public discourse. In one incarnation, it imagines conversation taking place between opponents engaged in verbal combat on specific issues. These opponents are armed with rhetoric—forms of persuasion and evidence—which they wield to sway an audience. These engagements are usually guided by a set of formal rules, such as time limits, and a moderator is often included to assure that the rules are followed. Debates are "won." The winner may be determined by an audience, a group of experts, or sometimes by the participants themselves (as in a legislature). Persuasiveness of argument is usually defined in terms of logic, evidence, coherence, and presentational style.

The notion of winning in the debate model is less compatible with the six principles than is the importance it places on rules and moderators. Researchers have found that actual public discourse is often characterized by negative, simple arguments; by power differentials that allow those with more argumentative resources to control the deliberative agenda; by feelings of enforced silence on the part of subordinate groups; and by bad uses of emotional appeals such as stereotypes and ad hominem attacks.[42] The result is often a reproduction of power relationships, the perpetuation of bad arguments, and, not surprisingly, bad deliberative outcomes. In its insistence on rules and moderators, the debate model remedies these abuses. It suggests that deliberation ought to entail a division of labor between speakers, moderators, and audiences. These actors are linked by formal rules of conduct and engagement. Rules and moderators are intended to prevent the intrusion of bad argument and inappropriate abuses of power into our public deliberations.

The family model makes us aware that public discourse might privilege values other than winning. Communitarians emphasize that Americans possess cultural traditions and shared idioms,[43] and these traditions lend coherence to public deliberations by providing a viewpoint from which to judge claims, evidence, and identities. Many studies have documented the power of a typically American viewpoint that includes individualism, egalitarianism, and pragmatism. While these values are sometimes appropriated by whites to discriminate against or indict other groups, they are held just as strongly by other ethnic and racial groups.[44]

The family model indicates that a good public discourse is not always directed at overcoming opposition. It may also reaffirm shared cultural values, or raise issues pertaining to those values. For instance, it is unlikely that conversations about racism—an entrenched tradition in the American culture—can be conducted profitably in a debate format. The issue cuts too close to our common identity and raises too many conflicting and heated emotions to be addressed in that form. In contrast, a conversation on race organized on the family model might usefully replace antagonism and frustration with intimacy and common purpose, stressing narrative rather than argument. It might be grounded in a basic assumption of the family model, that despite differences, participants belong to a common history and tradition. The result may not be a win for one position or another, but a sense of reciprocity in the discussion of race that remains elusive.

Of course, the danger of the family model is its inherent conservatism.

In foregrounding history and tradition, it implies that the past is inevitably reproduced in the present. Change does not come quickly in the family model of discourse. The therapeutic model addresses this shortcoming. In the academic literature, therapy is routinely disparaged as a narcissistic, individualistic, and corrupting influence on our public culture,[45] and there is some truth in these criticisms. Historically, the therapeutic idiom has been connected to consumerist orientations.[46] But therapy may be more useful than its historical manifestations imply. The therapeutic model is above all a process of identity construction. In conversation with experts, individuals engage in the construction of new narratives of the self. This process requires guidance (much like debate), but also openness, interpretation, and intuition. It demands that individuals deal with inappropriate or unhelpful emotions, beliefs, values, and actions by situating them in constructive self-understandings.

As Mark Warren argues, this process may be eminently beneficial to our public discourse.[47] Many studies have found that American values are often jumbled and contradictory,[48] and positions on the issues are often developed in a haphazard manner in the light of the most recently available information. Through conversation, the therapeutic model promises to raise contradictory values and beliefs to the public consciousness. The point of this form is not to win an argument, or to reaffirm historical commonality, but to create new collective narratives. Experts would guide the construction of these narratives, but the process relies on public participation. Their intent would be to raise for discussion the emotions and values that implicitly guide much public activity, and to construct new narratives that allow individuals to master these emotions and employ them in more profitable directions. Of the three models, therapy is certainly the most controversial. But given the pervasiveness of therapeutic discourse and the need to develop new collective narratives to deal with complex issues laden with deep emotions, therapy promises to institutionalize qualities of openness and imagination that are sorely needed in our public life.

Several of the qualities that characterize these three forms are incompatible with one another; others are so disparate that they are difficult to achieve in a single forum. But together, they may help us create a multiplicity of sites for institutionalizing the six principles of good public discourse. As Nancy Fraser suggests, our public deliberation may best proceed at multiple sites, animated by different qualities, serving particular principles, oriented to different goals, but all engaged in the construction of a vibrant national conversation.[49] The vision of numerous sites committed to various forms of deliberation, dedicated to some combination of our six principles, is a heady one. Can this vision ever come to pass? Many scholars and professionals think so, and have offered specific proposals for realizing it.

Making Good Public Discourse a Reality

There are as many proposals for reforming public discourse as there are critics. In general, these proposals have addressed one of four areas: politics, the mass media, economics, or society. Broadly, one might characterize the range of reforms as oriented to one of two goals: reducing the distance between people, or increasing the time people spend together talking and deliberating. Agreeing with Hannah Pitkin and Sara Shumer that a democratic politics is best conceived on the basis of face-to-face interactions,[50] political reformers seek in one way or another to slow down public interactions and to make them more intimate. For instance, proposals for reforming politics attempt either to slow down the process of deliberation, or to make representatives more responsive to citizens. This rationale is evident in several of the most popular campaign reforms. Campaign finance reform posits that representatives could spend more time on deliberative activities and their constituents if they could spend less time raising money. Advocates for free television time for candidates argue that this reform would create a richer conversational space for candidates that would inhibit sound bites and negative advertising. A shortened election season would make the election process a more intimate and focused affair, and limit candidates' fundraising demands. Reductions in committee responsibilities and staff for members of Congress might prevent members from delegating deliberative responsibilities and give them time to focus on this task.[51] Public financing of deliberative forums would close the distance between the public and the presidency.[52] Finally, advocates for strengthening parties at the local level argue that these parties might then organize and moderate public deliberation in a more intimate manner than the current system of mass mediation.[53]

Reform proposals aimed at the mass media reveal a similar logic. The most influential of these proposals—public journalism—argues that journalists ought to be more active in facilitating good public discourse.[54] According to public journalists, if an interested and committed public seems to have all but disappeared today, it is incumbent upon journalists to create a more conducive environment. The notion that better public discourse requires more elite responsiveness to the citizenry guides the public journalism movement. In the techniques they employ—facilitating discussions, convening focus groups, and sampling public opinion—public journalists demonstrate a desire to make journalists a surrogate of the deliberative process. Like other institutional reformers, public journalists view mass mediation as corrosive of good public discourse, but the journalists imagine the news media as playing a stronger role in facilitating more intimate, and more reflective, public deliberations. In a sense, it is as if public journalists want local newspapers to fill the coordinating role that local party representatives once played in the nineteenth century. But instead of focusing on winning elections, as their nineteenth-century ancestors did, these new leaders would concentrate on the deliberative process.

It is precisely this embrace of a strong mediating role that concerns critics of public journalism. Besides the question of practicality (responsiveness is expensive), critics of this movement observe that the key difference between journalists and other political actors is that the news media have not been elected to their position. Simply put, journalists cannot be voted out of office. This crucial distinction threatens the legitimacy of the news media at a time when that legitimacy has already been seriously eroded. Still, the willingness to instill face-to-face kinds of deliberative ideals within the mass media is telling. It indicates the degree to which the notion that more time and less distance equals better discourse has gained legitimacy in reform circles.

The principles of more time and less distance are perhaps most significant in reforms pertaining to civil society. Much of this conversation has been instigated by the work of Robert Putnam,[55] who argues that vibrant democracy depends upon the presence of thick social networks. Civic activity, as measured by participation in voluntary associations, enhances democracy by producing greater social capital in the form of trust, networks of relationships, and shared social norms.[56] This analysis implies that participation in myriad voluntary associations—from political parties to bowling leagues—is the best barometer of a healthy public life. Several studies support this contention. Christopher Kenny and Robert Huckfeldt and his colleagues have found that social networks serve as a powerful filter of political information.[57] Stephen Knack has determined that among all the reasons people vote, civic norms are often more influential than strictly material considerations.[58] James Youniss and his colleagues have found that youth participation in organized activities and civic behavior is a strong predictor of their civic activity fifteen years later.[59] This work implies that reforms of civic life are necessary to produce better public discourse. These reforms might include public funding for voluntary associations or the creation of more opportunities for voluntary associations to handle government responsibilities.[60] Or they might take the form of James Fishkin's deliberative polls, which bring together a randomly selected sample of the public for face-to-face discussions of pressing social issues—and then poll them on their more reflective, considered opinion.[61]

Putnam's thesis suggests that ordinary people must spend more time together, in face-to-face interactions, if democracy is to be enhanced. Indeed, his theory's support for the face-to-face sensibility in political communication may explain its popularity in scholarly circles. However, some scholars are more skeptical. Much of their criticism notes the difficulty inherent in specifying variables of social capital and establishing causal connections between them and better democracy.[62] Others have argued that while civil society may be a necessary condition for good democracy, it is not sufficient.[63] Instead, political institutions are at least as important as civic associations for the creation of vibrant democracy.[64] For instance, John Scholz and Wayne Gray (1997) find that government agencies are crucial for facilitating cooperation between private parties.[65] Peter Wielhouwer and Brad Lockerbie argue that the parties continue to be primary institutions for connecting citizens to the political process.[66] And Jan Leighley has found that participation in politics itself may enhance the political views of individuals.[67] While not discounting the importance of civic culture, this work contends that better public discourse is produced in the interaction between civic culture and political institutions. Reform of the one arena without the other is not likely to achieve the desired effect.

If not discussed much in the literature, two final reforms are still implied by our six principles of public discourse. They pertain to the economy and education. Scholars have perhaps been loath to focus on economic reforms because we live in a climate of fiscal austerity and a globalized economy. However, a case can be made that an economic safety net is crucial to achievement of a good public discourse. Academic research has determined that knowledge of and participation in politics is strongly conditioned by income level.[68] If this is so, then a certain level of economic stability is necessary to enforce any substantive notion of political equality. Moreover, if one accepts the premise that political participation produces better selves, then denial of access to public life is tantamount to a denial of self-development. As Carol Gould argues, freedom in this sense should be understood not only as a capacity for choice, but also as an activity of self-development.[69] Thus, to guarantee that fundamental democratic principles of equality and freedom are met, a minimal welfare state is necessary.

Similarly, academic research has determined that the process of public deliberation is often controlled by those with the best deliberative skills. Today, attainment of those skills is strongly associated with education level, which in turn is correlated with income level. To break this chain, a strong program of public argumentation might be put in place at the primary and secondary levels. This program would differ from traditional forensics classes in several ways. First, it would be a required course, not an elective one. Second, it would begin in primary, not secondary schools. Third, it would teach not only techniques of debate and argument, but also our principles of public discourse: moderation, reciprocity, grounded rationality, and so forth. And finally, it would include a substantive consideration of current social issues in the context of a larger understanding of U.S. history and society. In this way, the program might be linked to other core classes, such as social studies and history. Such a program would provide all students with the necessary tools for entering public deliberations. While not erasing the gap between better and less able public speakers, it would equip all citizens with a minimal set of skills for monitoring the public discourse.

Open Questions

What is good public discourse? Academic researchers have been much better at answering this question in theory than in practice. The vibrant theoretical conversation over public discourse has not been complemented by a similar depth of empirical analysis. Does participation in public discourse actually make for better citizens? The evidence collected thus far is mixed. At times, individuals are inspired by engagements in the public's business. At others, however, especially on issues that are central to one's core value system, or closely connected to one's livelihood, participation is as likely to produce stridency and unreasonableness. Is language used to identify individuals in certain ways, and through this identification, to exclude and discriminate in the public sphere? Yes. But individuals have a remarkable capacity for slipping through the cracks of this exclusion, and for turning oppressive language to their own advantage. Unfortunately, we know very little about how this process happens, or about initiatives that would make it happen more often. Which qualities of public discourse make people better citizens, and under what conditions? Which kinds of issues are likely to occasion moderation and reciprocity? What kinds of activities or practices break down language of exclusion and discrimination, and under what conditions? All these questions might be investigated empirically.

As I have suggested, most thinking on public discourse adheres to a basic logic: less distance and more time equals better deliberation. Scholars have smuggled into their studies an implicit seventh principle of public discourse: size matters. Like Montesquieu before them, contemporary scholars have been unable to imagine a democratic conversation that does not take place among a small group, in face-to-face communication.[70] As a corollary, they have been unable to imagine a mass-mediated conversation characterized by true relationality and reciprocity, a respect for radical difference and moderation. It seems that mass mediation requires performers and audiences, and thus necessarily produces many of the conditions of a degraded public discourse: lack of accountability, artificial publicity, separation of performers and audiences, and passive kinds of participation. While there is certainly much to recommend this view, it assumes that mass mediation necessarily corrodes public discourse. But are there principles of mass mediation that might foster better discourse? Is it necessary to reduce the distance between participants, and increase the time for reflection? Perhaps a new turn on James Madison's *Federalist X* is in order: Is good public discourse possible in a large, fragmented, *mass-mediated* society?[71] Answers to these questions are difficult to come by, but given that mass mediation and commercial media are facts of life in our society, they seem worthy of some reflection.

Chapter 15

A Paradox of Public Discourse and Political Democracy

Neil Smelser

High standards of public discourse are not in any natural way assured in a political democracy. In fact, given democracy's treasured values of freedom of speech and expression and its traditions of political campaigning, opportunities for debased or deteriorated discourse and behavior abound. Furthermore, once low standards find their way into the public dialogue and the political process, purposive intervention into that process is inhibited by the very democratic principles we embrace. To put the matter most baldly, there is a tension—if not a contradiction—between the culture of a democracy, on the one hand, and the public discourse and behavior that democracy permits, on the other. To elaborate this paradox, consider the constraints experienced by government officials, societal leaders, and institutional spokespersons who may want to improve the level of civil discourse or to sustain, support, or build institutional arrangements that foster good civil discourse.

First, the Bill of Rights of the Constitution guaranteed a number of rights that have come to be regarded as sacred traditions in the American polity. Among these are freedom of religion, freedom of assembly, freedom of speech, and freedom of the press. All of these, as stated and as interpreted by the courts, establish a burden-of-proof situation: the norm is not to interfere in public speech and expression because citizens are thus protected, and if interference is to be justified—as in the cases of shouting "Fire!" in a crowded theater, pornography, fighting words, and hate speech—the burden of proof lies with those who would intervene. This condition strongly inhibits legal and political action against expression and defines highly specific circumstances and complex and difficult procedures under which intervention is possible. These circumstances are codified in laws relating to libel and slander, sedition and treason, inciting to riot, and so on. As a general rule, Americans are proud of traditions that ensure freedom of expression and are not inclined to change them. Because ordinary discourse—civil or uncivil—is thus normally beyond legal and political interference, the burden of improvement is shifted to direct mechanisms of public opinion and moral suasion or indirect mechanisms of establishing institutional settings and practices that facilitate civil and civilized expression.

In connection with this general point, the press merits special comment. At the time the Bill of Rights was enacted, the press was, by and large, printed materials distributed locally, and was available to only certain segments of the population because of limited literacy. Over the years, the republic has witnessed the near universalization of literacy, the wider distribution of printed materials, the invention and universal spread of first radio and then television, and now electronic communication and the Internet. These developments have given a completely new definition and scope to the press and have multiplied the extent and potency of communication in ways beyond the dreams of the founders of the republic. All these media are and continue to be protected in different ways, but each time a new technological stride is made, a new alarm about the media's power to corrupt arises. Witness the recent widely voiced concerns about pornography on the Web and about the Web as an avenue for hate group propaganda. The general point is that, whether or not the quality of civil behavior and civil discourse has changed, its power to reach ever larger segments of the population on an instantly available basis has multiplied dramatically and will continue to do so.

Closely related to the tradition of inhibiting interventions on matters of expression is a more general American cultural principle: a skepticism about, and possibly an antagonism toward, authority and authorities. There is a general cultural appreciation that laws and rules ought to be obeyed by citizens, but there is an equally impressive array of mechanisms to attack those laws and rules: institutionalized mechanisms of challenge and appeal in administrative rules, the power of legal challenge in the courts, referendum initiatives, and, in some places, recall of responsible political figures. The anti-authority ingredient in American culture tends to inspire opposition and defiance when leaders exhort people to obey the rules. Once again, while we may regard the consequences of this cultural ingredient with some ambivalence, on balance, it does not seem to be an unwelcome element in the culture of any civilization.

The arena of the private, as contrasted with the public arena, is especially protected from intervention. When some item can be defined as falling within the private sphere, anyone who attempts to intrude on the behavior or action will be met with the response "mind your own business." Furthermore, since the line between private and public is ambiguous and continuously contested, citizens and groups resist intervention over their discourse or behavior by claiming that the item under question is private. Thus, the private-public distinction constitutes a political strategy in and of itself. In considering the issue of directed intervention in general, we must remind ourselves of the well-established principle of unintended consequences. In arena after arena—educational reform, enforcement of laws, evaluation studies of public policies, impact of advertising and propaganda—attempts to change people's behavior either fail to reach the intended targets, are ignored or undermined, or paradoxically create new ways to deviate from established rules and procedures. To put the point most generally, efforts to change human behavior introduce a new causal element into the social fabric, which combines with a multiplicity of other causal forces already at work, and the effort's intended effects are deflected or changed accordingly.

Practical Possibilities

These paradoxes might lead those committed to the improvement of discourse and behavior in our society to throw in the towel, so great and entrenched do the obstacles to change appear. A more appropriate conclusion is more complex. Direct efforts to change behavior and public discourse are indeed likely to fail or backfire because of the cultural and institutional obstacles to them. Other lines of reform, however, are more encouraging. They include various indirect means of improving conditions through cultural contexts, institutional contexts, and even infrastructure. These indirect means might facilitate and nurture better, more productive civil and political discourse, and increase the likelihood that such discourse will take root. Some of the indirect conditions and norms that might encourage better public discourse are already present. They exist in the American version of parliamentary democracy, in the tradition and form of debate, in the procedures that govern Congressional business, and in the traditions—however frail and ineffectual they might seem—of media responsibilities toward the public.

There are a number of other indirect lines of reform activity that might improve public discourse. They include selected reforms in educational institutions. The range of possibilities for educational reform is great. School districts could reorient the teaching of American history in primary and secondary schools away from assuring standardized knowledge about significant dates and events, and in the direction of highlighting decisive changes in history that have created opportunities for enlightened public discourse. Schools might reform the tradition of teaching civics courses in high schools, courses that typically have been required in the junior or senior year, but which have been less than ideal on account of their dry content and formality. For example, such courses might include applied sessions of deliberative public opinion formation, in which students are able to act and interact in the development of positions on public issues and also to observe this process. Each year many students engage in a version of public deliberation and discourse via student government and other such decision-making bodies. School districts might explore ways to make student government less "sandboxy" and more relevant to and engaged with the educational institutions in which they are lodged. Student government might also play some role in municipal and state political institutions.

Several other reforms in schools, colleges, and universities might lay an indirect foundation for better public discourse. Most colleges require some courses in American history or American studies. These courses could be revitalized with an eye to imparting the skills and critical faculties required in a deliberative democracy. Students in high school and college would benefit from expanded opportunities for participation in municipal and state government through fellowships, internships, and summer work programs. Finally, in both the K-12 and college settings, students would benefit from practicing good public discourse. Among other opportunities, classes could combine television viewing of significant political events in the classroom with organized student discussions and debates on the issues raised by the events.

Several indirect initiatives in the media might positively influence public discourse. We could increase the number and kind of media discussions and debates during campaigns. Currently, the main form of these is the presidential and vice-presidential debates prior to presidential elections, though the process has spread to some extent to gubernatorial and mayoral races as well. The format of these debates is often tightly orchestrated, however, so that candidates are able to give mini-campaign speeches as responses to questions, and little in the way of sustained argument and exploration of the issues occurs. Several possibilities exist for supplementing these forums, through which citizens, as well as the press, could become more involved in the presidential, vice-presidential, gubernatorial, and mayoral debates as organizers, participants, discussants, and so on, thereby thickening the political culture. For example, citizens might conduct parallel debates on relevant campaign issues, in coordination with the debates among politicians. If the debates were scheduled immediately after the political candidates' debates and were focused explicitly on issues, this might conceivably have the indirect effect of shaping up or otherwise improving the politicians' presentations. Community organizations could institutionalize public debates so that they are scheduled regularly; incipient and potentially divisive issues in the community would thus find a reliable forum for discussion and discourse. These periodically scheduled debates and forums might help stave off or defuse the political polarization that often occurs when groups take early, militant stands on issues and the public has few arenas for the consideration of other positions or views. Communities should consider the adoption of the speaker's corner in the tradition of the venerable March Arch in London, where on Sunday morning for the last 150 years citizens have been free to speak and debate with each other on issues of the day. These speaker's corners, located in parks or other accessible, public places, would continue the oral tradition and create additional spaces for public discourse and deliberation. To the extent possible, these reforms should neither be organized nor financed by governmental officials, but supported by foundations and citizen groups. These kinds of initiatives would not only generate a wider range of participation in public events, but would minimize the likelihood of their political manipulation and exploitation.

Organizational life in the United States is honeycombed with a great range of institutions that are meant to facilitate fair and equitable treatment of members who have grievances or are involved in conflicts. These take the form of ombudspersons, grievance procedures, administrative law, investigatory bodies (for example, Fair Employment and Housing Commissions), and the civil courts. These are all civilizing arrangements, in that they guide grievances and conflicts into institutionalized channels that have clear and often orderly procedures for handling the concern. Civil and administrative laws, for example, are explicit mechanisms for dealing with individual conflict, such as collective bargaining, grievance procedures, and the right to sue. These laws channel conflict into regulated settings, and in that way discourage it from taking more uncontrolled forms. It may well be the case that the United States has enough of these institutional mechanisms for grievance resolution, but it is appropriate to ask where these institutions do not exist. Are there interstices in society, located outside the organizational fabric, that have escaped the effects of past reforms? Even in places where grievance and conflict management arrangements are visible, is it the case that, in practice, it proves too costly in time, effort, frustration, and money to use them effectively?

It has been claimed that with the weakening of traditional parties (by the establishment of direct, binding primaries, by the emergence of large super-corporations that can wield their influence without the help of political parties, and so on), popular politics have migrated, to some degree, to social movements and protest groups that are less definitely institutionalized than parties, and have fewer institutionalized mechanisms to make their political voice heard—beyond using the press, conducting marches, and mobilizing write-in campaigns. Compared with earlier periods in American history, social movements are certainly more institutionalized and hence tamed, but they are still more fluid and unpredictable in their political activity than some other parts of the polity. We might work toward having more formal means of listening to and engaging with these social movements.

It is evident that despite the webs of political machinery in this country, there are a number of conspicuous groups that remain relatively voiceless. The most salient of these is the urban underclass, for whom many others speak and act, but whose own political life is relatively unorganized and not often heard directly. Other groups that might fall in this category are marginal rural populations (for example, in Appalachia) and recent immigrants. These groups are seldom politically vocal, but it would serve a democratic society well to be vigilant in identifying voiceless groups and contriving more effective means of incorporating them into the polity.

Unexamined Assumptions

There are many popular assumptions concerning public discourse and civility that shape our attitudes towards their roles in a democratic society. For example, our usual operating assumption is that uncivil behavior is degrading to the person, community, and society, but it is largely unknown whether this is so, to what extent, and in what ways. Thus, there is a need for more systematic study of the personal, group, and social consequences of uncivil behavior. Scholars might usefully assess what constitutes acceptable, effective, and productive public argumentation and what does not. Nor do we know enough about the appeal to emotion in public discourse. How can emotion be manipulated in these circumstances? What are the consequences? Again, many share the conviction that appeal to emotion is undesirable, but as is the case with every unexamined assumption, we can be certain only if we ask objective questions and gather reliable data that bears on the issue. Finally, additional research might explore the processes by which issues move from the public to the private sphere and vice versa. It seems erroneous to regard the public and the private as real, concrete, and separate things; rather, what is public and private is better regarded as a complex legal and political process, often subject to disputation and contestation. A better understanding of all these processes will contribute greatly to our understanding of the dynamics of public discourse and provide a stronger empirical foundation for efforts to thicken it.

Chapter 16
The Practice of Public Discourse:
A Study of Sixteen Discourse Organizations

David M. Ryfe

This essay examines how the principles of good public discourse are advanced by the activities of sixteen organizations in the discourse field (see Table 1). In an earlier chapter,[1] I found that scholars identified six principles of good public discourse: (1) it is structured by formal democratic procedures; (2) it involves both reason-giving and relationship-building activities; (3) it includes reflective mechanisms for examining its own values and assumptions; (4) it engages reciprocally with alternative views; (5) it allows individuals to speak in many different voices so as to convey the range of their experiences; and (6) it encourages a moderate rhetoric. In this chapter, I examine how these principles come into play in the activities of sixteen discourse organizations. I have analyzed materials that describe the work and methods of the organizations, accessed on their websites or collected by mail. When possible, I also talked with organization representatives and solicited other sorts of data, such as videotapes of actual interactions and evaluation studies. The product of this analysis is not a comparison or evaluation of the programs, but a first attempt to compare discourse practice with abstract scholarly principles of good discourse.[2]

Practitioners and academics both believe in the power of ordinary citizens to engage in deliberations that lead to public action. But this analysis reveals that there is a great deal of tension between the deliberative ideal and the representative system, primarily because that system works to filter public participation in political decision-making. This tension often goes unrecognized in the scholarly literature, where deliberative democracy is often discussed separately from the representative political system. Perhaps because they are on the front lines of public deliberation, and therefore must bridge this divide more often, discourse organizations illuminate these tensions more clearly. In so doing, they also show that principles of good public discourse interact in complex ways with a representative model of politics.

TABLE 1. DISCOURSE ORGANIZATIONS

Organization	Description
Americans Discuss Social Security (ADSS)	A project that developed both small-group and large-scale forums for public deliberation on the issue of social security reform. See http://www.americaspeaks.org/projects/adss.html.
Annenberg Institute for School Reform (AISR)	An initiative begun in 1994 which has sought to engage the public about issues related to education reform. See http://www.annenberginstitute.org.
The Aria Group	A group located at Antioch College which has developed an action-evaluation approach to conflict resolution. See http://www.ariagroup.com.
The Center for Deliberative Polling	A center that is dedicated to the use of deliberative polls as a preferred method of gauging public opinion. See http://www.la.utexas.edu/research/delpol/.
The Jefferson Center	A center that is dedicated to the use of the "jury model" as a method for deliberating on public issues. See http://www.jefferson-center.org.
The Common Ground Network for Life and Choice	A network that employs a therapeutic model for facilitating discussions between individuals and groups in conflict over the issue of abortion. See http://www.cpn.org/topics/families/prolife.html and http://www.sfcg.org/networkm.htm.
Democracy Is a Discussion	A project that produced two booklets containing short essays by scholars on various elements of democracy, for distribution to schools around the country. See http://www.civnet.org/news/full_articles/myers.htm.
The Harwood Group	A for-profit company established in 1988 which has created deliberative techniques for assisting local communities in developing solutions to public problems. See http://www.theharwoodgroup.com.
The Keystone Center	A nonprofit organization based in Keystone, Colorado, which uses deliberative techniques to assist communities in conflict over issues related to science and the environment. See http://www.keystone.org.
The National Issues Forums Institute (NIFI)	A small-group model of deliberation developed by the Kettering Foundation for community groups interested in using discourse to solve pressing public problems. See http://www.nifi.org.
The NEH National Conversation	A four-year project conducted by the National Endowment for the Humanities

	which sought to assess the usefulness of deliberation for creating greater public understanding of issues of identity, race, and ethnicity.[a]
The Pew Center for Civic Journalism	An institution dedicated to the dissemination of public journalism techniques and tools within the American news media. See http://www.pewcenter.org.
President Clinton's Initiative on Race	An initiative established in 1997 which used deliberative methods to identify ways of building a more racially integrated American society.[b]
The Project on Public Life and the Press	A project conducted from 1994 to 1997 which sought to foster the public journalism movement.[c]
The Public Conversations Project (PCP)	An organization created by the Family Institute of Cambridge, Massachusetts, which employs family therapy methods to facilitate public deliberation. See http://www.publicconversations.org.
The Study Circles Resource Center (SCRC)	A center established in 1990 which has popularized a study circles method for fostering public deliberation in local communities. See http://www.studycircles.org.

a. See Hackney, *One America Indivisible.*
b. See President's Initiative on Race, "Advisory Board's Report," "One America Dialogue Guide," and "Pathways."
c. See Rosen, "Part of Our World," "Making Things More Public" and *What Are Journalists For?*

There is a tendency in the scholarly literature to invoke binary conceptual oppositions. Often, in the heat of rhetorical battle, scholars draw lines between good and bad deliberation. Good deliberation, a scholar will argue, is characterized solely by rational argumentation; or good deliberation involves speaking solely from one's own personal experience. Of course, in practice there is no one correct mode of public discourse. Scholars know, or at least should know, this to be true. But, perhaps because they deal in highly abstract, conceptual categories, or are pushed to extremes in argumentative debate, or because they are concerned to develop logically clear and internally consistent arguments, this point gets lost. If the practice of public discourse has anything to teach scholars, it is this mundane, but important truism: different kinds of discourse are appropriate to different contexts.[3] That is, factors such as the goals, size, and composition of the groups involved will shape the discourse that is produced. In the following discussion, I assess what discourse organizations know and do not know about good public discourse. I end by listing several kinds of activities and specific projects that might be pursued to continue the good work that is being done on both the theory and practical aspects of public discourse.

Mapping the Practice of Public Discourse

The discourse organizations included in this study were selected according to three basic criteria. (1) They are nationally, as opposed to locally or internationally, focused. The field of discourse work is enormously varied. There are hundreds of local, state, and national organizations that work in the field of public discourse. This study draws on organizations that employ their talents on a national scale. (2) The organizations are discourse-based. Many initiatives include some discourse work in their activities but are primarily interested in community-building. That is, they focus on such things as building local parks and restoring neighborhoods rather than on stimulating community conversations. All the organizations in this study perceive discourse to be a principal tool and outcome of their activities. (3) The organizations are publicly focused. There is an enormous industry centered on alternative dispute resolution (ADR) and conflict resolution. However, many of these organizations concentrate their energies on private industry—disputes between corporate clients, for instance, or between individuals involved in a private disagreement.[4] The organizations included in this study make an explicit choice to work in public arenas on community-wide issues.

Although all our organizations fit these basic criteria, there is enormous variety among them. A number are nonprofit and foundation-funded; others reside at centers on university campuses; and a few are for-profit companies. Some promote methods usable in conversations on any issue; others develop methods that address specific issues, such as education or the news media; and still others have no method at all, save for a series of readings and activities. A few deal solely with very small groups of five to fifteen individuals, while others are intended to involve mass publics. In developing their approaches, the organizations draw from diverse sources, including family therapy, conflict resolution, the legal system, humanities education, and political philosophy.

All discourse organizations possess scarce resources and so must make choices as to the kinds of community groups with which they will work. Two primary criteria by which they make these choices are the size of a given community and its ultimate goal in practicing discourse. Community goals are usually one of five: education, conflict resolution, cooperation, action, and policy. Thus, some types of communities seek to educate their members. Others may wish to catalyze more cooperation, or work toward particular kinds of actions (taken by group members) or policies (taken by local governments). Discourse organizations tend to concentrate their attention on some subset of these goals. For instance, the reading packets distributed by Democracy Is a Discussion are intended to educate students through thoughtful reflection on key themes and issues related to democracy.[5] In contrast, the Keystone Center focuses solely on science policy issues.[6] Through its Science and Public Policy program, it facilitates discussions between decision-makers in government, the environmental community, industry, and citizen organizations, and these discussions are intended to result in a particular policy outcome.

These discourse organizations work with groups as small as five to fifteen individuals, or as large as a mass public. Discourse organizations develop methods that are appropriate to groups of a particular size. For instance, the Public Conversations Project (PCP) has devised a methodology stemming from the family therapy literature.[7] This methodology leads PCP to work closely with small groups to mediate value conflicts over sensitive issues. A great deal of face-to-face interaction between PCP and the participants is involved in this effort, even before actual conversations between the group members takes place. Several other organizations have developed different methods appropriate to small or medium-sized groups. For the Americans Discuss Social Security (ADSS) project, which was funded by the Pew Charitable Trusts and run by America*Speaks*, a conversation packet was created for small groups facilitated by local neighborhood leaders.[8] America*Speaks*, whose executive director Carolyn Lukensmeyer implemented ADSS for Pew, has also developed another method based on the use of satellite technologies and the Internet to convene discussion groups of several hundred individuals located in different physical spaces.[9] Similarly, the Annenberg Institute for School Reform (AISR) has created television programs designed to link together groups of several hundred people, but has also cooperated with the Study Circles Resource Center (SCRC) to produce a conversation packet for small-group discussion purposes.[10] Organizations that seek to foster large, community-wide conversations generally do so by using local and national news media. The Pew Center for Civic Journalism, the Project on Public Life and the Press, and the Harwood Group have all worked with local news organizations to foster better community discourse. Through his deliberative polls, James Fishkin has combined polling technologies with media coverage to instigate large-scale conversations.[11] And the President's Initiative on Race held a series of nationally and regionally televised forums to stimulate mass deliberations on the issue of race.

Discourse and Citizenship

When examined as a whole, it is clear that these discourse organizations prefer to work with smaller groups. Of the sixteen organizations in this analysis, thirteen work with small groups of less than fifty members. Only six of the organizations work with medium-sized groups of fifty to several hundred members, and five work with entire communities or national publics. Moreover, even when organizations work with medium-sized and large groups, they usually do so in the hope of inspiring conversations that are more local. We have seen that ADSS used satellite technology and the Internet to organize simultaneous conversations among several hundred individuals,[12] but the intention of these larger meetings is to inspire participants to become leaders of smaller conversations in their local communities. As Lukensmeyer states (quoting Margaret Mead) in the video that accompanies the ADSS conversation toolkit: "Never doubt that a small group of thoughtful, committed citizens can change the world; indeed, it's the only thing that ever has." Similarly, although the Aria Group is currently developing Internet-based software to facilitate wider and larger conversations, its director, Jay Rothman, considers this technology to be a "poor substitute" for face-to-face interactions, the proper site of democratic deliberation.[13] And, for all its national visibility, President Clinton's Initiative on Race developed a dialogue guide for local conversations, and Advisory Board members spent much of their time participating in small, face-to-face discussions.[14] It seems then, that scholars and discourse practitioners both imagine good public discourse in terms of face-to-face interactions.

Along with a preference for small groups, discourse organizations also leave the decision to participate up to the individuals and groups involved. That is, most of the community groups that convene conversations are self-selected.[15] This is not to say that discourse organizations do not practice a significant amount of outreach. Most distribute their materials and promote their models as widely as possible. Many work very closely with local community leaders to organize conversations. But the final decision to participate in these discourse activities generally lies with individual members themselves. For example, groups organized through Common Ground, SCRC, National Issues Forums Institute (NIFI), PCP, and ADSS all come together through word of mouth—friends recruit friends, fellow workers recruit fellow workers. Due to the sensitivity of the issues that they discuss (such as abortion and race), Common Ground and PCP require that individuals select themselves, because their willing participation in the process is a key determinant of the conversation's success.

The significance of this tendency to employ self-selection techniques is best understood in the context of an observation made by political scientist W. Russell Neuman: in terms of political sophistication, participation, and interest, only about 5 percent of Americans can be considered activists; another 75 percent can be considered part of an apathetic but primed middle group; and the last 20 percent are unabashedly apolitical.[16] Other scholars shift these numbers somewhat, but the three-part division remains the same.[17] That is, if one were to divide the American public in terms of political interest and participation, a small percentage (perhaps 5 to 10 percent) may be considered active; another 50 to 75 percent are capable of political action, but generally cynical and apathetic; and the other 20 to 40 percent are apathetic.

It is the middle group of Americans, which possesses certain kinds of civic skills but is not linked to civic life in any sustained manner, that discourse organizations tend to focus upon. Possessing the economic and intellectual resources to participate, but little motivation, individuals in this middle group often become very inspired and participatory when given opportunities to "make a difference." Organizations reach these kinds of individuals through word of mouth (participants recruit their more apathetic friends, family, and neighbors), by facilitating meetings at familiar public institutions such as libraries or town halls, and by advertising in local media. None of these methods is likely to reach the truly apathetic, who are often working class or poor, and thus isolated from more middle-class institutions, have few friends or coworkers involved in public life, and do not read newspapers or watch television news. Even when organizations like the Deliberative Polling Center actively seek out these individuals as part of their search for a representative sample of the population, they must go to extreme lengths—like driving them to the local airport because they have never been on a plane.[18] For the most part, it is difficult enough to attract the apathetic but primed middle; neither discourse organizations nor local community leaders have the resources to reach much further into the local population.

If discourse organizations tend to focus on small, self-selected groups, they also tend to concentrate their resources on serving the goals of conflict resolution, cooperation, and action. Twelve of the organizations assist groups with these goals. In contrast, only four organizations deal with policy-making groups, and another four assist communities interested in educating their constituencies. In part, this focus on conflict, cooperation, and action is compelled by the members of the groups involved. For instance, in a roundtable discussion, a group of NIFI facilitators agreed that, as Gregory Hall and Donald Kimelman put it, "one of the barriers preventing people from regularly attending forums is their expectation that there should be some form of resolution or call to action by the end of each discussion."[19] Even the NEH National Conversation, which was mainly devoted to educating the public on issues of diversity, warned its conversation leaders to "make sure that everyone knows that these are not 'bull sessions.' "[20] This stress on action is also encouraged by foundations that fund many discourse organizations.[21] In return for their money, foundations want to see deliverables. This means that organizations must show that their work is having real—defined as observable— effects on the community. This orientation to action raises the bar for measuring the success of discourse efforts. Simple education—helping people learn to be better citizens—is generally not enough to satisfy either funders or potential participants, and discourse organizations spend relatively little time teaching participants good civic skills. Instead, participants must come to conversations with a certain amount of knowledge and skill gained elsewhere (a key aspect of the apathetic but primed middle population). At the same time, conversations geared to action rarely reach the level of policy-making arenas.[22] Thus, discourse organizations are faced with a difficult challenge: on the one hand, they must convince participants that their efforts will be rewarded with concrete actions; on the other hand, they must acknowledge that this action rarely will take place in the conventional political system. In this context, a good deal of work is needed to frame actions as real and demonstrable, if not effective in policy-making circles.

Beyond this particular challenge, there is a paradox raised by the kinds of groups with which discourse organizations tend to work. This paradox has to do with the preferred image of citizenship embedded within the field of discourse practice. All these organizations imagine citizenship as participatory and civic-minded. Citizens are understood to be people who are willing to get involved, who care about pressing political issues and the state of their communities. Yet, individuals often refuse to participate unless they feel some emotional connection to the group. This connection might take an abstract form, as individuals are inspired by a generic notion of good citizenship. But more often the connection is made through some sort of boundary-marking exercise: I identify myself with this group because they are like me in some essential way.[23] Thus, I feel comfortable with my group because its members speak, look, or act in familiar ways, or because they tend to think about the world in ways that are familiar to me.

This kind of boundary-marking activity may create a comfortable space in which reflexivity, moderation, and reciprocity are nurtured. But it may also be a relatively narrow space, open only to certain kinds of identities, or to the expression of particular issues or conversational styles. Broadening these spaces entails an incredible amount of work. The best example of this is the extent to which PCP and Common Ground must go to open communities organized along racial or religious lines. Simply to get individuals to participate in a broadened community discussion, these organizations conduct a great deal of pre-meeting exercises with individual participants.[24] This work is intended to probe individual values and expectations, to confront participants with opposing views before the group meets, and to allow the organizations to develop a plan for actual discussions.

Of course, most discourse organizations do not have the resources to conduct such intensive exercises. Instead, they skirt the issue by dealing mainly with self-selected groups whose members already feel themselves to be part of a cohesive community. Or, if outreach is conducted, it is limited to the apathetic but primed middle-class, which ostensibly already has certain kinds of experiences, or possesses particular kinds of knowledge and skills that form a basis for commonality. Alternatively, discourse organizations may develop a heavily structured format in which principles of good citizenship are already embedded. For instance, ADSS, Jefferson Center Citizens Juries, and Center for Deliberative Polling groups are randomly selected to represent a wider community. But it is telling that these forums are heavily structured by the discourse organizations. Participants are told explicitly what is required of them and activities are tightly focused.[25] Within this structure—specifying the issues to be discussed and the method of discussion—are embedded specific criteria for appropriate ways of behaving. Because ADSS, Citizens Juries, and Deliberative Polling give participants information on specific issues and devise particular tasks for considering those issues, the organizations invite discussants to assume very specific roles.

Short of dealing with self-selected groups or adopting a heavily rule-bound structure, discourse organizations might work solely with action or policy-oriented groups that themselves are founded upon implicit assumptions of identity and goals and require appropriate behavior for reaching those goals in common. However organizations choose to deal with this paradox of citizenship, it is clear that an implicit notion of citizenship is often linked with other substantive notions of community identity. Without a Herculean effort by the discourse organization, these notions of identity work against inclusiveness and the consideration of issues that might threaten community norms. For the most part, discourse organizations simply avoid this paradox, either by working with small, self-selected groups, or by constructing heavily rule-bound formats that are grounded in particular conceptions of citizenship. But neither of these choices is likely to engage the 20 to 40 percent of Americans who simply refuse to participate in public life.

Good Public Discourse and the Demands of Representation

Aside from this paradox of citizenship, there are other tensions raised by the pressure to achieve particular actions or policies through public discourse. As one moves across group goals from education to policy-making, a stress on the scholarly principle of relationality slowly gives way to an emphasis on reason-giving. For example, organizations that emphasize education and conflict resolution tend to devote a great deal of time to relationship-building. In the NEH National Conversation kit distributed to community groups, discussion leaders were taught to allow participants to make the ground rules, to encourage individuals to speak from their experience, to allow time for participants to reflect on what has been said, and to avoid debates in which group members "try to score points or prove each other wrong."[26] PCP explicitly distinguishes dialogue from debate: dialogue occurs when "the atmosphere is one of safety"; "participants speak from their own unique experience," and they "gain insight into the beliefs and concerns of others."[27] Similarly, Common Ground describes its method as one that stresses a "spirit of dialogue," "looking beyond labels and stereotypes," "connective thinking," "sharing of personal experience," and recognition of a "shared member-ship in society."[28]

As one moves toward cooperation, action, and policy-making, this stress on relationship-building gives way to sifting through policy-oriented infor-mation. For instance, in the SCRC process, groups are encouraged to spend a first session on relationship-building. In the second to fourth meetings, however, groups quickly move to setting goals and developing an action agenda.[29] In its moderator's guide, NIFI encourages its con-versation leaders to "move the conversation beyond sharing . . . stories to looking at costs and consequences of the options."[30] Indeed, it advises leaders to spend no more than fifteen minutes on relationship-building. This contrast is nicely captured by the pre-meeting activities of PCP and Deliberative Polling: where PCP spends a great deal of pre-meeting time in building shared values and norms among the participants, the Delib-erative Polling Center asks its participants to digest packets of informa-tion on the issue at hand. Of course, Fishkin and other action-oriented practitioners might argue that relationships get built precisely by work-ing toward group goals. Without relevant data, it is difficult to assess this claim, but organizations that stress action and policy-making clearly de-vote much less attention to the explicit task of relationship-building. Thus, as groups move toward explicit actions, they spend more time sift-ing through information that will help to produce better decisions, and less on ensuring that the group develops a shared sense of community.[31]

Along with this movement from relationality to reason-giving across group goals, there is a movement from embracing a principle of radical difference (speaking for oneself) toward representation (speaking for larger groups). At a PCP, Common Ground, or NEH National Conversa-tion forum, participants are required to speak from their own unique ex-perience, but this emphasis is absent in an ADSS or Citizens Jury forum oriented to action. Sifting through materials related to social security, it is perfectly appropriate for participants to speak as an "older person who relies on social security to make ends meet" or a "younger person who is skeptical that social security will be there for them." Indeed, in a Citizens Jury or deliberative poll, participants are chosen explicitly because they are intended to be representative of a given community. During the large-group forums of President Clinton's Initiative on Race, participants routinely spoke in the name of entire ethnicities, races, or communi-ties.[32] Participants at Keystone Center meetings are expected to repre-sent stakeholder groups, be it an environmental group, a public agency, or a concerned community. The pressure to action appears to require that participants relinquish the personal view and adopt a more community-minded or representative perspective. One might conclude then, that as one moves across group goals, from education to action, the deliberative model gives way to more representative forms of conversation.

Something very similar occurs as one moves from smaller to larger groups. The key here is the interaction of size, time, and public exposure. Smaller groups are by nature more intimate and informal. Organizations that work with very small groups stress the need for moderation, reciprocity, and reflection. Often, groups are encouraged to begin by setting ground rules. Suggested rules include listening thoughtfully, speaking only for oneself, disagreeing with others in a respectful manner, and seriously reflecting on the views of others. Common Ground encourages groups to create a planning committee which is charged with setting the goals of the group, inviting participants, deciding meeting content, structure and logistics, and establishing dialogue ground rules. The NEH National Conversation instructed its conversation leaders to ensure that discussions are "civil" and that participants show "respect for the views expressed by others." When something potentially inflammatory is said, the guide urges moderators to "ask the participants if they are comfortable with the level of conflict or if the ground rules should be invoked."[33] In the Aria Group's "Action Evaluation" program, reflexivity is put at the center of the process as groups are taught to engage in a constant reflective process on its values and goals.[34] In these smaller group environments, moderation and reciprocity are of paramount concern because the cohesion of the group is of such importance.

Organizations that work with larger groups have greater difficulty in ensuring that moderation, reciprocity, and reflection characterize the proceedings. Reflexivity is difficult to achieve because of time constraints. In an evaluation of a large ADSS forum, Fay Lomax Cook and Lawrence Jacobs found that participants were dissatisfied with the amount of time available to deliberate and reflect upon policy options.[35] Similarly, large-group dynamics make moderation difficult to achieve. In large groups it is hard to get one's point heard, which leads people to be more insistent, and less willing to listen and respond to others. Moderators may also have greater difficulty in controlling these kinds of outbreaks. For instance, many of the meetings of President Clinton's Initiative on Race were disrupted by individuals intent on dominating the proceedings or asserting a particularly combative point.[36] Finally, the larger the group and the more publicity it accrues, the more the proceedings may serve as a platform for individuals wishing to speak for particular constituencies. It is not surprising that the most public of discourse efforts—President Clinton's Initiative on Race—was continually dominated by individuals wishing to speak for particular groups.

There is deep tension, then, between the requirements of deliberative democracy as outlined by the scholarship and as practiced by discourse organizations, and the wider representational political system in which policies are made. The pressure to enter the arena of action may lead groups to dispense with the very relationship-building activities that inspire moderation, relationality, a respect for difference, and reflection.

Large-group dynamics also shape deliberation in ways that may be antithetical to good public discourse. Yet, the representational system functions largely outside the purview of these organizations and the groups they facilitate. It operates by different rules, privileges different kinds of resources, and recognizes different forms of power. The result is a great deal of friction as discourse groups seek to effect positive change in the midst of the representational system.

This tension is nicely demonstrated when actual representatives enter into these deliberative formats. For the most part, discourse organizations prefer to exclude political representatives from their conversations. However, when they are invited, politicians are usually constrained to one of two roles: listening—and only listening—to discussants, or answering questions. For instance, the ADSS teleconferencing manual cautions organizers to constrain elected officials to "listening to the discussion and answering citizen questions."[37] Several organizations go further. The Center for Deliberative Polling, the Jefferson Center, AISR, the Harwood Group, ADSS, NIFI, and SCRC routinely invite representatives to speak with discussion participants. But as Kimelman and Hall found in their study, the resulting conversations are rarely good models of public discourse.[38] Politicians prefer to assume the role of experts in the political process, and seek to educate participants into the logic of group politics. Participants feel that they do not know enough about the relevant issues to engage with representatives as equals. The result is a teacher-pupil form of exchange that rarely moves beyond a question-and-answer session. Moreover, when more sustained conversations are achieved, they may breed more public cynicism. For instance, in a discussion facilitated by the Harwood Group and the League of Women Voters, politicians succeeded so well in convincing participants that Congress would do nothing about campaign finance reform, that "citizens . . . turned bitter and cynical" and questioned the value of deliberation that would not lead to policy change.[39] In the end, participants abandoned principles of good public discourse in favor of stridently criticizing representatives for their inaction.

What Discourse Organizations Know

The contradictions, ambiguities, and uncertainties discussed in the last few pages ought not be taken as an absolute indictment of the discourse practice field. Indeed, discourse practitioners know a great deal about what it takes to practice good public discourse. Perhaps, above all, they know that there is no such thing as one form or format of good discourse. Discourse is inherently rooted in context, and different kinds of context demand different kinds of conversations. In particular, discourse organizations have learned that conversations about values ought to be organized differently from conversations about actions. For instance, disagreements between pro- and anti-abortion activists are not likely to be reduced by the distillation of more policy information or the convening of a debate. In the same way, conversations about action plans and policy proposals generally assume that fundamental values are already shared. When there is a mismatch between format and group goals, conversations break down very quickly. President Clinton's Initiative on Race illustrates this point. For a conversation about race—an issue on which there is a great deal of value conflict—President Clinton convened a commission of experts to devise a series of policy proposals. Given the amount of value conflict, it is not surprising that the Commission's large-group conversations with the community went awry. The more the Commission sought information about the issue, the more communities refused to address it on those terms.

At the same time, discourse organizations (at least) implicitly know that good public discourse almost always begins with relationship-building. No public conversation can succeed without a minimal common recognition of shared values. This is true as much for community groups oriented to civic education as it is for groups geared to policy discussions. Even the most action-oriented discourse organizations build time into their formats for sharing experiences, building relationships, and discussing basic values. Often, this is very little time, but this is due more to the desires of group participants than to the wishes of the organizers themselves. Most participants want to see real results and become impatient with conversations that do not immediately satisfy this desire.

Whatever the desires of group participants, however, discourse organizations know that the most important result of these interactions is the construction and maintenance of a shared sense of belonging. All of the evaluation studies I have reviewed found that participants come out of the experience feeling more informed and more connected to public life and to their communities. As Michael Delli Carpini found with respect to the Harwood Group's forums, "participants became significantly more informed about politics, significantly more likely to say that they were engaged in political action of various kinds, and significantly more efficacious about their ability to understand and affect their government."[40] This feeling remained for at least six months at the time of follow-up interviews. Of course, these Citizens Assemblies had no success in pressuring Congress to reform campaign finance laws. By this measure, they were failures. But discourse organizations know that this is not the final, or even the most important, measurement of success. Instead, discourse organizations make their most important impact in the excitement over community involvement, the feeling of being personally empowered, and the instigation to public action, to reaching out beyond one's private life to share in issues of common concern. For at least the 50 to 75 percent of the population targeted by these organizations, relationship-building is the key positive virtue to emerge from participation in these initiatives.

What Discourse Organizations Don't Know

Of course, the knowledge that discourse organizations have produced may pertain only to that apathetic but primed middle group. For all that they have learned about engaging the public, discourse organizations have not discovered a way to reach that third of the public which simply does not participate in public life.[41] Creating representative samples of the population, as ADSS, Deliberative Polling, and Citizens Juries have done, is one method of ensuring that these groups are represented. But while it puts an individual or two at the table, this method is not likely to stimulate wider involvement among this population. These conversations are singular events, and do not speak to the conditions—economic, political, cultural, and social—which structure nonparticipation within these populations. Other models, such as that of SCRC, have achieved better results by turning to local institutions such as churches and schools to reach these individuals.[42] No data exist yet on the usefulness of this method. However, to the extent that less participatory people are isolated from leading social institutions, this approach is not likely to draw out a significant part of this population. It is therefore fair to say that discourse organizations have not yet devised proven methods for reaching the hard core of the population which resists community involvement.

In terms of the formats themselves, discourse organizations also do not know which discourse practices work in what contexts and why. Aside from the NIFI, initiated in 1982, the discourse organizations in this study were all begun in the last ten years, and many of them in the last five years. Given this timeline, it is not surprising that few have conducted rigorous evaluations to determine whether or not and under what conditions their programs work. Of the sixteen organizations in the study, five have conducted significant evaluations: NIFI, the Harwood Group, the Pew Center for Civic Journalism, the Deliberative Polling Center, and ADSS. SCRC has commissioned several evaluation efforts that are not yet completed. The primary method of these evaluations has been pre- and post-test attitudinal surveys. That is, evaluators survey participants before and after participation in the program to determine relevant attitudinal changes. This method is intended to determine the size of the format's effect on individual participants, but this is only one measure of program success and does not reveal how discourse practices achieve their results. SCRC has initiated just such a study, aptly named the Best Practices Evaluation. But this evaluation, involving an ethnographic investigation of six study circles projects, has only just begun and data will not be available for some time. Absent this kind of research, discourse organizations may have intuitions about what works and why, but cannot substantiate those intuitions with rigorous social science research.

More broadly, the lack of evaluation means that these programs cannot answer several crucial questions: Does discourse produce better political outcomes? Does participation in these programs produce better citizens? Are actions or policies initiated on the basis of discursive interactions better than actions and policies taken on the basis of traditional politics? As I discussed in my earlier survey of principles, some scholars have warned that political outcomes derived from discourse may be no better than those reached by other means.[43] Of course, these questions are unanswerable without the necessary research, but it is unclear that discourse organizations even want to know the answers. After all, what if it were found that deliberation produces worse outcomes, that is, more intolerant or illiberal decisions? The foundations that bankroll most discourse organizations would not take kindly to being associated with efforts that were found to produce morally unsatisfying political outcomes. Discourse organizations have been slow to commission work that addresses these issues.

Finally, discourse organizations do not know how to integrate deliberative and representative models of politics into a unified deliberative format. Aside from the issue of evaluation, this is the most crucial dilemma facing these organizations. Citizens may be cynical about the political system, but it is in the arena of group politics that most policy-making gets done. This form of politics, with its stress on coalition-building and bargaining, is in many ways antithetical to the deliberative ideal: a community of individuals reaching, if not political consensus, then at least political compromise, through dialogue. Preaching the power of deliberation may get citizens into the tent of these formats, but participants anticipate that their conversations will end in concrete political outcomes. Even if they go away from the process feeling more informed and connected to the public sphere, they still demand that actions flow from their participation. Sometimes this demand is satisfied: new programs are initiated, public parks are built, and policy options are pursued. But more often these conversations do not end in new policies. Indeed, given the role of interest group politics in the political process, it is surprising that discourse communities ever have an impact. This is a significant obstacle to the continued growth of the public discourse movement. To capture the imagination of a wide public, these organizations will either have to form stronger links to the political system or convince a skeptical public that conversation without this link is still worthwhile.

What Needs to Be Done

To solve these sorts of problems, there is a pressing need for more research on these organizations, and public discourse generally. In six

months of research, I discovered exactly two scholars who have devoted
attention to these organizations: Michael Delli Carpini, then of Brown
University and as of July 2003 Dean of the Annenberg School of Communication at the University of Pennsylvania, and John Gastil of the University of Washington. Aside from the Center for Democracy and Citizenship
at the University of Minnesota (Harry Boyte, director), and the Walt
Whitman Center for the Culture and Politics of Democracy (Benjamin
Barber, director), which also conduct some research in this area, that is
the extent of the academy's interest in these organizations. Of course,
there are many other organizations involved in the practice of public discourse and community-building.[44] But in the midst of this activity there is
precious little data collection and knowledge-building. Rigorous evaluation is therefore a pressing need in this field. Researchers must move beyond the pre- and post-test attitudinal methodology that has been favored
in the past to conduct more extensive, multimethod, longitudinal studies.
Comparative ethnographic research would be helpful, as would careful
discourse analyses of the ways in which deliberative formats have structured language use, role-playing, and conversational outcomes. These,
however, are just two suggestions; evaluation is presently a wide-open issue in the field and any number of methodologies would be appropriate.

A number of individuals who work in the field have also indicated a
desire to link discourse efforts across localities, regions, and the nation as
a whole. Currently, most communities organize discourse groups either
as short-term affairs or as preeminently local forums. The result is that
they have very little connection to other discourse efforts, and therefore
cannot draw from the wisdom and power of collaborative efforts. In the
SCRC process, for instance, communities across the nation hold study
circles, and many of them link individual study circles across the city. But
study circles are not linked nationally or even across regions. The same
can be said for most of the other discourse organizations in this study.
The ADSS project and its sister organization America*Speaks* (which ran
ADSS for the Pew Charitable Trusts) has done the most in this area.
ADSS has convened discussions on Social Security that link communities
regionally and nationally, and has produced a guide for conducting regional and national teleconferences.[45] America*Speaks* has provided technical support for a Web-based community discourse process in Washington
state (called Sno-Net), and has held a series of conferences with partners
from Limestone, Maine, Englewood, New Jersey, Chattanooga, Tennessee, and several other communities to make connections and share
experiences. But more work of this kind is needed—more thinking on
how to use technology to link larger groups in deliberation, and how to
structure these discussions so that they abide by principles of good public
discourse.

The extension of public discourse in this manner requires both scholarship and the practical wisdom of discourse practitioners. Unfortunately,

however, there has been little interaction between these two groups. To stimulate more and better exchanges, scholars and practitioners might be recruited to participate in a common project, such as a "state of public discourse" indicators initiative. Indicators are statistics, or aggregates of statistics, that illuminate trends within particular social domains.[46] For example, local and national groups have developed sets of indicators to track trends in environmental and social conditions that contribute to community sustainability.[47] This kind of project might be conducted for the health of our nation's public discourse. A working group of scholars and practitioners could be brought together to develop a list of key indicators; researchers assisting this group would then collect time series data on these indicators to develop a picture of the state of public discourse and where it is heading in the near future. The group might even publish a report card on public discourse, to be issued annually as a gauge for how well the country is doing in this area. Not only would this project serve as a barometer of our public discourse, and thus as a guide to action, it would also function as an opportunity to bring scholars and practitioners together. Together, this group could work to reach consensus on what a good public discourse is, how it is best achieved, and which indicators might illuminate the successes and failures of discourse efforts.

It might also participate in solving one of the most difficult issues facing the deliberative democratic model: how to reach that 20 to 40 percent of the population that currently falls outside the purview of discourse organizations. What is the exact size of this group? What prevents them from participating in public life? How might programs be developed to reach them in an effective manner? Discourse organizations have found that relationship-building is key to reaching the primed but apathetic middle of our population. That is, before action can take place, trust and solidarity must be built. One hypothesis might be that this equation is reversed for the obdurately apathetic. Deeply suspicious of dominant institutions and social groups, this population initially might be reached only through effective action, such as the redevelopment of neighborhoods. Through action, a certain degree of trust might be built, which could then serve as a foundation for better deliberation in the future. In this case, action must precede deliberation. This is only a hypothesis. The point is that a working group of scholars and practitioners might build a research agenda based in scholarship and practice to achieve what heretofore has been impossible to accomplish: the creation of deliberative models that are truly inclusive and thus truly democratic.

Chapter 17

Lessons from the Field: Practitioner Perspectives on Public Discourse Programs

A Roundtable Discussion with Members of the Penn National Commission

Led by Jay Rosen

What elements are essential in creating and sustaining meaningful dialogue about complex and often controversial public issues? Members of the Penn National Commission on Society, Culture and Community examined this question on 9 November 1999 in a plenary discussion with representatives from four exemplary discourse organizations—America*Speaks*, the Common Ground Network for Life and Choice, the Kettering Foundation, and the Study Circles Resource Center. Selected on the basis of David M. Ryfe's systematic review of sixteen such organizations,[1] these four participants represented both the variety of approaches to public discourse and community dialogue and some of the nascent national discourse movement's most experienced and successful practitioners.

- **Study Circles Resource Center**
  The Study Circles Resource Center, directed by Martha McCoy, brings large numbers of citizens in communities together for "democratic discussion and problem solving" at the local level on key issues, including race relations, diversity, education reform, crime and violence, and immigration. The program creates small study circles of people who talk about public issues in a community setting. McCoy described the Study Circles Resource Center as a program to think about how "face-to-face discussion" could become "an ongoing part of the way a community does its business." The Study Circles Resource Center has worked in 150 communities of various sizes in every region of the country, in groups ranging from hundreds to thousands. McCoy described the Study Circles as "laboratories of democracy."

* **Common Ground Network for Life and Choice**
  Mary Jacksteit directed the Common Ground Network for Life and
  Choice, a project of Search for Common Ground, based in Washington, D.C. Common Ground intervenes in the politics of abortion by
  creating a space for dialogue between pro-choice and pro-life people. They have worked in more than twenty states to create a dialogue between people who are ordinarily on opposing—and highly
  combative if not armed—sides of an issue. Common Ground starts
  with an intense conflict and, as Jacksteit explained, "believes that if
  we can change the conversations going on between the opponents,
  then we can change the conflict" through changing the discourse
  about it. Jacksteit envisioned the project as moving the debate, and
  its parties, "from one that's defined solely by their disagreements to
  one in which the disagreements are there, but their relationship can
  encompass areas of agreement, areas of common values, and a real
  understanding of the issues." Once common interests and values are
  identified, Common Ground hopes to redirect resources and energy
  to human and social problems about which there is some agreement.
  People can then begin to think about "the things around the abortion issue," not just the irresolvability of the issue itself.

* **America*Speaks***
  Carolyn Lukensmeyer founded America*Speaks*, which aims to create
  deliberative and genuine face-to-face dialogue among citizens that
  can be "taken to scale"—that is, register at the national level, or connect to national policy-making in a way envisioned by the country's
  founders. America*Speaks* uses technology to link citizen dialogues on
  issues such as Social Security, education, and the environment to national policy-makers and members of Congress. America*Speaks* cele-
  brates the "extraordinary foundation" of democracy in "small,
  face-to-face, authentic dialogue, the original New England town hall
  meetings." This concept, according to Lukensmeyer, "has resonance.
  Citizens have pride in it." Yet the town meeting clashes with the media time cycle and Congressional processes for decision-making.
  America*Speaks* convenes demographically diverse groups of citizens
  in cities across the country to discuss issues such as Social Security
  and then share their positions with national political leaders. Citizens
  develop their positions in follow-up meetings and share their views
  with national political leadership via interactive, two-way satellite
  connections. America*Speaks* inverts the hourglass of political discourse
  so that citizens "are on top and the politics are on the bottom."

* **Kettering Foundation Public Policy Institutes and National Issues
  Forums**
  Robert McKenzie works with the Kettering Foundation's Public

Policy Institutes, which train people in the art of moderating and cultivating public deliberation in National Issues Forums held across the country. The National Issues Forums are an ongoing network of community-based groups that create deliberative face-to-face dialogue led and moderated by facilitators trained by Kettering. The Kettering Foundation's work deals centrally with the question of "what it takes to make democracy work."

Linking Talk and Action

All panelists agreed that citizens will not participate in "talk for the sake of talking," as Lukensmeyer characterized it. "The first thing people ask about a program like this," McCoy of Study Circles said, "is, 'Is this just more talk or is it going to lead to change in the community?' " For large numbers of people to participate, McCoy concluded, conversations must be linked to action, change, and decision-making. Jacksteit of Common Ground observed that entrenched opponents on even as contentious an issue as abortion will have a dialogue if, quite simply, they are asked to do so. If "you invite people into something that is new, and you say it is new," Jacksteit commented, they will participate in good faith. As McCoy observed of the Study Circles, participants in Common Ground dialogues have "had lots of debates with each other, and they are not interested in more of the same." Jacksteit emphasized that sponsors must "make it very clear that this will be different, and make sure that it is different." Be "plain, open, intentional, and responsible about inviting people to a conversation that will be something other than what they've had." Lukensmeyer traced this frustration with "talk for talk's sake" to citizens' awareness of a "break in the fabric" between talk and action, especially at the national level. Because the panelists perceived a rupture between the discourse of citizens and effective political action, they emphasized that public discourse and deliberation must be linked to some concrete actions or outcomes, on a local or national scale. In order for deliberation to be connected to action, public deliberations should be coordinated with organizations that can effect change. McCoy noted that deliberations should be sponsored by "large groups of institutions, broad-based coalitions of institutions at the community level that would bring people into the deliberation and prepare, during the deliberation, to connect it back to change in institutions and policy-making at the community level." This action component must be built into the process itself, and participants in the conversation should take part in implementing the solutions that they develop.

Study Circles combine the strengths of small-group processes with those of large-group processes. Community coalitions sponsor small-group study circles, which are going on all over the community at the same time. This capitalizes on the small-group process, but also connects to the possibility for "community-wide institutional change and policy change at the local level." Like McCoy, Lukensmeyer urged that dialogues should not be initiated "unless they . . . link to the people who make decisions at the front end." Given high levels of cynicism toward citizen action, "we do a disservice to people to invite them once more to the table to talk, unless there's a link to people who can do something about it." This goal requires that universities, corporations, government, media, and other institutions must be prepared and readied to "take citizen voices seriously." Indeed, Lukensmeyer sensed more skepticism among people that they can make a difference in the media than the government, noting that participants have not been educated to believe that they can put demands on the way a newspaper or television station covers issues. Lukensmeyer sees that "Americans still fundamentally believe in our system enough that they're not demanding a total change in structure in order to participate, but they have to see an impact or an influence of their work."

Jacksteit cautioned, however, that the link between public discourse and action may be an obstacle, not an enticement, on some topics and themes. "To start with an end in mind is actually counterproductive in a difficult issue like abortion," she observed. Although Common Ground aims to link public discourse with long-term positive changes, "even the thought of being possibly identified as a working partner with someone else is extremely threatening" in the lethally divisive abortion debate. In these cases, "low commitment is exactly what you need to promise people." Common Ground makes clear to participants that they are not committing themselves to "doing anything other than coming here and talking."

Learning to Talk: Designing Good Public Discourse

Panelists articulated a paradox that public discourse is both a natural act, in Robert McKenzie's terms, and something that must be taught, practiced, cultivated, and heavily facilitated to be truly effective and meaningful. All agreed that good talk or effective public discourse does not just naturally emerge once citizens are placed in a room to discuss an issue. McKenzie elaborated, "Deliberative democracy is a recessive gene in the political makeup," easily overpowered by "other ways of thinking about politics." Although "deliberation is a natural act," performed each day as citizens make decisions about, say, where to go to dinner, "we tend to forget that we know how to deliberate when we get into politics." Good discourse "doesn't just happen," McCoy observed. "You can't just walk up to somebody at the post office and say, 'Hey, what do you think of race? Let's sit down and talk about it.'" Although good political discourse has atrophied, McKenzie argued, "citizens have responsibilities" in a democracy "that can be delegated to no one else. Democracy requires citizens," he noted, "and we have to build those citizens." Deliberation must be reintegrated into politics as the first step in a process whereby citizens learn to "talk together" so that they can "think together," so that they can "choose together," so that, eventually, they can "act together" politically, as democracy requires. How is an effective deliberative citizenry achieved?

All panelists noted that good public discourse requires a great deal of structure and forethought. Lukensmeyer dismissed as an excuse the claim that Americans are apathetic about politics, and argued instead that they have not been "invited to talk in a way that is meaningful." Leaders "are not designing or structuring" such discourses for citizens and are "not linking them to the institutional fabric" that makes decisions. Panelists identified several specific structures for good public discourse. First, the design of the room and the deliberative space communicates expectations about the event to follow. America*Speaks*, for example, in its Americans Discuss Social Security (ADSS) project, "upended the design" of the contemporary town hall meeting. It reversed the paradigm of "experts up front," auditorium style, with two microphones, where the "panel takes 80 percent of the time, and the audience gets 20 percent, at best," in a question-and-answer session. Instead, the room with its round tables suggested a level playing field. Members of Congress traveled from table to table and then listened to summaries of the conversations and reacted to those comments. Lukensmeyer counted as one of the deepest successes of America*Speaks* that "twenty-two members of Congress took what we did seriously enough that they will never run a town hall meeting again the way they had been trained to run them."

McCoy designs study circles with many key features in mind. She underscored that meetings must convene diverse participants—"racially diverse, socioeconomically diverse, ideologically diverse, gender diverse, all sorts of diversity within the group, and also role diverse." Counterintuitively, McCoy found, this means that organizations in the community with particular constituencies or points of view—for example, a church, a branch of the NAACP, and so on—are not necessarily the best organizations to sponsor conversations. The discourse should be structured, instead, so that participants "are not sitting with their interest group or specialization. They are sitting there as community members in all their diversity." Lukensmeyer agreed that individuals and organizations facilitating public discourse on difficult issues must be "honest neutral brokers," from both citizens' and Congress's point of view. Initially America*Speaks* feared that their absolute neutrality on Social Security would render them irrelevant to Congress, but "it turned out to be our largest asset."

Beginning the Conversation

Panelists emphasized that to facilitate effective discourse and talking together, issues must be framed initially and introduced with the greatest
care to create what McKenzie called an "emotional and intellectual public
space" for citizens to do their work. Before conversation or deliberation
even begins, issues must be framed "relative to what the people consider
valuable. That's not in a polarized fashion, and that's not in an ideological fashion."

Creating this "emotional and intellectual public space" may entail approaching topics from new and more inviting perspectives. McCoy found
that small group conversations have "to begin where people are." In effective public discourse, people have a chance initially to talk about why
they care about the issue, what it means in their lives, and what their experiences with the issue have been. This establishes an entirely different—
and ultimately richer and more productive—dynamic than beginning the
conversation by declaring, for example, "Today we're going to talk about
affirmative action." In that case, McCoy commented, "people will draw
the same lines they will draw in almost any political debate." But "if you
first sat down together to say, 'Tell me your experiences with racism and
race relations,' and then by session two or three, talk about affirmative
action, the discussion will be very different."

Similarly, on contentious issues such as abortion, participants may first
need to reorient their thinking to identify shared values and concerns.
Common Ground envisions their discourse as a "Venn diagram—two
overlapping circles," Jacksteit said. "Our assumption has been that pro-
choice and pro-life advocates don't live in totally separate worlds, although their perception is that they do. But in fact, they overlap, and
while there are significant areas of difference, there is this area of common ground which has been obscured and the existence of which is denied for all kinds of reasons by the prevailing debate."

Ground Rules for Deliberation

Panelists all agreed that effective public discourse requires clear ground
rules for how participants talk to one another, and benefits from heavy
facilitation and guidance. Again, since public discourse is both a natural
act and an acquired skill. As McKenzie described, National Issues Forums established "guidelines for deliberation that allow people to learn
together . . . and there's an art and a science to that." Lukensmeyer also
observed that conversations must be heavily facilitated, especially since
participants are not "taught to discourse" in school or society. Common
Ground, for example, asks participants to "make a commitment to how
they will treat other people, the kind of language they will use," and to

recognize that "this is not an opportunity to try to convince people of their point of view," according to Jacksteit. With those ground rules in place, she has seen that "a new conversation absolutely will happen." In fact, Jacksteit was astonished in her work with people's willingness to have a dialogue on abortion, and to participate in a new kind of conversation, once they were given an opportunity to do so. "These conversations are not difficult for people who have been given an opportunity to have them," she concluded. In the course of deliberation, participants need opportunities to consider and reflect upon all points of view; otherwise, McCoy described, the conversation "will tend toward the extreme," with few opportunities for citizens to reflect on others' positions and, perhaps, change their own. Deliberation differs from "drive-by conversation," as McCoy called it, because "people actually listen to each other and have a chance to consider different points of view."

In order to build relationships, trust, and honesty among participants in public discourse, conversations should occur over several meetings and extended periods of time. Good discourse requires, as McKenzie noted, "repetitive getting together" so that citizens can build genuine and more complex relationships with one another. McCoy also discovered that "one time isn't enough" to cultivate effective public discourse. "People need opportunities to sit down together face to face in groups over time," she said. Sponsors of public discourse may need to acknowledge the risks and chances that some participants take in simply talking with different constituencies. Common Ground openly acknowledges the consequences for participants in their dialogues. "They may not find themselves as comfortable in their own movement as they have before, and that's just part of being a responsible intervener. They may no longer be trusted, they may have to spend a lot of time explaining what they're doing, giving credibility to the other side," Jacksteit said. Leaders and organizations that sponsor better public discourse on difficult topics "need to support the people who will embrace it, because they will find themselves part of a new movement with no constituency," she argued.

Scaling for Impact: What Difference Can Talk Make?

Jacksteit noted the difficulty of bringing good public discourse to scale, a problem that also emerged from David Ryfe's review of discourse organizations.[2] But Jacksteit recognized that impact can be measured in a variety of ways aside from the political process itself. Other positive goals and benefits of good public discourse on divisive issues include lessening the tension in communities around that topic—the level of civility—and fostering a reallocation of energy away from destructive debates between entrenched parties and toward the fulfillment of social services that both sides agree are important. The project contributes to sustaining communities faced with possibly irresolvable differences: "How do you live in a community which may be your town, your state, or your nation in the presence of an irresolvable conflict? That's really what it's about" with the abortion question, she concluded. Lukensmeyer's initiative did link local, face-to-face discourse with national policy leaders and discourse. It changed both the particular discourse about Social Security and other general features of political discourse. Among other things, its conversations "set a different standard for polling" on Social Security, encouraging a move away from "quick read" questions to more neutral and thoughtful questions.

Principles for Effective Public Discourse

Panelists agreed that much of the effort to create effective public discourse begins before the deliberation itself. All the participants and the four exemplary discourse organizations they represented underscored that good discourse is surprisingly easy, in some cases, if citizens are invited to participate in a new kind of conversation with one another. They agreed that potential participants will not respond to an event that promises "talk for the sake of talk." They emphasized the importance of convening a truly diverse group of deliberators, who sit not with their constituencies but with others from the community, and having "honest, neutral brokers" to sponsor the deliberation. The design of the room should communicate a link between talk and action, and should reduce status disparities among citizens, experts, and national policy-makers. Goals and outcomes should be clear for participants at the outset, whether these goals are increased civility in the local community or citizen impact on national policies.

The conversation itself should be heavily facilitated, with trained moderators. Panelists agreed that the issue under discussion must be framed and introduced very carefully, to create an "emotional and intellectual public space," in McKenzie's terms, as well as a literal public space, for discourse. This means introducing contentious and difficult topics with an eye toward common values rather than opposing views, and allowing participants to start their conversation by reflecting on what the issue has meant to them personally. Panelists concurred that simply asking participants to "talk about abortion," for example, will not yield new or productive public discourse. To build genuine deliberative relationships of trust, participants should meet several times, not just once. Panelists emphasized that it is critical to establish ground rules for effective conversation. Although, paradoxically, discourse is a natural act, it is what McKenzie calls a "recessive gene" in political discourse. Participants should learn the art of public discourse through a commitment to rules and guidelines for how they will treat each other throughout the conversation. The dividends for good public discourse, however difficult to achieve, are immense. "Deliberation produces public knowledge," McKenzie reported, "that can be obtained in no other way. It reveals what people are thinking, not just what they think." Rather than underscore opinions and sides, deliberation raises awareness of trade-offs and other knowledge that is particularly valuable in the democratic process.

Part Six

Creating Community Through Public Discourse

Chapter 18
Building Community in the Twenty-First Century

Joyce Appleby

While many Americans express despair about a lost community spirit, a new breed of community-builders has taken on the task of using new centers and modes of public discourse to bring people together to shape their own environments and to express both shared and disparate values and experiences. Forward-looking, tough-minded, and pragmatic, these men and women (most of them under fifty) are reshaping the meaning of community at the start of a new century. Rather than lament the passing of archetypal neighborhoods, they are exploring the potential for community-building by accepting the complexity and diversity of American towns and cities.

Nodes for new types of sustained interaction—an antiseptic way of defining community—are multiple. They include museums, historical societies, labor action groups, welfare recipients meetings, mothers, associations, and environmental societies. These new efforts at bringing people together have in common a realistic vision of the future, an acceptance of changes in American society, and a conviction that ordinary men and women can be effective in building communities, given a little help. What they provide, in many cases, is an outsider's assist to start the conversations, canvass effective ways of building networks, and provide the necessary moral and financial support.

Museums, many of them anchored to buildings in deteriorating urban zones, have reconceptualized what museums are for, reaching out to families through their children. Even more remarkable, they are laying out paths to participation in our national culture through the byways of ethnic identities. The downtown location of museums has prompted decades of hand-wringing about mission, yet it is proving to be a new strength as museums become centers for urban renewal. The riches of old collections and the generous architecture of earlier periods have given museums entries into city life as the sites for community gatherings. But none of these changes has evolved naturally; they have taken years of thinking about the challenges posed by an increasingly mobile and fragmented population. Most important, new initiatives have begun with finding ways to talk about what is needed and turning those needs into challenges. Committed to preserving traditions, both established museums and start-up, shoestring societies to preserve a small group's unique customs have discovered the power of diverse artistic expressions in bringing people together in common acts of appreciation.

For foundations, community-building has become the mantra of the past decade, the catchphrase for efforts to close the distance between knowledgeable professionals and the poor families they serve. With whole neighborhoods assaulted by unchecked violence, asocial teenagers, toxic environments, fleeing jobs, deteriorating schools, and indifferent public officials, foundations have responded to the imperatives of urban decay. Foundations have many things to offer: guidance in how to start to address problems, experience in creating the sites for people to come together in the community's interest, backing for innovative nonprofit groups, and know-how in formulating plans for redressing grievances, whether it be checking the proliferation of neighborhood liquor stores or agitating against toxic waste dumping.

While many people have found communal comfort in their churches, synagogues, and mosques, they and others have also responded enthusiastically to the efforts of foundational community-builders to engage local residents in cooperative projects in the civic realm. These impromptu organizations, usually formed to correct a particular situation, strengthen communities indirectly. They create the social experiences and collective memories that lengthen and strengthen social ties. They have also led to coalitions that cross religious and racial lines. The separatism promoted by the ethnic identity movements of two decades ago has given way to a recognition that real social change will require a common front and a lot of mutual patience. It is difficult not to be impressed by the yeasty proliferation of action groups in all our cities, but their ultimate success remains uncertain. Working outside the framework of municipal governance, they encounter both resistance and indifference from officials. The pressured schedules and organized leisure of urban professionals work against mobilizing more affluent volunteers. Even within their own organizations, innovators struggle with the rigidities put in place by institutional regulations.

Foundations, for instance, are normally confined to funding organizations with 501(c)(3) federal tax status, leaving inventive, new enterprises without the funds to experiment in a field where experimentation is very much needed. It is a fertile mix: professional students of community action and the latent talent for leadership among those living in troubled neighborhoods. Development of communication skills frequently acts as the critical catalyst in moving proto-communities into successfully organized groups, whether brought together by problems, ethnicity, or an affinity of interests. These developments are racing ahead of efforts to collect and analyze information on their success and failure.

This essay examines community-building efforts that began with political action and social engagement sponsored by a wide variety of institutions. It examines how foundations are revising their philanthropic approaches, how outreach programs from museums have cemented community ties, and how activists have reinvigorated political consciousness among America's poorest citizens. It summarizes the obstacles that professionals have encountered in their efforts to help towns and cities attain the *e pluribus unum* of American hopes. The efforts described, heroic as they are in many cases, reflect an unwillingness on the part of the public and its elected officials to address many of the problems affecting poorer communities and the life chances of their members. Without the imaginative outreach of a new group of professionals in museums, universities, foundations, and other philanthropies, American neighborhoods would be in much worse condition. To say this is not to subscribe to the idea that other private sector entities can successfully nurture American civic life without the help of government.

American Communities in Historical Perspective

Nostalgia is the price that Americans pay for their mobility, and community has been its focus. Over the years, pundits and their audiences have invested the idea of community with an elusive and evocative appeal. Towns may be neutral and cities dangerous, but a community is good, so good that the word does constant duty as a metaphor. Nostalgia is pervasive, but rests on a weak factual foundation when it suggests that in a different era people stayed put, raised their families, fought and had fun together, and knew themselves to be a corporate entity.

While the pace of change was once slower, Americans have always been on the move. Mining and industrial employers expected workers to move to where the jobs were, not vice versa as in Europe. Landless Americans who wanted farms had to move where land was cheaper, and many kept moving with each opening of the national domain. The twentieth-century service economy has repeatedly lured people to move with opportunities and promotions. The appeal of the frontier has consistently pulled Americans west. Foreigners have never ceased to be amazed at the ease with which we pull up stakes. Most men and women in the United States— of all backgrounds—have, over the past four centuries, known what it means to be uprooted, willingly or not. Immigrants in this nation of immigrants became Americans by the act of breaking the ties of custom and traveling a long distance. Sometime in the last quarter century, LAX surpassed Ellis Island as the recipient of the largest aggregate number of immigrants, and the flow continues. Families churn through America's cities and suburbs. Even when people stay put, their neighborhoods undergo transformation under them, with new ethnic configurations in the nation's still largely segregated housing or turns of the gentrification-decay wheel of fortune.

To speak of community building at the dawn of the twenty-first century is to take on the legendary "lost community" myth and replace it with a franker look at Americans and their social interactions. In the absence of residential permanence, Americans have developed a variety of pre-dominant associational capacities: They have developed their talent for making, unmaking, and remaking social ties, whether based on religious denominations, parent-school groups, or hobbies. More age-conscious than other societies, Americans change their patterns of conviviality as the age and composition of their families change. Americans show a strong preference for voluntary and informal activities over those that are pre-scribed, official, or compulsory. Institutions never sank deep footings in American soil, and the successful American Revolution left an ideological legacy that stresses independence over dependence and individual initia-tive over collective action. Americans know how to cooperate easily with people they do not know. The British historian, Dennis Brogan, once commented that only in the United States was "stranger" a friendly greeting, as in "Howdy, Stranger." Americans have a healthy apprecia-tion of friendliness, even the commercial friendliness that started them telling one another, "Have a good day." Americans can easily form volun-tary groups for concerted action and just as easily abandon them, keep-ing only one or two friendships or none. They prefer communities of affinity and choice.

This sunny list of American predispositions represents the optimal so-cial qualities from which communities in the twenty-first century can be built. Impermanence should be accepted as a deep cultural tendency, if not an actual preference. Unhappily, alongside these predispositions ex-ist lingering racial prejudices, flourishing hate groups, and the routine ne-glect of those left behind in the movable feast of American living. Tapping into Americans' real skills at ad hoc action and impromptu organizing, the new community-builders promote a civic identity for the twenty-first cen-tury that is as flexible as it is portable. Nostalgia for lost communities or efforts to establish these legendary homes will only make theirs a Sisy-phean task.

Foundation Community-Building Efforts

Community-building has been the topic of the decade in the foundation world, engaging people from the most prestigious and established orga-nizations, as well as those acting on fresh ideas of their own. When efforts foundered on the lack of a social framework for the implementation of programs on the ground, some of them turned to building community infrastructures, a more complicated, time-intensive approach, but one with great potential for long-term effects. Those foundations and non-profit groups have discovered as well that developing latent community resources must be a first priority. Along with the discourse of community-building has come the concept of "stakeholders," a term that refers to those in the communities, or more accurately, the residential locations, who are affected by the problems being addressed. Identifying stake-holders, who may well be parents, chamber of commerce officials, or even local gang members, has required considerable preparatory study. Only with a familiarity built up through extensive conversations can community-builders work effectively with stakeholders to prepare plans of action. Fresh as an approach, genuine partnerships with stakeholders have challenged the hierarchical practices of the foundation world, and in some instances created a demand for a new cadre of professionals ca-pable of this hands-on work.

Pushed to the fore is the question of whether foundations can success-fully focus on community-building as an end in itself without using the resolution of particular problems as their means. Questions have arisen about what community capacity is or should be. Such refinements in ap-proach and terminology measure the momentum gathering behind community-building efforts. Constructing a community infrastructure, particularly in neighborhoods with serious problems, requires a longer commitment of time and money than is usually given to the completion of a specific project, with fewer conspicuous results. The more ambitious, even elusive, goal of promoting civic life and political skills has necessi-tated more realistic timetables. The scope of operation has also encour-aged coalitions among like-minded groups, greater communication to all interested parties, and, above all, the nurturing of leadership at the local level.

The premier example of community-building comes from the Casey Foundation–funded Comprehensive Community Initiatives. Operating in almost all major cities in the United States, the CCIs have been able to unify the efforts of more than twenty foundations. CCIs promote eco-nomic development and improve social services by cultivating local tal-ents and using professionals to help volunteers build their own support groups. The Roundtable of Comprehensive Community Initiatives meets periodically to evaluate the CCIs, assessments that end up stressing both the slow rate of progress and the frustration traditional funders feel about this pace.

The Pew Partnership for Civic Change is another national initiative di-rected to smaller cities in the country. Reporting to it are the Pew Civic Entrepreneur Initiatives, which support local leaders in ten cities for a period of two years in a program carefully designed to address urban problems while crossing the fault lines of race and ethnicity. Longer-term Pew funding for civic change has sustained partnerships with cities willing to share the financial burden. More clearly directed toward the development of enterprise and credit facilities in poorer neighborhoods are the Ford Foundation's programs in asset building and community development. Attention paid to building communities has yielded unexpected insights on what makes certain problems intractable and why outsiders can only do so much.

As communities have been reimagined, so has there been a parallel reimagining of community-building itself. On paper, getting stakeholders involved stands out as simple common sense; in practice, the imbalance in skills between professionals and stakeholders has strained partnerships and threatened to turn good intentions into fig leaves. At the same time, the creation of new community groups to work in partnership with outside professionals has inspired resentment among those in existing organizations. In all cases, the attention given to troubled neighborhoods by outsiders has had a mixed and unpredictable impact.

A small foundation like Liberty Hill of Los Angeles has been giving grants to local groups on a competitive basis, funding shoestring operations like a young Hispanic women's cooperative, a low-wage Korean janitorial workers' association, and an after-school family center. Encouraging these small groups to form clearinghouses of information and sociability, Liberty Hill has built communities of activists within the many communities of Los Angeles. Perhaps Liberty Hill's greatest long-term success has come from the cultivation of dozens of community leaders, some of whom have benefited from yet another initiative, the Community Scholars Program, which awards one-quarter fellowships to the UCLA urban planning department. Community-building has also cast into high relief the critical role that communication plays in enhancing community action and creating civic identity. Both informal conversations and public discussions can focus attention, provide safe conduits for emotions, and bring out the range of opinion in any given group. Forming interpretive communities has proved to be an essential first step in community-building as a whole.

Foundations have funded imaginative, ad hoc programs to foster public discourse. Over one hundred grants have been given annually since 1996 to improve civic life through stimulating debate, raising the level of informed opinion, and enriching public discourse. Some of these initiatives have directly addressed community fragmentation by providing safe spaces for exploring religious differences or getting school children to discuss violence. The multiculturalism much talked about in the United States has more recently become a fulcrum for leveraging communication among diverse groups.

New Museum Initiatives

Museums are taking on new responsibilities as community-builders, a portmanteau term that covers an array of civic-minded activities from supplementing school programs to providing sites for town forums and forging coalitions with other local groups concerned about their city's health. The success of many museums in reassessing their mission and becoming support centers for their cities stems in part from a widely felt longing for safe, public space. Museums, once thought of as hallowed repositories of precious artifacts of art and science, have become major generators of community-building energy. Three reasons explain museum involvement in new outreach and pull-in programs. Museums are often physically tied to inner city neighborhoods in trouble; their most loyal supporters are graying; and their professional staffs have imbibed deeply a new philanthropic ethic that foregrounds the elusive physical and moral place that we call community.

Many museums like the Brooklyn Children's Museum found themselves in the center of deteriorating parts of old downtown areas. When prospective subscribers viewed their location as unsafe and unattractive, they faced declining attendance and community support. To turn this situation around, some museum directors have grabbed the nettle of inner city problems and devised ways to become part of a solution. While jobs drained away, hastening the conversion of the old steel belt into the new rust belt, museums, libraries, and zoos in such cities as Boston, Baltimore, Cincinnati, and Brooklyn reassessed their physical assets and discovered in their location opportunities to revitalize their adjacent neighborhoods. In a mobile society, museums have inadvertently demonstrated the power of permanence. Forced to remain with their buildings and collections, they have increasingly sought to halt urban decay as a new responsibility.

Popular tastes have changed as well. Standard exhibitions and performances in music, art, history, and science that once drew steady crowds no longer do so. Museums have had to become more attuned to a larger, more comprehensive audience with tastes more popular than classical. Taking on new assignments has netted new critics at the same time. Many historical museums found themselves in the center of brouhahas, as Americans engaged in a contentious debate about the preferred presentation of the nation's past.

When thrown on the defensive, museums have reacted in various ways, but in all cases, they have become aware of their new communities. In the absence of a consensus about what museums should preserve and display, and with a succession of high-profile, thoroughly politicized controversies, museum directors have had to find better ways to communicate with the public. At worst, they have become timid; at best, they have unpeeled the exterior of their exhibits and revealed how they are put together, along with what their own understandings and assumptions are. In doing this, they have reconstrued their missions in ways that have broadened their "natural" constituency.

Throughout the 1980s and 1990s, attentive Americans became increasingly aware of the consequences of urban neglect, welfare dependency, working class poverty, and the faltering performance of our public schools. The steady media coverage of civic decline has produced a new philanthropic spirit evident in the leaders of public institutions. Having concrete resources at their disposal and being able to draw on the benign image of their institutions, museum directors and their staffs have added community-building to their agendas. Evidence of the new importance placed upon civic outreach in the museum world is the National Award for Museum Service that the Institute of Museum and Library Services (IMLS), based in Washington, D.C., started giving in the early 1990s. As the 1997 citation for the Children's Museum of Indianapolis (CMI) noted, the museum went beyond traditional museum programs "to serve as a catalyst to help our neighborhood be strong, healthy, and vital." At CMI a special department has been established for community initiatives, in partnership with residents and social service agencies, on such developments as an intergenerational day care facility, urban landscape beautification projects, housing developments, and a master urban planning feasibility study.

Working with a different set of possibilities for community-building, the Montshire Museum of Science in Norwich, Vermont, won the IMLS award in 1995 for getting communities to look ahead at the environmental issue of solid waste disposal, gathering information and ideas before mandates came down from government. In this case, the museum helped local residents create a discourse for examining their situation with a series of meetings for the public to engage experts on the subject. Acting on the conviction that communities cannot solve problems without advance planning, the museum made it possible for local residents to get a five-year head start on a problem that would otherwise capture their attention only as a catastrophe featured on the front page of the local paper.

Rallying his fellow high school teachers to the cause of introducing school children to performances and exhibitions of Mexican art, Carlos Tortolero founded the Mexican Fine Arts Center Museum (MFACM) in Chicago in 1982. Working through the city's parks department, the MFACM got an unused building after demonstrating its capacity to mount shows that would educate the local community of Mexican-Americans about their heritage and disseminate to a larger audience knowledge and appreciation of Mexican art, artifacts, and artistic performances. Demonstrating the importance of having sites for community building, the museum has also provided space for political debates and bought a radio station with a six-mile radius to disseminate art news and programming. Fundamentally committed to art education, the MFACM's leadership has been animated by the conviction that the best way to teach is through the hands-on experience that museums can best provide. Tortolero believes in "equity in art," which means challenging two assumptions: that only those of high social status appreciate art, and that only those with special talents enjoy it.

At Chicago's Field Museum, President John McCarter has found that working with the city's United Neighborhood Organizations has plunged the museum into the center of public festivals, swearing-in ceremonies for new citizens, and parent-children activities. The Field also works with nine museums in an after-school program for the city's children that integrates modeling activities with museum visits where model-makers are confronted with the museum's authentic prototypes. Noting that the Field Museum had 72 staff members with Ph.D.s, McCarter stressed the power of his museum to contribute to teacher training and after-school programming. At the same time, the Field is doubling its volunteer force in order to strengthen the infrastructure for its many outreach programs.

Another national leader, Executive Director Robert Archibald of the Missouri Historical Society in St. Louis, is transforming his history museum into what might be called a community center with a memory. Convinced that "history is not a set of facts," Archibald has used the museum to promote "conversations among the living" about what in the past "we've done poorly and what we've done well." This philosophy has helped him make a key fundraising point: "Investment in history is investment in the long-term health of a community."[1]

New initiatives and roles, however, place unusual demands on a museum's staff. The rapid pace of change has made it harder for museums to sustain their conventional efforts as well as their fresh initiatives. On the bright side, museums have become forums for public discussions in a variety of forms. Most museum people want to use their spaces to connect their constituencies with history, with art, with themselves, while also helping them explore different heritages. Paradoxically, mobility has increased people's desire to feel connected to their past and its artifacts.

Tapping into community needs, museums have discovered that it takes someone to do the listening and convening, provide the lunch and the forum through which people can come together, and keep things moving. Without an active agent, momentum slows. Reminding people that museums have safe, attractive urban space has put them in the center of civic life. Do museums have the necessary infrastructure to continue to reach out? Can metropolitan areas keep the support of people in distant suburbs and the new edge cities, while they are cultivating their residential core? Slow to wake up to the diverse communities they serve and need, museum directors are an unlikely set of frontline workers in community building, but that is where they now are.

Conclusions About Contemporary Community-Building Efforts

It would be foolish to underestimate the obstacles and roadblocks confronting the new cadre of professionals who are working with neighborhood stakeholders to build communities in the country's most embattled living areas. On top of a culture of mobility and novelty are piled the problems spawned by poverty. Yet it would be equally unwise not to see that the impetus behind community-building comes from a sound recognition that it is essential to involve those most intimately connected with urban trouble and most likely to benefit from urban development. In focusing attention upon the creation or strengthening of neighborhood networks of concerned residents instead of programs solely administered by professionals, foundations have had to give much greater thought to the social, intellectual, and moral capital in their communities. Equally important has been the attention paid to public discourse. Planners have devised strategies aimed at getting people to express their views, share their understandings, and articulate means for addressing problems. New leaders have emerged from these preparatory acts, as well as unexpected ideas. The latent capacities of local residents have given substance to the claims that working in communities is a two-way learning process. Those foundations or foundation-sponsored efforts that tackle problems yielding only to long-term efforts have inadvertently enhanced the civic capacities of communities: moving entrenched interests and hidebound bureaucracies are tasks of years, even decades—just the kind of sustained involvement that thickens community connections.

Those working to improve the environment, create drug-free zones, or bring social services to neglected areas we could call indirect community-builders. The most recent example of this has come from responses to welfare reform. Recognizing the potential for glitches or even abuses in hastily crafted work programs, electronic check payments, and welfare deadlines, impromptu groups have emerged all over the country. One of their most conspicuous practical entailments has been raising the political consciousness of those imperiled by state and federal changes in welfare provisions. With states awash in money earmarked for the poor, grassroots organizations emerged to initiate programs to establish free savings accounts to receive digital payments, extend child care hours and sites, and even demonstrate the need to augment welfare office equipment in the light of new demands for monthly applications for aid. All of these efforts required the discussions, planning, and social action that enhance civic identity and promote collective responsibility.

Confronting a new regime of philanthropy, those on the front line of community-building efforts isolated six major problems: unrealistic expectations from funders, diversion of time to fund-raising to sustain their efforts, the difficulty of enlisting candidates of color into professional positions, the indifference of wealthier members of affected communities, the fragility of alliances formed, and the current beltway view that private philanthropy can do the tasks formerly assumed by government.

On the positive side, the greatest contribution that those on the front line could imagine would be regular exchanges of information about successes and failures in the community-building effort. Museum directors spoke frankly about the pitfalls of the programs they were championing. Many foundations, they said, had unrealistic expectations of what can be done in community-building, a point underscored by those in foundations who were working on the issue. With more elusive goals and less precise indices of achievement, funders grow restless even though sustainability is a key to ultimate success, with benefits accumulating beyond the life of the funding.

There is a strong sense that social change comes slowly. There have been failures following the infusion of money into an area after some well-publicized disaster had attracted attention. We heard again and again that people with experience need to be frank about the need for longer-term projects, to speak honestly to funders, to accept stricter oversight, and to develop livelier connections between institutional leaders and the people they seek to help. The difficulty of getting and sustaining funding made fund-raising a more necessary and time-consuming task, diverting the attention of museum directors as well as the grassroots organizations that rely upon foundation support.

Directors spoke, too, of the changes that have come with the creation of new wealth that is divorced from the community. Some, however, reported that good community programming made fundraising easier because many donors preferred supporting community programs rather than cultural ones, which are often perceived as a frill. Others agreed that museums' infrastructural support was being eroded because potential donors tended to restrict their giving, donating to outreach educational projects while ignoring the cost of maintaining the institution or mounting the exhibits, both essential to the educational purpose.

The globalization of the American economy, one museum director felt, had undermined the civic leadership once provided by local business men and women and those in the professions. Others drew attention to the changing character of corporate leadership. Where once it came from an elite that took support of the arts for granted, today that sense of responsibility has eroded, if not disappeared altogether. As one professional directing a nonprofit group explained, "In the years that we've been working on the community, there has been a real change, in that when we started there was a clear leader or spokesperson in each of the towns in our cluster, and if you could get to that person you could make things work." Not only is that no longer true, according to him, but he also felt that leaders were not being replaced and that there was more divisiveness at the political level.[2] On the brighter side, some corporations are taking a leading role in new programs for civic improvement and social change. Business for Social Responsibility has enlisted the talents of top management in Rhino Records, Pep Boys, Creative Artists Agency, Time-Warner, Mattel, Ben & Jerry's, Edison International, Taco Bell,

Sony, Amgen, Reebok, Levi-Strauss, and Target Stores, among its 800 members.

While time-consuming and sometimes dispiriting in the short run, the fund-raising efforts of museums and foundations have had the unintended effect of nurturing a new generation of American philanthropists. Every time a foundation, museum, or university seeks funding for its community-building efforts, they are starting a conversation about public needs and civic responsibility. Whether through civic action or cultural expression, their programs advertise the power of shared values and experiences.

The biggest challenge for nonprofit organizations, one museum director maintained, was to cultivate young people, particularly among minority groups. Except for top management, salaries are not high in the nonprofits, which rely upon the intrinsic worth of the work to attract idealistic men and women. Long the preserve of cultivated white men, the venerable institutions that are now in the process of changing their agendas and constituencies need to give more thought to recruitment among minority populations.

Related to the need for a diverse core of professionals in community-building is the lack of trust that many nearby residents feel for their museum. When institutions began to work more actively with their communities, they encountered hostility because of what was perceived as their former indifference or, worse, their maintenance of literal and figurative walls around their white enclave. In addition to the broader social issues arising from racial, class, and value differences, many museums have a history of past neglect of their residential area which must be overcome before they can build the solid partnerships necessary for sound community relationships.

Other museum people have used their physical resources to work directly on the problem of creating civic identity through open forums, city celebrations, and giving access to local associations. Emerging communities, like emerging markets, are extremely fragile. Neighborhoods with serious problems experience even more mobility than those without them. Community activists are subject to more distractions. Even the outsiders running programs are subject to change. "Ours is a changing society with people who have less time, and yet mobile communities need more, not fewer conversations," remarked one director. The challenge, she said, was getting the community "to respond to our initiatives that are in fact the ones that help people cope with change," noting that there "is a feeling of insecurity with constant change." Volunteers, like the people they are reaching out to, come and go. They burn out, or move out, as tougher demands are placed on them, sometimes with insufficient psychic rewards.[3]

The plurality of social and cultural groups with different agendas and aspirations has also weakened community ties. The American dream is seen as having once held Americans together, but now those ties appear frayed. On the move, many families fail to connect with the institutions in their new location. Someone who cares, one person claimed, has to stay put to know who to bring together and how to mediate among the potential participants. As part of the ongoing professionalization of community-building, that person is more and more likely to be a university official, museum director, nonprofit employee, or foundation officer. After two decades of hearing government programs belittled, Americans are inclined to think that charitable institutions and churches can do a better job of dispensing care than state or federal agencies.

Professionals working in the field see significant drawbacks to such an abnegation of public responsibility. As their own long-term community-building projects suggest, poor neighborhoods need more than stopgap aid. With more and more women in the workforce, there are fewer people with substantial amounts of time to donate, and the severity of problems demands the kind of investments that only government can make. The best of all possible worlds would involve a mix of structural assistance from government and bold initiatives from private associations. Both government agencies and private, nonprofit groups have been criticized: the foundations for changing their funding patterns with changing philanthropic trends, if not fads, and government for generating a succession of programs without a clear sense of priorities. As one community service provider said, looking back on the past twenty years, "Without our own endowment, we have always had to chase chic money." Equally daunting has been the issue of race, which is omnipresent in most community-building programs, but rarely addressed directly.[4]

In many cities, the severity and persistence of urban problems have overcome old hostilities among ethnic groups. Over time, too, communication has improved between the largely white cadre of professional program directors and the people of color whose collaboration they seek. Here, more than in any other aspect of community-building, communication must be addressed as a specific program that makes demands on participants' capacity to listen, as well as their speaking ability. What these criticisms point to is the difficulty of the challenges undertaken. Community-builders have revealed that there is a great wealth of latent social capital in all American towns, cities, and suburbs. Intellectual capital has not been depleted, but more could be created. It is actual capital that is in short supply; only long-term, well-funded community organizations can develop the local talent, hands-on knowledge, and personal commitment necessary to do the job. This is particularly important when cultivating civic responsibility among young people. Where there have been programs geared to their needs and abilities, they have responded. One leader said that the public needs to know more about virtuous capital, like that created by the Boston Children's Museum, whose programs have demonstrated the powerful impact of converging efforts in community-building and educational and literacy reform.[5]

Many of the social entrepreneurs, as they are sometimes called, use the latest technology to bind their groups together. Indirectly, they are preparing their participants to use computers and Internet services. With all this innovation, communication among community-builders lags behind individual inventiveness. Everyone whom we talked to in the field urged more sharing of experience among the tens of thousands of professionals and volunteers working on community projects in the United States today. They all seem to have websites, but lack the linkages that would create their own communities of purpose. Exchanges of information about successes and failures are not sufficient to prevent repeated reinventions of the wheel, they reported. Real or virtual symposiums might start a knowledge exchange for these professionals.

If, indeed, community-building is simultaneously a proven corrector of neighborhood deterioration and a Sisyphean task, this fact needs airing. The goal of creating a civic identity to flourish alongside our many other identities is both grand and imperative. Sound public policy also means addressing deep personal yearnings. Americans on the move have difficulty generating communities spontaneously, yet they feel keenly the need for them. Professionals in the nonprofit world are now addressing the next century's signature conundrum: that a vigorous public realm is ever more desired as its creation becomes more problematic.

Recognizing that cultural and nonprofit institutions not traditionally considered the loci of American civil society—universities, museums, libraries, and private and community foundations—have become the new centers of vibrant, diverse discourse communities is a first and essential step toward helping both citizens and the nonprofit professionals who work in those institutions to create such a vigorous and inclusive public culture.

Chapter 19
The Myth of Academic Community

Don M. Randel

University and community have an uneasy and shifting relationship to one another. At one extreme, the university has been thought to be an ideal community—the model community for a larger, usually national community. At the university, this view holds, reason prevails, communication is direct and transparent, and the young are educated to be good citizens and to know how to behave. By extension, literally and figuratively, the university in this view can teach others how to build similar communities with similar virtue. In the process, it can cure a broad range of ills that afflict modern society. At another extreme, the university has been accused of aiding and abetting, in the aftermath of the late 1960s, the breakdown of precisely those notions of community that have justified the university's existence as the model for the larger community. At the university today, the argument goes, there is no respect for the sacred texts and symbols that are presumed to undergird community and national culture; all values, perspectives, and morals are relative, and the whole enterprise, furthermore, costs too much.

Of course, there are many more than two positions, and these two come in a variety of flavors. But it is important to note that these two positions are readily collapsed onto one another. The second position subscribes to the first in principle, but simply locates it in some idealized past and laments that the university today has strayed from the ideal. The argument about the university and community, then, is about history at least as much as it is about the present state of affairs. This history can certainly be profitably studied, and such study is likely to lead to the conclusion that the ideal university shared by these two positions never really existed. In any case, if we are concerned with what to do in reality about the university in relation to society, culture, and community in the twenty-first century, we can perhaps afford to set aside the argument about history, however interesting it may be. How are we doing today and what are our options?

William Readings puts the matter bluntly: "Anyone who has spent any time at all in a University knows that it is not a model community, that few communities are more petty and vicious than University faculties. . . .

And yet the story persists. The University is supposed to be the potential model for free and rational discussion, a site where the community is founded in the sharing of a commitment to an abstraction, whether that abstraction is the object of a tradition or of a rational contract."[1] Dominick LaCapra points out in response that in Readings the leftist critique (according to which the university has become a market-oriented corporation) merges with the critique of the neoconservatives (such as Allan Bloom and others, who see the university as a repository of culture overwhelmed by, or giving in to, various kinds of relativism) and that Readings "is himself so marked by the ideal of the university of culture that he is unable to inquire into the extent to which it was always a phantasm."[2] But that does not make the skepticism of Readings toward the university as a model community wrong. His insight suggests that before worrying about the university's ability to develop communities outside of itself, and before worrying even about whether university students too often contentiously self-segregate along racial and other lines, as has often been lamented, we should think some about how university faculties and administrations behave and what bearing this might have on what our students and society at large could learn from us.

The dominant feature of the culture of the university is the set of disciplines that it embodies and the relationships of these disciplines to one another. This is one of the respects in which the university is sometimes said to be a community of communities. But this set of disciplines has its own history, and it is "a history of conflict," as Gerald Graff observes. "A university is a curious accretion of historical conflicts that it has systematically forgotten. Each of its divisions reflects a history of ideological conflicts that is just as important as what is taught within the divisions yet is prevented from being foregrounded by the divisions themselves."[3] This suggests at a minimum that if universities have something to teach about community building it is not something based on the demonstrated willingness of rational people to put aside their differences and get along with one another for the common good. But it might be something even more important than that: namely, the ability to articulate the struggles between and among disciplines and to demonstrate how these differences are negotiated. This would require that many of the university's apologists and critics become less fearful of our differences and instead come to terms with their inevitability and irreducibility.

The character of individual disciplines and the degree to which each constitutes and forms part of a community has its internal and external aspects. Internally, a discipline, or rather a university department that represents one, is most likely to behave like a community if it has a collective challenge or objective that is clearly beyond the ability of any single individual to meet—that is, when in some sense prosperity, if not survival, for both the individual and the community depends on the ability of the individuals to function as a community. A good example is the large physics department that operates an accelerator. There are leaders, to be sure. But no one person can claim the credit for the scientific results. Papers are published with tens of coauthors. And these departments must even figure out how to decide on tenure for people who have only functioned as part of a collective enterprise and whose individual contribution is not always easy to isolate.

Disciplines or departments in which individual accomplishment predominates over collaborative effort are likely to exhibit different behaviors in the academic and nonacademic spheres. The study of the humanities has largely been a very solitary activity even when there has been some measure of agreement about what ought to be studied and by what method. Simultaneously, the humanities have usually been thought to bear the primary responsibility for transmitting those ideas and values that define the model community, especially as some of the social sciences attempted more and more to emulate the natural sciences in method and degrees of specialization. Thus, it is perhaps not surprising that the humanities receive the harshest criticism for the failure of the university to model community. As both subject and method in humanities were challenged to broaden, incorporating noncanonical topics and new critical theory, the self-image of these fields threatened to dissolve and with it some of the behaviors that might be thought essential to community. Departments of English, for example, regularly became divided into opposing camps on issues such as what to teach, how to teach it, and who ought to be appointed and promoted. As LaCapra observes, "The fragility of disciplinary definitions often breeds intolerance and a penchant for ostracism in those who desire a secure professional identity and identity-forming disciplines at any price."[4] Fields that have resisted pressures on their self-definition may give the impression of being, in LaCapra's phrase, "complacently intolerant." None of this is to suggest that universities have turned out to be worse examples of community than many others. It is just that they have not turned out to be much better. Universities have their very own versions of low voter turnout and uncivil discourse, even when employing a greater-than-average density of Latinate polysyllables.

Universities are, of course, not only the products of internal forces. The structure of the disciplines and their relationships to one another respond in considerable degree to external forces. To the extent that those external forces have expressed themselves with money, universities have been quite responsive and have in consequence become the site of some of the same behaviors produced elsewhere when money is made the measure of all things. Even when professing devotion to the ideals of the university as transmitter of civic virtue and the values of community, society in the United States has most wanted universities to contribute to national economic well-being and to personal economic well-being for their graduates. Only the national defense might be said (though usually quite speciously) to have occupied anything approaching a similar place in the nation's hopes for higher education. There never has been any money in the business of teaching civic virtue in and of itself, and that is why disciplines that could get out of this business did so and those that did not have anywhere else to go retreated into their own kinds of specialization, got paid less for teaching more, and watched their enrollments decline steadily and steeply. The social sciences in general moved in the direction of more quantitative methods, behaving and competing for resources more in the fashion of the natural sciences, and away from the broader study of the political institutions through which society actually functions. Many in literature departments became preoccupied with fundamental philosophical questions about how and whether literary texts could mean anything at all and thus did not treat the canon of Western literature as a set of exemplary texts for the edification of the young. Enrollments for classes in European literature in the original languages were hardest hit.

Parents are more accurately the customers or consumers of higher education than are the students, at least at expensive institutions where the terms are perhaps most often invoked, and parents, too, have had a lot to do with what universities have become. Many of the behaviors for which university students are criticized are behaviors with which those students arrived at the university. Parents sometimes want the university to make their sons and daughters behave in ways that the parents themselves could not make them behave in the first seventeen years of their lives. And with all due respect for the sacrifices imposed on families by the high price of higher education, especially private higher education, the consumerism with which higher education is often approached has contributed notably to undermining the values whose decline in universities is so often lamented.

The university's embrace of the consumer or market model in the allocation of its resources has become increasingly explicit and even fashionable. Yet if the leaders of universities determine that resources cannot be allocated on the basis of academic principle but only on the basis of revenue and expense, discipline by discipline, what hope is there that universities, their faculties, and their students will model any behavior or sense of community that the market itself does not produce? What does it mean to say that because the graduates of the school of divinity or architecture do not in general become as wealthy as the graduates of the business school or the law school, that students of the former should study in shabbier quarters than students of the latter or, better still, that the university should simply get out of the business of educating the former at all? What do students and faculty learn about community from this and how will they behave with one another as a consequence?

There is a great tradition of public service in American higher education. It is quite explicit in the land-grant tradition (which, to be sure, has much to do with serving economic interests), but it is widely represented as well in both public and private institutions. That tradition should be nourished and strengthened with all available means. It will produce notable successes as well as failures in the building of communities outside the university. It would be nice if we engaged in these activities even when government agencies and foundations did not give us money to do so. And it would be especially nice if more of our students and faculty took part and came to regard such activities as central to their own intellectual formation and vocation.

But there is more that we need to do at the heart of our universities if we wish to claim the ability or perhaps even the right to teach others about community. We must first teach one another and by that method (if not alone) teach our students. Who would dare to embark on a community-building enterprise outside the university and claim that the goal was to replicate the degree to which their own department or university functions as a community? Who would dare to say with a straight face that the only trouble with our political institutions is that they do not exemplify community, civil discourse, and other values as well as the faculty of their own university?

Graff has described part of what we could do even within and among our own disciplines. We could study and teach the very conflicts that many would have us erase or deny. This would not be to prize conflict over consensus or to lapse into paralyzing indecision. It would be at the very least, however, to take the disciplines as they actually are rather than to dwell, rancorously or not, on a mythology of the past. And it would prize inquiry and critical examination as central to the life of the university rather than unexamined devotion to whatever circumstances and forces beyond reason might otherwise be the sole definers of community. Let the curriculum incorporate the challenges to the disciplines from within and without rather than ignore those challenges either through the proliferation of more and more specialized offerings or through mere exclusion.

LaCapra has described part of what we could do in evaluating the faculty and administrators' contribution to the life of the university. We could recognize the value of "critical intellectual citizenship," of contributions to "discussion and debate about issues that are not confined to one discipline or area of expertise."[5] This would, after all, be the university's version of the kind of discussion and debate that one would hope to see prevail in society at large. All of these changes would have to begin, however, with members of the university community asking whether as individuals and as colleagues they exemplify, in any way that our students might actually notice, the values and behaviors that we would like to see at work in the society around us.

Chapter 20
The University as Discourse Community

Judith Rodin

On September 26, 1999, the *Philadelphia Inquirer* published an editorial addressing the controversy over Australian ethicist Peter Singer, newly appointed to the Princeton faculty. "What's the point of a university?" the editorial begins. "Is it only to cram a society's settled opinions into the minds of young adults, to prepare them to ease smoothly into the workplace once they've snagged a diploma? Or is it also to spur those minds to become more agile and powerful, capable of challenging and improving upon the received wisdom, able to stretch the boundaries of theory and research?"[1] The failure to address this fundamental question marks some of the most dangerous episodes in the modern history of American higher education. It certainly should have been asked more strongly during the era of McCarthyism and witch-hunting for communists in the 1950s—and whenever a culture of political correctness becomes a reality of intellectual coercion. The same question should be asked today in the wake of the recent controversy at the University of North Carolina over the required reading by incoming freshmen of a book about Islam. Indeed, the question of what a university is *for* is a perennial one. "Spurring minds to become more agile and powerful" sounds just like the business universities want to be in. And, by some measures, universities are succeeding in this endeavor. Undergraduate applications continue to skyrocket, research advances garner headlines and greater funding, college graduates have multiple career opportunities, and endowments continue to grow. But have we challenged ourselves to *answer* the question "What is a university?" for the new century, just as Cardinal Newman did for the late nineteenth century.[2]

As he began a life sentence in South Africa's Robben Island prison, Ahmed Kathrada, an apartheid political prisoner with Nelson Mandela, wrote to his family: "When Ma or anyone at home starts worrying about me, they must just imagine that I'm not in jail but at university."[3] This was more than hyperbole or a way to calm his parents. What is a university at its best, after all, but people learning from one another, communicating, and thinking, even if they are breaking rocks on a chain gang? Indeed, Kathrada would later become the first prisoner to earn a university degree while incarcerated at Robben Island.[4] Just as a prison can be a university, so too can a university be a prison, one whose bars are orthodoxy, indifference, or disengagement from the larger community. The world is a more dangerous place than ever after 11 September 2001. The need to prepare university students for a mercurial society and an unpredictable future is greater than it ever was. I no longer believe that it is enough for universities to expand the intellect and talents of their students. It is not enough to provide a great education. That is still central and essential to our mission, but it is not sufficient. We cannot hope to cope with the complex threats and challenges we face today if we "silo" our knowledge and faculty, or our students, inside carefully constructed and vigorously defended disciplinary, institutional, and cultural walls. Our problems are too complex and there are too many other things—about the world and about themselves—that university students need to learn and that we need to learn from them.

Universities can and should be the exemplars of a new kind of thoughtful civic engagement and robust public discourse. This kind of civic engagement is neither easy nor accidental. It is strategic, comprehensive, intense, and purposeful. At its best, it weaves itself in and through every aspect of campus life, from medical research and particle physics to classical studies, student volunteerism, and economic development. To cultivate active citizenship and civic engagement, universities must pursue multiple initiatives in every aspect of their activities, from student life to the classroom to business practices and investment. Universities are in a unique position to bridge communities, cultivate leadership, and model effective public discourse.

Universities can develop academic service-learning courses that find synergy in the combination of scholarship and service. Such courses feature a direct and conscious link between the application and social value of knowledge and the academic core of the university. These are not second-rate, watered-down, "applied" field sessions. They are not academic credit for what should properly be volunteer activities. When well conceived and well implemented, they are high-order creations of intellectual sophistication and public spirit that teach students how to engage actively with those they may never otherwise come to know and work with. For example, the University of Pennsylvania has developed service-learning courses that bring about enduring community improvements such as effective public schools, neighborhood economic development, and vital community organizations. These academic programs find synergy in the combination of scholarship and service, in their application of theories to practice, and the stimulation of new theorizing out of practical experience. In a typical Penn program, a student performs service as part of an internship that is coordinated with scholarly research—to the mutual benefit of research and service.

This program is well illustrated by the work of Robert Giegengack, a geologist, chair of Penn's department of Earth and Environmental Science, and past director of Penn's Institute for Environmental Studies. His class in Environmental Studies covers basic research in environmental toxins, and in that respect is a traditional arts and sciences course. In addition, however, members of the class help public school students and their families, most living below the poverty line, to identify sources of lead in and around their homes. Undergraduates work with students from a nearby middle school to test soil samples from their yards, and dust and paint samples from their homes, and assist in mapping the risk of lead exposure in the neighborhood. In addition, the middle school students work with the undergraduates to design materials that are disseminated to parents and neighbors warning them of the dangers of lead exposure and how to decrease the chances of lead ingestion by the group most at risk of its ill effects, preschool toddlers. As a short-term program of outreach and information dissemination, the program has been a dramatic success. School children are now far more knowledgeable about the problem of lead exposure in their homes and neighborhood, and middle schools now have a unit of study installed in their curriculum that focuses on the lead problem. But the educational benefits of this program to our undergraduates are also enormous. Moreover, the findings of the program have enabled us better to understand the epidemiology of lead exposure in Philadelphia and other cities, and may help other schools in Philadelphia and elsewhere adopt the program with similar success. This course and many others like it connect the university and the world outside in transformative ways that build new communities and create new forms of public engagement.

A second critical form of civic engagement is the commitment that universities, as citizens themselves, make to the quality of life in their neighboring communities. Universities shoulder extensive civic duties, and the manner in which they do so, once again, is an example to their students and to other institutions. The willing participation of universities and their neighbors in the conversations of democracy—which are rarely smooth and rarely easy—is the only way to gain the long-term benefits of mutual trust and understanding without the unrealistic expectation of perpetual agreement. Real progress requires a new mindset, asking not what should we do *to* the community, or even *for* the community, but rather what should we do *with* the community. What work do we have to do *together*, in virtue of our shared situation? The conversations that follow must be ongoing, open-ended, and constantly renewed, focused on the tasks we share; they must welcome our divergent responses to that common agenda. Sustained community partnerships will help define successful universities in the twenty-first century, and such partnerships will fail in the absence of a continuous civic dialogue about the urgent tasks we must undertake together. In another such initiative, a new University-assisted pre-K–8 neighborhood school in West Philadelphia opened in the fall of 2001—the result of a unique partnership between Penn, the Philadelphia public school system, and the teachers union. The school features small classes and learning communities, active professional development for teachers, a cutting-edge curriculum, and other important innovations. It is not a Penn lab school. Nor is it a charter school. It is a *neighborhood* public school intended to bolster efforts to enhance the West Philadelphia community.

Universities can also play important community-building roles when they act in more traditional ways as clearinghouses for credible information and analysis in an age of information overload. Universities can sort out what we know and do not know, so that people are able to make sense of all the data and convert information into knowledge. By providing clear information, in certain cases, we may help to explode negative popular myths that breed unfounded cynicism, and we help to provide good data to inform public policy debates. Universities should do more to interpret and publicize the fruits of their research to the general public; this would benefit public policy and the common good. At Penn today, we are doing this through the formation of a new interdisciplinary Institute for Strategic Threat Analysis and Response, as we struggle to address the uncertainties and instant mythologies of the "War on Terrorism."

The most important form of civic engagement for universities may be their own evolution as strong and lively "discourse communities," shaped in the crucible of their members' intense engagement with issues of personal and public moment. We can only create real, solid community by engaging—even arguing—with each other over important matters, not by ignoring or suppressing those concerns, especially when we disagree. We must form communities of serious conversation around the most compelling issues of the day—issues such as the maintenance of civil liberties in the wake of the 9/11 terrorist attacks, the continuing legal struggles over affirmative action, the challenges of immigration and religious tolerance in a dangerous and frightening world, and the long-unresolved domestic crises in health care, retirement security, and welfare reform. The university is an obvious setting for robust and thoughtful discourse on such hot-button topics. By fostering these conversations, the university will offer students valid experiences of active, engaged public discourse and civic involvement that will serve as lifelong prototypes. But when discussions grow hot and ill tempered, as they sometimes do, the university must also model how heat and anger can be handled and utilized for positive change.

Most universities have now concluded that we cannot legislate away undesirable behavior and incivility with codes, policies, and regulations. Campus speech codes and similar regulations failed to reduce levels of intolerance or incivility on campuses, and they certainly will not moderate the ideological polarizations of our politics. Such measures send fundamentally the wrong message, one that reinforces the sense of powerless individuals and monolithic institutions, of cultural orthodoxy and paternalistic authority, and of ideological conformity and political correctness. Universities must learn to use the robust discourse permitted by our society's fundamental commitment to the freedoms of ideas and expression to educate rather than to wound. The university administration's job is to support, foster, and facilitate such dialogue and debate, not to cut it off; to create an environment in which we can educate each other, not one in which doctrine or orthodoxy are legislated from on high; to encourage voluntary engagement over boundaries of difference, not silence the expression of unpopular ideas through moral intimidation from a privileged bully pulpit.

University presidents, to be sure, must provide "moral leadership" on campuses. But moral leadership requires suasion not censorship, conscience not coercion, engagement not intimidation. Most of all, it requires an insistence that we—all of us—talk about what troubles us. Words are the lifeblood of a university. For all their limitations, even if they sometimes drive us apart, words are what bind us together in the academy and in our larger communities. Free and robust expression and debate are essential to an academic community. Tempting as the mantle of moral leadership may be, it is too often a comfortable excuse for imposing quietude and conformity where raucous debate and energetic engagement should flourish. Academic leaders too often feel the temptation to quietude, but we must not fall prey to it. Students cannot retreat to their computers, their courses, and their careers. We all have to engage. Universities bear the responsibility to create a context in which actual diversity of views and opinions, persons and groups, politics and perspectives, is nurtured, valued, and shared.

Universities can raise the level of the discourse. Basic academic values that we already hold—respecting complexity, posing substantive rather than rhetorical questions when framing a discussion, welcoming real input and participation, holding open the possibility that we may be in error, and, of course, refraining from ad hominem arguments—are not only guidelines for good public discourse. They also create in modern universities a readily accessible model for workable communities. By modeling this kind of public discourse and behavior in universities, we will take an important step toward fulfillment of our leadership responsibilities. Universities are transformative places. They have the capacity to change people's expectations of others and of themselves. If Mandela and his fellow prisoners in their university of the mind could have conceived new forms of democracy while breaking rocks, imagine what those institutions more typically thought of as universities have the potential to create.

Chapter 21
Creating Community in Cyberspace: Criteria for a Discourse Technology Project

Stephen P. Steinberg

Are virtual communities real? Few issues regarding the social impact of the Internet received more media attention or were more widely discussed during the Internet boom of the 1990s than the interrelated debates over whether being online is an inherently isolating or connecting experience and whether communities could truly be said to have formed in what has become known as cyberspace. Initial studies of the psychological and behavioral impacts of living online suggested that excessive engagement with the virtual reality of the Internet increased social isolation, with concomitant increases in feelings of loneliness and depression.[1] However, more recent studies suggest that these deleterious consequences may be neither permanent nor inevitable.[2] In the long run, the final verdict on the psychosocial impact of heavy involvement with the Internet will have major implications for the closely related question about the reality of virtual communities. Likewise, if true communities can be formed in cyberspace, some of the negative impacts of heavy Internet involvement may be ameliorated and ultimately outweighed by the strengthened senses of connection and community.

Thus, the design and creation of effective, engaging, and enduring virtual communities poses an important challenge—and opportunity—to those concerned with the central roles of public discourse and strong, inclusive communities in both the American and global social fabrics of the twenty-first century. The challenge lies in the potential for online interactions at a distance to erode further the sense of local, personal connection to a concrete community.[3] The opportunity lies in the potential for innovative forms of virtual community to offer uniquely new and valuable experiences of community that were not even conceivable prior to the advent of the Internet.[4] With these challenges and opportunities in mind, the staff of the Penn National Commission on Society, Culture and Community undertook a Discourse Technology Project to think through the notion of cybercommunity from the ground up, as it were, on the basis of the Commission's insights into the nature of contemporary communities and the central role of public discourse in creating and sustaining them. The following is a report of the results of that effort.[5]

In attempting to model a cybercommunity that recruits technology not only to facilitate, but also to enhance and expand opportunities for effective public discourse, it is helpful to examine some of the fundamental issues faced by online communities—and how the findings of the Penn National Commission provide critical insights into ways in which one might successfully address those issues. This summary will discuss those connections, as well as other concerns that affect the tone, tenor, and overall robustness of online communities. It will then propose a new model for a true cybercommunity and identify some of the provocative challenges that would need to be addressed in bringing such a model cybercommunity to realization.

The State of Online Community

While many people are deeply skeptical about the possibility that something truly resembling a community can exist in cyberspace, precisely because of its virtual character, in November 1999 Lawrence Lessig pointedly told the Penn National Commission that "in fact, there are already such things as communities existing in cyberspace, in all the senses that you would identify as relevant for a community. There are places where people spend an extraordinary amount of time devoted to communal goods, to bringing about things that are of value to a collection of people, where they feel identified and feel like they have a role and responsibility in shaping that space. There are extraordinary collections of people who work in common on problems that they consider their problems and problems of society in general. There are these places you would recognize as communities."[6]

But Lessig also reminded the Commission that in cyberspace architecture is destiny: "Cyberspace is not automatically a community," he said. There is an "extremely delicate relationship that exists between particular architectures or designs of cyberspace and the communities that they bring" into being.[7] As this comment suggests, the a priori design of a cybercommunity largely predetermines and limits what can occur in it, unlike most real communities, which tend to be more open-ended and evolutionary. Of course, situational factors, such as geographical features, climate, and location, play a limiting and determining role in real communities, as well as virtual ones.

While a comprehensive review of the burgeoning literature on community in cyberspace is beyond the scope of this chapter, two well-documented incidents may be useful as touchstones for the discussion that follows.[8] The first of these—which was offered to the Commission as a "proof-of-concept or existence-proof of the phenomenon of community online"[9]—is the now notorious story of "A Rape in Cyberspace," told by Julian Dibbell in his book *My Tiny Life*.[10] "A Rape in Cyberspace" is the story of what happens when one member of an online community undertakes to repeatedly subvert the community through the online enactment of violent sexual acts attributed to other participants. It powerfully demonstrates the intensity that participants can bring to the virtual world of MUDs—multiuser dungeons—and other technologies of online community, and the complex issues of governance and freedom of expression that then ensue. (Just like, we might add, in the real world.) As Dibbell noted in relating this case to the Penn National Commission, "A Rape in Cyberspace" is especially compelling because it shows what can happen when a community is formed without any common task to focus the energies and constrain the behavior of its members.[11]

The other recent occurrence that is useful to keep in mind is the extraordinary level of online activity and the formation of instant communities on the Internet following the 11 September 2001 terrorist attacks.[12] In the wake of the tragedy, unprecedented numbers of Americans turned to the Internet, in all its forms, including email, chat rooms, bulletin boards, online forums, polls, information sites, and commemorative sites. A study by the Pew Internet and American Life Project found that nearly three-quarters of Internet users turned to email in the wake of the tragedy "to display their patriotism, contact family and friends to discuss events, reconnect with long-lost friends, discuss the fate of the victims, and share news," and one-third turned to the virtual commons of chat rooms, bulletin boards, and online forums to discuss the events.[13] The post-9/11 use of the Internet to reestablish the senses of community and connection shattered by the events of that day is significant because it is one of the few examples of online community that is both open-ended and inclusive in nature, and thus, more similar to what we usually consider a community. It also demonstrates the power of an externally imposed, shared circumstance to create the inclusive situational framework in which a diverse community of individuals can be built.

However, a shared situation is not enough, by itself, to create a community. As the Penn National Commission discovered, a true community must also have *real work to do together* in responding to that situation.[14] As Marc Ewing told the Commission, many efforts at forming online communities demonstrate that professional or single-task communities, like the open source software movement, have flourished, but multitask, open-ended communities, which are closer analogues to real, geographically based communities, generally lack the enduring common situation (usually determined by extrinsic factors) that is needed to subtly coerce members to continue to do productive work together.[15]

As Joel Fleishman pointed out during the Commission's plenary discussion, the Internet is a very effective tool for "creating communities of like-minded people," who already have a professional or social task in common, but yet unproved is its utility in bringing diverse populations of "differing-minded people" together into a single community.[16] "The typical geographic area has people who have different views on everything," he added. "We've been very much concerned, whether it's a town or institution or a university or a nation, with how you foster a greater sense of community there in overcoming differences of opinion. Where do you make that connection between people who are drawn to the Internet because they share the same views on a particular issue and those who don't, who differ on those issues? How do you create community across those groups?"[17]

Thus, both recent events and early experience with Internet-based communities have underscored the central importance of an identifiable common situation and the shared tasks such situations define in creating true communities, whether in the real world or online. Yet, whether a good idea or a bad one, it is clear that efforts at forming, and levels of participation in, various kinds of so-called communities online are likely to continue to grow in the years ahead. Anticipating this growth, now is the moment to step back and think through the normative features and practices that should characterize a true cybercommunity.

Conceptualizing Community in Cyberspace

The central question posed to the staff of the Penn National Commission's Discourse Technology Project was how to translate the Commission's findings about the key elements of effective public discourse—particularly the element of *real work to do together*—into a thriving online cybercommunity. While many so-called online communities already exist, upon closer examination there continues to be a notable lack of both diversity and enduring cohesion in these groups. Thus, in order to realize—in a virtual setting—the Commission's vision of strengthening diverse and inclusive communities through public discourse, it was critical to understand where and how existing cybercommunities fall short.

WORK TO DO TOGETHER

Most existing online communities address the notion of *real work to do together* only partially, if at all. There are, indeed, websites that focus on the work aspect, such as Grassroots.com, which encourages citizens to work for social and political change and provides e-mail petitions, online research resources, political contact lists, and other technological tools.[18] While this type of website provides invaluable tools for citizens searching to make their voices heard on a variety of meaningful topics, these sites are primarily geared toward large numbers of people acting alone, carrying on their work asynchronously and ultimately as individuals. A visitor to such a website need not even make contact with other individuals occupying the same virtual space in order to participate in the work at hand, and visitors who choose to focus on other issues of particular interest to them are generally sent offsite, to websites created and maintained by interest groups completely unrelated to the original site host.

Another variant of this type of asynchronous, aggregated, individual work model appears in the ratings features of sites such as eBay.com, Epinions.com, and Amazon.com.[19] Visitors are asked to provide ratings about a variety of topics, such as consumer products (or, in the case of eBay, about each other). By gathering, computing, and displaying information about how individual visitors rated specific items or their interactions with fellow participants, these websites allow visitors to glean a form of collective wisdom from the aggregated responses—paradoxically, without ever compelling either viewers or contributors to interact directly with others.

Of course, there do exist virtual loci in which visitors are encouraged to share and discuss their thoughts and opinions, engaging each other on topics of civic or political interest. Some of these are simply the designated discussion areas of action-oriented sites (such as Grassroots.com); others are discussion areas of portals or online media outlets (as seen in discussion groups on Yahoo.com or Salon.com respectively).[20] In addition to this common subsector model, there are some sites completely dedicated to open, online, public discussion. The most notable of these is Abuzz.com, the discussion site venture acquired by the *New York Times* in 1999.[21] While the site sought to capitalize on the preexisting knowledge community of *New York Times* readers, it has since failed to engage participants to a meaningful degree, a fact underscored by the subsequent downsizing of the entire *New York Times Online* unit.[22]

An underlying problem with the aforementioned cybercommunity models is that participants are either not compelled to contribute toward some sort of discernible end (i.e., there is no *real work* to do, merely talk for talk's sake), or participants can make substantive contributions to the completion of a communal task, but are free to do so in isolation (i.e., the end result is not contingent upon the *collective* performance of the task). In other words, they are missing some critical component of *real work to do together*, which the Penn National Commission identified as the focal point for the kind of productive, engaged public discourse that is central to building and strengthening diverse, inclusive communities.

In the absence of robust, enduring communities of conversation online, what else occurs? The sites mentioned above, as well as others, provide us with some interesting clues. Many community sites tend to level off in participation, despite continuing gains in recruitment, due to participant attrition. While they may retain a small core of dedicated users, they fail to grow and thrive due to lack of interest and activity on the part of early adopters and newcomers alike; over time, even recruitment of newcomers becomes more difficult, once such sites have saturated their target populations and the population dwindles as unengaged members depart.

The notable exceptions to this pattern are the transactional websites, such as eBay and Amazon, in which the primary goal of most participants is an economic transaction. While the user base for these sites continues to grow, they can only be termed "communities" in the loosest and most dilute sense of the word. The majority of participants do not tend to self-identify as community members during their participation online, nor do online community discussions extend in any depth beyond essentially self-referential content—talk about the online community at hand, its rules and regulations, and helpful pointers for engaging in successful transactions therein.

To Be or Not to Be . . . Online

Although the notion of *real work to do together* provided the staff of the Penn National Commission's Discourse Technology Project with both a clear mandate and a meaningful way of distinguishing its model from other online proto-communities, it did not address a more fundamental question: Why should a person join a community in an online, technology-mediated, or virtual space, rather than in real space and in real time? Advocates of cybercommunity will need to answer this question if proposed cybercommunities are to do more than simply establish a market share by siphoning off a portion of the existing participant base for all online communities. A successful cybercommunity, worthy of the name, will have to expand the very notion of the relationship between technology and the dynamics of traditional communities. We have identified several types of individuals whose interest in community engagement might be particularly well facilitated by the Internet and other new communications technologies.

- **The Geographically Isolated**
  Individuals in isolated locations can find gatherings in virtual space more convenient than those in real life, and they can sometimes locate others with shared interests more easily in the denser online locale.

- **The Differently Abled**
  Technologies that support online exchanges, such as auditory text readers for the visually impaired, or even the written medium itself for the hearing-impaired and some of the physically impaired, can enable many individuals with physical handicaps to participate more actively in a virtual space than they otherwise might be able to in a face-to-face setting.

- **The Nonnative Speaker**
  The emergence of the first successful translation engines provides a unique opportunity for native speakers of different languages to communicate with one another in a way that might otherwise be impossible in the absence of some mediating technology.

- **The Overbooked or Oddly Scheduled**
  The ability to conduct meaningful exchanges on their own time, rather than in complete temporal synchrony, makes virtual space attractive to those with extremely tight schedules, or those with schedules that are out of sync with the majority of their physical neighbors.

- **The Physically Immobile or Hypermobile**
  Virtual space provides a readily accessible venue for individuals who may lack full logistical mobility, such as senior citizens and young people, as well as individuals whose lives are marked by extreme logistical movement, such as those who relocate frequently or whose travel schedules do not give them a clear physical home base.

- **The Prodigal Participant**
  A ready group of participants already exists among individuals who have previously attempted to join online communities, but who have fallen away due to the attrition caused by the lack of continually engaging content and interaction in these virtual settings.

The creation of an electronically mediated communal life at a distance for these types of individuals has obvious advantages, and prima facie, seems especially appropriate and desirable in the light of their special needs.

THE "I" IN IDENTITY

The consistent experience of online community organizers has been that allowing users complete anonymity, and hence a lack of personal accountability, can have a deleterious effect on the overall levels of civility and constructive engagement in virtual space—the story of "A Rape in Cyberspace," cited above, being the classic example of the risks of allowing such anonymous participation.[23] Though most users tend to abide by implicit or explicit cybercommunity norms, the lack of a stable, singular, ongoing individual identity makes it difficult for cybercommunity leaders actually to enforce those norms, and can allow a very small minority of participants to disproportionately color the overall canvas of community interactions. Perhaps more important, the absence of richly elaborated, real, and enduring individual identities is a fundamental obstacle to the realization of online communities. In short, after some initial exchanges, few people will find a sense of community in continuing exchanges with an anonymous, perhaps fraudulent interlocutor. The necessity of moving from anonymity to identity in online dating exchanges is a good example of this at the level of one-to-one interpersonal relationships.

Rather than grappling with the issue of how to maximize individual freedom vis-à-vis online identity while maintaining a robust community, we believe that online endeavors should begin from a point of best facilitating *real work to do together*, and to control the variables which have (based upon the experiences of other online community experiments) proven empirically problematic in their most unrestricted form (total anonymity being chief among them). While cybercommunities need not require full disclosure on the part of participants, neither should participants be allowed to assume multiple identities or to conceal factual information about themselves from their fellow community members. The concept of a stable, continuing, individual identity is central to the very notion of a community of individuals, and getting to know and appreciate the identities of other individual community members and recognizing their persistence over time are critical elements in binding individual members into the continuing community. Individual identities, and the values, experiences, and knowledge that come with them, are the raw materials of *real work to do together* out of which communities are formed.

THE LIFE CYCLE OF A CYBERCOMMUNITY CITIZEN

These considerations suggested that to be successful, the cybercommunity envisioned by the Discourse Technology Project would have to be specifically designed to avoid the pitfalls evidenced in existing sites and address the need for real and engaging *work to do together*, which stands at the center of any enduring community. Such a model cybercommunity is perhaps best presented longitudinally, through the life cycle of a typical participant in the cybercommunity we envisioned.

The Curious Visitor. During an initial get-acquainted stage, viewers can visit the community's website and view publicly available content. This should include features such as:

- Introductory information about the structure and nature of the site.
- The ability to view (but not participate in) open, general-public, cybercommunity discussions.
- Links to work results such as resource collections and tools created by cybercommunity members and groups.
- A registration area in which visitors can volunteer to join the cybercommunity by submitting a member profile.

The Welcome Newcomer. Once an individual has registered to become a community member, they should be welcomed into the cybercommunity and given newcomer status. By registering to join the community, participants would be given access to a set of members-only privileges, such as:

- The ability to participate in general-public cybercommunity discussions.
- The opportunity to attend real-time community events, such as interviews, concerts, and other gatherings.

As newcomers, the participants should also receive special assistance to help them learn about their new cybercommunity:

- Each newcomer should become part of an orientation group of fellow newcomers, creating a safe haven where even the most rudimentary questions are welcome. Groups would be facilitated by community leaders (see below), and newcomers would also be given contact information for at-large community leaders who could also assist them in getting oriented in the cybercommunity.
- Newcomers should have the opportunity to participate in online exercises and role-playing to help them learn about community standards and norms, and to familiarize them with available community resources.
- After newcomers have successfully completed an orientation period, their online status would be upgraded to that of a full-fledged member.

By giving newcomers the opportunity to learn about community norms and self-governance through direct interaction with community leaders from the outset, and by engaging newcomers in elements of the cybercommunity at-large before granting them participatory access in more specialized interest groups, this model addresses three major deficiencies that the Penn National Commission identified as undermining effective public discourse: a failure of leadership, the fragmentation of communities, and a culture of intolerance.

The Full-Fledged Member. Full-fledged members should have the opportunity to avail themselves of the full complement of community privileges and services, including:

- Access to special communications services and technologies (e.g. instant messaging, PDAs) available only upon completion of orientation.
- The opportunity to contribute archived feedback and ratings regarding fellow participants and website features and content.

- The ability to participate interactively (rather than simply as a viewer) in special cybercommunity live events.
- The opportunity to participate in and contribute to many of the self-maintenance and self-governance functions of the community.
- The opportunity to participate in workgroups focusing on special-interest topics.

The Community Leader. After participating in the cybercommunity for a certain length of time, and having received a sufficient level of positive feedback (or lack of negative feedback) about their own personal participation, an individual should become eligible to earn community leader status. Drawing upon the wealth of discourse leadership resources available online, the community provides an exciting new venue for developing and training aspiring discourse leaders. Privileges and opportunities for cybercommunity leaders would include:

- Training sessions and tutorials in discourse facilitation methods, customized for use in cyberspace.
- Participation in regular leadership summits, which include exclusive access to visiting experts and small-scale special events.
- The opportunity officially to orient newcomers to the cybercommunity.

Critical Questions

In order to implement an online community such as that suggested above, effective responses must be fashioned to a small set of core challenges. Not only do these important issues present themselves at the outset, but the ways in which they are addressed would fundamentally inform and shape the identity of the community. Any true cybercommunity will have to answer the following critical questions.

- **What is the nature of the work that members are asked to accomplish, and how will they accomplish it together?**
  It is clear that the inability to realize the central notion of *real work to do together* in currently existing virtual communities has diluted their effectiveness, endurance, and robustness. While participants should be asked to do work, it must be work of sufficient meaning and impact to motivate their communal participation and engagement on a continuing basis. It is also critical that work platforms and venues are constructed in such a way that participants obtain the most productive results by interacting with one another, rather than by accumulating a tally of individual inputs.

- **What qualities will attract new participants to the cybercommunity, and what incentives will keep existing members active?**

Successfully addressing the work challenge outlined above would already distinguish a model cybercommunity constructed on these lines from other existing online sites. What must also be considered is the need to identify what incentives or rewards can be provided to active community members to encourage and support their continued participation. In the for-profit sector, this is often accomplished by giving visitors free gifts or cash-value discounts; in a nonprofit context, one must determine what resources, services, features, or other benefits can be provided to reward active community participants.

This question of how to attract and retain community members in the absence of financial or material rewards is a particularly pointed one, especially given the notable number of recent failures to retain strong online customer bases in the commercial sector—even with such incentives. The most obvious attempts to address this issue have centered on the civic value of talk for talk's sake and its potential influence on other minds, government policies, and individual behaviors. While broadcast media and even certain facets of existing online communities implicitly embody this promise of effective amplification, allowing individuals to present their opinions to far larger audiences, the frequent lack of change in publicly visible outcomes as a result of such a process renders such promises problematic as continuing, long-term motivators of participation.

While a strong cybercommunity cannot at this point hope to compete with broadcast media in terms of sheer numerical reach, what it can offer is better consequentialist amplification: by effectively channeling the energies and synergies of participants' efforts, a model cybercommunity can attempt to deliver a greater resultant level of observable, sustainable change. While this emphasis on impact is, in fact, already part of the driving force behind some of the aforementioned work sites (with Grassroots.com employing the tagline "Online Action and Impact"),[24] little apparent attention has been devoted to the question of how impact can be enhanced through shared and robust interactions among participants. Consequentialist amplification as a result of collective participation can act as both a powerful and necessary motivator for individual participants, as well as an identifying hallmark of the community as a whole.

Thus, the multiplier effects of successful community action must be the ultimate reward and motivation for continued participation. If these outcomes address the fundamental, shared situation of the community's members, and if they are brought about as direct consequences of members' collective efforts, then there is reason to think that they will engender continuing participation and create a strong, enduring, online community.

- **How will a commonweal be maintained within the cybercommunity in the face of the strong tendencies toward self-segregation and community fragmentation in most online communities?**

  Gradual self-segregation into ever more specialized narrowly based interests groups can create online communities with very strong bonds among members. Unfortunately, this does not always enhance each group's diversity, nor does it teach members how to progress— despite differences and dissent—to doing *real work* together across a wide spectrum of concerns. The nature of cyberspace is also such that it is not difficult for highly specialized groups to relocate and splinter off entirely from their founding locus. A key identity issue, then, is how, despite a high degree of specialization, will a cybercommunity maintain a consistent branding that continually reinforces participants' connections to the community and their desires to stay within it.

- **How will the cybercommunity ensure that members receive a significant *return on participation* (ROP), proportionate to their investment of time, energy, and thought in building and participating in the life of the community?**

  Among individuals considering how best to use their discretionary time and energy, we have noted the strong interest in receiving good value and in optimizing return on investment for their attention and contributions. This is both a common and rational response to the need to allocate limited personal resources in an era of ever escalating demands and interests.

Conclusion

In closing, it may be useful to make explicit what has been implicit throughout this conceptual analysis of the normative features of a community in cyberspace: the creation of a true community in cyberspace does not appear to be primarily a technological challenge. Indeed, nothing that we have suggested as a functional characteristic of such a community appears to us to be particularly difficult to realize in hardware and software, given the current state of information and communications technologies. Rather, our thought experiment has made clear that the real challenges of creating cybercommunities are conceptual and strategic. Identifying the specific *work to do together* that will bind such a community together over time and foster real dialogical and multilateral engagements amongst its members is the very difficult—and as yet unanswered challenge—that still faces the would-be creators of cybercommunities.

Epilogue: The Centrality of Public Discourse

Stephen P. Steinberg

As the papers in this volume have shown, the problems of incivility, intolerance, and community fragmentation are not new phenomena in American history—though they are certainly amplified by the advent of mass-market entertainment, mass media, and instant, global communications. The Penn National Commission on Society, Culture and Community concluded that these problems are less worrisome than the absence of a richer and more engaged, honest, and productive public discourse. In the past, such a discourse surrounded and counterbalanced the incivility and intolerance that sometimes in recent years have seemed so dramatic and overwhelming. Motivated by this insight—and in sharp contrast to some of the other national groups concerned with civility and civic renewal—the Penn National Commission took as its objective the creation of "a robust and diverse public culture in which reasoned and reasonable discourse can flourish."[1] We chose this course, instead of condemning incivility or moralizing about it, because productive conversations are central to both the creation and the successful functioning of diverse and inclusive democratic communities.[2] Consider, for example, the often uncivil and quite robustly engaged conversations that the founders had over independence, slavery, federalism, taxes, and other issues, through which they brought thirteen colonies together to form a single nation and later created a functional and effective national government.

It is our hope that the essays in this volume will stimulate continuing efforts toward these ends and focus both popular and scholarly attention on the growing community of practitioners and citizens actively engaged in promoting productive and engaged public discourse as a means of building and strengthening American communities and public life more generally. To survive and prosper, any democratic society must be able to accomplish certain basic activities that are essential to its efficient functioning, its adaptability to new circumstances, and its fundamental democratic character. When successfully carried out, these activities enable and foster the engagement of its citizens with the civic and political life of their communities and nation. When a society fails to perform these tasks successfully, its civic fabric frays and it can lose the recognition of a common situation, the acceptance of a shared responsibility, and the mutual willingness to participate in public life that must ultimately underlie any well-functioning and enduring democratic society. As this volume has argued, engaged and productive public discourse is a central—and often overlooked—variable in determining these outcomes.

Four Essential Faculties

In the Commission's work, at least four basic capacities were identified as critical to democratic life in the emerging society of the twenty-first century.

- **The ability to undertake sustained and reasoned social and political deliberation on important communal and cultural issues.**
  Reasoned political and social deliberation differs from public performance and from private conversation. Effective public conversation is not simply a matter of displaying deeply held convictions, but presupposes a willingness to consider modifying those beliefs. It should be expected and assumed that new information and new arguments will generate new attitudes and new policy positions. In the political arena, public discourse is at its best when the participants are diverse and engaged, and the context is neutral, fair, and optimistic. Yet today, sustained and reasoned political deliberation has been attenuated by the contemporary phenomena of mass media and political polling, among others, which make serious discussion and debate among political candidates a rarity and frame political campaigns more as sporting events or horse races than opportunities to deliberate on important issues. Thus, new forms of public discourse, new styles of discourse leadership, and new technologies will need to be harnessed if the general public is to be successfully encouraged to engage in thoughtful and sustained discussion of public issues.

- **The ability to attract and enable effective social and political leaders.**
  Leaders are made—they are educated, trained, recognized, selected, mentored, and promoted. Though leaders often possess natural talents and abilities, there are ample opportunities to identify and cultivate leaders in every professional field, academic discipline, political and civic setting, and influential cultural arena. Through educational programs and professional societies, positive peer pressure, and the exemplary behavior of those who model leadership for others, patterns of leadership behavior are readily amenable to modification. Focusing these potential leaders on their responsibilities for improving public discourse, modeling positive public behavior, and mentoring future leaders is no more difficult than ensuring that every lawyer knows torts, every business student has a grasp of mi-

croeconomics, and every politician can read an opinion poll. Just as the failures of contemporary leaders inhibit the creation of a more vigorous public conversation, the emergence of a cadre of more effective discourse leaders in politics, the media, and elsewhere in civic and professional life can energize and expand the domain of effective public discourse.

- **The ability to create viable, inclusive discourse communities for the emerging American society.**
  Our democratic society cannot thrive, or even truly be said to exist, unless it recognizes the enormous cultural changes that the nation is experiencing. Ethnicities and races are mixing and blending more than ever in every facet of our society—from the playground to the classroom, in our families and in our communities, at work and at prayer. Without creating a discourse that comprehends and affirms this fundamental change, our public conversation will become increasingly static, elitist, exclusive, and ultimately unproductive. As David M. Ryfe has argued,[3] to understand where people come from and where they are—to acknowledge that race and ethnicity today are almost as individual as the person—is a crucial requirement of good public conversation. This tenet, which Ryfe calls "radical difference," asserts that individuals must have the right to speak in the voice of any of the groups to which they belong, as they offer their differing responses to a shared communal situation.[4] The Chinese grocer on the corner, the Salvadoran roofer in the next town, and the Mexican educator at the local university will differ in their opinions, but recognizing what each has to offer as individuals and as part of any number of cultural groups will foster a more dialogical public discourse and create a more inclusive sense of community. This concept is particularly central to often divisive and factious conversations on race.

- **The ability to create and sustain relatively clear and generally accepted cultural and behavioral boundaries between the public and private spheres.**
  The unprecedented commercialization of almost every facet of our culture has all but eliminated the boundaries that once separated a vaguely definable private sphere from public scrutiny or exposure. Even in the Gilded Age of the late nineteenth century, some areas remained off limits. Today, by contrast, the dynamics of mass-market media, financial influence in politics, and flourishing technological innovation have opened virtually any area of life, including higher education, criminal justice, and health care, to public exposure and commercial exploitation. Simultaneously, the behavioral standards of the mass marketplace have come inevitably to dominate private

life as well. While there is no turning back the clock or preventing the cultural transformations wrought by new technologies, an open and engaged public conversation can help locate the ever shifting boundary between public and private and enable both ordinary citizens and their leaders to navigate this demarcation more comfortably in their daily activities.

These four capacities can be usefully thought of as the social "faculties" by means of which a democratic society fulfills some of its most vital functions: conflict resolution, problem-solving, civic education, social and political debate, social interaction, and community formation. These capacities are to the body politic what the mental faculties of knowing, feeling, imagining, perceiving, and judging were to the human mind of eighteenth- and early nineteenth-century philosophical psychology.[5] They are the basic functions that any healthy social organism must be able to perform in order to sustain itself in a hostile environment.

Indeed, the metaphor of faculties plays a role here analogous to that which it played in the development of modern experimental psychology. Only by identifying specific core capacities of the human organism did it become possible to develop ongoing lines of scientific research into the cognitive and neuro-biological processes by which those macro capacities are realized.[6] Examining the largely ignored role of public discourse in the concrete social processes of a democracy can foster the study of democratic society in ways that parallel the nineteenth-century shift in psychology from phenomenological description and philosophical speculation to creative experimentation and rigorous empirical research.

Thinking of these capacities as the faculties of a democratic society is doubly appropriate in the context of our examination of American public discourse, since each also plays a central role in the cultural, political, and social ideologies upon which American society and its political system are founded. Enlightenment political philosophy held that all human beings are capable of rational deliberation.[7] On this view, the task of an enlightened society was to nurture and instrumentalize this capacity through education, freedom of thought and expression, and representative government—leading inevitably to the advancement of human society[8]

Yet, along with this Enlightenment optimism went the realization that no society can rely solely on mass democracy to find its way. Thus, the founders struggled to craft, especially in the Constitution, a balance between democratic "chaos" and the need for responsible leadership. The two centuries of intervening history have made evident the degree to which this vision also relied upon unspoken assumptions of cultural (as well as racial and gender) commonality, which enabled democratic government to function successfully. The formation of a stable, relatively homogenous community was both the precondition and the product of

successful democratic government, and it contributed to the maintenance of a well-ordered and well-functioning society.

The Centrality of Public Discourse

In such a community, both independent leadership and popular values
played important roles in the rational deliberation of social ends and
means. In today's more inclusive and self-conscious context, energetic
public discourse can once again play an essential role in creating the kind
of inclusive contemporary communities so necessary to a democratic society. However, while emphasizing this dependence of our society's crucial democratic faculties on spirited and productive public conversation,
several caveats must be kept in mind.

First, these faculties are concerned exclusively with the interactions
that occur in the public sphere, where civic or communal activities are at
issue, and discourse is the central means through which those civic activities are carried out. The preconditions, conduct, content, and leadership
of public discourse stand squarely at the center of the cultural crisis that
some have alleged. This relationship is reciprocal. Each of the four social
faculties outlined above relies upon the exercise of effective public discourse to support and enable its realization, and such a discourse cannot
itself survive and flourish without the full and sustained exercise of these
faculties.

Second, in emphasizing the central role of productive public discourse
in the functioning of a well-ordered democratic society, we must not lose
sight of the link between public discourse and hot-button issues—the
most polarized and tendentiously debated issues of the day. In recent
years, those issues have been immigration, race, abortion, and affirmative action. In earlier eras, they were taxes, trade, and ideology. Today,
they are war, terrorism, civil liberties, and the role of religion in politics
and government. But whatever the hot-button issues of the moment, the
goal of focusing on the context, conduct, and content of public discourse
is to find more productive ways of discussing such issues and arriving at
socially useful outcomes. At the very least, a productive public conversation should be a vehicle for desensitizing such issues and facilitating co-
existence, even in the face of irresolvable disagreements. In short, the
action is at the intersection of public talk and the important social issues,
cultural concerns, and political debates of the day. To talk about public
discourse is to talk about how we talk about (and then potentially solve)
public issues.

Third, it is equally important to note what is not implicated in this description of democratic faculties. Effectively excluded as a primary focus
of study are such issues of private behavior as drugs, divorce, religion,
and "family values." Our analysis accepts the contemporary condition of
private life as a given, relevant only in so far as it becomes a subject for

debate in the public arena, as when private behavior is the subject of public regulation. However, understanding the impact of these formerly private issues on the public sphere—indeed, their virtual domination of much recent public discourse—is a prerequisite for strengthening our capacity to deliberate effectively on important public matters.

Finally, the cultivation of a more robust and reasoned public dialogue, more effective discourse leadership, and more inclusive communities offers the most realistic prospects for effecting positive change—short of ill-considered (and often politically motivated) attempts to transform or reverse the basic social and cultural paradigms of the twenty-first century, or to reproduce the mythic historical communities for which so many are nostalgic. Effective public dialogue permits and encourages those who hold competing values to remain at the table, where they can argue for their differing visions of society without ruling other competing visions out of the conversation. In this connection, it is instructive to compare the failed dialogue of President Clinton's 1997 national conversation on race, in which participants worked toward no concrete outcome and were intimidated by the President's predetermined agenda, with the extraordinary discourse that took place before South Africa's Truth and Reconciliation Commission. In the latter, all shared—albeit painfully and despite the most profound differences—in a common, crucial task of social reconstruction. Thus, more effective public discourse can facilitate a more productive consideration of public issues, whether in the political, social, cultural, international, or economic sphere.

Conversely, it is impossible to imagine the effective resolution of conflicts among communities without the creation of some kind of productive public dialogue. The alternative to such a productive public discourse is isolation, fragmentation, and dissolution. The absence of a clear understanding of the preconditions and requirements of effective public discourse undercuts serious deliberations on important public policy issues. Nowhere is this more evident than in most discussions of race and affirmative action. The failure to establish neutral settings and to acknowledge the powerful emotional dimensions of these discussions tends to push them toward either cliché or self-parody. When this happens, the needs of individual citizens, disadvantaged minorities, and society as a whole are ill served—with predictable consequences.

Looking Forward

What would strengthen the core faculties of our democratic society? Four questions need to be answered to identify the means for doing better: What does good public discourse look like and what factors determine its success? What institutional practices create communities of conversation across boundaries of difference, particularly among groups predisposed to conflict? What are the characteristics of effective discourse leadership? How can cultural boundaries (such as that between private and public spheres) be created, reinforced, and altered in ways that support effective public discourse—and how can such discourse contribute to the formation of clearer and more stable cultural demarcations?

First, we must recognize that improvement in public life must come from the creation of new, more vigorous, and more engaged forms of public discourse, consistent with the key faculties of democratic society, rather than from the reform or elimination of the negative phenomena that attract so much attention. The goal of creating better, more productive forms of public discourse differs from the approach of some scholars and commentators, who have instead called for the suppression, or at least the condemnation, of uncivil rhetoric, or have responded to incivility by moralizing about individuals' private behaviors and values. For example, the final report of William Bennett's National Commission on Civic Renewal offered data on rates of divorce, non-marital births, youth murder, fear of crime, church attendance, charitable giving, and similar variables to measure "America's civic condition" and as evidence of the "civic disengagement" of "a nation of spectators."[9] Instead of moralizing and sermonizing about the decline of private values and public culture, we should attempt to foster a public conversation in which uncivil behaviors are not eradicated but submerged in a wealth of constructive and energetic public debate and deliberation. It is not necessary that rational deliberation dominate public conversation, but only that there be sufficient rationality and clear enough boundaries between the private and public spheres for civil society to function efficiently and effectively.

Second, these improvements must be essentially forward-looking and creative, not backward-looking and restorative. No conceivable coalition of forces can restore the eighteenth- and nineteenth-century world—or even that of the 1950s. Those worlds have been swept away by the forces of the past half century. The Penn National Commission's approach offers an alternative to the usual analysis of "civil society" and the familiar suggestions for curing its ills.[10] While it is certainly useful to examine the decline of such traditional institutions as labor unions, political parties, churches, and even families, the underlying social dynamics that have reduced their role in civil society are here to stay. Those who are concerned with the construction of a viable social order for the twenty-first century would do better to look to the new opportunities, communities, and institutions that are emerging all around us.[11] We cannot revitalize old communities or institutions, but we do have it within our power to use new forces of mass communication, globalization, democratization, and urbanization to create a social counter-dynamic, the outcomes of which will be as unpredictable and positive as were the promotion of public libraries, women's suffrage, and land-grant colleges in the nineteenth and twentieth centuries.

Third, we must seize those opportunities for creative innovation that present themselves. Today, American public culture is widely regarded as the unfortunate by-product of mass communications, Madison Avenue values, and unbridled capitalist self-striving. Yet it is precisely these features of contemporary public culture—aided and abetted by new technologies—that make it susceptible to influence and positive change. The overwhelming influence of mass communications presents not only a challenge, but also an opportunity. A single incident in the news, a charismatic personality, or a clever advertising slogan or product can capture—and repeatedly have captured—the public imagination. Public culture can be influenced as readily for productive discourse as for un-civil discourse. Indeed, the widespread revulsion against so much of con-temporary mass communications has created the conditions for change; only an appropriate catalyst is required.

Fourth, the continuing fragmentation of traditional communities, which were based largely on relatively stable and homogenous geo-graphic units (whether ethnic urban neighborhoods, small towns, or rural communities), has created an increasing sense of individual isola-tion and alienation. But this too presents new opportunities to enrich our public conversation. The forces that have broken down traditional communities are precisely the ones that open possibilities for creating new and very different senses of affiliation and shared existence. Intensi-fied urbanization, increased mobility, higher levels of education, bur-geoning professional communities, alternative forms of identification such as gender and sexual orientation, ease of communication at a dis-tance, and competition from new forms of affiliation such as interest groups, all offer new kinds of communal experiences. It may be that we will have to re-educate ourselves in order to recognize and appreciate fully the communal nature of such affiliations and interactions, and to break with our romantic visions of historical communities that cannot be re-created. But what is most dramatic about these new possibilities for community is their dependence on and contributions to, not the geographic focus of traditional community, but various forms of public dialogue. One of the striking features of our situation is that public dis-cussion and debate is now central to our sense of community. This fact opens new discourse-centered avenues for the creation of new kinds of communities, including cybercommunities.[12]

Finally, while the more egregious examples of incivility and intoler-ance, magnified by mass media and mass markets, may give us a momen-tary sense of despair, the same developments in technology and mass communications offer ample opportunity—if we seize them with ener-getic creativity and imagination—to balance the incivility with a more dialogical and useful discourse. The accumulating changes of two cen-turies of urbanization, exploration, economic expansion, social and po-litical development, technological invention, and explosive growth in knowledge and professional expertise are bearing fruit. From within the dominant paradigm of mass-market democratic capitalism, now almost global in acceptance, these forces are creating a world of enormous risk—but also enormous potential.

Thus we must recognize that each of these changes has an equally important positive dimension. For example, opinion polling is arguably a great boon to the realization of a truly representative democracy in which the will of the people matters more than special interests and money. The diversification of leadership in every realm of endeavor has brought new and different voices into our public conversation—voices that are often willing to challenge the received wisdom and accepted social and cultural attitudes of earlier, more homogenous times. The relaxation of cultural norms has arguably produced an environment in which much greater freedom of expression and creativity are possible. Technological advances in computing and communications have vastly increased public awareness of important issues and developments, and have forced leaders to be more accessible and responsive to their constituents. Our communities are more diverse, and our awareness and openness to cultural and social differences is generally greater.

All these developments are reasons for optimism. But the challenge they present is to ensure that the positive consequences of irreversible social, cultural, and technological changes outweigh the negative consequences. They present an opportunity—as yet not fully realized—for the creative use of new capacities and new dynamics. If we seize these opportunities, we can expand the participation of citizens in spirited and productive public discourse on important public issues and thereby strengthen the core faculties of democratic society—our essential capacities for deliberation, community, leadership, and the maintenance of a thriving public culture.

Notes

Prologue: The Work of the Penn National Commission

1. A comprehensive electronic archive of the Commission's work, including plenary transcripts and videos, papers, commissioned research, and a comprehensive, annotated bibliography of the literature on public discourse by David M. Ryfe, is available on the Internet at http://www.upenn.edu/pnc (15 October 2002).

2. Boorstin, *Decline of Radicalism*, 98.

3. Franklin, "Proportion of Representation and Votes," 1134.

Introduction: Incivility and Public Discourse

1. Marks, "Uncivil Wars."

2. See Putnam, "Bowling Alone," later expanded into the book, Putnam, *Bowling Alone*.

3. Morin and Balz, "Americans Losing Trust," the first article of a six-part series on "the politics of mistrust." More recently, similar trends of declining trust were found in the *Voice of the People* global public opinion survey conducted between July and September 2002 for the World Economic Forum by Gallup International and Environics International Ltd. Available on the Internet at http://www.weforum.org/site/homepublic.nsf/Content/Annual+Meeting+2003%5CResults+of+the+Survey+on+Trust (2 May 2003). See World Economic Forum, *Voice of the People*.

4. See, e.g., National Commission on Civic Renewal, *Nation of Spectators*.

5. Paul Begala, "Politics and the Culture of Contempt," plenary presentation to the Penn National Commission on Society, Culture and Community, Philadelphia, 9 December 1996.

6. Karl Rove, from a plenary roundtable discussion on "Improving Political Discourse in the Twenty-First Century," with Kathleen Hall Jamieson, Paul Begala, Tom Luce, and the members of the Penn National Commission on Society, Culture and Community, Philadelphia, 9 November 1999. Available on the Internet at http://www.upenn.edu/pnc/trans.html (2 May 2003).

7. Bill Bradley, "Government and Public Behavior," plenary presentation to the Penn National Commission on Society, Culture and Community, Washington, D.C., 8 December 1997. Available on the Internet at http://www.upenn.edu/pnc/trans.html (2 May 2003).

8. Bradley, "Government and Public Behavior."

9. James S. Fishkin, "Surmounting Conflict and Building Community: Rational Discourse in the 1990s," plenary presentation to the Penn National Commission on Society, Culture and Community, Philadelphia, 10 December 1996. See Fishkin, *Voice of the People*.

10. See Kathleen Hall Jamieson and Erika Falk, "Civility in the House of Representatives," a series of reports from the Annenberg Public Policy Center at the University of Pennsylvania, 1997–2001. Available on the Internet at http://www.appcpenn.org/political/civility/ (20 December 2002).

11. Karl Rove, from a plenary roundtable discussion on "Improving Political Discourse in the Twenty-First Century," with Kathleen Hall Jamieson, Paul Begala, Tom Luce, and the members of the Penn National Commission on Society, Culture and Community, Philadelphia, 9 November 1999. Available on the Internet at http://www.upenn.edu/pnc/trans.html (2 May 2003).

12. Kevin Phillips, "The Market, the State, and the Dynamics of Public Culture," plenary presentation and roundtable discussion with members of the Penn National Commission on Society, Culture and Community, Philadelphia, 11 June 1997. Available on the Internet at http://www.upenn.edu/pnc/phillips.html (20 December 2002).

13. Cass Sunstein, from a plenary roundtable discussion on "National Leadership and the Conversation on Race," with Ward Connerly, William H. Gray, III, and the members of the Penn National Commission on Society, Culture and Community, Chicago, 4 June 1998. Available on the Internet at http://www.upenn.edu/pnc/trans.html (2 May 2003).

14. Ibid.

15. Judith Rodin, "The University and Public Behavior," plenary presentation to the Penn National Commission on Society, Culture and Community, Washington, D.C., 8 December 1997. Available on the Internet at http://www.upenn.edu/pnc/ptrodin.html (11 September 2002).

16. See Kant, *Critique of Judgement*, 1: 152–53 (lines 294–95).

17. Lawrence Lessig, from a plenary roundtable discussion on "Cybercommunities: A New Discourse for a New Century," with panelists Ken Deutsch (Internet Strategic Communications), author Julian Dibbell, Marc Ewing (Red Hat Software, Inc.), and the members of the Penn National Commission on Society, Culture and Community, Philadelphia, 8 November 1999. Available on the Internet at http://www.upenn.edu/pnc/trans.html (2 May 2003).

Chapter 1. The Thinning of American Political Culture

1. The best analysis of contemporary American politics is Dionne, *Why Americans Hate Politics*.

2. Schudson, *Good Citizen*.

3. In formulating my argument, I have been especially indebted to the fine work of three historians: Gurstein, *Repeal of Reticence*; Wiebe, *Self-Rule*; and McGerr, *Decline of Popular Politics*.

4. For a fine account of politics in cities, see Ryan, *Civic Wars*.

5. Shklar, *American Citizenship*.

6. See Ethington, *Public City*.

7. See Sproat, *Best Men*.

8. Norton, "Intellectual Life in America," 321.

9. Parkman, "Failure of Universal Suffrage."

10. See Godkin, "Democratic View." For further discussion and documentation, see Bender, *New York Intellect*, 184–91. See also Quigley, "Reconstructing Democracy."

11. On the "sinking" of the working classes, see Wiebe, *Self-Rule*, part II.

12. See Habermas, *Structural Transformation*; Arendt, *Human Condition*; and Calhoun, *Habermas and the Public Sphere*, especially Ryan, "Gender and Public Access"

and Eley, "Nation, Publics, and Political Culture." The relation of these different perspectives is discussed in Bender, "New Metropolitanism," especially 72–74.

13. Actually, the revival of immigrant and working class participation began with the presidential candidacy of Al Smith in 1928. See Degler, "American Political Parties."

14. Tocqueville, *Democracy in America*, ed. Bender, 102, 409–11.

15. Baker, *Advertising*.

16. See Lippmann, *Public Opinion*; Lippmann, *Phantom Public*; Dewey, "Public Opinion"; and Dewey, *Public and Its Problems*.

17. Dewey, *Public and Its Problems*, especially chaps. 4 and 5. For a contemporary argument favoring the intelligence of the people, see Lindblom and Cohen, *Usable Knowledge*. In *Inquiry and Change*, Lindblom affirms his faith in the intelligence of democracy, while criticizing Dewey for not being democratic enough.

18. Gurstein, *Repeal of Reticence*.

19. Susman, *Culture as History*, chap. 14.

20. This discussion draws on Westbrook, "Politics as Consumption," quote from 145.

21. Quoted in ibid., 155.

22. Ibid., 164.

23. Tocqueville, *Democracy in America*, ed. Bender, 399–402.

Chapter 2. Primary Tensions in American Public Life

1. See Sunstein, *Democracy*, especially 121–65.

2. See Rodriguez, "The North American," this volume.

3. See Putnam, "Bowling Alone," later expanded into the book, Putnam, *Bowling Alone*.

4. See Sandel, "Procedural Republic."

5. See Bellah et al., *Habits of the Heart*.

6. See Ryfe, "The Principles of Public Discourse," this volume.

Chapter 3. Deliberative Democracy and Public Discourse

1. While it may be incorrect to characterize the United States as wholly liberal (see Hartz, *Liberal Tradition*), the liberal tradition is nonetheless a key strand of the American political culture.

2. See Schudson, *Good Citizen*, on the framers' distaste for political talk outside government.

3. Deliberation is not fundamental to the ideal model of politics presented in Rawls, *Theory of Justice* and Rawls, *Political Liberalism*.

4. On rights over public discourse in a democracy, see Lindblom, *Intelligence of Democracy* and Dahl, *Democracy and Its Critics*.

5. Various combinations of these liberal criticisms have been leveled at deliberative politics in Burnheim, *Is Democracy Possible*; Burtt, "Psyche"; Burtt, "Politics of Virtue"; Johnson, "Arguing for Deliberation"; Frohock, "Boundaries"; Fullinwider, "Citizenship"; Lund, "Communitarian Politics"; Sanders, "Against Deliberation"; Warren, "Self-Transformation"; Warren, "Better Selves"; Warren, "More Democracy"; and Warren, "Deliberative Democracy and Authority."

6. For social choice theorists on politics, see Arrow, *Social Choice*; Kelly, *Theorems*; Sen, *Collective Choice*; and Elster and Hylland, *Social Choice Theory*.

7. On "good enough" outcomes for social agents, see Simon, *Bounded Rationality*.

8. On deliberation as unnecessary, even if theoretically preferable, see Riker, "Political Trust" and Riker, *Liberalism Against Populism*.

9. For pitfalls of deliberation, see also Przeworski, "Deliberation."

10. See Moon, "Constrained Discourse," on the circularity of arguments for deliberative democracy. See also van Mill, "Rational Outcomes."

11. On deliberative democracy's bias in favor of those who practice the deliberative arts, see Berkowitz, "Debating Society."

12. For the possible negative effects on broad public participation, see also Hoyt, "Manipulation."

13. For the communitarian view of people in communities, see Sandel, *Limits of Justice*; Sandel, *Critics*; and MacIntyre, *After Virtue*.

14. On individuals' sense of themselves as derived from community, see Portis, "Citizenship."

15. For the fragmentation of shared cultural traditions in contemporary America, see Bellah et al., *Habits of the Heart* and Reynolds and Norman, *Community*.

16. For the effect of fragmentation on achieving good political outcomes, see Gutmann and Thompson, *Democracy and Disagreement*.

17. On the importance of communication, see Etzioni, *New Golden Rule*.

18. On the value of democratic deliberation, see Habermas, *Structural Transformation*; Miller, "Citizenship"; Elster, *Deliberative Democracy*; Farrell, *Norms*; Rowland, "Purpose"; Myerson, *Rhetoric*; and Nino, *Constitution*.

19. For the source of this assessment of deliberation's value, see John Stuart Mill, *On Liberty*.

20. On deliberation and legitimacy, see Habermas, *Legitimation Crisis*.

21. For representation as a means of shielding deliberation from dominating elites, see Gargarella, "Full Representation."

22. On deliberation as producing better citizens, see Habermas, *Structural Transformation* and Gutmann and Thompson, *Democracy and Disagreement*.

23. For social interaction as cultivating the civic virtues, see Aristotle, *Politics*; Wolin, *Politics and Vision*; and Pocock, *Machiavellian Moment*.

24. But for one example of empirical data related to deliberation, see Dryzek and Berejikian, "Reconstructive Democratic Theory."

25. On the increase in U.S. poverty in the 1980s, see Danzinger and Gottschalk, *Uneven Tides*.

26. For statistics on poverty in the 1980s, see Wolff, "Increasingly Richer."

27. On numbers of people in the middle class in the 1980s, see Harrison and Bluestone, *Great U-Turn*.

28. On relatively stable wealth inequality in the United States, see Shammas, "New Look."

29. For the relation between socioeconomic status and political knowledge, see McLeod and Perse, "Direct and Indirect Effects"; and Viswanath and Finnegan, "Knowledge-Gap Hypothesis."

30. For socioeconomic status and political participation, see Verba et al., "Citizen Activity"; Brady, Verba, and Schlozman, "Beyond SES"; and Schlozman et al., "Gender."

31. For socioeconomic status as it relates to education and intolerance, see Davis, "Black Political Intolerance"; Golebiowska, "Individual Value Priorities"; Tom Smith, "Misanthropy"; and Kuhn, *Skills of Argument*.

32. On the isolation of inner city and suburb, see Massey, Gross, and Shibuya, "Migration."

33. For racial exclusivity in the American suburbs, see Danielson, *Politics of Exclusion*; Jackson, *Crabgrass Frontier*; and Lipsitz, *Possessive Investment*.

34. On gated communities, see Blakely and Snyder, *Fortress America*.

35. On integration, see Thernstrom and Thernstrom, *America in Black and White*.

36. On malls and the erosion of public spaces, see Cohen, Hanchett, and Jackson, "Shopping Malls."

37. For the effects of social fragmentation on social discourse, see Putnam, *Making Democracy Work*; Putnam, "Bowling Alone"; and Putnam, "Strange Disappearance."

38. For social fragmentation and discrimination, see Tom Smith, "Misanthropy."

39. Surveys documenting exacerbated traditions of discrimination are described in Citrin, Reingold, and Green, "American Identity"; Gilens, "Racial Attitudes"; Gilens, "Race Coding"; Giles et al., "Reactions"; and Nelson and Kinder, "Issue Frames."

40. On stereotypes, discrimination, and public behavior, see Weissberg, *Political Learning*.

41. On Americans holding liberal values, see Brooks and Manza, "Social and Ideological Bases"; Polanyi, *Telling the American Story*; Hogan, "Rhetoric and Community"; Wolfe, *One Nation*; Hochschild, *Facing Up*; Lindblom and Hall, *Falling Apart*; de la Garza et al., "Please Stand Up"; and Dimaggio, Evans, and Bryson, "Social Attitudes."

42. On the contradictory American value system, see Rogers Smith, "American Creed."

43. On a preference for helping the disadvantaged without forming policies in the language of groups, see Nelson and Kinder, "Issue Frames."

44. For Americans' acceptance of immigrants who themselves favor assimilation, see Giles et al., "Reactions" and Link and Oldendick, "Social Construction."

45. For Americans' lack of interest in conventional political institutions, see Leighley, "Attitudes"; Shienbaum, *Beyond the Electoral Connection*; Avey, *Demobilization*; and Crotty, *Political Participation*.

46. For participation in nineteenth-century elections, see McGerr, *Decline of Popular Politics*.

47. On multinationals, see Lash and Urry, *End of Organized Capitalism*.

48. For the rise of Washington interest groups, see Walker, "Origins and Maintenance."

49. Statistics for Washington lobbyists are drawn from Rauch, *Demosclerosis*.

50. For politics as bazaar, see Baumgartner and Talbert, "Interest Groups."

51. For exclusive professionalism, see Fischer, "Policy Discourse."

52. On lobbyist jargon, see Thelen, *Becoming a Citizen* and Zinni, Mattei, and Rhodebeck, "Structure of Attitudes."

53. On the framers' intentions for a deliberative Congress, see Bessette, *Mild Voice of Reason*.

54. For the career concerns of members of Congress, see Ehrenhalt, *United States of Admiration*.

55. See King, *Running Scared*, for activities required to retain Congressional office.

56. For the presidency as a rhetorical force, see Wilson, *Constitutional Government* and Tulis, *Rhetorical Presidency*.

57. See Daniel Boorstin, *Image*, on image politics.

58. On provisions for image politics, see Maltese, *Spin Control*.

59. See Wattenberg, *American Political Parties*; Aldrich, *Why Parties*; and McGerr, *Decline of Popular Politics*, on the demise of the parties.

60. For television campaigning, see Luntz, *Candidates*.

61. On consultants in politics, see Sabato, *Political Consultants* and Kelley, *Professional Public Relations*.

62. On parties, television campaigning, and consultants in politics, see Bennett, *Governing Crisis*.

63. See Ansolabehere and Iyengar, *Going Negative*, on negative ads.

64. For critiques of polling, see Mann and Orren, *Media Polls*; Ginsberg, *Captive Public*; and Glasser and Salmon, *Public Opinion*.

65. On media framing of politics, see Gitlin, *Whole World* and Hallin, *Uncensored War*.

66. For characteristics of framing, see Just, *CrossTalk*.

67. For networks taken over by conglomerates, see Auletta, *Three Blind Mice*.

68. On cable and satellite television, see MacDonald, *One Nation*.

69. For entertainment techniques in television news, see Matusow, *Evening Stars*; Boyer, *Who Killed CBS*; and Gunther, *House That Roone Built*.

70. For dramatized news formats, see Hirsch, *Talking Heads* and Kurtz, *Hot Air*.

71. For changes in the economics of the newspaper industry, see Bagdikian, *Media Monopoly*; Underwood, *When MBAs Rule*; and McManus, *Market-Driven Journalism*.

72. On the news media as the central site of political deliberation, see Hallin and Mancini, "Speaking of the President" and Patterson, *Out of Order*.

Chapter 4. Affirmative Action and the Culture of Intolerance

1. For an example of such a matrix, see Edley, *Not All Black and White*, 20–21.

Chapter 8. Leadership in a Complex Democratic Society

1. Peirce and Johnson, *Boundary Crossers*.

2. Useem, *Leadership Moment*, 270–71.

3. Barber, *Passion for Democracy*, 113, from an essay originally published in 1975.

4. Garment, *Scandal*, 9. On the increase in ethics laws, see 109; on the rise of federal inspectors general, see 112–13.

5. Ibid., 29.

6. Nye, "Decline of Confidence," 1.

7. Rothman, *Strangers at the Bedside*, 1.

8. Ibid., 108–9, 126–28, 145–47, 158, 257.

9. Bryce, *American Commonwealth*, 1: 73–80.

10. See Rosen, "Part of Our World," this volume.

Chapter 9. Political Leadership in the Great Health Care Debate of 1993–1994

1. For the text of Clinton's 22 September 1993 speech to Congress, see Eckholm, *Health Care Crisis*, 301–14.

2. Quoted in Skocpol, *Boomerang*, 5.

3. Center for Public Integrity, *Well-Healed*, 1.

4. Annenberg Public Policy Center, "Role of Advertising," 2.

5. Skocpol, *Boomerang*, 118.

6. Ibid., 123.

7. Blendon, Brodie, and Benson, "What Happened," 18.

8. Skocpol, *Boomerang*, 164.
9. Yankelovich, "Debate That Wasn't."
10. Columbia Institute, *What Shapes.*
11. Robert Blendon et al., "American Public," 1543.
12. See Bok, *State of the Nation*, 235–55.
13. Stout, "Many Don't Realize."

Chapter 10. Part of Our World: Journalism as Civic Leadership

1. Lippmann, *Public Opinion*, 364.
2. Lasch, "Lost Art."
3. MacNeil, "Regaining Dignity."
4. Broder, "Democracy and the Press."
5. Broder, "New Assignment."
6. Merritt, *Public Journalism and Public Life*, 83.
7. Oppel, "We'll Help You Regain Control of the Issues."
8. Ibid.

Chapter 11. Modeling Public Discourse in Popular Culture

1. See Gabler, *Life, the Movie*, 48.
2. Kael, "Trash, Art, and the Movies," 104.
3. See Dahl, *Who Governs?*
4. See Cannon, *President Reagan.*

Chapter 12. Creating a National Discourse: Truth and Reconciliation in South Africa

1. Garton Ash, *File.*
2. Renan, "What Is a Nation?" 190.
3. See Plutarch, *Cicero*, in *Plutarch's Lives* 2: 436.
4. Churchill, "Tragedy of Europe," speech at Zurich University, 19 September 1946.
5. Televised address marking release of the Chilean Truth and Reconciliation Commission report, 4 March 1991.

Chapter 13. Political Apologies and Public Discourse

1. Levy, "Symbolism," 238.
2. Shriver, *Ethic for Enemies*, 6.
3. Dumas, "Foregiveness and Politics," 43, quoted in Love, *Peace Building*, 12.
4. I would like to thank Ian Lustick for sparking my interest in political apologies and supervising my work on a research project on which this chapter is based.
5. Tavuchis, *Mea Culpa*, 15.
6. Owen, *Apologies*, 109.
7. Tavuchis, *Mea Culpa*, 36.
8. Ibid., 121.
9. Ibid., 16–24.

10. Ibid., 33–34.

11. Ibid., 108.

12. Ibid., 29.

13. See Ryfe, "Principles of Public Discourse," this volume.

14. Tavuchis, *Mea Culpa*, 20.

15. Ibid., 45.

16. Ibid., 46. Tavuchis acknowledges that outsiders such as interested third parties may play a role. For example, they can help to reconfigure the status of the offender, the offended, or even the offense itself (50).

17. Ibid., 48.

18. A comprehensive list of political apologies is available on the Penn National Commission website at http://www.upenn.edu/pnc under "Resources."

19. Tavuchis, *Mea Culpa*, xiii.

20. Cohen, "French Church."

21. Thoreson et al., "Science and Forgiveness Interventions," 164–65.

22. Bronkhorst, *Truth and Reconciliation*, 38.

23. Dorff, "Elements of Forgiveness," 35.

24. Ibid., 44–45.

25. Azar et al., "Propensity to Forgive."

26. Worthington, *Dimensions of Forgiveness*, 2.

27. See Nietzsche, *Genealogy of Morals*, 65, 76, 84, 90–92, 124–25, and passim.

28. See Arendt, *Human Condition* (1959), 212–19.

29. Baumeister, Exline, and Sommer, "Victim Role," 80.

30. Murphy and Hampton, *Forgiveness and Mercy*, 6, 12, 89.

31. Baumeister, Exline, and Sommer, "Victim Role," 81.

32. Ibid., 102.

33. McCullough et al., "Annotated Bibliography," 306. See Zillman et al., "Effect of Timing."

34. McCullough et al., "Annotated Bibliography," 271. See Ohbuchi et al., "Apology as Aggression Control."

35. See discussion in Boraine, "Creating a National Discourse," this volume.

36. Pross, *Paying for the Past*, viii.

37. McCullough et al., "Annotated Bibliography," 218. See Darby and Schenkler, "Children's Reactions."

38. McCullough et al., "Annotated Bibliography," 299. See Weiner et al., "Public Confession."

39. McCullough et al., "Annotated Bibliography," 198, on Axelrod. See Axelrod, "Effective Choice."

40. Goffman, *Relations in Public*. See Tavuchis, *Mea Culpa*, 127.

41. Goffman, *Relations in Public*, 143–44, quoted in Owen, *Apologies*, 19–20.

42. Minow, *Between Vengeance and Forgiveness*, 116. Among de facto apologies is the Nuremberg International Military Tribunal, which the Allied powers established to prosecute Nazi leaders for war crimes, crimes against humanity, and crimes against peace. From 1945 to 1949, roughly 200 defendants were tried. Although I do not consider the Nuremberg trials a form of apology, they do constitute a response to the wrongs committed, albeit a response dictated by the victorious powers rather than the defeated offender.

43. Traverso, *Jews and Germany*, 136–37.

44. Pross, *Paying for the Past*, 21.

45. Schwerin, "German Compensation," 48.

46. Serotta, *Jews, Germany, Memory*, 37.

47. Ibid., 37.

48. Schwerin, "German Compensation," 49.

49. Segev, *Seventh Million*, 201.

50. Frohn, *Holocaust and Shilumim*, 4.

51. Cited in ibid., 5.

52. Ibid., 2.

53. *Guardian*, "Leaders' Apologies."

54. Schiller, "World Bids Final Farewell."

55. Massie, "Why Losers."

56. Statue of Liberty-Ellis Island Foundation, "America's Concentration Camps."

57. Telephone interview with Tom Keaney, Chief of Staff for Representative Robert Matsui (D, Calif.), 16 September 1999.

58. Shriver, *Ethic for Enemies*, 165.

59. Civil Liberties Public Education Fund, *Personal Justice Denied*, x.

60. Telephone interview with Tom Keaney, 16 September 1999.

61. Statue of Liberty-Ellis Island Foundation, "America's Concentration Camps."

62. Civil Liberties Public Education Fund, *Personal Justice Denied*, xi.

63. The Commission's financial recommendations were based on its estimate that (in 1983 dollars) between $810 million and $2.0 billion was lost in income and property. Ibid., xii, 456.

64. Telephone interview with Tom Keaney, 16 September 1999.

65. Matsui's district was only 9 percent Asian American at the time, and no district had an Asian population of over 20 percent. Ibid.

66. Ibid.

67. Tavuchis, *Mea Culpa*, 107.

68. Shriver, *Ethic for Enemies*, 166.

69. *Economist*, "Japan's War."

70. Dower, "Bombed," 141.

71. Chang, *Rape of Nanking*, 4.

72. Zhigeng, *Lest We Forget*, 7.

73. The term "comfort women" is of course a euphemism. In Korean, it is *wianbu*; in Japanese, it is *ianfu*. Another term used in Korea is *chongshindae*, which translates literally as "voluntarily offered body corps." See Howard, *True Stories*, v.

74. Hicks, *Comfort Women*, 17.

75. Ibid., 11.

76. Tanaka, "Why Is Asia Demanding?"

77. Noboru, "Japanese War Apology." This letter to the editor notes that Japan had in fact apologized for wartime atrocities.

78. Pilkington, "Yeltsin Learns."

79. Gluck, "Idea of Showa," 2, 12; Burress, "Most Japanese"; Tachibana, "Quest," 168–73. Shriver claims that "after 1945, the mending of American-Japanese political relations was rapid and pragmatic, as American leaders saw the defeated country as their trans-Pacific front against the Soviet Union and (soon after) Communist China and North Korea." Shriver, *Ethic for Enemies*, 139. See also Hogan, *Hiroshima*, 8; Jameson, "Hosokawa Outlines Reforms"; Hein and Selden, *Living with the Bomb*, 22; Dower, *Bombed*, 141; Hicks, *Comfort Women*, 11, 15–17, and 21; and Howard, *True Stories*, vi.

80. Desmond, "Finally."

81. Shriver, *Ethic for Enemies*, 137.

82. Mukae, "Japan's Diet Resolution."

83. Hein and Selden, *Living with the Bomb*, 49.

84. Tavuchis, *Mea Culpa*, 39.

85. Email correspondence with Steven Benfell, 18 August 1999. However, on 15 August 2001, Prime Minister Koizumi made an apology to China and used the term *ware-ware*, which means "we," thereby invoking a broader admission of responsibility than previous apologies had used.

86. Hein and Selden, *Living with the Bomb*, 180; Desmond, "Finally"; and Tavuchis, *Mea Culpa*, 42–43.

87. I am indebted to Steven Benfell for the main point and examples here, as well as for providing me with a wealth of helpful background information on Japanese political apologies.

88. Burress, "Most Japanese."

89. "Between October 1939 and June 1941, the Soviet Union additionally deported some 1.5 million Poles to various locations within the Soviet Union. More than a million of these were never heard of again. This was out of a Polish population of 36 million." Murphey, "Katyn."

90. Slowes, *Road to Katyn*, xxv.

91. Lauck, *Katyn Killings*, 87–88 and Paul, *Katyn*, 335–37.

92. Paul, *Katyn*, 335–37.

93. Ibid., 339.

94. Fein, "Upheaval."

95. Ibid.

96. *Los Angeles Times*, "Joy and Sorrow."

97. Boyes, "Yeltsin Snubs."

98. *Los Angeles Times*, "Joy and Sorrow"; Paul, *Katyn*, 340; and Sikorski, "Haunting Russia."

99. Tolz, "Katyn Documents."

100. Boyes, "Yeltsin Snubs" and Nagorski, "At Last."

101. Bobinski, "Yeltsin Seeks to Heal."

102. Boyes, "Yeltsin Snubs."

103. Minow, *Between Vengeance and Forgiveness*, 114.

104. Tavuchis, *Mea Culpa*, 5.

105. Ibid., 98.

106. Ibid.

107. Ibid., 97, 103.

108. Ibid., 100.

109. Ibid.

110. Ibid., 97.

111. Levy, "Symbolism," 242-43.

112. Tavuchis, *Mea Culpa*, 100.

113. Ibid.

114. Noboru, "Japanese War Apology."

115. Speirs, "Atonement."

116. Shriver, *Ethic for Enemies*, 141; and Chang, *Rape of Nanking*, 224.

117. Burress, "Most Japanese" and *Economist*, "Cold Comfort."

118. Minow, *Between Vengeance and Forgiveness*, 105.

119. Tanaka, "Why Is Asia Demanding?"

120. *Economist*, "War Shadows."

121. I am indebted to Steve Benfell for this point.

122. Dower, "Bombed," 142.

123. *Economist*, "War Shadows."

124. I am indebted to Ellen Kennedy for this point.

125. Tavuchis, *Mea Culpa*, 47

126. Ibid., 22.

127. Ibid., 13. Note that, insofar as political apologies work because of the assumption of a greater moral community, these apologies support the academic liberal paradigm in international relations; realism cannot be correct if political apologies indicate the existence of widely shared norms of conduct.

128. Ibid., 71.

129. If "the head of one state apologizes to another in camera to reduce political tensions arising from some incident while remaining publicly silent or denying fault," this does not qualify as a political apology, as (1) the apology is not truly on behalf of the group whose representative gives it, and (2) the recipient of the apology is not truly a group, but rather only an individual. See ibid., 102.

130. Ibid., 109 and Minow, *Between Vengeance and Forgiveness*, 115–16.

131. Tavuchis, *Mea Culpa*, 109.

132. Ibid., 117.

133. *Los Angeles Times*, "Joy and Sorrow."

134. Tavuchis, *Mea Culpa*, 8.

135. Ibid., 18.

136. Minow, *Between Vengeance and Forgiveness*, 115.

137. Tavuchis, *Mea Culpa*, 45, 23.

138. Enright and Coyle, "Researching the Process Model," 141.

139. Tavuchis, *Mea Culpa*, 115.

140. Ibid.

141. Ibid., 87.

142. Ibid., 88.

143. Ibid., 12.

144. *Los Angeles Times*, "Joy and Sorrow."

145. Paul, *Katyn*, 342.

146. Berger, "Hidden Japanese."

147. Sontag, "Israel."

148. Levy, "Symbolism," 240.

149. In a legal context, consider the "excited utterance" exception to the hearsay rule of evidence. Hearsay is generally not admissible, but utterances made in a state of excitement immediately after a startling event are admissible, on the theory that excitement precludes the kind of reflection necessary to lie, so such statements are sufficiently reliable to be used in a court of law. For example, someone who shouts, "I'm sorry, it was all my fault" after an automobile collision may be held culpable because of that admission. Aviva Orenstein has argued against this exception on feminist grounds, and there may be reason to oppose it on the grounds that it inhibits the sort of easy apology that can facilitate good-natured resolutions of minor difficult situations. See Orenstein, "My God!" I am indebted to Kim Scheppele for this point.

150. Levy, "Symbolism," 239–40.

151. Minow, *Between Vengeance and Forgiveness*, 117.

152. Tavuchis, *Mea Culpa*, 107. Ackerman also recommends that new states establish a special compensation fund, but his rationale is mainly that such funds enable new states to cement their administrative control. See Ackerman, *Future of Liberal Revolution*, 93.

153. Serotta, *Jews, Germany, Memory*, 37, quoted in Segev, *Seventh Million*, 215.

154. Ackerman, *Future of Liberal Revolution*, 97.

155. Bronkhorst, *Truth and Reconciliation*, 40.

156. Tavuchis, *Mea Culpa*, 94.

157. Ibid., 63.

158. *New York Times*, "Australia Apologizes."

159. *New York Times*, "No Apology to Orphans."

160. DePalma, "Canada's Indigenous Tribes."
161. Totsuka, "Commentary" and *New York Times*, "Japan: Koreans, Plea Rejected."
162. Gluck, "Idea of Showa," 14.
163. Rose, "Down Under."
164. Gonzalez, "Killing Shocks Jamaicans."

Chapter 14. The Principles of Public Discourse: What Is Good Public Discourse?

1. This turn toward issues of language and discourse has been described in various terms, as may be seen from the following titles: Rorty, *Linguistic Turn*; Simons, *Rhetorical Turn*; Fischer and Forester, *Argumentative Turn*; Chaney, *Cultural Turn*; Jameson, *Cultural Turn*; Best and Kellner, *Postmodern Turn*; Hassan, *Postmodern Turn*; and Seidman, *Postmodern Turn*.

2. On the relation of language to personal and social identities, as it has been studied across several disciplines, see Cherwitz and Hikins, *Communication and Knowledge*; Fairclough, *Language and Power*; van Dijk, *Communicating Racism*; and Gumperz, *Language and Social Identity*.

3. For new, deliberative theories of democracy that have emerged from a focus on communication, see Habermas, *Structural Transformation*; Gutmann and Thompson, *Democracy and Disagreement*; Dryzek, *Discursive Democracy*; Elster, *Deliberative Democracy*; and Bohman and Rehg, *Deliberative Democracy*.

4. On deliberative theory's view that the relation between the state and individuals is too narrow a focus, see Elster, *Deliberative Democracy*.

5. For the necessary relation between good democratic politics and good public discourse, see Cohen, "Democracy and Liberty."

6. On argumentation as the best deliberative model for public discourse, see the extensive work in rhetoric, such as Toulmin, *Uses of Argument*; Perelman and Olbrechts-Tyteca, *New Rhetoric*; Perelman, *Realm of Rhetoric*; van Eemeren et al., *Reconstructing Argumentative Discourse*; Willard, *Theory of Argumentation*; Williams and Hazen, *Argumentation Theory*; and Farrell, *Norms*.

7. For argumentation in sociology, communication, and history, see Bohman, "Communication" and Calhoun, *Habermas and the Public Sphere*. For the communicative model of rationality on which these approaches depend, see Habermas, *Structural Transformation* and Habermas, *Theory of Communicative Action*.

8. The work on argumentation in linguistics has been guided by the conversational maxims in Grice, "Logic in Conversation."

9. On thinking as basically argumentative, see Billig, *Ideology and Opinions* and Billig, *Arguing and Thinking*.

10. For postmodernism on inevitable irrationality and the abuses of reason, see Foucault, *Madness and Civilization* and Derrida, *Of Grammatology*. For the resulting revisions in the view that argumentation is a model of good public discourse, see Zarefsky, "Spectator Politics" and Schrag, *Resources of Rationality*.

11. For a critique of Habermas's view that ordinary language is inherently rational, see McCarthy, "Practical Discourse."

12. For the relaxation of Grice's four maxims of conversation, see Harris, "Pragmatics and Power."

13. The move away from abstract accounts of argument has returned the discussion to a conception outlined in Toulmin, *Uses of Argument*; Perelman and Olbrechts-Tyteca, *New Rhetoric*; and Perelman, *Realm of Rhetoric*.

14. For even postmodern argument as principally based in reason, see Myer-

son, *Rhetoric*; Schrag, *Resources of Rationality*; Rowland, "Purpose"; Spragens, *Reason and Democracy*; and Aronovitch, "Political Importance."

15. On propositions, evidence, and counterarguments in postmodern argument, see van Eemeren et al., *Reconstructing Argumentative Discourse*.

16. For reason in individuals, see Kant, *Critique of Pure Reason*; for reason's multiple manifestations, see Beer, "Words of Reason." But for its enduring place in public communication and in the Western tradition, see Canary, et al., "Toward a Theory" and Gellner, *Reason and Culture*.

17. On argument entailing emotion, see Abu-Lughod and Lutz, "Introduction" and Gallois, "Group Membership."

18. For the feminist analysis of reason and emotion, see Benhabib and Cornell, *Feminism as Critique*; Young, *Justice*; Condit, "Opposites"; and Fraser, *Unruly Practices*.

19. On gender domination in linguistic interactions, see Coates, *Men and Language* and Tannen, "Introduction."

20. For the role of emotion in gaining assent, see Frank, *Passions Within Reason*.

21. On emotion as a key to character in argument, and its function in gaining assent, see also Smith and Hyde, "Rethinking."

22. On the good and bad effects of emotion in argument, with case studies, see Walton, *Place of Emotion*.

23. On misleading appeals to emotion, see also Gallois, "Group Membership."

24. For survey data that demonstrates the role of an appeal to emotion in attracting participants' attention, see Theiss-Morse, Marcus, and Sullivan, "Passion and Reason."

25. On storytelling as crucial to sustaining dialogue, see Schiffrin, *Everyday Argument* and Schiffrin, "Management of a Cooperative Self."

26. On narrative and common understanding based in experience, see Foss and Griffin, "Beyond Persuasion"; on narrative and collective identity, see Somers, "Narrative Constitution."

27. On narrative, relationships, and commitment, see Sullivan and Goldzwig, "Relational Approach."

28. For tolerance as a liberal ideal, see Fletcher, "Case for Tolerance" and Murphy, "Tolerance."

29. On tolerance and accommodation to alternative views, see Chong, "How People Think."

30. For a liberal view of tolerance and its conservative, democratic, and postmodernist critics, see Kautz, "Liberalism."

31. On the weakness of tolerance when moral disagreements are deep, see Langerak, "Pluralism."

32. On reciprocity in deliberative democracy, see Gutmann and Thompson, *Democracy and Disagreement*.

33. For reciprocity as a form of engagement between isolation and appreciation, see Gutmann and Thompson, "Moral Conflict" and Gutmann, "Challenge."

34. On politeness as a universal feature of human communication, see Brown and Levinson, *Politeness*.

35. For a critique of politeness as a way of avoiding potentially divisive topics, see Eliasoph, "Close to Home" and Eliasoph, *Avoiding Politics*.

36. On the reluctance to confront controversial issues in certain settings, see also Kochman, "Politics of Politeness" and Loury, "Self-Censorship."

37. On compassion in good public discourse, see Nussbaum, *Fragility of Goodness* and Nussbaum, "Compassion."

38. On compassion in gift exchange as a guarantee of individuality, see Wuthnow, *Acts of Compassion*.

39. For the failure to be compassionate when information is scarce, see the work of social choice theorists such as Margolis, *Selfishness* and Elster and Hylland, *Social Choice Theory.*

40. On activists sustained by the image of a compassionate society, see Teske, *Political Activists* and Teske, "Beyond Altruism."

41. For a rare description and assessment of the actual forms of good public discourse, see Fishkin, *Democracy and Deliberation.*

42. Researchers have found that actual public discourse is hampered by a range of problems. On negative, simple arguments, see Capella and Jamieson, *Spiral of Cynicism* and Cobb and Kukinski, *Changing Minds.* For power differentials that permit those who argue well to control the agenda, see Gumperz and Cook-Gumperz, "Introduction"; Gumperz, "Communicative Competence Revisited"; Hosman and Siltanen, "Attributional and Evaluative Consequences"; Gallois, "Group Membership"; Skillington, "Politics and the Struggle"; van Dijk, "Social Cognition"; and Stokes, "Pathologies of Deliberation." For the enforced silence felt by subordinate groups, see Huspek and Kendall, "Withholding Political Voice" and Gibson, "Political Freedom." For the use of stereotypes and ad hominem attacks to influence emotions, see Link and Oldendick, "Social Construction"; Gilens, "Racial Attitudes"; Gilens, "Race Coding"; Jamieson, *Dirty Politics*; and Cappella and Jamieson, *Spiral of Cynicism.*

43. For the communitarian emphasis on Americans' cultural traditions and shared idioms, see Sandel, *Limits of Justice*; Sandel, *Critics*; and MacIntyre, *After Virtue.*

44. On American individualism, egalitarianism, and pragmatism as broadly embraced by members of ethnic and racial groups, see Giles et al., "Reactions" and de la Garza et al., "Please Stand Up."

45. For the common academic view that therapy is a narcissistic, individualistic, and corrupting influence on our public culture, see Rieff, *Triumph of the Therapeutic*; Lasch, *Culture of Narcissism*; and Cloud, *Control and Consolation.*

46. On consumerism and the therapeutic idiom, see Lears, "From Salvation."

47. On possible benefits of the therapeutic model in public discourse, see Warren, "Better Selves" and Warren, "Self-Transformation."

48. For the broad consensus that American values are contradictory, see Chong, "Tolerance and Social Adjustment"; Converse, "Nature of Belief Systems"; Conover, Crewe, and Searing, "Nature of Citizenship"; Gamson, *Talking Politics*; Hochschild, "Disjunction and Ambivalence"; Herbst, *Numbered Voices*; and Neuman, Just, and Crigler, *Common Knowledge.*

49. For public deliberation at multiple sites, see Fraser, *Justice Interruptus.*

50. On the face-to-face interactions that reformers also find compelling, see Pitkin and Shumer, "On Participation."

51. On systematic ways of encouraging members of Congress to devote personal attention to their deliberative responsibilities, see Bessette, *Mild Voice of Reason.*

52. On public financing of deliberative forums, and the possible effect on the relationship between the public and the presidency, see Jamieson, *Dirty Politics.*

53. On the possible benefits of stronger parties at the local level, instead of the current system of mass mediation, see Sabato, *Party's Just Begun* and Aldrich, *Why Parties.*

54. On public journalism and good public discourse, see Rosen, *Getting the Connections Right* and Rosen, "Part of Our World," this volume.

55. For seminal work on the principles of more time and less distance as they pertain to civil society, see Putnam, *Making Democracy Work*; Putnam, "Tuning In; and Putnam, "Strange Disappearance."

56. On participation in voluntary associations and the production of greater social capital, see Rothenbuhler, "Process of Community Involvement"; Karen Jones, "Trust"; and Newton, "Social Capital."

57. On social networks filtering political information, see Huckfeldt et al., "Political Environments" and Kenny, "Political Participation."

58. On civic norms as a more important motive than material considerations when people vote, see Knack, "Civic Norms."

59. On youth participation as a strong predictor of later civic activity, see Youniss, McLellan, and Yates, "What We Know."

60. For public funding of voluntary associations and opportunities for voluntary associations to handle government responsibilities, see Hirst, *Associative Democracy* and Cohen and Rogers, "Secondary Associations."

61. On deliberative polls, see Fishkin, *Democracy and Deliberation.*

62. On the difficulty of specifying variables of social capital and establishing causal connections between the variables and better democracy, see Levi, "Special Section."

63. On civil society as a necessary but not a sufficient condition for good democracy, see Berman, "Civil Society" and Jackman and Miller, "Renaissance."

64. On the importance of political institutions in the creation of vibrant democracy, see Schudson, "Sending a Political Message."

65. For the role of government agencies in cooperation between private parties, see Scholz and Gray, "Can Government Facilitate."

66. For the claim that parties are still the primary institutions for connecting citizens to the political process, see Wielhouwer and Lockerbie, "Party Contacting."

67. On possible enhancement of political views by participation, see Leighley, "Participation as a Stimulus."

68. For the academic finding that political knowledge and participation are conditioned by income level, see Muller and Seligson, "Civic Culture."

69. On freedom as an activity of self-development, see Gould, *Rethinking Democracy.*

70. For his views on democratic conversation and face-to-face communication, see Montesquieu, *Spirit of the Laws.*

71. On good public discourse in a fragmented society, see Hamilton, Madison, and Jay, *Federalist Papers*, X.

Chapter 16. The Practice of Public Discourse: A Study of Sixteen Discourse Organizations

1. See Ryfe, "Principles of Public Discourse," this volume.

2. For other reviews of this scholarship, see Gastil, "Undemocratic Discourse"; Warren, *Democracy and Association*, especially chapter 4; and Mendelberg, "Deliberative Citizen." Recently, researchers have begun to put the claims of this theoretical literature to empirical test. See, for instance, Cook and Jacobs, *Deliberative Democracy*; Gastil, "Democratic Citizenship" on NIFs; Kimelman and Hall, "Critical Study"; Button and Mattson, "Actually Existing"; Delli Carpini, "Impact of Money+Politics"; Pearce and Littlejohn, *Moral Conflict*; Walsh, "Democratic Potential"; Denver, Hands, and Jones, "Fishkin and the Deliberative Opinion Poll"; Gastil and Dillard, "Increasing Political Sophistication"; Mendelberg and Oleske, "Race and Public Deliberation"; Hibbing and Theiss-Morse, "Deliberation as a Source"; Sulkin and Simon, "Habermas in the Lab"; Hendriks, "Institutions"; and Fung and Wright, "Deepening Democracy."

3. This point emerged for me in a personal conversation with Richard Harwood of the Harwood Group and during a panel discussion at the International

Communication Association Conference, 23–27 May 1999, in San Francisco, which centered on a discussion of Schudson, "Why Conversation."

4. An excellent example of this kind of privately oriented program is the Dialogue Project at MIT. Headquartered at the Center for Organizational Learning on the MIT campus, this project has analyzed discourse within complex organizations like large corporations. As far as I have been able to discern, the Center has yet to apply this method to more public concerns.

5. See the Democracy Is a Discussion packets: Myers, *Civic Engagement* and Myers, *Challenges and Promise*.

6. For the Keystone Center focus on science policy issues, see Keystone Center, "Publications List."

7. For PCP's methodology, see Chasin and Herzig, "Creating Systemic Interventions."

8. See ADSS, "Discussion Leader Kit."

9. For the ADSS use of satellite technologies and the Internet, see Lukensmeyer and Goldman, "National Town Hall."

10. The AISR and SCRC conversation packet for small-group discussion is AISR, "Local Conversations."

11. See Fishkin, *Voice of the People*.

12. See Lukensmeyer and Goldman, *National Town Hall*.

13. Interview with Jay Rothman, conducted 4 February 1999.

14. See President's Initiative on Race, "Dialogue Guide." For board participation in small-group discussion, see President's Initiative on Race, "Advisory Board's Report," 19.

15. This is not true for a few of the organizations. The Jefferson Center and the Center for Deliberative Polling carefully select and recruit their participants for Citizens Juries and Deliberative Polls. Other organizations, like the Keystone Center, the Aria Group, and the Harwood Group, identify relevant stakeholders and bring them to the table. Finally, the participation of some groups is determined by their respective leaders. For instance, a local school principal or newspaper editor may decide to institute a civics or civic journalism program using Democracy Is a Discussion or Pew Center materials. In these cases, the students and journalists involved have little choice with regard to their participation.

16. See Neuman, *Paradox of Mass Politics*, 171. These numbers mirror a comment made by political scientist Samuel Popkin at the Penn National Commission on Society, Culture and Community plenary meeting in Los Angeles on 17 December 1998, to the effect that the 15 percent of Americans with advanced degrees produce more votes on election day than the one-third of Americans who have not finished high school. A transcript is available on the Internet at http://www.upenn.edu/pnc.

17. Other scholars shift these numbers somewhat (see Berelson, Lazarsfeld, and McPhee, *Voting*; Dahl, *Modern Political Analysis*; and Verba and Nie, *Participation*), but the three-part division remains the same.

18. See Fishkin, *Voice of the People*, 180.

19. Kimelman and Hall, "Critical Study," 2. Similarly, in their study of meetings organized by the League of Women Voters and the Harwood Group on the issue of money and politics, Mark Button and Kevin Mattson found that "most of the people we interviewed [did] not believe that deliberation would have a direct impact on public policy." See Button and Mattson, "Actually Existing," 37. This feeling of ineffectuality greatly stunted participants' enthusiasm for the meetings.

20. NEH (1996), "Handbook of Tips," 9.

21. This point was made by a number of individuals I interviewed, including

Mary Jane Hollis, the Study Circles Coordinator in Aurora, Illinois (interview conducted on 12 May 1999) and Rona Roberts, a consultant in Lexington, Kentucky, who is doing an ethnographic analysis of six study circles as part of the SCRC Best Practices evaluation program (interview conducted 5 May 1999).

22. As the Harwood Group instructed members of its discussion groups: "The purpose of this project is *not* to create a new package of legislative reforms. Instead, this is about us working through these issues and setting a general direction for action." See Harwood Group, "Money+Politics," 7, emphasis in original. Even the Jefferson Center's Citizens Jury process, a format that has often been used by policy-making agencies, produces no more than recommendations for policy action.

23. See Eliasoph, *Avoiding Politics*.

24. This point was emphasized for me both by Mary Jacksteit, director of the Common Ground Network (interview conducted on 2 April 1999) and by Maggie Herzig, program coordinator for PCP (interview conducted on 18 May 1999).

25. See Fishkin, *Voice of the People*; Jefferson Center, "Citizen Jury"; and Lukensmeyer and Goldman, "National Town Hall."

26. NEH (1996), "Handbook of Tips," 10–12.

27. Becker et al., "Stuck Debate," 150.

28. Jacksteit and Kaufmann, "Finding Common Ground," 6.

29. See SCRC, "Building Strong Neighborhoods." This kit for study circles on the issue of education describes four conversation sessions: The first session is devoted to a simple description of participants' neighborhoods. By the second session, however, participants are invited to brainstorm solutions to particular problems, such as how they can make their neighborhood safer. The third session is devoted to planning solutions to identified problems, and the final session asks participants to respond to the following question: "How can we move from words to action?"

30. NIFI, "For Convenors and Moderators."

31. Given that participants generally desire to make such decisions, it is not surprising that they chafe when having to spend time building relationships. For instance, a study of an ADSS large-group forum found that participants were frustrated at having to begin their discussions with values, and wanted to move directly to policy options for reforming social security. See Cook and Jacobs, "Deliberative Democracy," 8–9.

32. See President's Initiative on Race, "Advisory Board's Report," 18, 33.

33. NEH, "Handbook of Tips," 14.

34. Rothman, "Action Evaluation."

35. Cook and Jacobs, "Deliberative Democracy," 11.

36. Something similar occurred during forums on energy restructuring in the Pacific Northwest that were observed by Kimelman and Hall. Over 300 people attended one such event, but most were not able to speak, and those that gained access to the microphone did little more than rattle off a prepared statement. See Kimelman and Hall, "Critical Study," 14.

37. Lukensmeyer and Goldman, "National Town Hall," 46.

38. Kimelman and Hall, "Critical Study."

39. Button and Mattson, "Actually Existing," 35.

40. Delli Carpini, "Impact of Money+Politics," 1.

41. This comment assumes that discourse organizations have intended to reach these groups. Several in this study clearly have not. The Keystone Center, the Aria Group, PCP, and Common Ground intend to work with groups that are in conflict, not necessarily ones that are apathetic. However, the other organizations intend for their methods to be useful for promoting better democracy, which implies that they wish to spur greater inclusion in public conversations. It is in this

sense that these organizations have failed to "discover" ways of reaching the hardened core of apathetic citizenry.

42. Leighninger and McCoy, "Mobilizing Citizens."

43. See Cargile and Giles, "Understanding Language Attitudes" and Kuklinski et al., "Thinking About Political Tolerance."

44. For a helpful, if partial list of these organizations, see Millennium Communications Group, *Communications as Engagement.*

45. Lukensmeyer and Goldman, "National Town Hall."

46. See Horn, *Statistical Indicators* and Rossi and Gilmartin, *Handbook.*

47. Miringoff and Miringoff, *Social Health.*

Chapter 17. Lessons from the Field: Practitioner Perspectives on Public Discourse Programs

1. See Ryfe, "Practice of Public Discourse," this volume.

2. Ibid.

Chapter 18. Building Community in the Twenty-First Century

This chapter, based on extensive interviews and discussions with community and institutional leaders, reflects the conclusions of the Working Group on Community in the Twenty-First Century of Penn National Commission on Society, Culture and Community. Professor Appleby chaired the Working Group.—Eds.

1. Interview with Robert Archibald, Executive Director, Missouri Historical Society, St. Louis, Missouri, 7 April 1998.

2. Interview with David Goudy, Montshire Museum of Science, Norwich, Vermont, 7 April 1998.

3. Interview with Bonnie Kroeger, Director of Grant Development, Cincinnati Zoo and Botanical Garden, Cincinnati, Ohio, 7 April 1998.

4. Interview with Tim Watkins, Watts Labor Community Action Committee, Los Angeles, 9 September 1997.

5. Interview with Lou Casagrande, Director and President, Children's Museum, Boston, 8 April 1998.

Chapter 19. The Myth of Academic Community

1. Readings, *University in Ruins*, 180–81.

2. LaCapra, "University in Ruins?" 39.

3. Graff, *Professing Literature*, quoted in LaCapra, "University in Ruins?" 49; see also Graff, *Beyond the Culture Wars.*

4. LaCapra, "University in Ruins?" 46.

5. Ibid., 54.

Chapter 20. The University as Discourse Community

An earlier version of this essay was delivered by Judith Rodin as the Visiting Chubb Fellow at Yale University on 12 October 1999.

1. *Philadelphia Inquirer*, "Speech and Challenges."
2. See Newman, *Idea of a University* and Newman, *Scope and Nature*.
3. Kathrada, *Letters from Robben Island*, 38–39.
4. Ibid.

Chapter 21. Creating Community in Cyberspace: Criteria for a Discourse Technology Project

1. See Markoff, "Newer, Lonelier Crowd"; Harmon, "Researchers Find"; and Rainie and Kalsnes, "Commons of the Tragedy."
2. See Cole and Lebo, "UCLA Internet Report"; Associated Press, "UCLA Study"; and Guernsey, "Professor."
3. See, e.g., Sunstein, *Republic.com*.
4. See, e.g., Harmon, "Vox Populi."
5. The thinking behind this chapter was very much the product of an interactive and dialogical group effort. I particularly want to express my appreciation to Ms Jennifer Yuan, who developed many of the criteria contained herein while working under my direction as the Assistant Director for Information Technology of the Penn National Commission on Society, Culture and Community. I also wish to thank Mr. Michael Strong, who preceded Ms Yuan in that position and educated me in the possibilities and technologies of the Internet. I also want to acknowledge the helpful background and stimulating commentary (some of which is cited in this chapter) offered by the guest panelists and Commission members who participated in "Cybercommunities: A New Discourse for a New Century," a plenary discussion of the Penn National Commission on Society, Culture and Community, 8 November 1999, in Philadelphia. The panel was organized and led by Lawrence Lessig (then of Harvard Law School), with panelists Ken Deutsch (Internet Strategic Communications), author Julian Dibbell, and Marc Ewing (Red Hat Software, Inc.). A transcript is available on the Internet at http://www.upenn.edu/pnc.
6. Ibid.
7. Ibid.
8. On cybercommunities more generally, see especially Horrigan, "Online Communities"; Reingold, *Virtual Community*; Smith and Kollock, *Communities in Cyberspace*; Doheny-Farina, *Wired Neighborhood*; and Holeton, *Composing Cyberspace*.
9. "Cybercommunities" plenary discussion.
10. Dibbell, "Rape in Cyberspace."
11. "Cybercommunities" plenary discussion.
12. Rainie and Kalsnes, "Commons of the Tragedy."
13. Ibid., 2.
14. See Bender, "Thinning."
15. "Cybercommunities" plenary discussion.
16. Ibid.
17. Ibid.
18. See http://www.grassroots.com (2 March 2003).
19. See http://www.ebay.com; http://www.epinions.com and http://www.amazon.com (2 March 2003).
20. See http://www.grassroots.com; http://www.yahoo.com and http://www.salon.com (2 March 2003).
21. See http://www.abuzz.com (2 March 2003).
22. Barringer, "Internet Unit Plans Layoffs."
23. Dibbell, "Rape in Cyberspace."
24. See http://www.grassroots.com (2 March 2003).

Epilogue: The Centrality of Public Discourse

1. See the Penn National Commission website at http://www.upenn.edu/pnc (15 October 2002).

2. For an example of the condemnatory approach, see National Commission on Civic Renewal, *Nation of Spectators*. For the Penn National Commission's approach, see Rodin, "Work of the Penn National Commission," this volume.

3. See Ryfe, "Deliberative Democracy," this volume.

4. Ibid.

5. See, e.g., Kant, *Anthropology*.

6. See Wundt, "Introduction," sec. 2, and especially n. 1 of the online version.

7. See, e.g., Kant, "What Is Enlightenment," in *On History*.

8. See, e.g., Kant, "Perpetual Peace," in *On History*.

9. See, e.g., National Commission on Civic Renewal, *Nation of Spectators*.

10. Putnam, "Bowling Alone"; later expanded into the book, Putnam, *Bowling Alone*.

11. See Appleby, "Building Community," this volume.

12. See Steinberg, "Creating Community," this volume.

Bibliography

Abu-Lughod, Lila, and Catherine A. Lutz. "Introduction: Emotion, Discourse, and the Politics of Everyday Life." In *Language and the Politics of Emotion*, edited by Catherine A. Lutz and Lila Abu-Lughod. Cambridge: Cambridge University Press, 1990.

Ackerman, Bruce. *The Future of Liberal Revolution*. New Haven, Conn.: Yale University Press, 1992.

ADSS. "Discussion Leader Kit." Washington, D.C.: Americans Discuss Social Security, 1998.

AISR. "Local Conversations on Education in Your Community." Providence, R.I.: Annenberg Institute for School Reform, 1998.

———. "Reasons for Hope, Visions for Change." Providence, R.I.: Annenberg Institute for School Reform, 1998.

Aldrich, John. *Why Parties? The Origin and Transformation of Political Parties*. Chicago: University of Chicago Press, 1995.

Annenberg Public Policy Center. "The Role of Advertising in the Health Care Debate. Part Two: Accuracy." Philadelphia: Annenberg Public Policy Center, 1994.

Ansolabehere, Stephen, and Shanto Iyengar. *Going Negative: How Attack Ads Shrink and Polarize the Electorate*. New York: Free Press, 1995.

Apter, David, ed. *Ideology and Discontent*. Glencoe, Ill.: Free Press, 1964.

Arendt, Hannah. *The Human Condition*. Chicago: University of Chicago Press, 1958; Garden City, N.Y.: Doubleday Anchor Books, 1959.

Aristotle. *The Politics*. Ed. and trans. Ernest Baker. Oxford: Oxford University Press, 1958.

Aronovitch, Hilliard. "The Political Importance of Analogical Argument." *Political Studies* 45 (1997): 78–92.

Arrow, Kenneth. *Social Choice and Individual Values*. 2nd ed. New York: Wiley, 1963.

Associated Press. "UCLA Study: Internet Doesn't Isolate Most People." Associated Press, 25 October 2000, available on the Internet at http://www.cnn.com/2000/TECH/computing10/25/internet.study.ap/index.html (2 March 2003).

Auletta, Ken. *Three Blind Mice: How the Television Networks Lost Their Way*. New York: Random House, 1991.

Avey, Michael. *The Demobilization of American Voters: A Comprehensive Theory of Voter Turnout*. New York: Greenwood Press, 1989.

Axelrod, Robert. "Effective Choice in the Prisoner's Dilemma." *Journal of Conflict Resolution* 24 (1980): 3–25.

Azar, Fabiola, et al. "The Propensity to Forgive: Findings from Lebanon." *Journal of Peace Research* (March 1999).

Bagdikian, Ben. *The Media Monopoly*. 5th ed. Boston: Beacon Press, 1997.

Baker, C. Edwin. *Advertising and the Democratic Press*. Princeton, N.J.: Princeton University Press, 1994.

Barber, Benjamin. *A Passion for Democracy*. Princeton, N.J.: Princeton University Press, l998.

Barringer, Felicity. "New York Times Company's Internet Unit Plans Layoffs." *New York Times*, 7 January 2001.

Baumeister, Roy, Julie Exline, and Kristin Sommer. "The Victim Role, Grudge Theory, and Two Dimensions of Forgiveness." In *Dimensions of Forgiveness: Psychological Research and Theological Perspectives*, edited by Everett L. Worthington, Jr. Philadelphia: Templeton Foundation Press, 1998.

Baumgartner, Frank, and Bryan Jones. *Agendas and Instability in American Politics*. Chicago: University of Chicago Press, 1993.

Baumgartner, Frank, and Jeffrey C. Talbert. "Interest Groups and Political Change." In *The New American Politics: Reflections on Political Change and the Clinton Administration*, edited by Bryan Jones. Boulder, Colo.: Westview Press, 1995.

Beck, Ulrich, Anthony Giddens, and Scott Lash. *Reflexive Modernization: Politics, Tradition, and Aesthetics in the Modern Social Order*. Stanford, Calif.: Stanford University Press, 1994.

Becker, Carl, Laura Chasin, Richard Chasin, Margaret Herzig, and Sallyann Roth. "From Stuck Debate to New Conversation on Public Issues: A Report from the Public Conversations Project." *Journal of Feminist Family Therapy* 17 (1995): 143–63.

Beer, Francis. "Words of Reason." *Political Communication* 11 (1994): 185–201.

Begala, Paul. "Politics and the Culture of Contempt." Unpublished plenary presentation to the Penn National Commission on Society, Culture and Community, Philadelphia, 9 December 1996.

Bellah, Robert, Richard Madsen, William M. Sullivan, Ann Swidler, and Steven M. Tipton. *Habits of the Heart: Individualism and Commitment in American Life*. Berkeley: University of California Press, 1985.

Bender, Thomas. "The New Metropolitanism and the Plurality of Publics." *Harvard Design Magazine* (Winter/Spring 2001).

———. *New York Intellect*. New York: Knopf, 1987.

Benhabib, Seyla, and Drucilla Cornell. *Feminism as Critique: On the Politics of Gender*. Minneapolis: University of Minnesota Press, 1987.

Bennett, Lance. *The Governing Crisis: Media, Money, and Marketing in American Elections*. 2nd ed. New York: St. Martin's Press, 1996.

Berelson, Bernard, Paul Lazarsfeld, and William McPhee. *Voting: A Study of Opinion Formation in a Presidential Campaign*. Chicago: University of Chicago Press, 1954.

Berger, Michael. "The Hidden Japanese; Rites of Summer." *New Leader*, 6 September 1993.

Berkowitz, Peter. "The Debating Society." *New Republic* 215 (25 November 1996): 36–42.

Berman, Sheri. "Civil Society and Political Institutionalization." *American Behavioral Scientist* 40 (1997): 562–74.

Bessette, Joseph. *The Mild Voice of Reason: Deliberative Democracy and American National Government*. Chicago: University of Chicago Press, 1994.

Best, Stephen, and Douglas Kellner. *The Postmodern Turn*. New York: Guilford Press, 1997.

Billig, Michael. *Arguing and Thinking: A Rhetorical Approach to Social Psychology*. Cambridge: Cambridge University Press, 1996.

———. *Ideology and Opinions: Studies in Rhetorical Psychology*. London: Sage, 1991.

Black, Jay, ed. *Mixed News: The Public/Civic/Communitarian Journalism Debate*. Mahwah, N.J.: Lawrence Erlbaum, 1997.

Blakely, Edward, and Mary G. Snyder. *Fortress America: Gated Communities in the United States*. Washington, D.C.: Brookings Institution, 1997.

Blendon, Robert J., Mollyann Brodie, and John Benson. "What Happened to Americans' Support for the Clinton Health Plan?" *Health Affairs* 14 (1995).

Blendon, Robert, et al. "The American Public and Critical Choices for Health System Reform." *Journal of the American Medical Association* 271 (1994).

Bobinski, Christopher. "Yeltsin Seeks to Heal Katyn Wounds." *Financial Times*, 26 August 1993.

Boggs, Carl. "The Great Retreat: Decline of the Public Sphere in Late Twentieth-Century America." *Theory and Society* 26 (1997): 741–80.

Bohman, James F. "Communication, Ideology, and Democratic Theory." *American Political Science Review* 84 (1990): 93–109.

Bohman, James F., and William Rehg, eds. *Deliberative Democracy: Essays on Reason and Politics*. Cambridge, Mass.: MIT Press, 1997.

Bok, Derek. *The State of the Nation: Government and the Quest for a Better Society*. Cambridge, Mass.: Harvard University Press, 1998.

Boorstin, Daniel J. *The Decline of Radicalism: Reflections on America Today*. New York: Random House, 1969.

———. *The Image: A Guide to Pseudo-Events in America*. New York: Atheneum, 1961.

Bowen, Sheryl Perlmutter, and Nancy Wyatt, eds. *Transforming Visions: Feminist Critiques in Communication Studies*. Cresskill, N.J.: Hampton Press, 1993.

Bowers, James R., Blair Claflin, and Gary Walker. "The Impact of Civic Journalism Projects on Voting Behavior in State-Wide Referendums: A Case Study of Rochester, N.Y." Paper presented at the Annual Meeting of the New England Political Science Association, Worcester, Mass., 1–2 May 1998.

Boyer, Peter. *Who Killed CBS? The Undoing of America's Number One News Network*. New York: St. Martin's Press, 1989.

Boyes, Roger. "Yeltsin Snubs Katyn Massacre Ceremony." *New York Times*, 6 June 1995.

Brady, Henry, Sidney Verba, and Kay Lehman Schlozman. "Beyond SES: A Resource Model of Political Participation." *American Political Science Review* 89 (1995): 271–94.

Broder, David. "Democracy and the Press." *Washington Post*, 3 January 1990, A15.

———. "A New Assignment for the Press." Press-Enterprise Lecture Series. Riverside, Calif.: Press-Enterprise, 1991.

Bronkhorst, Daan. *Truth and Reconciliation: Obstacles and Opportunities for Human Rights*. Amsterdam: Amnesty International, 1995.

Brooks, Clem, and Jeff Manza. "The Social and Ideological Bases of Middle-Class Political Realignment in the United States, 1972–1992." *American Sociological Review* 62 (1997): 191–208.

Brown, Penelope, and Stephen Levinson. *Politeness: Some Universals in Language*. Cambridge: Cambridge University Press, 1987.

Bryce, James. *The American Commonwealth*. 2nd ed. Vol. 1. Chicago: Charles H. Sergel, 1891.

Burnheim, John. *Is Democracy Possible? The Alternative to Electoral Politics*. Cambridge: Polity Press, 1985.

Burns, Nancy, Kay Lehman Schlozman, and Sidney Verba. "The Public Consequences of Private Inequality: Family Life and Citizen Participation." *American Political Science Review* 91 (1997): 37–89.

Burress, Charles. "Most Japanese Support Apology." *San Francisco Chronicle*, 18 August 1995.

Burtt, Shelley. "The Good Citizen's Psyche: On the Psychology of Civic Virtue." *Polity* 23 (1990): 23–38.

———. "The Politics of Virtue Today: A Critique and a Proposal." *American Political Science Review* 87 (1993): 360–68.

Button, Mark, and Kevin Mattson. "Actually Existing Deliberative Democracy: Challenges and Prospects for Civic Deliberation Within a Representative System." Unpublished manuscript prepared for the Kettering Foundation. Walt Whitman Center for the Culture and Politics of Democracy, New Brunswick, N.J., 1998.

Calhoun, Craig, ed. *Habermas and the Public Sphere*. Cambridge, Mass.: MIT Press, 1992.

———. *Social Theory and the Politics of Identity*. Cambridge: Blackwell, 1994.

Canary, Daniel, Jeanette Brossmann, Brent Brossmann, and Harry Weger. "Toward a Theory of Minimally Rational Argument: Analyses of Episode Specific Effects of Argument Structures." *Communication Monographs* 62 (1995): 183–212.

Cannon, Lou. *President Reagan: The Role of a Lifetime*. New York: Simon & Schuster, 1991.

Cappella, Joseph, and Kathleen Hall Jamieson. *Spiral of Cynicism: The Press and the Public Good*. New York: Oxford University Press, 1997.

Cargile, Aaron Castelan, and Howard Giles. "Understanding Language Attitudes: Exploring Listener Affect and Identity." *Language and Communication* 17 (1997): 195–217.

Center for Public Integrity. *Well-Healed: Inside Lobbying for Health Care Reform*. Washington, D.C.: Center for Public Integrity, 1994.

Chaney, David C. *The Cultural Turn: Scene-Setting Essays on Contemporary Cultural History*. London: Routledge, 1994.

Chang, Iris. *The Rape of Nanking: The Forgotten Holocaust of World War II*. New York: Basic Books, 1997.

Charity, Arthur. *Doing Public Journalism*. New York: Guilford Press, 1995.

Chasin, Richard, and Margaret Herzig. "Creating Systemic Interventions for the Sociopolitical Arena." In *The Global Family Therapist: Integrating the Personal, Professional, and Political*, edited by Benina Berger Gold and Donna Hilleboe Demuth, 149–91. Boston: Allyn and Bacon, 1994.

Cherwitz, Richard, and James Hikins. *Communication and Knowledge: An Investigation in Rhetorical Epistemology*. Columbia: University of South Carolina Press, 1986.

Chong, Dennis. "How People Think, Reason, and Feel About Rights and Liberties." *American Journal of Political Science* 37 (1993): 867–99.

———. "Tolerance and Social Adjustment to New Norms and Practices." *Political Behavior* 16 (1994): 21–53.

Chubb, John E., and Paul E. Peterson, eds. *The New Direction in American Politics*. Washington, D.C.: Brookings Institution, 1985.

Churchill, Winston S., "The Tragedy of Europe." In *The Sinews of Peace: Post-War Speeches*, edited by Randolph S. Churchill. London: Cassell, 1948; also in *Finest Hour* 92 (Autumn 1996): 14, and available on the Internet at http://www.winstonchurchill.org/unite.htm (29 April 2003).

Citrin, Jack, Beth Reingold, and Donald Green. "American Identity and the Politics of Ethnic Change." *Journal of Politics* 52 (1990): 1124–54.

Civil Liberties Public Education Fund. *Personal Justice Denied*. Washington, D.C.: Civil Liberties Public Education Fund, 1997.

Cloud, Dana. *Control and Consolation in American Culture and Politics: Rhetoric of Therapy*. Thousand Oaks, Calif.: Sage, 1998.

Cmiel, Kenneth. *Democratic Eloquence: The Fight over Popular Speech in Nineteenth-Century America*. New York: William Morrow, 1990.

Coates, Jennifer. *Women, Men, and Language: A Sociolinguistic Account of Gender Differences in Language.* 2nd ed. London: Longman, 1993.

Cobb, Michael, and James Kukinski. "Changing Minds: Political Arguments and Political Persuasion." *American Journal of Political Science* 41 (1997): 88–121.

Cohen, Joshua. "Democracy and Liberty." In *Deliberative Democracy*, edited by Jon Elster, 185–231. Cambridge: Cambridge University Press, 1998.

Cohen, Joshua, and Joel Rogers. "Secondary Associations and Democratic Governance." *Politics and Society* 20 (1992): 393–472.

Cohen, Lizabeth, Thomas W. Hanchett, and Kenneth T. Jackson. "Shopping Malls in America." An American Historical Review Forum. *American Historical Review* 101 (1996): 1049–121.

Cohen, Roger. "French Church Issues Apology to Jews on War." *New York Times*, 1 October 1997.

Cole, Jeffrey, Harlan Lebo, et al. "The UCLA Internet Report: Surveying the Digital Future." Directed by Jeffrey J. Cole, written by Harlan Lebo. Los Angeles: Regents of the University of California, October 2000. Available on the Internet at http://ccp.ucla.edu/UCLA-Internet-Report-2000.pdf (3 March 2003).

Columbia Institute. *What Shapes Lawmakers' Views? A Survey of Members of Congress and Key Staff on Health Care Reform.* Washington, D.C.: Columbia Institute, Kaiser Family Foundation, Harvard School of Public Health, 1995.

Condit, Celeste Michelle. "Opposites in an Oppositional Practice: Rhetorical Criticism and Feminism." In *Transforming Visions: Feminist Critiques in Communication Studies*, edited by Sheryl Perlmutter Bowen and Nancy Wyatt, 205–30. Cresskill, N.J.: Hampton Press, 1993.

Connor, Steve. *Theory and Cultural Value.* Oxford: Blackwell, 1992.

Conover, Pamela, Ivor Crewe, and Donald Searing. "The Nature of Citizenship in the United States and Great Britain: Empirical Comments on Theoretical Themes." *Journal of Politics* 53 (1991): 800–832.

Converse, Philip. "The Nature of Belief Systems in Mass Publics." In *Ideology and Discontent*, edited by David Apter. Glencoe, Ill.: Free Press, 1964.

Cook, Fay Lomax, and Ronald Jacobs. *Deliberative Democracy in Action: Evaluation of Americans Discuss Social Security.* Washington, D.C.: Pew Charitable Trusts, 1999.

Cook, Timothy E. *Governing with the News: The News Media as a Political Institution.* Chicago: University of Chicago Press, 1998.

Craig, Bob. "The Keystone Center." Keystone, Colo.: Keystone Center, 1998.

Crotty, William. *Decision for Democrats: Reforming the Party Structure.* Baltimore: Johns Hopkins University Press, 1978.

Crotty, William. *Party Reform.* New York: Longman, 1983.

———, ed. *Political Participation and American Democracy.* New York: Greenwood Press, 1991.

Dahl, Robert A. *Democracy and Its Critics.* New Haven, Conn.: Yale University Press, 1989.

———. *Modern Political Analysis.* Englewood Cliffs, N.J.: Prentice-Hall, 1963.

———. *Who Governs? Democracy and Power in an American City.* New Haven, Conn.: Yale University Press, 1961.

Danielson, Michael N. *The Politics of Exclusion.* New York: Columbia University Press, 1976.

Danzinger, Sheldon, and Peter Gottschalk, eds. *Uneven Tides: Rising Inequality in America.* New York: Russell Sage Foundation, 1993.

Darby, B. W., and B. R. Schenkler. "Children's Reactions to Apologies." *Journal of Personality and Social Psychology* 43: 742–53.

Davidson, Roger H. "Subcommittee Government: New Channels for Policymaking." In *The New Congress*, edited by Thomas E. Mann and Norman J. Orenstein. Washington, D.C., American Enterprise Institute for Public Policy Research, 1981.

Davis, Darren. "Exploring Black Political Intolerance." *Political Behavior* 17 (1995): 1–22.

Degler, Carl E. "American Political Parties and the Rise of the City: An Interpretation." *Journal of American History* 51 (1964): 41–59.

de la Garza, O. Rodolfo, Angelo Falcon, and F. Chris Garcia. "Will the Real Americans Please Stand Up: Anglo and Mexican-American Support for Core American Values." *American Journal of Political Science* 40 (1996): 335–51.

Delli Carpini, Michael X. "Impact of Money+Politics: Citizen Assemblies on Assembly Participants." Unpublished manuscript, 1997.

Delli Carpini, Michael X., Leonie Huddy, and Robert Y. Shapiro, eds. *Political Decision-Making, Deliberation, and Participation*. Amsterdam: JAI Press, 2002.

Denver, D., G. Hands, and B. Jones. "Fishkin and the Deliberative Opinion Poll: Lessons from a Study of the Granada 500 Television Program." *Political Communication* 12 (1995): 147–56.

DePalma, Anthony. "Canada's Indigenous Tribes Receive Formal Apology." *New York Times*, 8 January 1998.

Derrida, Jacques. *Of Grammatology*. Trans. Gayatri Chakravorty Spivak. Baltimore: Johns Hopkins University Press, 1976.

Desmond, Edward W. "Finally, a Real Apology." *Time*, 28 August 1995.

Dewey, John. *The Public and Its Problems*. New York: Henry Holt, 1927.

———. "Public Opinion," *New Republic*, 3 May 1922, 286–88.

Dibbell, Julian. "A Rape in Cyberspace, or TINYSOCIETY, and How to Make One." In *My Tiny Life: Crime and Passion in a Virtual World*. New York: Henry Holt, Owl Books, 1999.

Dimaggio, Paul, John Evans, and Bethany Bryson. "Have Americans' Social Attitudes Become More Polarized?" *American Journal of Sociology* 102 (1996): 690–755.

Dionne, E. J., Jr. *Why Americans Hate Politics*. New York: Touchstone Books, 1992.

Doheny-Farina, Stephen. *The Wired Neighborhood*. New Haven, Conn.: Yale University Press, 1996.

Dorff, Elliot N. "The Elements of Forgiveness: A Jewish Approach." In *Dimensions of Forgiveness: Psychological Research and Theological Perspectives*, edited by Everett L. Worthington, Jr. Philadelphia: Templeton Foundation Press, 1998.

Dower, John W. "The Bombed: Hiroshima and Nagasaki in Japanese Memory." In *Hiroshima in History and Memory*, edited by Michael J. Hogan. Cambridge: Cambridge University Press, 1996.

Dryzek, John. *Discursive Democracy: Politics, Policy, and Political Science*. Cambridge: Cambridge University Press, 1990.

Dryzek, John, and Jeffrey Berejikian. "Reconstructive Democratic Theory." *American Political Science Review* 87 (1993): 48–60.

Dumas, André. "Forgiveness and Politics," *Evangile Aujourd'hui* 77 (June 1973).

Eckholm, Erik, ed. *Solving America's Health Care Crisis*. Washington, D.C.: Cato Institute, 1993.

Economist. "Cold Comfort: Japan." *Economist*, 18 May 1996.

———. "Japan's War with China, Revisited." *Economist*, 6 September 1997.

———. "War Shadows: Japan." *Economist*, 20 August 1994.

Edley, Christopher, Jr. *Not All Black and White: Affirmative Action and American Values*. New York: Hill and Wang, 1996.

Ehrenhalt, Alan. *The United States of Ambitions: Politicians, Power, and the Pursuit of Office*. New York: Times Books, 1991.

Eley, Geoff. "Nation, Publics, and Political Culture: Placing Habermas in the Nineteenth Century." In *Habermas and the Public Sphere*, edited by Craig Calhoun, 289–339. Cambridge, Mass.: MIT Press, 1992.

Eliasoph, Nina. *Avoiding Politics: How Americans Produce Apathy in Everyday Life.* New York: Cambridge University Press, 1998.

———. " 'Close to Home': The Work of Avoiding Politics." *Theory and Society* 26 (1997): 605–47.

Elster, Jon. "Introduction." In *Deliberative Democracy,* edited by Jon Elster. Cambridge: Cambridge University Press, 1998.

———, ed. *Deliberative Democracy.* Cambridge: Cambridge University Press, 1998.

Elster, Jon, and Aanund Hylland, eds. *Foundations of Social Choice Theory.* New York: Cambridge University Press, 1986.

Enright, Robert D., and Catherine T. Coyle. "Researching the Process Model of Forgiveness Within Psychological Interventions." In *Dimensions of Forgiveness: Psychological Research and Theological Perspectives,* edited by Everett L. Worthington, Jr. Philadelphia: Templeton Foundation Press, 1998.

Ethington, Philip. *The Public City: The Political Construction of Urban Life in San Francisco, 1850–1900.* New York: Cambridge University Press, 1994.

Etzioni, Amitai. *The New Golden Rule: Community and Morality in a Democratic Society.* New York: Basic Books, 1996.

Fairclough, Norman. *Language and Power.* New York: Longman, 1989.

Farrell, Thomas. *Norms of Rhetorical Culture.* New Haven, Conn.: Yale University Press, 1993.

Fein, Esther B. "Upheaval in the East." *New York Times,* 14 April 1990.

Fischer, Frank. "Policy Discourse and the Politics of Washington Think Tanks." In *The Argumentative Turn in Policy Analysis and Planning,* edited by Frank Fischer and John Forester. Durham, N.C.: Duke University Press, 1993.

Fischer, Frank, and John Forester, eds. *The Argumentative Turn in Policy Analysis and Planning.* Durham: N.C.: Duke University Press, 1993.

Fishkin, James. *Democracy and Deliberation: New Directions in Democratic Reform.* New Haven, Conn.: Yale University Press, 1991.

———. *The Voice of the People: Public Opinion and Democracy.* New Haven, Conn.: Yale University Press, 1995.

Fletcher, George. "The Case for Tolerance." *Social Philosophy and Policy* 13 (1996): 229–39.

Foss, Sonja, and Cindy Griffin. "Beyond Persuasion: A Proposal for an Invitational Rhetoric." *Communication Monographs* 62 (1995): 2–18.

Foucault, Michel. *Madness and Civilization: A History of Insanity in the Age of Reason.* Trans. Richard Howard. New York: Vintage Books, 1965.

Fox, Charles, and Hugh Miller. *Postmodern Public Administration: Toward Discourse.* Thousand Oaks, Calif.: Sage, 1995.

Fox, Harrison W., Jr., and Susan Webb Hammond. "The Growth of Congressional Staffs." In *Congress Against the President,* edited by Harvey C. Mansfield. *Proceedings of the American Academy of Political Science* 32 (1975): 112–24.

Fox, Richard Wightman, and T. J. Jackson Lears. *The Culture of Consumption: Critical Essays in American History, 1880–1980.* New York: Pantheon Books, 1983.

Frank, Robert. *Passions Within Reason: The Strategic Role of the Emotions.* New York: Norton, 1988.

Franklin, Benjamin. "Speech in a Committee of the Convention on the Proportion of Representation and Votes, June 11, 1787." In *Benjamin Franklin: Writings,* edited by J. A. Leo Lemay. New York: Library of America, 1987.

Fraser, Nancy. *Justice Interruptus: Critical Reflections on the Post-Socialist Condition.* New York: Routledge, 1997.

———. *Unruly Practices: Power, Discourse, and Gender in Contemporary Social Theory.* Minneapolis: University of Minnesota Press, 1989.

Frohn, Axel, ed. *Holocaust and* Shilumim*: The Policy of* Wiedergutmachung *in the Early 1950s.* Washington, D.C.: German Historical Institute, 1991.

Frohock, Fred. "The Boundaries of Public Reason." *American Political Science Review* 91 (1997): 833–44.

Fullinwider, Robert. "Citizenship, Individualism, and Democratic Politics." *Ethics* 105 (1995): 497–515.

Fung, Archon, and Erik Olin Wright. "Deepening Democracy: Innovations in Empowered Participatory Governance." *Politics & Society* 29 (2001): 5-41.

Gabler, Neal. *Life the Movie: How Entertainment Conquered Reality.* New York: Alfred P. Knopf, 1999.

Gallois, Cynthia. "Group Membership, Social Rules, and Power: A Social-Psychological Perspective on Emotional Communication." *Journal of Pragmatics* 22 (1994): 301–24.

———. "The Language and Communication of Emotion." *American Behavioral Scientist* 36 (1993): 309–38.

Gamson, William. *Talking Politics.* Cambridge: Cambridge University Press, 1992.

Gargarella, Roberto. "Full Representation, Deliberation, and Impartiality." In *Deliberative Democracy*, edited by Jon Elster, 260–80. Cambridge: Cambridge University Press, 1998.

Garment, Suzanne. *Scandal: The Crisis of Mistrust in American Politics.* New York: Times Books, 1991.

Garton Ash, Timothy. *The File: A Personal History.* New York: Random House, 1997.

Gastil, John. "Democratic Citizenship and the National Issues Forums." Ph.D. dissertation, University of Wisconsin-Madison, 1994.

———. "Undemocratic Discourse: A Review of Theory and Research on Political Discourse." *Discourse and Society* 3 (1992): 460–500.

Gastil, John, and J. Dillard. "Increasing Political Sophistication Through Public Deliberation." *Political Communication* 16 (1999): 3-23.

Gellner, Ernest. *Reason and Culture: The Historic Role of Rationality and Rationalism.* Oxford: Blackwell, 1992.

Gibson, James. "Political Freedom: A Socio-Psychological Analysis." In *Reconsidering the Democratic Public*, edited by George Marcus and Russell Hanson. University Park: Pennsylvania State University Press, 1993.

Giddens, Anthony. *Modernity and Self-Identity: Self and Society in the Late Modern Age.* Stanford, Calif.: Stanford University Press, 1991.

Gilens, Martin. " 'Race Coding' and White Opposition to Welfare." *American Political Science Review* 90 (1996): 593–604.

———. "Racial Attitudes and Opposition to Welfare." *Journal of Politics* 57 (1995): 994–1014.

Giles, Howard, Angie Williams, Diane M. Mackie, and Francine Rosselli. "Reactions to Anglo- and Hispanic-American Accented Speakers: Affect, Identity, Persuasion, and the English-Only Controversy." *Language and Communication* 15 (1995): 107–20.

Ginsberg, Benjamin. *The Captive Public: How Mass Opinion Promotes State Power.* New York: Basic Books, 1986.

Gitlin, Todd. *The Whole World Is Watching: Mass Media in the Making and Unmaking of the New Left.* Berkeley: University of California Press, 1980.

Gittell, Marilyn. *Limits to Citizen Participation: The Decline of Community Organizations.* Thousand Oaks, Calif.: Sage, 1980.

Glasser, Theodore, and Charles Salmon, eds. *Public Opinion and the Communication of Consent.* New York: Guilford Press, 1995.

Gluck, Carol. "The Idea of Showa." In *Showa: The Japan of Hirohito*, edited by Carol Gluck and Stephen R. Graubard. New York: Norton, 1992.

Gluck, Carol, and Stephen R. Graubard, eds. *Showa: The Japan of Hirohito*. New York: Norton, 1992.

Godkin, E. L. "Democratic View of Democracy." *North American Review* 101 (1865): 103–33.

Goffman, Erving. *Relations in Public: Microstudies of the Public Order*. New York: Basic Books, 1971.

Gold, Benina Berger, and Donna Hilleboe Demuth, eds. *The Global Family Therapist: Integrating the Personal, Professional, and Political*. Boston: Allyn and Bacon, 1994.

Golebiowska, Ewa. "Individual Value Priorities, Education, and Political Tolerance." *Political Behavior* 17 (1995): 23–48.

Gonzalez, David. "A Killing Shocks Jamaicans into Soul-Searching." *New York Times*, 18 October 1999.

Gould, Carol. *Rethinking Democracy: Freedom and Social Cooperation in Politics, Economy, and Society*. Cambridge: Cambridge University Press, 1988.

Graff, Gerald. *Beyond the Culture Wars: How Teaching the Conflicts Can Revitalize American Education*. New York: Norton, 1992.

———. *Professing Literature: An Institutional History*. Chicago: University of Chicago Press, 1987.

Grice, Paul. "Logic in Conversation." In *Studies in the Way of Words*, 22–40. Cambridge, Mass.: Harvard University Press, 1989.

———. *Studies in the Way of Words*. Cambridge, Mass.: Harvard University Press, 1989.

Grimshaw, Allen D., ed. *Conflict Talk: Sociolinguistic Investigations of Arguments in Conversations*. Cambridge: Cambridge University Press, 1990.

Guardian. "The Leaders' Apologies." 13 October 1993.

Guernsey, Lisa. "Professor Who Once Found Isolation Online Has a Change of Heart." *New York Times*, 26 July 2001.

Gumperz, John J. "Communicative Competence Revisited." In *Meaning, Form, and Use in Context: Linguistic Applications*, edited by Deborah Schiffrin, 278–89. Washington, D.C.: Georgetown University Press, 1984.

———., ed. *Language and Social Identity*. Cambridge: Cambridge University Press, 1982.

Gumperz, John J., and Jenny Cook-Gumperz. "Introduction: Language and the Communication of Social Identity." In *Language and Social Identity*, edited by John J. Gumperz, 1–21. Cambridge: Cambridge University Press, 1982.

Gunther, Marc. *The House That Roone Built: The Inside Story of ABC News*. Boston: Little, Brown, 1994.

Gurstein, Rochelle. *The Repeal of Reticence*. New York: Hill and Wang, 1996.

Gutmann, Amy. "The Challenge of Multi-Culturalism in Political Ethics." *Philosophy and Public Affairs* 22 (1993): 171-206.

———. "Civic Education and Social Diversity." *Ethics* 105 (1995): 557–79.

Gutmann, Amy, and Dennis Thompson. *Democracy and Disagreement*. Cambridge, Mass.: Belknap Press, 1996.

———. "Moral Conflict and Political Consensus." *Ethics* 101 (1990): 64–88.

Habermas, Jürgen. *Legitimation Crisis*. Boston: Beacon Press, 1975.

———. *The Structural Transformation of the Public Sphere: An Inquiry into a Category of Bourgeois Society*. Trans. Thomas Burger. Cambridge, Mass.: MIT Press, 1989.

———. *The Theory of Communicative Action*. Trans. Thomas McCarthy. Boston: Beacon Press, 1984.

Hackney, Sheldon. *One America Indivisible: A National Conversation on American*

   Pluralism and Identity. Washington, D.C.: National Endowment for the Human-
   ities, 1998.
Hallin, Daniel. *The Uncensored War: The Media and Vietnam.* New York: Oxford
   University Press, 1986.
Hallin, Daniel, and Paolo Mancini. "Speaking of the President: Political Structure
   and Representational Form in U.S. and Italian Television News." *Theory and
   Society* 13 (1984): 829–50.
Hamilton, Alexander, James Madison, and John Jay. *The Federalist Papers.* New
   York: Bantam, 1982.
Harmon, Amy. "Researchers Find Sad, Lonely World in Cyberspace," *New York
   Times*, 30 August 1998, Technology section.
———. "Vox Populi, Online and Downtown," *New York Times*, 26 September
   2002, Circuits section, G1.
Harris, Sandra. "Pragmatics and Power." *Journal of Pragmatics* 23 (1995): 117–35.
Harrison, Bennett, and Barry Bluestone. *The Great U-Turn: Corporate Restructuring
   and the Polarizing of America.* New York: Basic Books, 1988.
Hartz, Louis. *The Liberal Tradition in America: An Interpretation of American Political
   Thought Since the Revolution.* New York: Harcourt, Brace, 1955.
Harvey, David. *The Condition of Postmodernity: An Enquiry into the Origins of Cultural
   Change.* Oxford: Blackwell, 1989.
Harwood Group. "Meaningful Chaos: How People Form Relationships with Pub-
   lic Concerns." Bethesda, Md.: Harwood Group, 1993.
———. "Money+Politics: People Change the Equation." Conversation Leader
   Handbook. Bethesda, Md.: Harwood Group.
———. "Political Fortunes: A Public Voice on Money and Politics." Bethesda,
   Md.: Harwood Group, 1996.
———. "Will Any Kind of Talk Do? Moving From Personal Concerns to Public
   Life." Bethesda, Md.: Harwood Group, 1996.
Hassan, Ihab Habib. *The Postmodern Turn: Essays in Postmodern Theory and Culture.*
   Columbus: Ohio State University Press, 1987.
Heelas, Paul, Scott Lash, and Paul Morris, eds. *Detraditionalization: Critical Reflec-
   tions on Authority and Identity.* Cambridge: Blackwell, 1996.
Hein, Laura, and Mark Selden, eds. *Living with the Bomb: American and Japanese
   Cultural Conflicts in the Nuclear Age.* Armonk, N.Y.: Scharpe, 1997.
Hendriks, Carolyn. "Institutions of Deliberative Democratic Processes and Inter-
   est Groups: Roles, Tensions, and Incentives." *Australian Journal of Public Ad-
   ministration* 61 (2002): 63-75.
Herbst, Susan. *Numbered Voices: How Opinion Polling Has Shaped American Politics.*
   Chicago: University of Chicago Press, 1993.
Hibbing, J., and E. Theiss-Morse. "Deliberation as a Source of System Delegiti-
   mation and Popular Disharmony." Paper presented at the annual meeting of
   the Midwest Political Science Association, Chicago, April 2000.
Hicks, George. *The Comfort Women: Japan's Brutal Regime of Enforced Prostitution in
   the Second World War.* New York: Norton, 1995.
Hirsch, Alan. *Talking Heads: Political Talk Shows and Their Pundits.* New York: St.
   Martin's Press, 1991.
Hirst, Paul. *Associative Democracy: New Forms of Economic and Social Governance.*
   Amherst, Mass.: University of Amherst Press, 1994.
Hochschild, Jennifer. "Disjunction and Ambivalence in Citizens' Political Outlooks."
   In *Reconsidering the Democratic Public*, edited by George Marcus and Russell Han-
   son, 187–210. University Park: Pennsylvania State University Press, 1993.
———. *Facing Up to the American Dream: Race, Class, and the Soul of the Nation.*
   Princeton, N.J.: Princeton University Press, 1995.

Hogan, Michael J. "Preface: Rhetoric and Community." In *Rhetoric and Community: Studies in Unity and Fragmentation*. Columbia: University of South Carolina Press, 1998.

———, ed. *Hiroshima in History and Memory*. Cambridge: Cambridge University Press, 1996.

———, ed. *Rhetoric and Community: Studies in Unity and Fragmentation*. Columbia: University of South Carolina Press, 1998.

Holeton, Richard, ed. *Composing Cyberspace, Identity, Community, and Knowledge in the Electronic Age*. Boston: McGraw-Hill, 1998.

Horn, Robert V. *Statistical Indicators for the Economic and Social Sciences*. Cambridge: Cambridge University Press, 1993.

Horrigan, John B. "Online Communities: Networks That Nurture Long Distance Relationships and Local Ties." Washington, D.C.: Pew Internet and American Life Project, 2001.

Hosman, Lawrence A., and Susan A. Siltanen. "The Attributional and Evaluative Consequences of Powerful and Powerless Speech Styles: An Examination of the 'Control over Others' and 'Control of Self' Explanations." *Language and Communication* 14 (1994): 287–98.

Howard, Keith, ed. *True Stories of the Korean Comfort Women: Testimonies*. Trans. Young Joo Lee. London: Cassell, 1995.

Hoyt, Paul D. "The Political Manipulation of Group Composition: Engineering the Decision Context." *Political Psychology* 18 (1997): 771–89.

Huckfeldt, Robert, Paul Allen Beck, Russel J. Dalton, and Jeffrey Levine. "Political Environments, Cohesive Social Groups, and the Communication of Public Opinion." *American Journal of Political Science* 39 (1995): 1025–54.

Hughes, Robert. *Culture of Complaint: The Fraying of America*. New York: Oxford University Press, 1993.

Hunter, James D. *Culture Wars: The Struggle to Define America*. New York: Basic Books, 1991.

Huspek, Michael, and Kathleen Kendall. "On Withholding Political Voice: An Analysis of the Political Vocabulary of a 'Non-Political' Speech Community." *Quarterly Journal of Speech* 77 (1991): 1–19.

Irons, Peter, ed. *Justice Delayed: The Record of the Japanese American Internment Cases*. Middleton, Conn.: Wesleyan, 1989.

Jackman, Robert, and Ross Miller. "A Renaissance of Political Culture?" *American Journal of Political Science* 40 (1996): 632–59.

Jackson, Kenneth. *Crabgrass Frontier: The Suburbanization of the United States*. New York: Oxford University Press, 1985.

Jacksteit, Mary, and Adrienne Kaufmann. "Finding Common Ground in the Abortion Conflict: A Manual." Washington, D.C.: Common Ground Network for Life and Choice, 1995.

Jacobs, Lawrence, and Robert Shapiro. "Issues, Candidate Image, and Priming: The Use of Private Polls in Kennedy's 1960 Presidential Campaign." *American Political Science Review* 88 (1994): 527–40.

Jameson, Frederic. *The Cultural Turn: Selected Writings on the Postmodern, 1983–1998*. New York: Verso, 1998.

Jameson, Frederic, and Masao Miyoshi, eds. *The Cultures of Globalization*. Durham, N.C.: Duke University Press, 1998.

Jameson, Sam. "Hosokawa Outlines Reforms for Japan But Omits Details." *Los Angeles Times*, 24 August 1993.

Jamieson, Kathleen Hall. *Dirty Politics: Deception, Distraction, and Democracy*. New York: Oxford University Press, 1992.

Jamieson, Kathleen Hall, and Erika Falk. *Civility in the House of Representatives*.

Philadelphia: Annenberg Public Policy Center, 1997–2001. The series of reports is available online at http://www.appcpenn.org/political/civility/ (3 March 2003).

Jefferson Center. "1994 Pennsylvania Gubernatorial Citizens Jury Final Report." Minneapolis: Jefferson Center for New Democratic Processes, 1994.

———. "The Citizen Jury: Effective Public Participation." Minneapolis: Jefferson Center for New Democratic Processes, 1999.

———. "Citizens Jury on Dakota County's Comprehensive Land Use Plan." Minneapolis: Jefferson Center for New Democratic Processes, 1997.

———. "Citizens Jury on Orono Public Schools 'Now and into the Future.' " Minneapolis: Jefferson Center for New Democratic Processes, 1998.

———. "Citizens Jury on Physician-Assisted Suicide." Minneapolis: Jefferson Center for New Democratic Processes, 1998.

Johnson, James. "Arguing for Deliberation: Some Skeptical Considerations." In *Deliberative Democracy*, edited by Jon Elster, 161–84. Cambridge: Cambridge University Press, 1998.

Jones, Bryan, ed. *The New American Politics: Reflections on Political Change and the Clinton Administration*. Boulder, Colo.: Westview Press, 1995.

Jones, Karen. "Trust As an Affective Attitude." *Ethics* 107 (1996): 4–25.

Just, Marion, Ann N. Crigler, Dean E. Alger, Timothy E. Cook, Montague Kern, and Darrell M. Wes. *CrossTalk: Citizens, Candidates, and the Media in a Presidential Campaign*. Chicago: University of Chicago Press, 1996.

Kael, Pauline. "Trash, Art and the Movies." In *Going Steady: Film Writings 1968–1969*. Boston: Little, Brown, 1970.

Kant, Immanuel. *Anthropology from a Pragmatic Point of View*. Trans. Victor Lyle Dowdell, rev. and ed. Han H. Rudnick. Carbondale: Southern Illinois University Press, 1978.

———. *Critique of Judgement*. Trans. James Creed Meredith. Oxford: Oxford University Press, 1952; reprint 1978.

———. *Critique of Pure Reason*. Trans. J. M. D. Meiklejohn. Buffalo, N.Y.: Prometheus Books, 1990.

———. *On History, Immanuel Kant*. Ed. and trans. Lewis White Beck, Robert E. Anchor, and Emil L. Fackenheim. Indianapolis: Bobbs-Merrill, Library of Liberal Arts, 1963.

———. "Perpetual Peace." In *On History, Immanuel Kant*. Ed. Lewis White Beck, trans. Lewis White Beck, Robert E. Anchor, and Emil L. Fackenheim. Indianapolis: Bobbs-Merrill, Library of Liberal Arts, 1963.

———. "What Is Enlightenment." In *On History, Immanuel Kant*, ed. Lewis White Beck, trans. Lewis White Beck, Robert E. Anchor, and Emil L. Fackenheim. Indianapolis: Bobbs-Merrill, Library of Liberal Arts, 1963.

Kathrada, A. M. *Letters from Robben Island: A Selection of Ahmed Kathrada's Prison Correspondence, 1964–1989*. Edited by Robert D. Vassen. Cape Town: Mayibuye Books in association with the Robben Island Museum; East Lansing: Michigan State University Press, 1999.

Kautz, Steven. "Liberalism and the Idea of Toleration." *American Journal of Political Science* 37 (1993): 610–32.

Kelley, Stanley, Jr. *Professional Public Relations and Political Power*. Baltimore: Johns Hopkins University Press, 1956.

Kelly, Jerry S. *Arrow Impossibility Theorems*. New York: Academic Press, 1978.

Kenny, Christopher. "Political Participation and Effects from the Social Environment." *American Journal of Political Science* 36 (1992): 259–67.

Kernell, Samuel. *Going Public: New Strategies of Presidential Leadership*. Washington, D.C.: Congressional Quarterly Press, 1986.

Keystone Center. "The Keystone Center and Its Programs." Keystone, Colo.: Keystone Center, 1999.

———. "Publications List." Keystone, Colo.: Keystone Center, 1999.

Kimelman, Donald, and Gregory Hall. "A Critical Study of Civic Deliberation and the Political Process." Unpublished manuscript prepared for the Kettering Foundation. Walt Whitman Center for the Culture and Politics of Democracy, New Brunswick, N.J., 1997.

Kinder, Donald, and Lynn Sanders. *Divided by Color: Racial Politics and Democratic Ideals*. Chicago: University of Chicago Press, 1996.

King, Anthony. *Running Scared: Why America's Politicians Campaign Too Much and Govern Too Little*. New York: Martin Kessler, 1997.

Knack, Stephen. "Civic Norms, Social Sanctions, and Voter Turnout." *Rationality and Society* 4 (1992): 133–56.

Kochman, Thomas. "The Politics of Politeness: Social Warrants in Mainstream American Public Etiquette." In *Meaning, Form, and Use in Context: Linguistic Applications*, edited by Deborah Schiffrin, 200–209. Washington, D.C.: Georgetown University Press, 1984.

Kritz, Neil J., ed. *Transitional Justice: How Emerging Democracies Reckon with Former Regimes*. Vol. 3. Washington, D.C.: U.S. Institute of Peace Press, 1995.

Krondorfer, Björn. *Remembrance and Reconciliation: Encounters Between Young Jews and Germans*. New Haven, Conn.: Yale University Press, 1995.

Kuhn, Deanna. *The Skills of Argument*. Cambridge: Cambridge University Press, 1991.

Kuklinski, James, Ellen Riggle, Victor Ottati, Norbert Schwarz, and Robert Wyer. "Thinking About Political Tolerance, More or Less, with More or Less Information." In *Reconsidering the Democratic Public*, edited by George Marcus and Russell Hanson, 225–47. University Park: Pennsylvania State University Press, 1993.

Kurtz, Howard. *Hot Air: All Talk All the Time*. New York: Random House, 1996.

LaCapra, Dominick. "The University in Ruins?" *Critical Inquiry* 25 (Autumn 1998): 32–55.

Langerak, Edward A. "Pluralism, Tolerance, and Disagreement." *Rhetoric Society Quarterly* 24, no. 1/2 (Winter/Spring 1994): 95–106.

Lasch, Christopher. *The Culture of Narcissism: American Life in an Age of Diminishing Expectations*. New York: Norton, 1978.

———. "The Lost Art of Political Argument." *Harper's*, September 1990, 17–22.

Lash, Scott, and John Urry. *The End of Organized Capitalism*. Cambridge: Polity Press, 1987.

Lauck, John H. *Katyn Killings: In the Record*. Clifton, N.J.: Kingston Press, 1988.

Lazarsfeld, Paul Felix. *The People's Choice: How the Voter Makes Up His Mind in a Presidential Campaign*. New York: Duell, Sloan and Pearce, 1944.

Lazear, Edward P. *Culture Wars in America*. Stanford, Calif.: Hoover Institution on War, Revolution, and Peace, 1996.

Lears, T. J. Jackson. "From Salvation to Self-Realization: Advertising and the Therapeutics of Consumer Culture, 1880–1920." In *The Culture of Consumption: Critical Essays in American History, 1880–1980*, edited by Richard Wightman Fox and T. J. Jackson Lears. New York: Pantheon Books, 1983.

Leighley, Jan. "Attitudes, Opportunities, and Incentives: A Field Essay on Political Participation." *Political Research Quarterly* 48 (1995): 181–210.

———. "Participation as a Stimulus of Political Conceptualization." *Journal of Politics* 53 (1991): 198–211.

Leighninger, Matt, and Martha McCoy. "Mobilizing Citizens: Study Circles Offer a New Approach to Citizenship." *National Civic Review* 87 (1998): 183–89.

Levi, Margaret. "Social and Unsocial Capital: A Review Essay of Robert Putnam's *Making Democracy Work*." *Politics and Society* 24 (1996): 45–55.

———, ed. "Special Section: Critique of Robert Putnam's *Making Democracy Work*." *Politics and Society* 24 (1996).

Levy, Jacob T. "Symbolism, Ethnic Politics, and Official Apologies." In *The Multiculturalism of Fear*. Oxford: Oxford University Press, 2000.

Lewin, Leif, and Evert Vedung, eds. *Politics as Rational Action: Essays in Public Choice and Policy Analysis*. Boston: Reidel, 1980.

Lindblom, Charles E. *Inquiry and Change: The Troubled Attempt to Understand and Shape Society*. New Haven, Conn.: Yale University Press, 1990.

———. *The Intelligence of Democracy: Decision-Making Through Mutual Adjustment*. New York: Free Press, 1965.

Lindblom, Charles E., and David K. Cohen. *Usable Knowledge: Social Science and Social Problem Solving*. New Haven, Conn.: Yale University Press, 1977.

Lindholm, Charles E., and John Hall. "Is the United States Falling Apart?" *Daedalus* 126 (1997): 183–210.

Link, Michael, and Robert Oldendick. "Social Construction and White Attitudes Toward Equal Opportunity and Multiculturalism." *Journal of Politics* 58 (1996): 149–68.

Lippmann, Walter. *The Phantom Public*. New York: Harcourt, Brace, 1925.

———. *Public Opinion*. New York: Harcourt, Brace, 1922.

Lipsitz, George. *The Possessive Investment in Whiteness: How White People Profit from Identity Politics*. Philadelphia: Temple University Press, 1998.

Loomis, Burdett A. *The New American Politician: Ambition, Entrepreneurship, and the Changing Face of Political Life*. New York: Basic Books, 1976.

Los Angeles Times. "Joy and Sorrow in Poland." 14 April 1990.

Loury, Glenn. "Self-Censorship in Public Discourse: A Theory of 'Political Correctness' and Related Phenomena." *Rationality and Society* 6 (1994): 428–61.

Love, Mervyn T. *Peace Building Through Reconciliation in Northern Ireland*. Brookfield, Vt.: Avebury, 1995.

Lukensmeyer, Carolyn, and Joseph P. Goldman. "A National Town Hall: Bringing Citizens Together Through Interactive Video Teleconferencing." Washington, D.C.: The Tides Center/Americans Discuss Social Security, 1999.

Lund, William R. "Communitarian Politics and the Problem of Equality." *Political Research Quarterly* 46 (1993): 577–600.

Luntz, Frank. *Candidates, Consultants, and Campaigns: The Style and Substance of American Electioneering*. Oxford: Blackwell, 1988.

Lutz, Catherine A., and Lila Abu-Lughod, eds. *Language and the Politics of Emotion*. Cambridge: Cambridge University Press, 1990.

MacDonald, J. Fred. *One Nation Under TV: The Rise and Decline of Network Television*. Chicago: Nelson-Hall, 1994.

MacIntyre, Alasdair C. *After Virtue: A Study in Moral Theory*. Notre Dame, Ind.: University of Notre Dame Press, 1981.

MacNeil, Robert. "Regaining Dignity," *Media Studies Journal* 9, no. 3 (Summer 1995): 110–11.

Maltese, John. *Spin Control: The White House Office of Communications and the Management of Presidential News*. Chapel Hill: University of North Carolina Press, 1992.

Mann, Thomas E., and Norman J. Orenstein. *The New Congress*. Washington, D.C., American Enterprise Institute for Public Policy Research, 1981.

Mann, Thomas E., and Gary Orren, eds. *Media Polls in American Politics*. Washington, D.C.: Brookings Institution, 1992.

Mansbridge, Jane. *Beyond Adversary Democracy*. New York: Basic Books, 1980.

Mansfield, Harvey C., ed. *Congress Against the President*. Proceedings of the American Academy of Political Science 32. New York: Academy of Political Science, 1975.

Marcus, George, and Russell Hanson, eds. *Reconsidering the Democratic Public*. University Park: Pennsylvania State University Press.

Margolis, Howard. *Selfishness, Altruism, and Rationality: A Theory of Social Choice*. New York: Cambridge University Press, 1982.

Markoff, John. "Portrait of a Newer, Lonelier Crowd Is Captured in an Internet Survey." *New York Times*, 16 February 2000, Technology section.

Marks, John. "The American Uncivil Wars: How Crude, Rude, and Obnoxious Behavior Has Replaced Good Manners and Why That Hurts Our Politics and Culture." *U.S. News and World Report*, 22 April 1996, 66–72.

Marty, Martin. "The Ethos of Christian Forgiveness." In *Dimensions of Forgiveness: Psychological Research and Theological Perspectives*, edited by Everett L. Worthington, Jr. Philadelphia: Templeton Foundation Press, 1998.

Massey, Douglas, Andrew Gross, and Kumiko Shibuya. "Migration, Segregation, and the Geographic Concentration of Poverty." *American Sociological Review* 59 (1994): 425–45.

Massie, Alan. "Why Losers Came to Win in the End." *Daily Telegraph*, 23 July 1994.

Matusow, Barbara. *The Evening Stars: The Making of the Network News Anchor*. Boston: Houghton Mifflin, 1983.

McCarthy, Thomas. "Practical Discourse: On the Relation of Morality to Politics." In *Habermas and the Public Sphere*, edited by Craig Calhoun, 51–72. Cambridge, Mass.: MIT Press, 1992.

McClain, Charles, ed. *The Mass Internment of Japanese Americans and the Quest for Legal Redress*. Volume 3. New York: Garland, 1994.

McCullough, Michael, Julie Juola Exline, and Roy F. Baumeister. "An Annotated Bibliography of Research on Forgiveness and Related Concepts." In *Dimensions of Forgiveness: Psychological Research and Theological Perspectives*, edited by Everett L. Worthington, Jr. Philadelphia: Templeton Foundation Press, 1998.

McGerr, Michael. *The Decline of Popular Politics: The American North, 1865–1928*. New York: Oxford University Press, 1986.

McLaughlin, John. "Democracy Is a Discussion: An Evaluation." Unpublished manuscript, 1998.

McLeod, Douglas, and Elizabeth Perse. "Direct and Indirect Effects on Socioeconomic Status on Public Affairs Knowledge." *Journalism Quarterly* 71 (1994): 433–42.

McManus, John H. *Market-Driven Journalism: Let the Citizen Beware?* Thousand Oaks, Calif.: Sage, 1994.

Mendelberg, Tali, "The Deliberative Citizen: Theory and Evidence." In *Political Decision-Making, Deliberation, and Participation*, edited by Michael X. Delli Carpini, Leonie Huddy, and Robert Y. Shapiro. Amsterdam: JAI Press, 2002, 151-94.

Mendelberg, Tali, and J. Oleske. "Race and Public Deliberation." *Political Communication* 17 (2000): 169–91.

Merritt, Davis, Jr. *Public Journalism and Public Life: Why Telling the News Is Not Enough*. Hillsdale, N.J.: Erlbaum, 1995.

Mill, John Stuart. *On Liberty*. Edited by Elizabeth Rapaport. Indianapolis: Hackett, 1978.

Millennium Communications Group. *Communications as Engagement: A Communications Strategy for Revitalization*. Prepared for the Rockefeller Foundation. Washington, D.C.: Millennium Communications Group, 1994.

Miller, David. "Citizenship and Pluralism." *Political Studies* 43 (1995): 432–50.

Minow, Martha. *Between Vengeance and Forgiveness*. Boston: Beacon Press, 1998.

Miringoff, Marc, and Marque-Luisa Miringoff. *The Social Health of the Nation: How America Is Really Doing*. Oxford: Oxford University Press, 1999.

Montesquieu, Charles de Secondat. *The Spirit of the Laws*. Edited and translated by Anne M. Cohler, Basia Carolyn Miller, and Harold Samuel Stone. Cambridge: Cambridge University Press, 1989.

Moon, J. Donald. "Constrained Discourse and Public Life." *Political Theory* 19 (1991): 202–29.

Moore, Gwen, and J. Allen Whitt. *Research in Politics and Society: The Politics of Wealth and Inequality*. Greenwich, Conn.: JAI Press, 1995.

Morin, Richard, and Dan Balz, "Americans Losing Trust in Each Other and Institutions, Suspicion of Strangers Breeds Widespread Cynicism." *Washington Post*, 28 January 1996, A1.

Moynihan, Daniel P. *Secrecy: The American Experience*. New Haven, Conn.: Yale University Press, 1998.

Mukae, Ryuji. "Japan's Diet Resolution on World War II: Keeping History at Bay." *Asian Survey* (October 1996).

Muller, Edward, and Mitchell Seligson. "Civic Culture and Democracy: The Question of Causal Relationships." *American Political Science Review* 88 (1994): 634–52.

Murphey, Dwight C. "Katyn: The Untold Story of Stalin's Polish Massacre." Review of Allen Paul, *Katyń : The Untold Story of Stalin's Polish Massacre. Journal of Social, Political, and Economic Studies* (Spring 1999): 124.

Murphy, Andrew R. "Tolerance, Toleration, and the Liberal Tradition." *Polity* 29 (1997): 593–623.

Murphy, Jeffrie G., and Jean E. Hampton. *Forgiveness and Mercy*. Cambridge: Cambridge University Press, 1988.

Myers, Sondra, ed. *Democracy Is a Discussion: Civic Engagement in Old and New Democracies*. New London, Conn.: Connecticut College, 1996, reprint 1998.

Myerson, George. *Rhetoric, Reason, and Society: Rationality As Dialogue*. Thousand Oaks, Calif.: Sage, 1994.

Nagorski, Andrew. "At Last, a Victory for the Truth; Moscow Admits to an Infamous Massacre." *Newsweek*, 26 October 1992.

National Commission on Civic Renewal. *A Nation of Spectators: How Civic Disengagement Weakens America and What We Can Do About It*. Chaired by William J. Bennett and Sam Nunn. Washington, D.C.: National Commission on Civic Renewal, 24 June 1998. Available on the Internet at http://www.puaf.umd.edu/Affiliates/CivicRenewal/finalreport/table_of_contentsfinal_report.htm (3 March 2003).

NEH. "A Handbook of Tips: How to Use the Conversation Kit." Washington, D.C.: National Endowment for the Humanities, National Conversation on Pluralism and Identity, 1996.

Nelson, Thomas, and Donald Kinder. "Issue Frames and Group-Centrism in American Public Opinion." *Journal of Politics* 58 (1996): 1055–78.

Neuman, W. Russell. *The Paradox of Mass Politics: Knowledge and Opinion in the American Electorate*. Cambridge, Mass.: Harvard University Press, 1986.

Neuman, W. Russell, Marion Just, and Ann Crigler. *Common Knowledge: News and the Construction of Political Meaning*. Chicago: University of Chicago Press, 1992.

Neustadt, Richard E. *Presidential Power and the Modern Presidents: The Politics of Leadership from Roosevelt to Reagan*. New York: Free Press, 1990.

Newman, John Henry. *The Idea of a University: Defined and Illustrated in Nine Discourses Delivered to the Catholics of Dublin in Occasional Lectures and Essays Addressed to the Members of the Catholic University*. Edited by Martin J. Svaglic. Notre Dame, Ind.: University of Notre Dame Press, 1982.

———. *The Scope and Nature of University Education*. New York: E.P. Dutton, 1958.

Newton, Kenneth. "Social Capital and Democracy." *American Behavioral Scientist* 40 (1997): 575–86.

New York Times. "Australia Apologizes for Treatment of Aborigines." 27 August 1999.

———. "Japan: Koreans' Plea Rejected." 31 August 1999.

———. "No Apology to Orphans, Quebec Church Says." 16 September 1999.

Nietzsche, Friedrich Wilhelm. *On the Genealogy of Morals*, trans. Walter Kaufmann and R. J. Hollingdale; *Ecce Homo*, trans. and ed. Walter Kaufmann. New York: Vintage Books, 1967; reprint 1989.

NIFI. "Alcohol: Controlling the Toxic Spill." Dayton, Ohio: National Issues Forums Institute, 1999.

———. "For Convenors and Moderators: Organizing for Public Deliberation and Moderating a Forum/Study Circle." Dayton, Ohio: National Issues Forums Institute, 1999.

Nino, Carlos Santiago. *The Constitution of Deliberative Democracy.* New Haven, Conn.: Yale University Press, 1996.

Noboru, Seiichiro. "Japanese War Apology." Letter to the editor. *Los Angeles Times*, 29 August 1995.

Norton, Charles Eliot. "The Intellectual Life in America," *New Princeton Review* 6 (1888).

Nussbaum, Martha. "Compassion: The Basic Social Emotion." *Social Philosophy and Policy* 13 (1996): 27–58.

———. *The Fragility of Goodness: Luck and Ethics in Greek Tragedy and Philosophy.* Cambridge: Cambridge University Press, 1986.

Nye, Joseph S., Jr. "Introduction: The Decline of Confidence in Government." In *Why People Don't Trust Government*, edited by Joseph S. Nye, Jr., Philip D. Zelikow, and David C. King. Cambridge, Mass.: Harvard University Press, 1997.

Nye, Joseph S., Jr., Philip D. Zelikow, and David C. King, eds. *Why People Don't Trust Government.* Cambridge, Mass.: Harvard University Press, 1997.

Ohbuchi, K., et al. "Apology as Aggression Control: Its Role in Mediating Appraisal of and Response to Harm." *Journal of Personality and Social Psychology* 56 (1989): 219–27.

Oppel, Rich. "We'll Help You Regain Control of the Issues." *Charlotte Observer*, 12 January 1992, A1.

Orenstein, Aviva. " 'My God!': A Feminist Critique of the Excited Utterance Exception to the Hearsay Rule." *California Law Review* (January 1997).

Owen, Marion. *Apologies and Remedial Interchanges.* New York: Mouton, 1983.

Page, Benjamin, and Robert Shapiro. *The Rational Public: Fifty Years of Trends in Americans' Policy Preferences.* Chicago: University of Chicago Press, 1992.

Parkman, Francis. "The Failure of Universal Suffrage," *North American Review* 127 (1878): 1–20.

Patterson, Thomas E. *Out of Order.* New York: Knopf, 1993.

Paul, Allen. *Katy´n : The Untold Story of Stalin's Polish Massacre.* New York: Charles Scribner's Sons, 1991.

Pearce, W. Barnett, and Stephen W. Littlejohn. *Moral Conflict: When Social Worlds Collide.* Thousand Oaks, Calif.: Sage, 1997.

Peirce, Neal, and Curtis Johnson, *Boundary Crossers: Community Leadership for a Global Age.* University Park, Md.: James MacGregor Burns Academy of Leadership, l997.

Perelman, Chaiz. *The Realm of Rhetoric.* Notre Dame, Ind.: University of Notre Dame Press, 1982.

Perelman, Chaiz, and L. Olbrechts-Tyteca. *The New Rhetoric of Argumentation.* Notre Dame, Ind.: University of Notre Dame Press, 1969.

Pew Center for Civic Journalism. "Civic Lessons: Report on Four Civic Journalism Projects Funded by the Pew Center for Civic Journalism." Philadelphia: Pew Charitable Trusts, 1997.

———. "With the People: A Toolbox for Getting Readers and Viewers Involved." Washington, D.C.: Pew Center for Civic Journalism, 1999.

Philadelphia Inquirer. "Speech and Challenges: Universities Must be Free to Inspire Both." 26 September 1999, Editorial section, E6.

Pilkington, Edward. "Yeltsin Learns Diplomacy of Contrition from His Hosts." *Guardian,* 13 October 1993.

Pitkin, Hannah F., and Sara M. Shumer. "On Participation." *Democracy* 2 (1982): 43–54.

Plutarch, *Cicero.* In *Plutarch's Lives,* 2 vols., translated John Dryden, ed. Arthur Hugh Clough, 408–40. New York: Random House, Modern Library, 1992, 2001. Available online from the Internet Classics Archive at http://classics.mit.edu//Plutarch/cicero.html.

Pocock, J. G. A. *The Machiavellian Moment: Florentine Political Thought and the Atlantic Republican Tradition.* Princeton, N.J.: Princeton University Press, 1975.

Polanyi, Livia. *Telling the American Story: A Structural and Cultural Analysis of Conversational Storytelling.* Norwood, N.J.: Ablex, 1985.

Polsby, Nelson. *Consequences of Party Reform.* Oxford: Oxford University Press, 1983.

Portis, Edward. "Citizenship and Identity." *Polity* 18 (1986): 457–72.

President's Initiative on Race. "The Advisory Board's Report to the President." Washington, D.C.: One America in the 21st Century, 1998.

———. "One America Dialogue Guide: Conducting a Discussion on Race." Washington, D.C.: One America in the 21st Century, 1998.

———. "Pathways to One America in the 21st Century: Promising Practices for Racial Reconciliation." Washington, D.C.: One America in the 21st Century, 1999.

Pross, Christian. *Paying for the Past.* Baltimore: Johns Hopkins University Press, 1998.

Przeworski, Adam. "Deliberation and Ideological Domination." In *Deliberative Democracy,* edited by Jon Elster, 140–60. Cambridge: Cambridge University Press, 1998.

Putnam, Robert. "Bowling Alone," *Journal of Democracy* 6, no. 1 (January 1995): 65–78.

———. *Bowling Alone: The Collapse and Revival of American Community.* New York: Simon and Schuster, 2000.

———. *Making Democracy Work: Civic Traditions in Modern Italy.* Princeton, N.J.: Princeton University Press, 1993.

———. "The Strange Disappearance of Civic America." *American Prospect* 24 (1996): 34–48.

———. "Tuning In, Tuning Out: The Strange Disappearance of Social Capital in America." *PS: Political Science and Politics* 28 (1995): 664–83.

Quigley, David. "Reconstructing Democracy: Politics and Ideas in New York City, 1865–1880." Ph.D. dissertation, New York University, 1997.

Rainie, Lee, and Bente Kalsnes. "The Commons of the Tragedy: How the Internet Was Used by Millions After the Terror Attacks to Grieve, Console, Share News, and Debate the Country's Response." Washington, D.C.: Pew Internet and American Life Project, 10 October 2001. Available on the Internet at http://www.pewinternet.org/reports/pdfs/PIP_Tragedy_Report.pdf (3 March 2003).

Rauch, Jonathan. *Demosclerosis: The Silent Killer of American Government.* New York: Times Books, 1994.

Rawls, John. *Political Liberalism*. New York: Columbia University Press, 1993.

———. *A Theory of Justice*. Cambridge, Mass.: Belknap Press, 1971.

Readings, Bill. *The University in Ruins*. Cambridge, Mass.: Harvard University Press, 1996.

Renan, Ernest. "What Is a Nation?" In *Modern Political Doctrines*, edited by Alfred Zimmern, 186-205. London: Oxford University Press, 1939.

Reynolds, Charles, and Ralph Norman, eds. *Community in America: The Challenge of Habits of the Heart*. Berkeley, Calif.: University of California Press, 1988.

Rheingold, Howard. *The Virtual Community: Homesteading on the Electronic Frontier*. New York: HarperCollins, 1994.

Rieff, Philip. *The Triumph of the Therapeutic: Uses of Faith After Freud*. New York: Harper and Row, 1968.

Riker, William. *Liberalism Against Populism: A Confrontation Between the Theory of Democracy and the Theory of Social Choice*. San Francisco: W.H. Freeman, 1982.

———. "Political Trust as Rational Choice." In *Politics As Rational Action: Essays in Public Choice and Policy Analysis*, edited by Leif Lewin and Evert Vedung, 1–24. Boston: Reidel, 1980.

Rorty, Richard, ed. *The Linguistic Turn: Recent Essays in Philosophical Method*. Chicago: University of Chicago Press, 1967.

Rose, Michael. "Down Under: Few Funds, No Apology." *World Press Review*, March 1998.

Rosen, Jay. "Getting the Connections Right: Public Journalism and the Troubles in the Press." New York: Twentieth Century Fund, 1996.

———. "Making Things More Public: On the Political Responsibility of the Media Intellectual," *Critical Studies in Mass Communication* 11, no. 4 (1994): 373-74.

———. "Project on Public Life and the Press, Report of Activities, 1994–1995." Unpublished manuscript, 1995.

———. "Project on Public Life and the Press, Report of Activities, September 1995–1996." Unpublished manuscript, 1996.

———. "Project on Public Life and the Press: Final Report." Unpublished manuscript, 1997.

———. *What Are Journalists For?* New Haven, Conn.: Yale University Press, 1999.

Rossi, Robert J., and Kevin J. Gilmartin. *The Handbook of Social Indicators: Sources, Characteristics, and Analysis*. New York: Garland STPM Press, 1980.

Rothenbuhler, Eric. "The Process of Community Involvement." *Communication Monographs* 58 (1991): 63–78.

Rothman, David J. *Strangers at the Bedside*. New York: Basic Books, 1991.

Rothman, Jay. "Action Evaluation: Integrating Evaluation into the Intervention Process." Unpublished manuscript, 1999.

Rowland, Robert. "Purpose, Argument Evaluation, and the Crisis of the Public Sphere." In *Argumentation Theory and the Rhetoric of Assent*, edited by David Williams and Michael Hazen. Tuscaloosa: University of Alabama Press, 1990.

Ryan, Mary P. *Civic Wars: Democracy and Public Life in the American City During the Nineteenth Century*. Berkeley: University of California Press, 1997.

———. "Gender and Public Access: Women's Politics in Nineteenth-Century America." In *Habermas and the Public Sphere*, edited by Craig Calhoun, 259–88. Cambridge, Mass.: MIT Press, 1992.

Ryfe, David M. *What Is Good Public Discourse? An Annotated Bibliography*. Prepared for the Penn National Commission on Society, Culture, and Community. Philadelphia: Trustees of the University of Pennsylvania, 1999. Available online at http://www.upenn.edu/pnc under "Resources" (15 May 2003).

Sabato, Larry. *The Party's Just Begun: Shaping Political Parties for America's Future*. Glenview, Ill.: Scott, Foresman, 1988, 2001.

———. *The Rise of Political Consultants: New Ways of Winning Elections*. New York: Basic Books, 1981.

Sandel, Michael J. *Liberalism and the Limits of Justice*. New York: Cambridge University Press, 1982.

———. "The procedural republic and the unencumbered self, *Political Theory* 12 (1984): 81-96.

———., ed. *Liberalism and Its Critics*. Oxford: Blackwell, 1984.

Sanders, Lynn. "Against Deliberation." *Political Theory* 25 (1997): 347–76.

Schiffrin, Deborah. "Everyday Argument: The Organization of Diversity in Talk." In *Handbook of Discourse Analysis: Discourse and Dialogue*, edited by Teun van Dijk, vol. 3, 35–46. London: Academic Press, 1985.

———. "The Management of a Cooperative Self During Argument: The Role of Opinions and Stories." In *Conflict Talk: Sociolinguistic Investigations of Arguments in Conversations*, edited by Allen D. Grimshaw, 241–59. Cambridge: Cambridge University Press, 1990.

———, ed. *Meaning, Form, and Use in Context: Linguistic Applications*. Washington, D.C.: Georgetown University Press, 1984.

Schiller, Ben. "World Bids Final Farewell to Conciliator Willy Brandt." *Toronto Star*, 18 October 1992.

Schlozman, Kay Lehman, Nancy Burns, and Sidney Verba. "Gender and the Pathways to Participation: The Role of Resources." *Journal of Politics* 56 (1994): 963–90.

Scholz, John, and Wayne B. Gray. "Can Government Facilitate Cooperation? An Informational Model of OSHA Enforcement." *American Journal of Political Science* 41 (1997): 693–717.

Schrag, Calvin. *The Resources of Rationality: A Response to the Postmodern Challenge*. Bloomington: Indiana University Press, 1992.

Schudson, Michael. *The Good Citizen: A History of American Civic Life*. New York: Free Press, 1998.

———. "Sending a Political Message: Lessons from the American 1790s." *Media, Culture, and Society* 19 (1997): 311–30.

———. "The Sociology of News Production Revisited." *Media, Culture, and Society* 11 (1989): 263–82.

———. "Why Conversation Is Not the Soul of Democracy." *Critical Studies in Mass Communication* 14 (1997): 297–309.

Schwerin, Kurt. "German Compensation for Victims of Nazi Persecution." In *Transitional Justice: How Emerging Democracies Reckon with Former Regimes*, edited by Neil Kritz, vol. 3. Washington, D.C.: U.S. Institute of Peace Press, 1995.

SCRC. "Building Strong Neighborhoods: A Study Circle Guide for Public Dialogue and Community Problem-Solving." Pomfret, Conn.: Study Circles Resource Center, 1998.

———. "The Busy Citizen's Discussion Guide." Pomfret, Conn.: Study Circles Resource Center, 1995.

———. "Facing the Challenge of Racism and Race Relations: Democratic Dialogue and Action for Stronger Communities." 3rd ed. Pomfret, Conn.: Study Circles Resource Center, 1997.

———. "Study Circles on Racism and Race Relations: A Report on the Focus Groups." Pomfret, Conn.: Study Circles Resource Center, 1997.

———. "Toward a More Perfect Union in an Age of Diversity." Pomfret, Conn.: Study Circles Resource Center, 1999.

Segev, Tom. *The Seventh Million: The Israelis and the Holocaust*. Trans. Haim Watzman. New York: Hill and Wang, 1993.

Seidman, Steven, ed. *The Postmodern Turn: New Perspectives on Social Theory.* New York: Cambridge University Press, 1994.

Sen, A. K. *Collective Choice and Social Welfare.* San Francisco: Holden-Day, 1970.

Serotta, Edward. *Jews, Germany, Memory: A Contemporary Portrait.* Berlin: Nicolai, 1996.

Shammas, Carole. "A New Look at Long-Term Trends in Wealth Inequality in the United States." *American Historical Review* 98 (1993): 412–29.

Shienbaum, Kim. *Beyond the Electoral Connection: A Reassessment of the Role of Voting in Contemporary American Politics.* Philadelphia: University of Pennsylvania Press, 1984.

Shklar, Judith. *American Citizenship: The Quest for Inclusion.* Cambridge, Mass.: Harvard University Press, 1991.

Shotter, John. *Conversational Realities: Constructing Life Through Language.* Thousand Oaks, Calif.: Sage, 1993.

Shriver, Donald W., Jr. *An Ethic for Enemies.* New York: Oxford University Press, 1995.

Sikorski, Radek. "Haunting Russia." *National Review*, 2 March 1994.

Silbey, Joel. *The American Political Nation, 1838–1893.* Stanford, Calif.: Stanford University Press, 1991.

Simon, Herbert. *Models of Bounded Rationality.* Cambridge, Mass.: MIT Press, 1982.

———, ed. *The Rhetorical Turn: Invention and Persuasion in the Conduct of Social Inquiry.* Chicago: University of Chicago Press, 1990.

Simpson, Andrea. *The Tie That Binds: Identity and Political Attitudes in the Post-Civil Rights Generation.* New York: New York University Press, 1998.

Skillington, Tracey. "Politics and the Struggle to Define: A Discourse Analysis of the Framing Strategies of Competing Actors in a 'New' Participatory Forum." *British Journal of Sociology* 48 (1997): 493–513.

Skocpol, Theda. *Boomerang: Clinton's Health Security Effort and the Turn Against Government in Politics.* New York: Norton, 1996.

Slowes, Salomon W. *The Road to Katyn: A Soldier's Story.* Ed. Wladyslaw T. Bartoszewski, trans. Naftali Greenwood. Cambridge, Mass.: Blackwell, 1992.

Smith, Craig, and Michael Hyde. "Rethinking 'The Public': The Role of Emotion in Being-with-Others." *Quarterly Journal of Speech* 77 (1991): 446–66.

Smith, Marc A., and Peter Kollock, eds. *Communities in Cyberspace.* London: Routledge, 1999.

Smith, Rogers. "The 'American Creed' and American Identity: Limits of Liberal Citizenship in the United States." *Political Research Quarterly* 41 (1991): 225–52.

———. *Civic Ideals: Conflicting Visions of Citizenship in U.S. History.* New Haven, Conn.: Yale University Press, 1997.

Smith, Tom. "Factors Relating to Misanthropy in Contemporary American Society." *Social Science Research* 26 (1997): 170–96.

Somers, Margaret. "The Narrative Constitution of Identity: A Relational and Network Approach." *Theory and Society* 23 (1994): 605–49.

Sontag, Deborah. "Israel: Apology for Crusades." *New York Times*, 16 July 1999.

Speirs, Rosemary. "Atonement Must Come from the Top." *World Press Review*, March 1998.

Spragens, Thomas. *Reason and Democracy.* Durham, N.C.: Duke University Press, 1990.

Sproat, John. *"The Best Men": Liberal Reformers in the Gilded Age.* New York: Oxford University Press, 1968.

Statue of Liberty-Ellis Island Foundation. "America's Concentration Camps." New York: Statue of Liberty-Ellis Island Foundation, 1998.

Stokes, Susan. "Pathologies of Deliberation." In *Deliberative Democracy*, edited by Jon Elster, 123–39. Cambridge: Cambridge University Press, 1998.

Stout, Hilary. "Many Don't Realize It's the Clinton Plan They Like." *Wall Street Journal*, 10 March 1994, B1, B6.

Sulkin, T., and A. Simon. "Habermas in the Lab: A Study of Deliberation in an Experimental Setting." *Political Psychology* 22 (2001): 809–26.

Sullivan, Patricia, and Steven Goldzwig. "A Relational Approach to Moral Decision-Making: The Majority Opinion in *Planned Parenthood v. Casey*." *Quarterly Journal of Speech* 81 (1995): 167–90.

Sunstein, Cass R. *After the Rights Revolution: Reconceiving the Regulatory State*. Cambridge, Mass.: Harvard University Press, 1990.

———. *Democracy and the Problem of Free Speech*. New York: Free Press, 1993.

———. *Republic.com*. Princeton, N.J.: Princeton University Press, 2001.

Susman, Warren. *Culture as History: The Transformation of American Society in the Twentieth Century*. New York: Pantheon Books, 1984.

Tachibana, Seiitsu. "The Quest for a Peace Culture: The A-bomb Survivors' Long Struggle and the New Movement for Redressing Foreign Victims of Japan's War." In *Hiroshima in History and Memory*, edited by Michael J. Hogan. Cambridge: Cambridge University Press, 1996.

Tannen, Deborah. *The Argument Culture: Moving from Debate to Dialogue*. New York: Random House, 1998.

———. "Editor's Introduction." In *Gendered and Conversational Interaction*, edited by Deborah Tannen. New York: Oxford University Press, 1993.

———, ed. *Gendered and Conversational Interaction*. New York: Oxford University Press, 1993.

Tanaka, Hiroshi. "Why Is Asia Demanding Postwar Compensation Now?" *Hitotsubashi Journal of Social Studies* 28 (1996).

Tavuchis, Nicholas. *Mea Culpa*. Stanford, Calif.: Stanford University Press, 1991.

Teske, Nathan. "Beyond Altruism: Identity-Construction as Moral Motive in Political Explanation." *Political Psychology* 18 (1997): 71–91.

———. *Political Activists in America: The Identity Construction Model of Political Participation*. Cambridge: Cambridge University Press, 1997.

Theiss-Morse, Elizabeth, George E. Marcus, and John L. Sullivan. "Passion and Reason in Political Life: The Organization of Affect and Cognition and Political Tolerance." In *Reconsidering the Democratic Public*, edited by George Marcus and Russell Hanson, 249–72. University Park: Pennsylvania State University Press, 1993.

Thelen, David. *Becoming a Citizen in the Age of Television: How Americans Challenged the Media and Seized Political Initiative During the Iran-Contra Debate*. Chicago: University of Chicago Press, 1996.

Thernstrom, Stephan, and Abigail Thernstrom. *America in Black and White: One Nation, Indivisible*. New York: Simon and Schuster, 1997.

Thoreson, Carl, Frederic Luskin, and Alex H. S. Harris. "Science and Forgiveness Interventions: Reflections and Recommendations." In *Dimensions of Forgiveness: Psychological Research and Theological Perspectives*, edited by Everett L. Worthington, Jr. Philadelphia: Templeton Foundation Press, 1998.

Tocqueville, Alexis de. *Democracy in America*. Ed. Thomas Bender. New York: Random House, Modern Library, 1981.

Tolz, Vera. "The Katyn Documents and the CPSU Hearings." *RFE/RL Research Report* 1, no. 44 (6 November 1992): 27–33.

Totsuka, Etsuro. "Commentary on a Victory for 'Comfort Women': Japan's Judicial Recognition of Military Sexual Slavery." Trans. Taihei Okada. *Pacific Rim Law and Policy Journal* 8, no. 1 (January 1999): 47–108.

Toulmin, Stephen E. *The Uses of Argument*. Cambridge: Cambridge University Press, 1958.

Traverso, Enzo. *The Jews and Germany: From the "Judeo-German Symbiosis" to the Memory of Auschwitz*. Trans. Daniel Weissbort. Lincoln: University of Nebraska Press, 1995.

Tulis, Jeffrey. *The Rhetorical Presidency*. Princeton, N.J.: Princeton University Press, 1987.

Underwood, Doug. *When MBAs Rule the Newsroom: How the Marketers and Managers Are Reshaping Today's Media*. New York: Columbia University Press, 1993.

Useem, Michael. *The Leadership Moment*. New York: Times Business, 1998.

van Dijk, Teun. *Communicating Racism: Ethnic Prejudice in Thought and Talk*. Newbury Park, Calif.: Sage, 1987.

———, ed. *Handbook of Discourse Analysis: Discourse and Dialogue*. London: Academic Press, 1985.

———. "Social Cognition, Social Power, and Social Discourse." *Text* 8 (1988): 129–57.

van Eemeren, Frans, Rob Grootendorst, Sally Jackson, and Scott Jacobs. *Reconstructing Argumentative Discourse*. Tuscaloosa, Ala.: University of Alabama Press, 1993.

van Mill, David. "The Possibility of Rational Outcomes from Democratic Discourse and Procedures." *Journal of Politics* 58 (1996): 734–52.

Verba, Sidney, and Norman Nie. *Participation in America*. New York: Harper and Row, 1972.

Verba, Sidney, Kay Lehman Schlozman, Henry Brady, and Norman Nie. "Citizen Activity: Who Participates? What Do They Say?" *American Political Science Review* 87 (1993): 303–18.

Viswanath, K., and John R. Finnegan, Jr. "The Knowledge-Gap Hypothesis: Twenty-Five Years Later." *Communication Yearbook* 19 (1996): 187–228.

Walker, Jack. "The Origins and Maintenance of Interest Groups in America." *American Political Science Review* 77 (1983): 390–406.

Walsh, Katherine Cramer. "The Democratic Potential of Civic Dialogue on Race." Paper delivered at the annual meeting of the Midwest Political Science Association, Chicago, 3-6 April 2003.

Walton, Douglas. *The Place of Emotion in Argument*. University Park: Pennsylvania State University Press, 1992.

Warren, Mark. "Can Participatory Democracy Produce Better Selves? Psychological Dimensions of Habermas' Discursive Model of Democracy." *Political Psychology* 14 (1993): 209–34.

———. *Democracy and Association*. Princeton, N.J.: Princeton University Press, 2001.

———. "Deliberative Democracy and Authority." *American Political Science Review* 90 (1996): 46–60.

———. "Democratic Theory and Self-Transformation." *American Political Science Review* 86 (1992): 8–23.

———. "What Should We Expect from More Democracy?" *Political Theory* 24 (1996): 241–70.

Wattenberg, Martin. *The Decline of American Political Parties, 1952–1984*. Cambridge, Mass.: Harvard University Press, 1996.

Weiner, B., et al. "Public Confession and Forgiveness." *Journal of Personality* 59 (1991): 281–312.

Weissberg, Robert. *Political Learning, Political Choice, and Democratic Citizenship*. Englewood Cliffs, N.J.: Prentice-Hall, 1974.

Westbrook, Robert. "Politics as Consumption: Managing the Modern American Election," In *The Culture of Consumption: Critical Essays in American History,*

1880–1980, edited by Richard Wightman Fox and T. J. Jackson Lears, 143–73. New York: Pantheon Books, 1983.

Wiebe, Robert H. *Self-Rule: A Cultural History of American Democracy*. Chicago: University of Chicago Press, 1995.

Wielhouwer, Peter W., and Brad Lockerbie. "Party Contacting and Political Participation, 1952–1990." *American Journal of Political Science* 38 (1994): 211–29.

Willard, Charles Arthur. *A Theory of Argumentation*. Tuscaloosa: University of Alabama Press, 1989.

Williams, David, and Michael Hazen, eds. *Argumentation Theory and the Rhetoric of Assent*. Tuscaloosa: University of Alabama Press, 1990.

Wilson, John. *Politically Speaking: The Pragmatic Analysis of Political Language*. London: Blackwell, 1990.

Wilson, Woodrow. *Constitutional Government in the United States*. New York: Columbia University Press, 1908.

Wolfe, Alan. *One Nation, After All*. New York: Viking, 1998.

Wolff, Edward N. "The Rich Get Increasingly Richer: Latest Data on Household Wealth During the 1980s." In *Research in Politics and Society: The Politics of Wealth and Inequality*, edited by Gwen Moore and J. Allen Whitt, 33–68. Greenwich, Conn.: JAI Press, 1995.

Wolin, Sheldon. *Politics and Vision: Continuity and Innovation in Western Political Thought*. Boston: Little, Brown, 1960.

World Economic Forum. *Voice of the People*. A global public opinion survey conducted by Gallup International and Environics International Ltd., 7 November 2002. Available on the Internet at http://www.weforum.org/site/homepublic.nsf/Content/Annual+Meeting+2003%5CResults+of+the+Survey+on+Trust (2 May 2003).

Worthington, Everett L., Jr., ed. *Dimensions of Forgiveness: Psychological Research and Theological Perspectives*. Philadelphia: Templeton Foundation Press, 1998.

Wundt, Wilhelm Max. "Introduction." In *Outlines of Psychology*, trans. Charles Hubbard Judd. New York: Stechert, 1897. Available on the Internet at http://psychclassics.yorku.ca/Wundt/Outlines/sec2.htm (5 March 2003).

Wuthnow, Robert. *Acts of Compassion: Caring for Others and Helping Ourselves*. Princeton, N.J.: Princeton University Press, 1991.

Yankelovich, Daniel. "The Debate That Wasn't: The Public and the Clinton Health Care Plan." *Brookings Review* 13 (Summer 1995).

Young, Iris. *Justice and the Politics of Difference*. Princeton, N.J.: Princeton University Press, 1990.

Youniss, James, Jeffrey McLellan, and Miranda Yates. "What We Know About Engendering Civic Identity." *American Behavioral Scientist* 40 (1997): 620–31.

Zaller, John. *The Nature and Origins of Mass Opinion*. New York: Cambridge University Press, 1992.

Zarefsky, David. "Spectator Politics and the Revival of Public Argument." *Communication Monographs* 59 (1992): 411–14.

Zhigeng, Xu. *Lest We Forget: Nanjing Massacre, 1937*. Beijing: Panda Books, 1995.

Zillman, D., J. R. Cantor, and K. D. Day. "Effect of Timing of Information about Mitigating Circumstances on Emotional Responses to Provocation and Retaliatory Behavior." *Journal of Experimental Social Psychology* 12 (1976): 38–55.

Zinni, Frank, Franco Mattei, and Laurie Rhodebeck. "The Structure of Attitudes Toward Groups: A Comparison of Experts and Novices." *Political Research Quarterly* 50 (1997): 597–626.

Contributors

Joyce Appleby is Professor Emerita of History at the University of California at Los Angeles. She is author most recently of *Inheriting the Revolution: The First Generation of Americans* and *Thomas Jefferson*.

Thomas Bender is University Professor of the Humanities, Professor of History, and Director of the International Center for Advanced Studies at New York University. He is author of *Intellect and Public Life*, *New York Intellect*, *The Unfinished City: New York and the Metropolitan Idea*, and *Community and Social Change in America*.

Derek Bok is President Emeritus of Harvard University and 300th Anniversary University Professor at the Kennedy School of Government. He is author most recently of *Universities in the Marketplace: The Commercialization of Higher Education*, *The Shape of the River: Long-Term Consequences of Considering Race in College and University Admissions* (with William G. Bowen), *The Trouble with Government*, and *The State of the Nation*.

Alex Boraine was Vice Chair of the Truth and Reconciliation Commission in South Africa and is currently founding President of the International Center for Transitional Justice in New York City. He is also the author of *A Country Unmasked* and Professor of Law at New York University, where he was director of the NYU Law School's Justice in Transition program.

Graham G. Dodds is a Research Fellow at the Brookings Institution and doctoral candidate in political science at the University of Pennsylvania, where he is completing a dissertation on the presidential use of executive orders. He has previously published articles on Thomas Hobbes and the relationship between presidents and the press.

Christopher Edley, Jr. is Professor of Law at Harvard University and is the founding co-director of the Civil Rights Project at Harvard. He has served as Senior Advisor to President Clinton for the Race Initiative, consultant to the President's Advisory Board on Racial Reconciliation, Associate Director for Economics and Government at the White House

Office of Management and Budget, and Special Counsel to the President, a capacity in which he led the Clinton White House's review of affirmative action programs. He is the author of *Not All Black and White: Affirmative Action, Race and American Values*.

Drew Gilpin Faust is the founding Dean of the Radcliffe Institute for Advanced Study and Professor of History at Harvard University. Prior to joining the Institute, she was the Annenberg Professor of History and the Director of Women's Studies at the University of Pennsylvania. She is the author of *Mothers of Invention: Women of the Slaveholding South in the American Civil War*, for which she won the prestigious Francis Parkman Prize.

Neal Gabler is a noted film critic, cultural historian, and author of *An Empire of Their Own: How the Jews Invented Hollywood*, which won the *Los Angeles Times* Book Prize for History, *Winchell: Gossip, Power and the Culture of Celebrity*, and most recently, *Life, the Movie: How Entertainment Conquered Reality*. A Guggenheim Fellowship recipient, he holds advanced degrees in film and American culture, has taught at the University of Michigan and Pennsylvania State University, and is currently a Senior Fellow at the Norman Lear Center for the Study of Entertainment in the Annenberg School of Communications at the University of Southern California.

Richard Lapchick was founder and Director of the Center for the Study of Sport in Society at Northeastern University and led the National Consortium for Academics and Sport. He is currently the DeVos Eminent Scholar and Chair of the DeVos Sport Business Management Program at the University of Central Florida. He is recipient of the Arthur Ashe Voice of Conscience Award and author of ten books, including *Smashing Barriers*, *Five Minutes to Midnight: Race and Sport in the 1990s*, *Broken Promises: Racism in American Sports*, and *Fractured Focus: Sport as a Reflection of Society*.

Don M. Randel is President and Professor of Music at the University of Chicago. He previously served as Provost, and earlier as Dean of Arts and Sciences, at Cornell University. A music historian, he has published widely on Mozarabic chant, fifteenth-century chansons, Arabic music theory, and Latin American popular music. He is also editor of the *New Harvard Dictionary of Music* and the companion *Harvard Dictionary of Musicians*.

Judith Rodin is President of the University of Pennsylvania. She is also Professor of Psychology, Medicine and Psychiatry at Penn. She convened and chaired the Penn National Commission on Society, Culture and Community. She served on President Clinton's Committee of Advisors on Science and Technology, and as Chair of the John D. and Catherine T. MacArthur Foundation Research Network on Determinants and Consequences of Health-Promoting and Health-Damaging Behavior. A psychologist widely known for her work on the relationship between psychological and biological processes in human health and behavior, she is the author of *Body Traps*, and previously served as Provost, Dean of the Graduate School of Arts and Sciences, and Chair of the Department of Psychology at Yale University.

Richard Rodriguez is an editor at Pacific News Service, an essayist for the PBS *News Hour*, and a contributing editor for *Harper's* and the *Los Angeles Times*. He is the author of *Brown: The Last Discovery of America*, *Hunger of Memory: The Education of Richard Rodriguez*, and *Days of Obligation: An Argument with My Mexican Father*, and he has received a George Foster Peabody Award for his *News Hour* essays on American life and the Frankel Medal from the National Endowment for the Humanities.

Jay Rosen is Associate Professor of Journalism and Mass Communication and former Director of the Project on Public Life and the Press at New York University. A leading figure in the "public journalism" media reform movement, he is co-author of *Public Journalism: Theory and Practice* and author of *Getting the Connections Right: Public Journalism and the Troubles in the Press* and, most recently, *What Are Journalists For?*

David M. Ryfe is Assistant Professor of Journalism at Middle Tennessee State University and a research consultant to the Kettering Foundation. He is the author of *The Interactive President: Presidential Communication in the Media Age*. His recent work, tentatively titled, *Deliberation, Policymaking, and Populism: Can Deliberative Forums Revitalize American Democracy?*, involves a historical and ethnographic investigation of deliberative forums.

Michael Schudson is Professor of Communication and Adjunct Professor of Sociology at the University of California, San Diego. He has been recipient of a MacArthur Foundation "genius" award and is Co-director of the UCSD Civic Collaborative. He is author of *The Good Citizen: A History of American Civic Life*, *The Power of News*, *Watergate in American Memory: How We Remember, Forget, and Reconstruct the Past*, *Advertising: The Uneasy Persuasion*, *Discovering the News: A Social History of American Newspapers*, and most recently, *The Sociology of News*.

Neil Smelser is Director Emeritus of the Center for Advanced Study in the Behavioral Sciences in Stanford, California, and University Professor Emeritus of Sociology at the University of California, Berkeley. He is the author of *Sociology*, *Problematics of Sociology*, and *The Social Edges of Psychoanalysis*.

Stephen P. Steinberg is Executive Director of the Penn National Commission on Society, Culture and Community and Lecturer in Philosophy at the University of Pennsylvania. A specialist in twentieth-century European philosophy and the philosophy of nationalism, he is also affiliated at Penn with the Solomon Asch Center for the Study of Ethnopolitical Conflict and the Institute for Strategic Threat Analysis and Response.

Robert H. Wiebe was, before his death in 2000, Professor Emeritus of History at Northwestern University. He was most widely known for his book *The Search for Order.* He was also the author of *The Opening of American Society, The Segmented Society*, and *Self-Rule: A Cultural History of American Democracy.* His most recent book, published posthumously in January 2002, is *Who We Are: A History of Popular Nationalism.*

Index

Members of the Penn National Commission on Society, Culture and Community, 1996–1999

K. Anthony Appiah
Department of Afro-American Studies
Harvard University

Joyce Appleby
Department of History
University of California, Los Angeles

Julius W. Becton, Jr.
District of Columbia Schools

Paul Begala *(1996–97)*
Former White House Counselor

Thomas Bender
Department of History
New York University

Derek Bok
Kennedy School of Government
Harvard University

Bill Bradley
Former U.S. Senator
New Jersey

David Bromwich
Department of English
Yale University

E. L. Doctorow
Department of English
New York University

Jean Bethke Elshtain
The Divinity School
University of Chicago

Drew Gilpin Faust
Radcliffe Institute for Advanced Study
Harvard University

James Fishkin
Department of Government
University of Texas

Mari Fitzduff
International Conflict Research (INCORE)
Derry, Northern Ireland

Joel Fleishman
Center for Ethics, Public Policy and the Professions
Duke University

Lani Guinier
School of Law
Harvard University

Rochelle Gurstein
The Bard Graduate Center

Amy Gutmann
Department of Politics
Princeton University

David Hamburg
Carnegie Corporation of New York

Teresa Heinz *(1996–98)*
Howard Heinz Endowment
Heinz Family Philanthropies

A. Leon Higginbotham, Jr. *(Deceased)*
Kennedy School of Government
Harvard University

William Hudnut
Urban Land Institute

Kathleen Hall Jamieson
Annenberg School for Communication
University of Pennsylvania

Randall Kennedy
School of Law
Harvard University

Linda K. Kerber *(1996–98)*
Department of History
University of Iowa

Richard Lapchick
School of Business Administration
University of Central Florida

Lawrence Lessig
School of Law
Stanford University

Tom Luce
Hughes and Luce, L.L.P.

Martin E. Marty
The Divinity School
University of Chicago

Abner Mikva
The Institute of Government and Public Affairs
University of Illinois

Michael J. Piore
Department of Economics
Massachusetts Institute of Technology

Don M. Randel
President
University of Chicago

Judith Rodin—*Chair of the Penn National Commission*
President
University of Pennsylvania

Jay Rosen
Department of Journalism
New York University

Karl Rove
Senior White House Adviser

Andras Sajo
Budapest College
Central European University

Michael Sandel
Department of Government
Harvard University

Michael Schudson
Department of Communication
University of California, San Diego

Martin E. P. Seligman
Department of Psychology
University of Pennsylvania

Neil Smelser
Center for Advanced Study in the Behavioral Sciences

Robert R. Spillane
U.S. Department of State

Claude Steele
Department of Psychology
Stanford University

Stephen P. Steinberg—*Executive Director of the Penn National Commission*
University of Pennsylvania

Cass Sunstein
The Law School
University of Chicago

Calvin Trillin
The New Yorker

Edna Ullmann-Margalit
Center for Rationality and Interactive Decision Theory
Hebrew University of Jerusalem

Michael Useem
The Wharton School
University of Pennsylvania

Paul Verkuil
Benjamin N. Cardozo School of Law
Yeshiva University

Robert H. Wiebe *(Deceased)*
Department of History
Northwestern University

William Julius Wilson
Kennedy School of Government
Harvard University

Robert Wuthnow
Department of Sociology
Princeton University

Acknowledgments

The editors wish to express their profound gratitude and appreciation to the members of the Penn National Commission on Society, Culture and Community, whose ideas, insights, and commitment are reflected in this volume. In addition, the many presenters and participants at the Commission's plenary and working group meetings, some of whose work is included in this volume, stimulated us to challenge preconceived notions and look forward rather than backward. Equally important was the unstinting and generous financial support of the Commission's work and the preparation of this volume provided by what is now known as The Atlantic Philanthropies. We are deeply indebted to them all.

The members of the Commission's staff, Dr. Stephen P. Steinberg, Dr. William D. Boltz, Dr. Cynthia M. Koch, Cheryl E. Faulkner, Michael Strong, George Stalle, Jennifer Yuan, and Lillian Rozin, as well as Jennifer Baldino and Ellen Epstein from the Penn president's office, performed the core intellectual and organizational work that made the Commission's meetings uniquely stimulating occasions. Much of what appears here was the direct or indirect product of their dedication and hard work.

A special thanks is also due to Professor David M. Ryfe, who prepared for the Penn National Commission an exhaustive and insightful review of the scholarly literature on public discourse, which forms the basis of Chapters 3 and 14 of this volume, and whose list of references constitutes the core of this book's Bibliography. A comprehensive annotated bibliography of the literature on public discourse through April 1999, "What is Good Public Discourse? An Annotated Bibliography," was also prepared for the Commission by Professor Ryfe and is available on the Penn National Commission website at http://www.upenn.edu/pnc.

Finally, we wish to express our appreciation to our development editor, Pamela Haag, and to Peter A. Agree, social science editor for the University of Pennsylvania Press, for a level of professionalism and engagement with this project that was as unanticipated as it was invaluable.